DATE DUE

DEMCO 38-296

J. William Fulbright was the longest-serving and most powerful chair of the Senate Foreign Relations Committee. Both an intellectual and an internationalist, Fulbright struggled ceaselessly against domestic anticommunism, the military–industrial complex, and a globalist foreign policy during the 1960s and 1970s.

Fulbright was also the most prominent, and the most effective, of the first American critics of the Vietnam War. Fulbright's criticism was particularly galling and damning to Lyndon Johnson because Fulbright was, like George Kennan, a principled internationalist who could not be dismissed as an ideologue. Fulbright used hearings by the Foreign Relations Committee as a forum in which to advance his powerful critique of the war. His books – which constitute an ongoing, comprehensive analysis of American foreign policy – sold hundreds of thousands of copies and together with the exchange program made him one of the best-known Americans of his time both at home and abroad.

This book is an abridgement of Randall Woods's prize-winning biography of J. William Fulbright. This edition presents the full story of Fulbright's role as one of the leading congressional opponents of the Vietnam War, and the author of an alternative approach to the cold war.

J. William Fulbright, Vietnam, and the Search for a Cold War Foreign Policy

J. William Fulbright, Vietnam, and the Search for a Cold War Foreign Policy

RANDALL BENNETT WOODS

University of Arkansas

CAMBRIDGE
UNIVERSITY PRESS

Riverside Community College
Library
4800 Magnolia Avenue
Riverside, CA 92506

E748.F88 W67 1998
Woods, Randall Bennett,
1944–
J. William Fulbright,
Vietnam, and the search for
a cold war foreign policy

OF THE UNIVERSITY OF CAMBRIDGE
ambridge, CB2 1RP, United Kingdom

CAMBRIDGE UNIVERSITY PRESS

The Edinburgh Building, Cambridge CB2 2RU, United Kingdom
40 West 20th Street, New York, NY 10011-4211, USA
10 Stamford Road, Oakleigh, Melbourne 3166, Australia

© Randall Bennett Woods 1998

This book is in copyright. Subject to statutory exception
and to the provisions of relevant collective licensing agreements,
no reproduction of any part may take place without
the written permission of Cambridge University Press.

First published 1998

Printed in the United States of America

Typeset in Times Roman

Library of Congress Cataloging-in-Publication Data
Woods, Randall Bennett, 1944–
J. William Fulbright, Vietnam, and the search for a
cold war foreign policy / Randall Bennett Woods.
p. cm.
ISBN 0-521-62059-7. – ISBN 0-521-58800-6 (pbk.)
1. Fulbright, J. William (James William), 1905– .
2. Legislators – United States – Biography.   3. United States,
Congress, Senate – Biography.   4. Vietnamese Conflict, 1961–1975.
5. United States – Foreign relations – 1945–1989.   I. Title.
E748.F88W67   1997
973.9'092 – dc21
[B]   97-17216
CIP

A catalog record for this book is available from
the British Library

ISBN 0-521-62059-7 hardback
ISBN 0-521-58800-6 paperback

Contents

J. William Fulbright, Vietnam, and the Search for a Cold War Foreign Policy

1

Taking the Stage

James William Fulbright was born in Sumner, Missouri, in 1905, the fourth of six children. His parents, Jay and Roberta Waugh Fulbright, were both descended from moderately well-to-do families and graduates of the University of Missouri. Jay inherited land from his father, a rough-hewn, hard-driving sort, but opted for a career in business, specifically, banking. In 1906 Jay settled his family in Fayetteville, Arkansas, a community of some three thousand souls nestled in the foothills of the Ozark Mountains and the site of the state university. During the next twenty years the patriarch of the Fulbright family built a small business empire, including a dry goods store, a lumber company, a bottling enterprise, a bank, the local newspaper, and numerous properties. Meanwhile, the gregarious Roberta carved out a niche in Fayetteville society, presiding over frequent soirees made up of prominent townspeople and faculty and administrators from the University of Arkansas.

To all of his friends and family James William Fulbright was never anything but "Bill." He was an intense, active child with an abundance of physical and psychological energy. Sticklers for education, Jay and Roberta decided to enroll Bill in the experimental grammar and secondary school operated by the university's College of Education. One of young Fulbright's classmates, Marguerite Gilstrap, recalled that the teachers at Peabody Experimental School were much influenced by the theories of educational pioneer John Dewey. Students were assigned material to master; in class they sat in embarrassed silence until they began to ask questions. The emphasis was on self-reliance and intellectual assertiveness. Gilstrap also remembered that the curriculum departed somewhat, though not entirely, from the classical. There were heavy doses of sociology, psychology, and political economy to go with language, math, and science. Apparently, the teachers at Peabody were particularly fond of the writings of Charles Beard.

Like his father, whom he admired greatly and whose approval he craved, Bill Fulbright was self-contained and independent even as an adolescent. And like Jay, Bill was regarded by his contemporaries as somewhat aloof. He did not run with a crowd but enjoyed the company of a few close friends, particularly Ed Stone, later known to the architectural world as Edward Durrel Stone.

Yet there was Huck Finn in Bill Fulbright as well as Tom Sawyer. Friends and family remember him as moody, at times given to an introspection that bordered on brooding. He also had a temper and knew how to fight. One of his life-long acquaintances recalled how ''Bill beat the hell out of me with his fists'' after they had quarreled over a girl.[1] Fulbright was seventeen at the time.

During Bill Fulbright's tenure there, the University of Arkansas embodied the term ''provincial institution,'' but he never considered attending another school, and nothing in his experience caused him to regret his choice. In addition to starring as a halfback on the football team and captaining the tennis squad, he was president of Sigma Chi and a member of virtually every other campus organization that counted, including Marble Arch, the ''A'' Club, the Arkansas Boosters' Club, and the Glee Club. He graduated with a ''B'' average in the days when a ''C'' was truly an average grade. In May 1923 he was elected student body president by a margin of one vote.

Even as late as his junior year in college, there is little indication that Fulbright was giving serious thought to his future. He spoke vaguely of either teaching or entering the consular service abroad. There was no mention of a political career. To his peers and family, he did not seem overly ambitious. He was not an avid reader, and he made respectable grades because his father and mother expected them of him.

One day in the fall of 1924 Bill Fulbright was making his way across the campus when he encountered Professor Clark Jordan, dean of the graduate school. Fulbright had had Jordan for several English classes, and the academic had become a regular at Roberta's soirees. Jordan stopped his young protégé and informed him that applications for the Rhodes Scholarships had just come in. The opportunity seemed tailor-made for him, Jordan declared enthusiastically. The program called for candidates who could exhibit both academic achievement and athletic prowess. What would he have to do, Bill asked? Nothing, Jordan replied. Selections were based on record, letters of recommendation, and an interview.[2] In his elegantly self-deprecating way, Fulbright recalled that there were only nine applicants all told, not one of whom, including himself, was particularly outstanding. When the Rhodes Scholarships were announced on December 14, Bill Fulbright's name was on the list. He attributed his selection to his exploits on the athletic field – ''since two or three had better academic records than I'' – and to his mother's considerable political influence.[3]

Bill Fulbright arrived at Oxford at a fortunate time. World War I had wrought great changes on English society and on Oxford. A spirit of egalitarianism

---

1 Quoted in Haynes Johnson and Bernard M. Gwertzman, *Fulbright: The Dissenter* (New York, 1968), 27.
2 Interview with J. William Fulbright, Oct. 11–18, 1988, Washington, D.C.
3 Ibid.

prevailed, and Oxford in the early 1920s was crowded with young men and women of the middle as well as the upper ranges of the social strata. "In January 1919," C. E. Mallett wrote in his three-volume history of Oxford,

> the Union Society was debating whether the world ought to be made safe for democracy or not. Undergraduates were returning to their old employments, their games, their clubs, their studies. In October 1919 there were gathered in Oxford more undergraduates than the University had ever seen before. The pressure on space was very great. The estimate of students in residence had risen in 1920 to four thousand, six hundred and fifty.[4]

Fulbright decided early on to attempt an Honors undergraduate degree in history and political science. He had the good fortune to have as his tutor Ronald Buchanan McCallum, a young Scotsman of singular intelligence and absolute commitment to his students. When he and Fulbright met in 1925, McCallum was in his maiden term at Pembroke. The college's newest fellow had spent the previous year on an Empire grant at Princeton and did not exhibit the anti-Americanism typical of so many of his colleagues. A Scottish Presbyterian and a devoted member of the Liberal Party, McCallum would earn a solid reputation as a scholar and teacher. His specialties were British elections and international organizations. He was, not surprisingly, a great admirer of Woodrow Wilson and throughout his long career would defend the concept of an international collective security organization as both practical and necessary. At twenty-seven, he was only seven years Fulbright's senior. "My tutor is a scotchman and very pleasant," Bill wrote his sister Anne. "He has not yet acquired the academic air."[5] Until the twilight of Fulbright's career and the death of McCallum in May 1973, the two would maintain a close intellectual and personal relationship.

During the next three years the young American, a fellow of Pembroke College, lived a typical Oxford experience. He played rugby and lacrosse, severely damaging both of his knees in the latter sport as a member of the combined Oxford–Cambridge team that toured America in the spring of 1926. He was accepted as a member of the Johnson Literary Society, named, of course, for Samuel Johnson. He spent his summers in France ostensibly studying but, in reality, soaking up French culture and café life.

Fulbright graduated from Oxford in June 1928 with a high second in modern history. He became convinced in later years that the university had done for him what Cecil Rhodes intended that it do: He had been stretched intellectually and culturally. Even had he been so inclined, Fulbright would never be able to retreat into a cocoon of complacency. The march of civilizations

---

4 Charles Edward Mallett, *A History of the University of Oxford* (London, 1948), 486.
5 J. William Fulbright [hereinafter referred to as JWF] to Anne Teasdale, Oct. 23, 1925, Personal Papers of J. William Fulbright, Mullins Library, University of Arkansas, Fayetteville, Ark. [hereinafter referred to as PPF].

across history had dazzled him. The complexities of other cultures and the rage of his tutors and his fellow students to learn about them left an indelible mark. Most important of all, those with whom he associated assumed that they were going to make a difference in the world. In Great Britain, Oxbridge alumni dominated Parliament, the press, academia, and big business. Coupled with his mother's belief in public service, Fulbright's years at Pembroke disposed him to seize any and every opportunity to enter public life. His education, however, was not yet complete.

Following a quick tour of the Continent with his mother, who had come over for graduation, Fulbright decided to visit Vienna for an extended period. He frequented the opera, read, roamed the city, and of course, spent his evenings in the cafés. Viennese café life was only slightly less brilliant than that of Paris. It attracted writers, painters, actors, and intellectuals of all types. Topics of discussion ranged from the merits of postimpressionist art to the plight of the Weimar Republic under the Versailles Treaty to the psychoanalytic theories of a Viennese doctor named Sigmund Freud. Significantly, Fulbright spent more and more time at the Café Louvre. Situated near the telegraph station, the Louvre was the favorite hangout of foreign correspondents. There one could see William L. Shirer, Walter Duranty, Dorothy Thompson, John Gunther, and Frazier Hunt. It was at the Louvre in October that the young American met and made friends with Mikhail Fodor.

A stocky, balding, garrulous Hungarian–American, Mike Fodor was then the Balkan correspondent for The *Manchester Guardian.* In addition to being an able reporter, Fodor was an intellectual who could discuss the complex political life of Eastern Europe in depth and place it in historical perspective. In the spring of 1929 Fulbright and Fodor toured the chanceries and palaces of Sophia, Belgrade, and Athens, interviewing prime ministers and other high-ranking officials. Had he not come down with a severe throat infection, the young American might well have followed Fodor into the world of international journalism. As it was, his brief tenure with his remarkable host constituted an education in itself, his introduction to the real world of international politics.

Fulbright returned to Fayetteville fully intending, after he recovered his health, to run the family businesses. His father had died in 1923 after a sudden illness when Fulbright was in his junior year of college. Roberta protected and even improved on the family empire, but she longed for help and looked to her youngest son for support. But during a business trip to Washington, Bill met Elizabeth Williams, the only daughter of a well-to-do Philadelphia Main Line family. Fulbright was smitten. To be near Betty, he enrolled in George Washington Law School. Despite the objections of Betty's mother, who had never been west of the Appalachians, the two were married on June 15, 1932. For the next half century the couple would complement each other as they worked to raise a family and carve out a niche in the political world. The outgoing, politically acute Betty was the perfect match for her, at times, introverted and acerbic husband.

Fulbright finished second in his class at George Washington and took a job with the Justice Department. During his brief tenure there, he helped try the famous *Schecter* case, which decided the constitutionality of the National Industrial Recovery Act. Early in 1935 Fulbright left Justice to take a position teaching at George Washington. If thoughts of running for public office crossed Fulbright's mind during this period, there is no evidence of it. He was not much given to taking his own temperature. Teaching seemed an admirable profession, in itself a form of public service, but as always he was open-minded about his future.

In 1937 Bill and Betty left Washington for Fayetteville. Roberta was again pleading for help with the family business, and northwest Arkansas seemed a good place to raise children. Within months of arriving, Betty gave birth to the second of two daughters, and Bill took a part-time teaching position with the University of Arkansas Law School. His mother, however, had bigger plans for him.

On September 12, 1939, the very eve of World War II, John C. Futrall, president of the University of Arkansas, was killed in an automobile accident. Roberta Fulbright was a close friend of the Futralls and, using the editorial page of the family-owned *Northwest Arkansas Times* as a platform, had become a political power in the state. During the weeks that followed Futrall's death, she used her considerable influence to have Bill named president of the University of Arkansas, making him the youngest college head in the United States. After two uneventful years in that post, during which he spent much time urging his fellow Arkansans to shake off their inferiority complex and move into the twentieth century, Fulbright was fired by Governor Homer Adkins. In axing Bill, Adkins was revenging himself on Roberta for opposing him in the 1940 gubernatorial election.

Six months following his dismissal as president of the University of Arkansas, Fulbright ran successfully for a seat in the House of Representatives. The third district, which he represented, included the top tier of northwest Arkansas counties, most of which epitomized the rural, upland South. The former Rhodes scholar did not know the names of all the counties and had never even visited six, but he and Betty set out in the family Ford, barnstorming through every hamlet and village. The initial run for Congress proved to be an invaluable political education for Fulbright. He learned firsthand about the principal concerns of his constituents, and most important, he learned to listen.

When Fulbright arrived in Washington in 1943, the Allied armies were on the attack on nearly every front. It was time, many congressmen and women believed, to begin planning for the peace. Fulbright decided that he was going to be part of that process. Like Theodore Roosevelt, who a half century earlier had decided that overseas expansion was an issue whose time had come, Fulbright sensed that America was at long last ready for Wilsonian internationalism. Perhaps if he could define and articulate the direction America should take, he could simultaneously advance his own interests and those of his country.

Fulbright's old Oxford tutor, Ronald McCallum, had long since convinced him that the concept of the League of Nations had been sound; the organization had not worked because political figures on both sides of the Atlantic had never been willing to make a true commitment to the principles that underlay it and had attempted to use it for their own selfish political purposes. Fulbright made that point repeatedly in various speeches during his first year in Congress and suggested that the great conflict then reaching its climax offered America and the world a second chance. Underlying Fulbright's internationalism was the assumption that there existed a body of ideas and a constellation of economic and political institutions that together defined Western civilization, that the United States shared in these ideals and institutions, and that, therefore, it had an obligation to defend them. Isolationism, he repeatedly declared, was just a facet of old-fashioned nationalism, and nationalism was chiefly responsible for the endless cycle of competition and conflict that marred world history.

In a speech to the American Bar Association, Fulbright outlined his ideal institution: a global organization with a collective security mandate and a police-keeping force sufficient to enforce that mandate. In agreeing to participate in such an organization, he declared, the United States must realize that it would have to surrender a portion of its sovereignty. Once the charter of the new organization was ratified, the president, through his representatives, would have the authority – without consulting Congress or anyone else – to commit American troops to military action authorized by the world body. To this end, the freshman congressman from Arkansas cosponsored the Fulbright–Connally Resolution, which placed Congress on record as favoring participation in a postwar collective security organization.

Using his new-found national reputation as an internationalist as a springboard, Fulbright defeated Homer Adkins for a seat in the U.S. Senate in 1944. Adkins was a Bible-thumping fundamentalist and a segregationist. During the campaign he accused his young opponent of being a ''nigger-lover'' and a communist sympathizer as well as a draft dodger. Using the University of Arkansas alumni roles as a constituent base, Fulbright managed to defeat Adkins in a bitterly contested runoff.

J. William Fulbright's political achievements since his dismissal from the presidency of the University of Arkansas were stunning. With no organization and no practical experience, he had defeated two entrenched Arkansas politicos and gained favorable attention from both the national and international media. Roosevelt, Hull, and other administration figures decided that the Arkansan was a southerner with whom the administration could take pride in being associated – for a change. The educated citizenry of Arkansas – liberal, moderate, and conservative – concluded that in Fulbright the state had a man that would possibly bring Arkansas the respect it had been so long denied. The parallels to Woodrow Wilson's symbolic importance to the South were striking. While reassuring voters that he would be mindful of their vested interests, Fulbright had campaigned and won as a "national" legislator. His victory over Homer Adkins reinforced his conviction that it was possible to immerse himself in the great questions of the day and simultaneously survive as an Arkansas politician.

Like many other Americans, Fulbright was disturbed by the apparent direction of U.S. foreign policy in 1945. To him the Yalta Accords seemed nothing more than a dressed-up spheres-of-interest deal, and the all-encompassing Security Council veto appeared to ensure that the projected world organization would be more of a four-policemen operation than a true collective security apparatus where each of the members surrendered a portion of its sovereignty for the common good. The Roosevelt administration, he decided, was not going to retreat from its commitment to internationalism if he could help it. "American foreign policy should have two anchors," he proclaimed in a March 1945 speech, "the Atlantic community [a concept then being touted by Walter Lippmann] and a collective security organization in which all nations were represented."[6]

At this, the very dawn of the cold war, J. William Fulbright saw no reason why the Western democracies and the Soviet Union could not coexist peacefully. The Russians, he said, had given no evidence that they intended to dominate the world through force, as the Germans had attempted to do. Let capitalism and communism compete peacefully. The best system would win. Indeed, he observed, "the highly emotional attacks upon communism and Russia by some of our public orators is an indication of the weakness of their faith in our system."[7]

Although Fulbright failed in his attempt to secure a seat on the Senate Foreign Relations Committee (SFRC), his preoccupation with the future of the United Nations continued. The United Nations Conference on International Organization (UNCIO) was scheduled to open in San Francisco in late April 1945, and like many other Americans, the junior senator from Arkansas had grave doubts about the new president's ability to lead the nation and the world at such a crucial time in its history. No less than Franklin Roosevelt, Harry S. Truman was first and foremost a politician – but without Roosevelt's education or contacts in the eastern establishment. The president had selected the Missourian to be his running mate in 1944, largely because he was ac-

6 J. W. Fulbright, "American Foreign Policy – International Organization for World Security," Mar. 28, 1945, BCN 24, F36, Senatorial Papers of J. William Fulbright, Mullins Library, University of Arkansas, Fayetteville, Ark. [hereinafter referred to as SPF].
7 Ibid.

ceptable to liberals as well as conservatives. By the time of Roosevelt's death, Harry Truman had earned a reputation for fairness, honesty, and some knowledge of Congress and budgetary matters, but no one would ever accuse him of being an expert on foreign affairs. Roosevelt had contributed to the problem by refusing to take Truman into his confidence and shutting him out of all discussions pertaining to war and postwar problems. To Fulbright's dismay, for the next year the new president oscillated back and forth between a policy of confrontation with and conciliation toward the Soviet Union. What he deplored most was the tendency of the United States to act unilaterally outside the confines of the United Nations.

Indeed, by the spring of 1946 Fulbright had become deeply disillusioned with the Truman administration's foreign policies. The White House and State Department seemed to be confused, distracted, and inept, unwilling or unable either to confront or to conciliate the Soviet Union. While Truman lectured Soviet Foreign Minister Vyacheslav Molotov in late 1945 on his country's failure to live up to the Yalta Accords and then sponsored Churchill's bellicose Iron Curtain speech at Westminster College in the spring of 1946, he at the same time presided over a dramatic weakening of the U.S. military establishment and a diplomatic campaign of conciliation at the various foreign ministers' conferences held in the aftermath of World War II. Against the advice of his Senate colleagues, his wife, and his chief of staff, the junior senator from Arkansas opened up on the Truman administration the first week in April. American foreign policy was in shambles, he told the Senate. While paying lip service to internationalism, the White House and State Department had crammed Argentina (that nation had remained neutral during World War II and acted as a haven for fugitive Nazis) and the Baruch plan (which would freeze the atomic status quo) down Moscow's throat at the UN. At the same time, Washington had demanded the right to retain exclusive possession of island bases in the Pacific captured during World War II while denying the right of other nations to do the same.

"The people in the country are very conscious of the lack of direction given to our policy by the President," Fulbright observed to a constituent. "My hope is that with a little prodding here and there, and with a little judicial criticism he may be encouraged to take a direct position and get some better men to advise him."[8] In the view of the White House, Fulbright's criticism became somewhat less than judicious when, following the election of Republican majorities in both houses of Congress in the fall of 1946, he suggested that President Truman resign. The man from Missouri demurred, of course, and from that point on referred to the junior senator from Arkansas as "that over-educated Oxford S.O.B."[9]

8 JWF to J. Q. Mahaffey, Dec. 1, 1945, BCN 6, F38, SPF.
9 Lucille Mock, "Truman and Fulbright, the Controversial Proposal for Resignation," Ms. on file, Harry S. Truman Library, Independence, Mo.

When exactly Fulbright began considering the idea of a foreign exchange program is unclear. He would claim that the atomic bombing of Hiroshima and Nagasaki focused his thoughts. In the new age of mass destruction, world leaders could not afford to miscalculate. Fulbright was not ready to abandon internationalism by any means, but over the fall and winter of 1945, he had begun to have doubts about the willingness of the nations of the world to rely on the collective security organization to safeguard their interests. Nationalism and unilateralism seemed more entrenched than ever. "I do not think that mere amendments to the Constitution or Charter or any other mechanical step will automatically bring about a system of law and order," he confided to a friend. "While these changes are necessary, they are only part of the picture. The prejudices and misconceptions which exist in every country regarding foreign people are the great barrier to any system of government." [10]

On September 27, 1945, Fulbright rose on the floor of the Senate. "I ask unanimous consent to introduce a bill . . . authorizing the use of credits established through the sale of surplus properties abroad," he requested of a near-empty chamber, "for the promotion of international good will through the exchange of students in the fields of education, culture, and science." [11] On April 12, 1946, just six weeks after subcommittee hearings, the Senate unanimously passed Fulbright's proposal with no debate and without a roll call vote. The House quickly followed suit. In 1948 the Fulbright exchange program got under way when 35 students and one professor came to the United States and 65 Americans ventured overseas. Two decades later, exchange programs had been set up with 110 countries and geographical areas under forty-nine formal exchange agreements. The total cost of the program to the United States during this period was $400 million, mostly in foreign currencies. Between 1948 and 1966, 82,585 individuals – 47,950 of them students – received Fulbright fellowships. Twelve million schoolchildren in the United States and abroad were taught by exchange teachers. As of 1987 the program could claim 156,000 alumni in the United States and abroad.

The exchange program was one of the few things in Fulbright's life that he felt passionately about. In its defense he could become emotional, irrational, and vindictive. During the course of his public life he would work assiduously to maintain and increase its funding. Those who wished to hurt him came quickly to realize that the way to do it was by damaging the exchange program. Indeed, international education became something of a religion for a man whom nearly everyone described as nonreligious. To his mind, it was a panacea for the world's problems. Its working would produce a kind of international talented tenth that would lead humankind into a new

10 JWF to George A. Horne, Feb. 6, 1946, BCN 24, F50, SPF.
11 Quoted in Johnson and Gwertzman, *Fulbright: The Dissenter*, 128.

era of cooperation based on mutual understanding. Its products would be public-spirited rationalists who would understand that war is the ultimate folly of *Homo sapiens*.

Despite his differences with the Truman administration, Fulbright enthusiastically supported the Truman Doctrine and the Marshall Plan. At this point in his career, again in spite of his misgivings about the quality of executive leadership, he believed in an active, powerful presidency with the ability and will to conduct the nation's foreign relations. The legislative branch should limit itself to consultation and articulation of broad principles. Increasingly disillusioned with the leading members of the United Nations, if not the organization itself, the Arkansan became a leading advocate of a United States of Europe (USE). Indeed, he believed that aid provided under the European Recovery Program ought to be used as leverage to force the nations of Europe to integrate. He readily admitted that communism flourished in conditions of economic and social insecurity, but the Marshall Plan was not a cure-all. America could provide a minimal amount of aid, but if Europe were to attain lasting prosperity, and thus democracy, its various national components would have to integrate their economies. Moreover, unification in the political sphere could very well solve the age-old problem of aggressive nationalism. Within a federation of Europe, the victors of World War II could control Germany, ensuring that it did not use its industrial and technical might in another insane attempt to conquer the world. In turn, with its fears concerning German aggression laid to rest, the Kremlin just might cease its expansionist policies and remove its boot from the nape of Eastern Europe's neck. Indeed, persuaded by Walter Lippmann, with whom he was forming an increasingly close relationship, Fulbright avoided portraying the envisioned European federation as an overtly anti-Soviet bloc. A United States of Europe would preserve existing power relationships until the UN had a chance "to succeed as a voluntary union of peoples" and "assist Russia to develop the self-restraint which is so patently lacking in her present philosophy of government."[12]

Fulbright frequently complained that his senatorial duties did not leave him enough time to read, but compared to the average politician, the Arkansan was a bookworm. During the crucial period from 1947 to 1950, he read everything he could get his hands on pertaining to foreign affairs. Fulbright was particularly impressed with the reasoning and arguments of George Kennan, who as head of the policy-planning staff in the State Department emerged after World War II as America's foremost expert on East–West relations.

In the wake of the Berlin blockade of 1948–9 Kennan had put forward

12 *Congressional Record*, Senate, Apr. 7, 1947, 3138.

three strategems for maintaining the global balance of power and containing Soviet expansion short of armed conflict. The United States should shore up those nations threatened by Soviet imperialism through programs of military and economic aid. It should by exploiting divisions within the communist world work to reduce Moscow's ability to project its power beyond its own borders. And America should attempt to modify, over time, the Soviet leadership's view of international relations, with the objective of bringing about a negotiated settlement of differences. The breakup of international communism was an irreversible trend, certain to proceed regardless of what the United States did, he believed. America need only to align itself with it.

In its defense policy, Kennan pointed out, the United States must match means with ends. Because American resources were limited, the nation could not blindly follow a policy of globalism, regarding communism anywhere and everywhere as an equally dangerous threat to American interests.

Although he regarded the foreign policies of the Soviet Union as inimical to the interests of the United States, Fulbright never accepted the idea of a monolithic communist threat. Like Kennan, he was able and willing to distinguish between communism as a political and economic principle and Soviet imperialism. "We are not fighting communists as a political party, but we are actually fighting the Chinese and the Russians," he wrote a friend of his mother's.

> The Russians have adopted the communist doctrine as an instrument to be used in their effort to dominate their fellowman. They use this doctrine much the same way as they might use airplanes or guns and have done so very effectively. In other words, if communists in a country have no connection with the Russians in their efforts to dominate the world, they can then be considered much like any other political party with which one violently disagrees.[13]

In 1950, as the administration was secretly embracing a globalist approach to containing communism vis-à-vis NSC-68, and neo-isolationists were calling for the removal of American troops from Europe and a defensive perimeter in Asia that excluded the mainland, Fulbright attempted to carve out a middle ground. Repeating the standard Atlantacist arguments concerning the indivisibility of cultures and the interdependence of economies, he addressed the foreign policy debate then raging in Congress:

> Broadly speaking, there may be said to be three policies that have been advanced in recent weeks. . . . First, the limitation of our commitments to the defense of the Western Hemisphere with emphasis upon air and sea power. Second, the so-called Truman doctrine of opposing aggression in every area where it appears. Third, participation in the creation of a land army in Western Europe, in addition to the defense of the

13 JWF to Lessie Read, Jan. 3, 1951, BCN 48, F11, SPF.

> Western Hemisphere. One may perhaps call this the Truman doctrine with limitations.''[14]

He left no doubt as to the approach he favored:

> It is my view that the safest and wisest policy for us to follow is neither the Hoover–[Joseph P.]Kennedy–Taft policy nor the Truman policy. The former is dangerous to our security and is morally wrong. The latter is beyond our capacity to carry out. I firmly believe, however, that by limiting our commitments to Europe and certain additional strategic areas as I have indicated, we can bring about the unity of the free world . . .''[15]

Fulbright campaigned unsuccessfully for Adlai Stevenson in the 1952 presidential campaign and then further endeared himself to American liberals by confronting Senator Joe McCarthy. Fulbright hated and feared demagogues. Charismatic figures who claimed divine or other kinds of inspiration and who pretended to embody the public interest in their person chilled and repelled him. For him, McCarthy was just such a person; indeed, he believed that the anticommunist witch-hunt spawned by the Wisconsin Republican constituted one of the gravest threats to democracy and civil liberty that the Republic had ever faced. Fulbright publicly defended State Department consultant Philip Jessup and others from attack and was the only member of the upper house to vote against appropriations for McCarthy's Permanent Subcommittee on Investigations. And this was after McCarthy had helped defeat several defiant senators for reelection in 1952. When finally the tide began to turn against the Wisconsin demagogue, the junior senator from Arkansas played a key role in the move to censure.

In the final analysis Fulbright was more frightened by the ism than the man. There would always be opportunists and charlatans ready to play on the public's fears and prejudices. Historically, the American people, optimistic and pragmatic, had resisted those who practiced the politics of fear. But the atomic age and the confrontation with the Soviet Union seemed to have unbalanced the popular mind. In the midst of the second Red Scare, the Arkansan speculated on its causes. Perhaps it was the anxiety of unresolved conflict, the siege mentality of a nation confronted with an apparently implacable enemy. Or more darkly, the breadth and depth of McCarthyism could reflect a burgeoning know-nothingism. In their frustration, his compatriots seemed ready to condemn any idea that they considered alien. According to McCarthyites, other cultures were by definition evil and potentially contaminating. Ideas and the questioning that produced them were portrayed as hidden avenues by which communism could gain access to America's psyche. During his jousts with McCarthy and his supporters, Fulbright felt

---

14 *Congressional Record*, Senate, Jan. 22, 1951, 521.
15 Ibid., 523.

compelled more than once to denounce "the swinish blight of anti-intellectualism." Most disturbing, Fulbright sensed that McCarthyism had merely subsided, that it lurked beneath the surface of American life, ready to burst forth in its consuming fury at the next crisis.

Liberal internationalists such as Henry Wallace and Eleanor Roosevelt assumed that their creed was based on a tolerance for other races, cultures, and religions. They associated isolationism with parochialism and nativism. Their vision of a parliament of humankind had no room for distinctions based on ideology, lifestyle, and particularly skin color. Ignoring the fact that southerners supported internationalism and multilateralism primarily for economic reasons, many northern liberals assumed that because of Fulbright's education and his views on foreign affairs he was one of a small breed of courageous southerners who opposed discrimination against African Americans and who were willing to risk their careers by participating in the burgeoning civil rights movement. The Arkansan's admirers had sadly miscalculated. During the late 1940s Fulbright had joined with Richard Russell (D–Georgia) and other southern senators to filibuster against legislation creating the Fair Employment Practices Commission. In 1956 he signed the Southern Manifesto, a document endorsed by southern senators and congressmen and women calling for all legal resistance to implementation of the Supreme Court's 1954 *Brown* decision denouncing segregation in public schools. Indeed, Fulbright would not openly support a civil rights measure until 1970.

That J. William Fulbright was a segregationist is indisputable. He would claim throughout his career that his position on civil rights was a matter of political expediency. "There's no mystery why the people from Georgia, Mississippi, and so on have been what they call bigots," he declared. "They inherited an historical situation. You couldn't be elected if you didn't have that view." That was no less true in Arkansas than elsewhere in the region, he insisted. "People in eastern Arkansas . . . couldn't see their daughter going to school with a black," he argued. "They always imagined the black would rape their daughter. This was the worst possible thing. They were scared of them actually."[16] He also justified his segregationist position on the traditional white supremacist grounds that a democracy should not, and could not, alter local prejudices through legislation. But Fulbright's conservatism on the race issue did not stem solely from political expediency. To his mind the blacks he knew were not equal to whites, nor could they be made so by legislative decree. Throughout his career, he would regard involuntary integration as anathema. Southerners, Fulbright believed, were trapped by their environment and history, and neither he nor Congress nor the Supreme Court could change that.

But Fulbright was no racist in the Vardaman–Talmadge–Bilbo tradition. He was no more hostile or resentful toward African Americans than he was

16 Fulbright interview.

toward Indonesians. On a personal level, he judged people by their manners, personal cleanliness, and education, not by their skin color. He did not, however, feel compelled by Christian duty or social conscience to use the power of the state to remedy historical wrongs, correct maldistribution of wealth, or legislate equality of opportunity. His racism was a combination of the blindness of the southern highlander who had not experienced black life and culture and the noblesse oblige of the planting aristocracy. One of his long-time aides recalled that ''he shares the class and caste consciousness of his planter friends from eastern Arkansas, but he does not share their fear of race-mixing.''[17]

Fulbright saw no contradiction between his views on international affairs and civil rights. Indeed, he was baffled by the slings and arrows sent his way by the leading internationalists of the day. What he favored was cultural autonomy for all peoples. He was an ardent Wilsonian, and like Arthur Link, he believed that Wilson's pledge to ''make the world safe for democracy'' indicated (at least by 1917) not a determination to export American culture and institutions but rather a commitment to the principle of national self-determination. As a southerner with a strong sense of class, kinship, and place, he believed it no less abhorrent that the North should impose its mores and social theories on the South than the United States should force its culture, political institutions, and economic theories on another society.

Fulbright shared the typical liberals' view of the Eisenhower administration. The president was a golf-playing, bourbon-drinking former general that had neither the qualifications nor the intellect to lead the nation. Indeed, for Fulbright as for Adlai Stevenson, Arthur Schlesinger, Jr., and John Kenneth Galbraith, Eisenhower epitomized the materialism and superficiality of the 1950s. The former Rhodes scholar took the typical liberal stance on Secretary of State John Foster Dulles as well, namely, that he was a self-righteous moralist that brought to anticommunism an extremism and rigidity that was frankly dangerous. Fulbright used his seat on the Senate Foreign Relations Committee (he had become a member in 1949) to rake the Republican foreign policy over the coals. Massive retaliation was an absurd concept, he declared, an approach that would lead to either nuclear war or a communist takeover of the developing world. Fulbright castigated the administration for not responding to conciliatory gestures coming from the Kremlin following Joseph Stalin's death in 1953. Dulles's offer to Egypt to help fund construction of the High Aswan Dam and subsequent withdrawal of that offer in response to Gamal Abdel Nasser's flirtations with the communist world epitomized the rigidity and bankruptcy of the Eisenhower–Dulles approach.

From its inception, the foreign aid program had received Fulbright's staunch support. He had voted for and spoken in behalf of Lend-Lease, the British loan, the Marshall Plan, Point Four, and the various mutual security

17 Interview with Lee Williams, June 20, 1989, Washington, D.C.

acts. He did so because he believed that foreign aid drove the exchange program but also because he was convinced that it served the national interest. Beginning in 1956, however, the Arkansan repeatedly criticized Dulles and Eisenhower for presenting a foreign aid program that stressed military aid at the expense of economic support and cultural exchange. In so doing, he argued, the United States was converting tribal and regional rivalries from minor military confrontations fought with primitive weapons into modern, deadly wars capable of wiping out entire populations. Given the fact that Nikita Khrushchev had targeted developing, Third World nations as potential Soviet client states, aid to alleviate social and economic problems was, and would continue to be, more important than tanks and bullets.

As the decade of the 1950s drew to a close, J. William Fulbright stood as one of liberal internationalism's shining stars, this despite the fact that he was at heart a nineteenth-century English liberal. In a 1955 column Walter Lippmann had christened him as the Senate's leading intellectual. He had stood against the forces of isolationism and McCarthyism and had led the way in denouncing the putative materialism and superficiality of the Eisenhower administration. Like Arthur Schlesinger, Jr., and John Kenneth Galbraith, Fulbright enjoyed the role of liberal gadfly. But history had other roles in store for him, roles replete with tragedy, triumph, and above all, irony.

2

Cuba and Camelot

In early 1959, ten years after his appointment to the Senate Foreign Relations Committee, J. William Fulbright became its chairman. Although from the beginning he had been closely identified with foreign affairs, Fulbright's rise to a position of influence on the committee was unusually swift. Through deaths, departures, and defeats, and through the seniority system he had initially deplored, he moved upward rapidly. By 1956 he was the number two man. Tom Connally, the chairman when Fulbright joined the committee, had left the Senate in 1952 at the age of seventy-five. Alexander Wiley of Wisconsin, who became the Republican chairman under Eisenhower, was sixty-nine and seventy during the two years he held the post. When the Democrats regained control of the Senate in 1954, Walter George assumed the reins at the age of seventy-seven. After Herman Talmadge took George's seat, the aged Theodore Francis Green became the chairman.

By 1959 Green was ninety years old and, not surprisingly, found it difficult to keep up with what day it was, much less the complexities of foreign affairs. The de facto chairman of the SFRC was Chief of Staff Carl Marcy. During the debates over the mutual security bills, it was customary for the press to be admitted to the committee room, where in executive session the members had "marked up," that is, made specific revisions in, the administration's proposed measure. "Senator Green loved to have the press come storming into the room so he could tell them what happened," Marcy remembered. The reporters would ask a question or two and then leave. As soon as Green departed, very pleased with himself, the press would return and get the real lowdown from Marcy.[1]

In an indiscreet moment Marcy remarked to Carroll Kilpatrick of the *Washington Post* that Green was getting so confused that in effect he, Marcy, was having to act in his place. Shortly thereafter, a story appeared in the Providence, Rhode Island, *Journal* declaring that the state's native son was senile and needed to step down. Deeply hurt, Green submitted his resignation as chairman of the SFRC to Lyndon Johnson in the middle of January 1959.

1 Interview with Carl Marcy, Oct. 10, 1988, Washington, D.C.

A week later Johnson ordered Marcy to gather the committee together. Although he was not a member of the SFRC, no one dared object when Johnson not only sat in but acted as chairman. He solemnly informed the assemblage that Senator Green had submitted his letter of resignation and, shedding copious crocodile tears, declared, "Theodore, you can't do this, it's the goddam press that's picking on you, you know they're a bunch of so-and-sos; you're the greatest chairman that the Committee has ever had. I plead with you to reconsider." That theme was echoed around the table, and it soon became apparent that LBJ had overdone it.

As Green wavered, Johnson whispered in desperation to Marcy: "Carl, I'm going to get him out of the room, you go out with him." Johnson put his arm around his aged colleague and said, "Theodore, you're feeling very strongly about this; I wish you'd go outside and think about it a little bit. It's a very important decision that you're making." As soon as the pair was out of the room, Johnson changed his tone. The old man was sick and tired, he told the members; if they did not get him out, he would continue to embarrass the party and probably die on their hands, to boot. Although he had not been told explicitly, Marcy knew what to do. He took Green into the back room where Eddy Higgins, the senator's longtime administrative assistant, was waiting. The two staffers argued that Green had submitted his resignation and ought to stick with it. Some very distinguished men had stepped down from the same post. It was up to Green to set an example, they said. The aged Rhode Islander made his way back to the committee and informed Johnson, with great solemnity, that he was standing by his decision.

A delighted Johnson slapped Green on the back, a gesture that sent the ninety-year-old into a fit of uncontrollable shaking, and proposed that he be made chairman emeritus. The committee voted unanimously to approve. The majority leader then turned to Fulbright and said: "Bill, you're the chairman." With that, the meeting broke up.[2]

For Fulbright his ascension to the chairmanship marked the end of one journey and the beginning of another. He had decided early on to be a "national" senator and to make his mark in the field of foreign affairs. That particular ambition could have but one goal: chairman of the SFRC. From his new vantage point, Fulbright – like Henry Cabot Lodge, William Borah, and Arthur Vandenberg – could critique and at times influence American foreign policy. He would be sought out for his opinions, courted by various administrations who were dependent on him to shepherd treaties and foreign assistance bills through Congress. What attracted Fulbright about his new post was that he could retain what he perhaps coveted most, his independence – independence of judgment, action, and to a certain extent, control over his time.

2 Donald A. Ritchie, interviewer, *Oral History Interviews: Carl A. Marcy* (Senate Historical Office: Washington, D.C., 1983), 96–100.

Although it was not apparent at the time, Fulbright's assumption of the post of chairman of the Senate Foreign Relations Committee in 1959 was a significant development in contemporary American history. No man since Henry Cabot Lodge brought such intellect, such vision, such ambition, and if his detractors are to be believed, such perversity to the position. It is true that the powerful progressive Republican William E. Borah intimidated presidents and secretaries of state from 1924 through 1932, but despite the claims of his defenders, the Idahoan was an isolationist emotionally, intellectually, and ideologically. He was both ignorant and fearful of foreign powers and cultures. His role in twentieth-century foreign affairs was that of a stubborn and effective reactionary.[3]

Like Lodge, who held a Ph.D. in history from Harvard, Fulbright revered the past and was determined to preserve American traditions and values from onslaughts by selfish special interests and materialistic know-nothings. Both saw themselves as national senators and the Senate Foreign Relations Committee as a full partner with the executive in the framing, if not the conduct, of American foreign policy. Like Lodge, Fulbright admired the British parliamentary system and believed that political parties in America ought to take clear-cut positions on vital issues, and when Congress and the executive were controlled by the same party, the legislative majority and the White House ought to work hand in hand to advance those positions; when they were not, the SFRC ought to hammer out an alternative foreign policy. The committee's two most formidable chairmen differed on substance, at least initially. Lodge was a Rooseveltian imperialist and a nationalist of the first order; Fulbright, a Wilsonian internationalist who continued to believe that the hope of the world lay, first, in regional groupings and then a world federation in which the member states surrendered a portion of their national sovereignty for the common good. Like Lodge, Fulbright was proud, stubborn, and intellectually arrogant. And like the New Englander, he was a natural dissenter. At the outset of his career as the SFRC's longest-reigning chairman, Fulbright believed that he could look forward to the same relationship with first John F. Kennedy and then Lyndon Johnson that Lodge had enjoyed with Theodore Roosevelt. He could not know that though they were of the same party, his relationship with Lyndon Johnson after the Texan became president would rather come to resemble that between Henry Cabot Lodge and Woodrow Wilson.[4]

In his effort to convert the SFRC into an effective, long-term critic and framer of foreign policy, Fulbright was aided and abetted by the committee's formidable chief of staff, Carl Marcy. The mustachioed, dapper Oregonian was a man of medium build but massive ego, the ultimate Capitol Hill ém-

---

3 See Robert J. Maddox, *William Borah and American Foreign Policy* (Baton Rouge, 1970).
4 William C. Widenor, *Henry Cabot Lodge and the Search for an American Foreign Policy* (Berkeley, 1980), 26–7, 30–1, 37–9, 48–50, 52–4, 266–300.

inence grise. He was educated, intelligent, organized, and ambitious to the point of obsession. He identified totally with the SFRC and, after Fulbright's accession to the chairmanship, with its chairman. In the junior senator from Arkansas, Marcy had found a man he could serve, indeed, a man worth serving. This was no provincial hayseed or tottering octogenarian but rather the architect of a massive educational exchange program and the author of the UN resolution. He was smart, sophisticated, and respected by the eastern establishment press. "I was already somewhat in awe of Fulbright by the time he became chairman," Marcy recalled.[5] Fulbright returned Marcy's loyalty with absolute trust. Each saw in the other a man who could help convert the SFRC into not only a forum for the discussion of contemporary foreign policy but a major contributor to the formulation of that policy.

From the time of his accession to the post of chief of staff in 1955, Marcy envisioned the SFRC as an institution that would reflect the attitudes and interests of the populace as a whole and that would command the respect, if not the admiration, of the State Department. Marcy believed that the Congress ought to be a coequal partner with the executive in the framing of American foreign policy. "There is no constitutional reason," he wrote Lindsay Rogers, "why the Senate should not be asked for its advice and consent prior to the signing of a treaty, especially one of significance."[6] Green's age, conservatism, and lack of stature made that impossible, however, and it was not until Fulbright took over the top spot that Marcy was able to make any headway.

From the outset Fulbright took the position that the SFRC ought to be above party politics, a stance that Carl Marcy enthusiastically endorsed. By that Fulbright did not mean that the Democrats should not dominate the positions and policies taken by the committee; that should occur naturally by virtue of the fact that his party was in the majority. However much the Democrats differed among themselves, they would not allow issues to be used against them for partisan advantage. But neither did he intend to permit representatives of either party to manipulate international crises and foreign policy issues simply to embarrass the opposition. The committee should take rational, enlightened positions rooted in a realistic internationalism and then let the chips fall where they might. Courtesy and consultation were the keys, he believed, to preserving what he called "unpartisan" foreign policy.[7] As a result, Fulbright made a great effort to get along with the stodgy, pedestrian Bourke Hickenlooper of Iowa. The Iowan was a conservative but not a reactionary, and he hated demagoguery. Each man believed that he possessed qualities that complemented those of the other. Hickenlooper valued Ful-

---

5 Marcy interview.
6 Marcy to Lindsay Rogers, Sept. 10, 1963, Box 4, Folder June–Sept., Papers of Carl Marcy, SFRC, RG 46 [hereinafter referred to as Marcy Papers], National Archives, Arlington, Va. [hereinafter referred to as NA].
7 Marcy to JWF, Feb. 24, 1959, Box 3, Folder Jan.–Dec., Marcy Papers.

bright's knowledge of history and foreign cultures, whereas Fulbright saw Hickenlooper as a simple, down-to-earth fellow, a farmer from the Midwest who was close to the people.[8]

Carl Marcy had a passion for anonymity, and he absolutely forbade members of the staff to write about the committee's operations for publication or to give interviews. Indeed, if interviews were to be given, not for attribution, of course, he would give them.[9] A past master at the strategic leak, Marcy spent hours each week cultivating and manipulating the press. Attracted by the chief of staff's forthcomingness and by Fulbright's ideals and charisma, a loyal band of congressional reporters attached themselves to the committee. The group included Ned Kenworthy and John Finney of the *New York Times* and Don Oberdorfer and Murray Marder of the *Washington Post*. They gathered outside the SFRC committee room before and after executive hearings to receive the official word from the chairman and then assembled in the staff offices for an off-the-record briefing from Marcy.[10] While Marcy's clandestine open door to the press enhanced Fulbright's image and gave the SFRC more clout, it occasionally got him and the chairman in hot water with Republicans on the committee and the executive branch.[11]

The SFRC–Fulbright groupies were simply reporters, of course, and ranked a cut below columnists and news analysts like Walter Lippmann and James Reston, whom Fulbright and Marcy regarded as full-fledged partners in the business of framing an alternative foreign policy. Fulbright continued to consult Lippmann on virtually every issue. Although he saw a variety of other columnists on a regular basis, no other pundit ever attained the same degree of intimacy with the chairman except, occasionally, Reston.[12]

"The SFRC under your chairmanship now has an opportunity to serve as a rallying point for critical and constructive opinion in this country," Chester Bowles wrote, "and I am confident that you will use this new opportunity with maximum effectiveness."[13] The foreign policy opening for which Fulbright and the Democrats had been waiting came finally in the late spring of 1960 when one of Eisenhower's greatest foreign policy disasters – the U-2 affair – emerged in the midst of what was to be one of its greatest triumphs – the Eisenhower–Khrushchev summit. That it threatened Fulbright's most cherished foreign policy goal – rapprochement between East and West – made for a welcoming conjoining of politics and principle.

8 Ritchie, *Interviews: Marcy*, 64–65.
9 Marcy to Roger Hilsman, Dec. 10, 1959, BCN 139, F2, SPF.
10 Ritchie, *Interviews: Marcy*, 122–3.
11 Hickenlooper to JWF, Oct. 11, 1963, Series 48:1, Box 5, F4, SPF.
12 Marcy, memorandum of conversation, June 24, 1959, Box 3, Folder Jan.–Dec., Marcy Papers.
13 Bowles to JWF, Feb. 7, 1959, BCN 135, F9, SPF.

In 1958 Khrushchev had threatened to sign a separate peace treaty with East Germany, thus turning over to that country the access route from West Germany to West Berlin. If Khrushchev made good on his threat, the Western allies would have to deal directly with the German Democratic Republic (GDR) in order to supply the ten thousand Western troops in Berlin across 110 miles of East German territory. In so doing, the North Atlantic Treaty Organization (NATO) would have to acknowledge the legitimacy of the East German regime and accept the permanent division of Germany, something the United States and its allies had steadfastly refused to do. East–West negotiations on a deadline dragged on through the remainder of 1958 and 1959. At the urging of British and French leaders, Eisenhower and Khrushchev agreed to a summit in the spring of 1960 on the German question.

Shortly before the president departed for Paris, the Soviets announced that they had shot down a U-2 reconnaissance plane over Sverdlovsk, and Khrushchev vehemently denounced the United States for violating Soviet airspace. When, subsequently, the State Department announced that the aircraft was a weather plane that had strayed off course, Khrushchev sprang his trap. The pilot, Francis Gary Powers, was in custody and had confessed to being a Central Intelligence Agency (CIA) operative. On May 11 Eisenhower publicly took full responsibility for the whole U-2 intelligence program, which dated back to 1956. Espionage was a "distasteful but vital necessity" to protect the United States and the free world "from another Pearl Harbor," he told a press conference.[14] The Paris summit opened as scheduled but then ended abruptly when Khrushchev angrily denounced the United States for spying on his country, demanded that Eisenhower punish those responsible, and walked out.

Shortly after the collapse of the Paris conference, Fulbright informed newspeople that he was going to ask the Senate to authorize the SFRC to investigate the U-2 affair. It would be "good for the soul of the country to get an understanding of what happened."[15] The Republicans, sensing an impending disaster, moved to seize the initiative. Everett Dirksen, the GOP's wavy-haired, honey-voiced hatchet man in the Senate, greeted Fulbright's request with an attempt to blame the summit debacle on Adlai Stevenson. Stevenson, who had repeatedly urged negotiations over Berlin, was "soft on communism," he proclaimed. After an unseemly partisan shouting match, the Senate authorized Fulbright to proceed with his investigation. For once on the defensive, Eisenhower pledged full cooperation with the Fulbright probe.[16]

The last week in June, Fulbright delivered the SFRC's verdict on the U-2

---

14 Chronology on U-2 Plane Incident, undated, BCN 147, F50, SPF.
15 Warren Duffee, "Fulbright Calls for U-2 Probe," *Washington Post,* May 22, 1960.
16 "GOP Charges Adlai Scuttled Summit," *Arkansas Gazette,* May 24, 1960; and "Ike Approves Congressional Probes of Summit Collapse, Promises Full Cooperation," *Arkansas Democrat,* May 26, 1960.

matter. His speech was a surgical strike that brought delight to the hearts of Democrats everywhere. The U-2 incident and the Eisenhower administration's handling of it "were the immediate cause of the collapse" of the summit. He spoke with "a heavy heart and some regret," Fulbright told the Senate, but it was clear that "we forced Khrushchev to wreck the conference by our own ineptness." The first mistake was not to suspend flights in mid-April; the second was for the president, "who embodies the sovereignty and dignity of his country," to have accepted responsibility; and the third was for the administration to self-righteously justify the flights and their continuance. Truth-telling was an admirable quality, as the president's defenders readily emphasized, but young George Washington, having admitted chopping down the cherry tree, did not go on to say: "Yes, I did it and I'm glad. The cherry tree was offensive to me, because it had grown so tall. I needed some cherries, and I shall chop down other cherry trees whenever I want more cherries."[17] There were many lessons to be learned from the U-2 incident, Fulbright declared solemnly, but he was not certain that the administration had learned any of them.

Although Fulbright had worked energetically in Jack Kennedy's behalf, he, like so many others, knew America's youngest president primarily by reputation. He remembered the Kennedy family's close ties to Joe McCarthy, but Fulbright was not one to begrudge a colleague his or her political expediency. Actually, during Kennedy's tenure in the Senate, Fulbright regarded him as a lightweight.[18] "I'd never really had a conversation with Jack to be frank about it – never had occasion," Fulbright later recalled. "He traveled in a different world."[19] But Kennedy's elevation to the presidency and Fulbright's tenure as chairman of the SFRC meant that the two would have to speak, would have to tread the same path even if they did not do it hand in hand.

There was some common ground. In appearance, they were opposites: Kennedy, with his flashy good looks, his aggressive, driving, if suave, style; Fulbright, reserved, sardonic, tweedy. But both men were attracted by words and ideas, they reveled in the pithy quote, they read and appreciated learning and art, they tolerated mistakes from talented subordinates, and they inspired loyalty and affection from followers who saw them as men of principle attempting to chart a firm course in a sea of expediency. Kennedy and Fulbright also detested pretentiousness and delighted in deflating overblown egos. In the end, each man viewed the other as someone to be reckoned with. Fulbright was an Arkansan and a senator, but he was a regional aristocrat with

---

17 *Congressional Record,* Senate, June 28, 1960, 14734–7.
18 Ritchie, *Interviews: Marcy,* 126.
19 Quoted in Haynes Johnson and Bernard M. Gwertzman, *Fulbright: The Dissenter* (New York, 1968), 195.

Oxford credentials – and he was chairman of the SFRC. Kennedy could, and did, play the role of a superficial young playboy, but he was smart and shrewd – and he was president of the United States.

In the aftermath of the 1960 election, rumors abounded in the national press that J. William Fulbright was being seriously considered for the post of secretary of state. They were true. As Bobby Kennedy later wrote, [Jack] "had worked with Fulbright, knew him better, was very impressed with the way he ran his committee." But there were problems. First and foremost was Fulbright's civil rights record. As soon as it became apparent that Kennedy was considering the Arkansan, John A. Morsell, assistant to the National Association for the Advancement of Colored People's (NAACP's) executive secretary, issued a public statement declaring that naming Fulbright secretary of state "would be one of the most colossal blunders of any administration." He called on the four-hundred-thousand-member organization to launch a nationwide campaign to keep Fulbright or any other signer of the Southern Manifesto out of the cabinet. Adding to Fulbright's woes was the fact that United Automobile Workers (UAW) chief Walter Reuther set up camp in Washington the last week in November and mounted a massive lobbying effort against one of organized labor's oldest and most consistent foes.[20] Perhaps the most powerful voices raised against Fulbright's candidacy for the top diplomatic post, however, were those of Israeli officials and American Zionists. In the aftermath of World War II Fulbright had supported the creation of the State of Israel, but he had been critical from time to time of the lobbying tactics employed by American Jewish groups on behalf of Israel. When in 1960 American labor unions refused to unload the Egyptian ship *Cleopatra* in retaliation for Nasser's closing of the Suez Canal to Israel, Fulbright dared to denounce them on the floor of the Senate.[21] During the weeks that followed, American Jews and officials of the Israeli embassy bombarded members of Kennedy's entourage with entreaties to pick anybody but Fulbright.[22] And so it was that the president passed over him in favor of Dean Rusk.

Fulbright was excited about the new administration, in part because he had had much to do with its composition. The chairman of the SFRC corresponded with, talked with, and played golf with Jack Kennedy throughout the last week in December and the first week in January.[23] He was responsible

---

20 *Kansas City Star,* Dec. 1, 1960.
21 *Fort Smith Southwest Times-Record,* Nov. 14, 1960.
22 Bill Gottlieb, American Council for Judaism, to JWF, Dec. 7, 1960; Lee Williams to Marshal D. Rothe, Jr., Dec. 9, 1960, Series 48:1, Box 1, F2, SPF; and "Dear Mr. President," Dec. 4, 1960, Fulbright Name File, Papers of John F. Kennedy, Columbia Point, Boston, Mass. [hereinafter referred to as Kennedy Papers].
23 "During Talks with President-elect Kennedy, Fulbright Hits on Arkansas Topics," *Northwest Arkansas Times,* Dec. 30, 1960.

for the appointment of George Ball, Adlai Stevenson's former campaign adviser, as undersecretary of state. He was among those who successfully urged Kennedy to appoint East Asian expert Edwin O. Reischauer as ambassador to Japan.[24] He championed the cause of William Benton as ambassador to the Court of St. James, a post that went to another Fulbright friend, David Bruce. He recommended Philip Stern, a Stevensonian from the 1952 campaign, as assistant secretary for congressional relations. He did not know the new secretaries of state and defense, Dean Rusk and Robert McNamara, but they were reputed to be men of integrity and vision. Neither was he acquainted with McGeorge Bundy, the dean of the faculty at Harvard, whom Kennedy selected to be his national security adviser, but the Arkansan had a weakness for academics from prestigious institutions. He did know Arthur Schlesinger and John Kenneth Galbraith, both of whom received appointments in the new administration.

There was from the outset a basic contradiction in the foreign policies of John Fitzgerald Kennedy. He and his advisers insisted that they were out to make the world safe for diversity, that under their leadership the United States would abandon the status quo policies of the past and support change, especially in the developing world. The Kennedy people did not object to Eisenhower's intervention into the internal affairs of other nations but to the fact that it usually intervened ineptly and always to prop up the status quo. According to Arthur Schlesinger, Jr., Kennedy fully understood that in Latin America "the militantly anti-revolutionary line" of the past was the policy most likely to strengthen the communists and lose the hemisphere. He and his advisers planned openings to the left to facilitate "democratic development."[25]

At the same time, the administration saw any significant change in the world balance of power as a threat to American security. Kennedy, Bundy, Rusk, and McNamara took very seriously Khrushchev's January 1961 speech offering support for "wars of national liberation"; it was, they believed, evidence of a new communist campaign to seize control of anticolonial and other revolutionary movements in economically underdeveloped regions. If the Third World was not to succumb to the siren's song of Marxism–Leninism, with all the implications that that would pose for the international balance of power, then the United States and other "developed" countries would have to demonstrate that economic progress could take place within a democratic framework. But the logic of this position, as John Gaddis has pointed out, was that the United States really would need a world resembling itself in order to be secure.[26]

Fulbright seemed to embrace the new administration's philosophy of for-

24 JWF to John F. Kennedy, Jan. 14, 1961, Series 1:1, Box 1, F4, SPF.
25 Arthur M. Schlesinger, Jr., *A Thousand Days* (Boston, 1965), 201.
26 John Lewis Gaddis, *Strategies of Containment: A Critical Appraisal of Postwar American National Security Policy* (New York, 1982), 208–9.

eign affairs enthusiastically. Consciously or unconsciously, Kennedy and his advisers were reacting to the criticisms of Eisenhower that Fulbright had voiced during the preceding six years. Here was an educated, interested president surrounded by activist intellectuals rather than unimaginative business-people. No longer would the foreign policy establishment surrender Third World areas to the communists in the name of a balanced budget. Galbraith, Schlesinger, and Rostow's advice appeared to reflect the Arkansan's notion that, given the balance of nuclear terror, the focus of competition between the communist and noncommunist worlds must shift to education, culture, and economic development. By all indications the White House and State Department recognized the crucial importance of the kind of people-to-people contact Fulbright had been advocating for a quarter of a century. The Peace Corps and the Alliance for Progress, a multi-billion-dollar, long-term aid program that the Kennedy administration hoped would do for Latin America what the Marshall Plan had done for Western Europe, seemed steps in the right direction to the Arkansan.[27] Indeed, Fulbright had been waiting for Kennedy's enlightened activism since 1945.

It was not surprising, then, that during the spring and summer of 1961 Fulbright more than any other figure associated with the Kennedy administration articulated the liberal activist philosophy that underlay Camelot's foreign policy. Effective resistance against the forces of international communism involved not only military strength, he told the Senate in June, but a willingness to help developing nations ''toward the fulfillment of their own highest purposes.'' Noting that the focus of the cold war was now on the undeveloped and newly emerging nations, Fulbright insisted that the United States could never guarantee the borders of a neutral country against infiltration or protect its villages from subversion. What it could do was instill in those people a willingness themselves to resist. What America had to offer was its values – ''liberty and individual freedom . . . international peace, law and order, and constructive social purpose.''[28]

Although one of the principal proponents of the liberal activism espoused by Schlesinger and Rostow, Fulbright perceived quite early the contradiction in the Kennedy foreign policy. He sensed, he told the Senate in the same speech in which he declared that the United States must align itself with the forces of social progress, that there were powerful voices abroad in the land declaring that any change in the status quo around the world was the result of a communist conspiracy and must be met by force. ''This is a dangerous doctrine,'' he warned. ''[N]othing would please communist leaders more than to draw the United States into costly commitments of its resources to peripheral struggles in which the principal communist powers are not themselves directly involved.'' The event that first created doubts in Fulbright's

27 *Memphis Press-Scimitar*, Mar. 17, 1961.
28 *Congressional Record*, Senate, June 29, 1961, 11703–5.

mind about the Kennedy administration's willingness to allow social revolutions to run their course was the abortive Bay of Pigs invasion.

Fulbright followed Fidel Castro's rise to power through the perceptive eyes of the SFRC's Latin American expert, Pat Holt. A tough, raw-boned Texan, his lean frame sheathed in skin that seemed perpetually sunburned and his angular face topped by a thatch of prematurely white hair, Holt was bluntly outspoken and almost as intolerant of fools as Fulbright. Intelligent without possessing a great deal of imagination, Holt was the stereotypical hard-bitten journalist. Although he had little empathy with ivory-tower academics such as Schlesinger and Rostow, the SFRC's Latin American specialist endorsed their stated determination to create openings to the democratic left and to identify the United States with peaceful change in Latin America.[29]

According to Holt, he, Fulbright, and the SFRC were quickly disabused of the idea that Castro was an enlightened social democrat with whom the United States could deal. The issue was not whether or not Castro was a communist, or whether he was a "tool of the Kremlin," Holt recalled. The problem was that Castro was "a mercurial, very unreliable, and largely unknown quantity."[30] Nonetheless, Fulbright and Holt were deeply committed to the principle of nonintervention except in the most dire consequences. "Of course I agree with you that our nationals are entitled to prompt, adequate, and effective compensation for their expropriated property in Cuba," Fulbright wrote a constituent. "What particularly troubles me is how we can effectively insist on this if the Cuban government proves obdurate. I think any kind of intervention in the manner of Teddy Roosevelt would only be self-defeating, not only in Cuba, but elsewhere in the hemisphere."[31]

By the fall of 1959 certain figures in the Eisenhower administration had come to the conclusion that Castro was a communist, a tool of the Kremlin, and a nationalist hell-bent on driving American interests out of Cuba. Over the protests of Fulbright's friend, Secretary of State Christian Herter, who argued that the unilateral use of force would "be inconsistent with our treaty obligations and would create widespread disillusionment, if not hostility, throughout Latin America and other areas of the world," the president decided to facilitate Castro's overthrow.[32] In 1960 the Eisenhower administration authorized the training and arming of a Cuban exile army of liberation under the direction of the CIA.

On January 20, 1961, John F. Kennedy inherited both the plan and an armed

---

29 Ibid., 118–19.
30 Ibid., 116–17; also Erickson to Holt, Apr. 6, 1960, and Holt to Erickson, Apr. 11, 1960, BCN 147, F44, SPF. See also Eugene Carusi to JWF, Mar. 9, 1959, and Holt to JWF, Apr. 24, 1959, BCN 140, F57, SPF.
31 JWF to W. W. Jackson, July 30, 1959, BCN 139, F4, SPF.
32 Herter to Dwight D. Eisenhower, June 30, 1960, Whitman File, Dulles–Herter File, Box 10, Papers of Dwight D. Eisenhower, Eisenhower Library, Abilene, Kans. [hereinafter referred to as Eisenhower Papers].

force already highly trained at secret Guatemalan bases and ready to go. The CIA authors of the scheme naturally advocated it, asking the president whether he was as willing as the Republicans to permit and assist these exiles to free their own island from dictatorship or whether he was willing to destroy well-laid preparations, leave Cuba to subvert the hemisphere, disband an impatient army in training for nearly a year under miserable conditions, and have it spread the word that Kennedy had betrayed its attempt to depose Castro.

During the winter of 1960–1 Pat Holt began to pick out straws in the wind that the CIA was training a brigade of Cuban exiles somewhere in Central America to overthrow Castro. He constructed a scenario that turned out to be close to the plan that was actually implemented. The problem was that he could not prove his suppositions and did not feel he should bother Fulbright with rumors. One did not persuade the chairman with gossip and innuendo. By chance, one day in early 1961 following a hearing, Fulbright, as was his custom, stayed in the SFRC room to chat with the staff. Apprehensively, Holt told him that he suspected the administration was going to support a Cuban exile invasion. "I don't think it will work," Holt ventured, "and I don't think we ought to try it if it would work." To Holt's surprise, Fulbright said, "I agree with you; I think that's what they've got in mind."[33]

Actually, the Cuban invasion was already an open secret. In Miami, talkative exiles were boasting of the forthcoming action, and the "secret" training camps in Guatemala were secret in name only. American reporters had filed on-the-scene dispatches about the camps, and Fidel Castro had for weeks been ostentatiously preparing for the CIA-sponsored invasion.

Fulbright ordered Marcy to prepare a memorandum outlining the pitfalls of a U.S.-sponsored re-infiltration. Meanwhile, he would work on the problem of how to bring it to President Kennedy's attention, he told his Latin American specialist. As luck would have it, on March 23, 1961, President Kennedy hosted a reception at the White House for thirty-three members of Congress, Fulbright among them. Although Kennedy had called Fulbright frequently, it was the first time the senator had been with the new president since the inauguration. During the coffee hour, the two men chatted:

"Where are you going for Easter?" Kennedy asked.

"We're going to Delray Beach [just below Palm Beach] to stay with Betty's aunt," Fulbright said.

"Well, I'm going to Palm Beach. How'd you like a ride?" the president asked.

Fulbright accepted. Here was his chance to present his views on the Cuban invasion.[34]

When he got back to the office, Fulbright summoned Holt and told him

33 Donald M. Ritchie, interviewer, *Pat M. Holt: Oral History Interviews* (Senate Historical Office: Washington, D.C., 1980) 151-3.
34 Quoted in Johnson and Gwertzman, *Fulbright: The Dissenter,* 204.

to redouble his efforts to get out a memo. Easter was in March that year, and it was just a matter of days until Fulbright would board Air Force One for Florida. Holt recalled that he worked night and day, consulting periodically with both Fulbright and Marcy. The United States, Fulbright and his staffers believed, faced two practical options in its dealings with Castro: to seek his overthrow or to tolerate his existence while working to isolate him and insulate the rest of the hemisphere from his revolution. Fulbright and Holt came down squarely in favor of the latter course. If the Cuban exiles succeeded, and the United States extended recognition, the operation would acquire a patina of legality, but this would do nothing to "lessen the universal popular impression that the whole operation was a brainchild and puppet of the United States." Most Latin American governments would be sufficiently intimidated to go along, but Washington's concern should not be with soldiers and politicians but with workers, peasants, and students. The Cuban revolution was already spreading, and a Yankee-led plot to overthrow Castro would give his revolution more credibility than it would otherwise have had.

On March 30, the day after the final memo was completed, Fulbright boarded Kennedy's plane to fly to Palm Beach. Several times during the course of Fulbright and Kennedy's wide-ranging talk, the president's aides broke in to discuss some aspect of the planned Cuban invasion. At last the Arkansan pulled the memo out of his pocket. "I have something to offer to the debate," he said. After Kennedy quickly scanned it, he and Fulbright mulled over the pros and cons of the enterprise. Fulbright emphasized his belief that the invasion would be a great mistake; Kennedy remained noncommittal. Minutes later, the plane landed and Bill and Betty Fulbright left for Delray Beach. The Arkansan departed, convinced that his arguments had fallen on deaf ears.

The Fulbrights were planning to return by commercial flight when the phone rang Easter Sunday. It was President Kennedy, and he wanted Fulbright to fly back to Washington with him on Air Force One on Tuesday, April 4. During the flight, nothing was said about Cuba until shortly before landing. Rather offhandedly Kennedy told Fulbright: "I'm having a meeting to discuss the subject of your memorandum at five o'clock this afternoon on the seventh floor of the State Department, and I'd like you to come along. I'm going to the White House first, then over to the [State Department] Auditorium for a press conference and from there I'll go on upstairs to join you. You can go to the press conference if you like."[35]

From his conversation with Kennedy, Fulbright had expected a small, perhaps informal meeting. Instead, he found confronting him as he walked into the State Department conference room as intimidating an array of American officials as had ever been assembled in one place. Three members of the Joint Chiefs of Staff (JCS), including Generals Lyman Lemnitzer and Thomas

---

35 Quoted in ibid., 207.

D. White, resplendent in their uniforms and campaign ribbons, were there. So was the pipe-smoking chief of the CIA, Allen Dulles. To his left was seated the secretary of defense, Robert McNamara, and his assistant, Paul Nitze. Adjacent to them were Secretary of State Dean Rusk and his assistant for Latin American affairs, Thomas Mann. Fulbright was momentarily cheered by the presence of his friend Douglas Dillon, now serving as Kennedy's secretary of the treasury. Old Latin American hand Adolph Berle was there. Completing the circle around a long table surrounded by maps and charts were two of Kennedy's special assistants, Richard Goodwin and Arthur M. Schlesinger.

"God, it was tense," Fulbright would remember. "I didn't know quite what I was getting into."[36] It was, in fact, the full-dress and final major policy review for the Bay of Pigs operation.

Kennedy waved Fulbright to a seat near him and directly in front of Dulles. Seated next to the CIA head was a heavyset man in civilian clothes who had just returned from the secret training camp in Guatemala. Dulles introduced him and said he was there to give "the very latest" word on the operation. The man spoke in glowing terms of the combat readiness of the Cuban soldiers, Brigade 2506, of their zeal and determination, and of the American belief that everything was ready for the successful invasion.

"Then Dulles took it up and made his pitch," Fulbright recalled. "He told what would happen in Havana and all over Cuba after the landing. After the landing their source in Havana believed there would be a sympathy uprising."

The CIA representatives argued forcefully that the invasion could not be abandoned at that late date. What would the president do with all those emotional Cubans the United States had trained and implicitly promised to support? They would be disillusioned and embittered and certainly would accuse the United States of going back on its pledge, of being weak, and perhaps even of being soft on communism.

Although it was the first time he had heard any details of the invasion plan, Fulbright was singularly unimpressed with the arguments advanced by the CIA. Dulles's contention that the United States would be placed on the horns of an unbearable dilemma if the invasion did not come off "didn't appeal to me a damn bit," he later recalled.

The president went around the table, calling on specific people for assessments – feasible or unfeasible. No one opposed the invasion until Kennedy reached Fulbright. The chairman of the SFRC later admitted that he was somewhat intimidated. Typically, intimidation turned to irritation and then defiance. "Fulbright," Arthur Schlesinger later recalled, "speaking in an emphatic and incredulous way, denounced the whole idea."[37]

---

36 Quoted in ibid.
37 Schlesinger, *Thousand Days*, 252.

The Bay of Pigs operation would damage the national interest no matter how one looked at it, he said. If it succeeded, Cuba would inevitably become a dependency of the United States, and the world would brand the members of the Kennedy administration as a band of brutal imperialists. If it failed, America would be made to appear weak and ineffective. Despite what he had heard, Fulbright said, he was unconvinced that the CIA's scheme was foolproof. More important, the projected invasion was a clear violation of America's principles and treaty obligations. No matter what the outcome, it would compromise the nation's moral position in the world. "He gave a brave, old-fashioned American speech, honorable, sensible and strong," Schlesinger later recounted, "and he left everyone in the room, except me and perhaps the President, wholly unmoved."[38]

In fact, neither Schlesinger nor Kennedy was all that moved. Early in the morning of Monday, April 17, 1961, the members of Cuban Exile Brigade 2506 – some 1,450 Cubans of every class, race, occupation, well trained and well led – landed at the Bay of Pigs, achieved tactical surprise, fought well, and inflicted heavy casualties upon Castro's forces until they ran out of ammunition. By nightfall of the following day, all of Cuba's would-be liberators had either been killed or imprisoned or were crawling through the swamps that ran inland from the Bay of Pigs.

Fulbright learned of the invasion while he and Pat Holt were returning with Douglas Dillon from a meeting of the Inter-American Development Bank in Rio de Janeiro. They were shocked. While the party was in Rio, Kennedy had told a press conference that American forces would not participate in any attempt to liberate Cuba. Fulbright and Holt interpreted this to mean that the Bay of Pigs operation had been canceled. At their stopover at Ramsay Air Force Base in Puerto Rico, they learned that the exiles had in fact landed. The chairman of the SFRC and his Latin American adviser returned to Washington in a somber and apprehensive mood.[39]

As Castro's forces were mopping up, President Kennedy was hosting, in white tie and tails, a White House reception for his cabinet and the members of Congress and their wives. Shortly before midnight he slipped away to meet privately with his top advisers and congressional leaders. They were all there, including Dulles, Lemnitzer, Johnson, McNamara, Rusk, Russell, Rayburn, and Fulbright.

Solemnly Kennedy reported that the Bay of Pigs operation was an abject failure. There would be no American rescue, and he, as president, would accept full responsibility. There were no excuses, no recriminations. As he passed Fulbright on his way out, he turned and said clearly enough for those present to hear: "Well, you're the only one who can say I told you so."[40]

---

38 Ibid.
39 Ritchie, *Interviews: Holt,* 153.
40 Quoted in Johnson and Gwertzman, *Fulbright: The Dissenter,* 210.

In late July 1962, shortly after a visit to Moscow by Raul Castro, Cuba's defense minister and brother to Fidel, the Soviet Union began sending weapons and personnel to Cuba. The Russians, citing the abortive Bay of Pigs invasion, explained that the arms they were shipping to the Caribbean would enable Fidel Castro to defend his regime against future American attacks. On the night of October 15 presidential advisers viewed new photographs from a U-2 flight showing a launching pad and other installations for medium-range nuclear missiles in a field near San Cristobal. After consulting with others, McGeorge Bundy decided that the matter could wait until the president awoke. Kennedy and his advisers interpreted the work of Soviet technicians, who were readying other sites, as a challenge to the Monroe Doctrine and an effort to shift the balance of power between the Soviet bloc and the West. Ruling out an air strike to destroy the missile sites on the grounds that it would kill thousands of civilians and further undermine America's moral position in the world, Kennedy decided, as a first step, to blockade Cuba. This would prevent entry of additional offensive weapons while the administration decided what to do about those already in place.

Eventually the rumors that swirled about Washington concerning the nature of the Soviet buildup in Cuba found their way to Arkansas, where Fulbright was campaigning for his fourth term in the Senate. When his opponent, Republican Kenneth Jones, asked where he stood on the communist threat that was being mounted against the United States, Fulbright assured the electorate that all weapons in Cuba were defensive in nature and that nothing would be accomplished if the United States smashed that ''poor, bedraggled country.''[41] And, in fact, on September 14 Holt cabled Fulbright that administration officials were assuring the Senate that the additional Soviet equipment that had recently arrived in Cuba ''is of an essentially defensive nature – as, for example, anti-aircraft weapons.'' He and his contacts in the State Department were confident that the real menace posed to U.S. interests by Castro was his determination to subvert friendly governments in Central and South America. Even there, Holt told Fulbright, the outlook was bright, because as the degree of Soviet intervention in Cuba became obvious, intensely nationalist Latinos were sure to sour on Castro.[42]

To deflect the Republican attacks on the administration's Cuban policy, the Democratic majority in Congress had passed on October 3 a joint resolution stating that the United States was ''determined . . . by whatever means may be necessary, including the use of arms,'' to prevent Cuba from subverting the other governments of the hemisphere or ''to prevent in Cuba the creation or use of an externally supported military capability endangering the

41 ''Jones Asks – and Fulbright Answers with Views on Cuba,'' *Arkansas Gazette,* Sept. 11, 1962.
42 Holt to JWF, Sept. 14, 1962, Series 48:1, Box 4:3, SPF.

security of the United States.''[43] Fulbright did not have to vote on the resolution and was thankful for it. "I agree that all of Latin America appears to be unstable and dangerous," he wrote his old friend Will Clayton, "but I have very little confidence in armed intervention. . . . [I]t won't work, just as it didn't work in Mississippi.''[44]

Then, late on the day of October 21, while he was touring Arkansas, Fulbright received an emergency phone call from the White House. He should return at once to Little Rock, where an air force plane would pick him up and bring him back to Washington for a top secret briefing on the Cuban situation. Congressional leaders gathered at the White House at five o'clock on the twenty-second, two hours before the president was scheduled to address a national television audience. Kennedy showed his guests the most recent U-2 photographs. According to Richard Russell's notes, the president confessed that there were in Cuba thirty medium-range missiles, forty MIG 21s, and twenty IL28 bombers with a range of twenty-two hundred miles. Clearly, Khrushchev was threatening the international balance of power. The real issue, Kennedy declared, was whether or not the United States would continue to be a first-class power. He and his advisers were afraid that Khrushchev was not bluffing. Air Force General Curtis LeMay assured him, Kennedy said, that his planes could go in and knock out the bases, but there was every chance the Soviets would retaliate against West Berlin. He then outlined his plans for a blockade; a naval picket line would prevent additional Soviet ships from landing hardware and personnel in Cuba while the United States worked through the United Nations and the Organization of American States (OAS) to force Cuba to dismantle existing facilities.

To Kennedy's surprise, Russell and Fulbright urged him to go further. The blockade would not remove the danger. Both Khrushchev and Castro had been repeatedly warned. The United States should either destroy the Russian missiles and planes through a surgical air strike or invade Cuba and by means of conventional ground action take out those weapons that posed a threat to the security of the United States. The fact that the principals had been warned negated the fears expressed by Robert McNamara that the United States would open itself to charges that it had staged a "sneak attack" à la Pearl Harbor. Kennedy listened courteously but reiterated his intention to follow the course he had outlined. All right, Russell responded, but why not use the word "quarantine" instead of blockade? Blockade is an

43 Marcy to Morse, Oct. 26, 1962, Box 4, Folder Jan.–May, Marcy Papers.

44 Federal marshals and National Guardsmen had earlier that year fought a pitched battle with segregationists in Oxford, Mississippi. The mob, egged on by the state's racist governor, had been attempting to prevent the integration of the University of Mississippi. JWF to Clayton, Oct. 5, 1962, Alpha File (1954–62), Folder FU, Papers of Will Clayton, Truman Library, Independence, Mo. [hereinafter referred to as Clayton Papers].

act of war, whereas there was no precedent or definition in international law for quarantine. It was the only bit of advice Kennedy accepted from the legislative leaders.[45]

The missile crisis moved to a denouement, the participants at times numb with anxiety. Through intermediaries, Khrushchev proposed a trade-off: The Soviet Union would remove the missiles from Cuba under inspection of the United Nations if the United States would lift the blockade and promise publicly not to invade Cuba. In this message and a subsequent letter, Khrushchev pressed Kennedy, in addition, to dismantle Jupiter missiles stationed in Turkey. Although he was prepared to consider a missile trade if the crisis dragged on into a third week, the president and his advisers offered a simple pledge not to invade Cuba in return for removal of the Soviet launchers and warheads. Khrushchev accepted.[46] The world had survived its first and perhaps greatest thermonuclear crisis.

It is possible that Fulbright and Russell's advice, if taken, would have touched off World War III. In the spring of 1992 American, Soviet, and Cuban participants in the 1962 missile crisis came together in Havana for a commemorative conference. During those proceedings it was revealed for the first time that there were tactical as well as strategic warheads in Cuba. Moreover, Soviet field commanders had permission to use tactical nuclear weapons against an American invasion without permission from Moscow. Robert McNamara, then secretary of defense, admitted that had the Soviets used such weapons against an American force, the demand for a nuclear response against the Soviet Union would have been overwhelming.[47]

It soon became public knowledge that Fulbright had reversed his Bay of Pigs position and urged an armed invasion of Cuba as part of an effort to destroy the missile sites. In a cruder version of Kennedy's interpretation, some charged that Fulbright, in the midst of his reelection campaign, had caved in to the perceived need to appear tough in the eyes of the home folks. Indeed, strident anticommunists inside and outside the Republican Party had spread the word that Fulbright had been personally responsible for holding back an American air strike that would have saved the Cuban brigade during the Bay of Pigs operation.[48] Fulbright continued to insist that his course was the one most likely to avoid World War III. If the Soviets had attempted to

45 Conference at White House, Oct. 23, 1962, General File, Box EE 3, Special Presidential File, Papers of Richard Russell, University of Georgia, Athens [hereinafter referred to as Russell Papers].

46 James N. Giglio, *The Presidency of John F. Kennedy* (Lawrence, Kans., 1991), 210–14.

47 On October 27, holed up in a bombproof bunker, Fidel Castro asked Khrushchev to authorize a preemptive nuclear strike against the United States to thwart an anticipated invasion. Arthur Schlesinger, Jr., "Four Days with Fidel: A Havana Diary," *New York Review of Books,* Mar. 26, 1992, 22–9.

48 Ned Curran, "Fulbright Switch? No Such Thing, Says the Senator," *Arkansas Gazette,* Oct. 28, 1962.

run the American naval blockade, or if U.S. personnel had attempted to board Soviet freighters headed for Cuba, he told reporters, it would have brought the Soviet Union and the United States into direct, cataclysmic conflict.

Actually, Fulbright's position had been worked out by his new speech writer, Seth Tillman. Congress was not in session at the time of the missile crisis. Pat Holt was in Brasilia at an Interparliamentary Union meeting shepherding a group of senators.[49] From Little Rock, before he departed aboard Air Force One for Washington, Fulbright called Tillman and told him to draft a memo for his forthcoming meeting with the president. Tillman desperately tried to find out what was going on, but, as he later put it, "the White House wasn't taking calls that day." From the newspapers and the *Congressional Record*, he managed to piece together an approximation of the crisis. "I came up with the idea that it might be wise to actually mount a force to dismantle the missiles," Tillman later recalled. "But the premise upon which I was proceeding was not that we do this in the most drastic confrontational mode, but rather that this would be a safer way than confronting the Russians directly. . . . We land a force which allows the Soviets to stand aside."[50] Fulbright later insisted that he bought the argument, flawed as it was, on its merits and only secondarily because it might stand him in good stead with his constituents. But as late as June 29 1962, he was warning against unilateral U.S. intervention in Cuba. "I suppose we would all be less comfortable if the Soviets did install missile bases in Cuba," he observed, "but I am not sure that our national existence would be in substantially greater danger than is the case today. Nor do I think that such bases would substantially alter the balance of power in the world."[51] It may have been that Fulbright recommended intervention because he unquestioningly accepted the recommendations of a novice staff member or that he was overly influenced by Richard Russell. Another explanation is that the Arkansan believed, ironically, that a "surgical" invasion would serve to outflank the Republicans and those Americans who were clamoring for World War III.

As was true throughout his tenure as chairman of the SFRC, Fulbright wanted to avoid a great power confrontation. He believed that the Bay of Pigs fiasco had so alarmed Castro and Khrushchev that they had staged the military buildup in Cuba to thwart future invasion attempts. Fulbright was also convinced that the Bay of Pigs humiliation had made John F. Kennedy more bellicose than he would otherwise have been, prompting him to confront the Soviets over Berlin and to overcommit the United States in such Third World areas as Vietnam. But Fulbright steadfastly refused to criticize the young president either publicly or privately. He urged Kennedy's detractors to be patient, for he was convinced that the president was well inten-

49 Ritchie, *Interviews: Holt,* 160.
50 Interview with Seth Tillman, Oct. 6, 1988, Washington, D.C.
51 Interview with J. William Fullbright, Oct. 11–18, 1988, Washington, D.C.

tioned and would mature in time. Perhaps most important, Fulbright believed that Kennedy needed all the help he could get in resisting pressure from a revived radical right. Indeed, the threat of a third Red Scare in America during the early 1960s ensured that the differences between the chairman of the SFRC and the White House remained minor.

3

"Freedom's Judas-Goat"[1]

Like Walter Lippmann, James Reston, and other observers of American foreign relations, Fulbright sensed that in the wake of the Berlin and U-2 crises,
the Bay of Pigs fiasco, and the Cuban missile confrontation the American
people were once again growing frustrated with and weary of the burdens of
world leadership. The great danger in all of this, he believed, was that the
country was ripe for an isolationist resurgence.

In the spring of 1961 Fulbright began to receive reports from friends and
admirers across the country that the U.S. military had embarked on a carefully
orchestrated campaign to acquaint the American public with the dangers of
communism. In the process, they were providing a forum for right-wing
Russophobes who not only denigrated the Soviet Union but equated liberalism with "socialism" and "communism." Fulbright first became concerned about the military's self-appointed role as a propaganda agency for
the right when James McCormick, an employee of *Stars and Stripes*, wrote
him complaining that members of the U.S. command in Germany had forbidden the paper to publish stories on recent SFRC hearings in which Fulbright and others had criticized aid to Turkey.[2] Fulbright immediately
complained to Secretary of Defense Thomas Gates and demanded that censorship of *Stars and Stripes* cease at once. Gates's reply was far from sat-
isfactory, but Fulbright assumed that with the election of John F. Kennedy,
the military would stick to purely military matters.[3] He was mistaken.

On April 19, 1961, Marcy passed Fulbright a letter that one of his contacts
in the Department of Defense (DOD) had given him. It was from a newly
reenlisted air force reserve officer who had attended a showing of the filmstrip
Communism on the Map. Portraying the United States as a bastion of freedom

---

1 *J. William Fulbright: Freedom's Judas-Goat* (Liberty Lobby: Washington, D.C., 1965). A
  "Judas goat" (or "Judas sheep") is "the animal that leads other animals to slaughter";
  William and Mary Morris, eds., *Morris Dictionary of Words and Phrase Origins,* 2d ed. (New
  York, 1962), 328.
2 James McCormick to JWF, Apr. 24, 1960, Series 4:19, Box 27:3, SPF.
3 JWF to Thomas Gates, May 4, 1960, Series 4:17, Box 27:3, SPF.

surrounded by a hostile world, the narrator of the film explained that countries like France, Sweden, and Norway were, for all practical purposes, already in the communist camp. USSR stood for Union of Soviet Socialist Republics, after all.[4] It was not so much the film that bothered him, the reservist wrote, but the harangues that followed. "The 'discussion' did not stop with criticizing past Presidents, but the speakers repeatedly called attention to and stated as a fact that welfarism leads to communism and that we were becoming more and more a welfare state. . . . [T]he whole tenor of the meeting was that the programs President Kennedy is for are programs which will lead us to communism."[5]

Then, on April 21, Willard "Lefty" Hawkins, a friend of John Erickson and Jack Yingling's, reported on three simultaneous Strategy for Survival conferences that had just been held in Little Rock, Fort Smith, and Fayetteville, Arkansas. The conferences, which drew fourteen hundred in Little Rock, a thousand in Fort Smith, and around a hundred in Fayetteville, saw members of the active-duty military and the Freedom Forum join hands to deliver a comprehensive "threat briefing" to the people of Arkansas. The crowd in Fort Smith, a mostly conservative community situated on the edge of the Fort Chaffee military reserve, cheered as the beribboned officers warned against the Soviet military menace abroad while Dr. George Benson, president of Harding College, a small fundamentalist institution located in Searcy, and his assistant, Dr. Clifton Ganus, equated liberalism with socialism and attacked members of the Arkansas congressional delegation.[6] In a talk entitled "The Moral Foundations of Democracy," Ganus declared that Congressman J. W. Trimble, a soft-spoken, well-liked, and generally conservative politician representing Fulbright's old district, "has voted eighty-nine percent of the time to aid and abet the Communist Party." Not all in attendance were amused.[7] Fulbright and his staff sensed that the Strategy for Survival seminars were evidence not only of a resurgent radical right rooted in McCarthyism but of the fact that the movement had penetrated the federal government.

Fulbright's fears were well founded. The 1960s began not only with the political triumph of a young, activist, progressive president but also, and perhaps not coincidentally, with the emergence of a new American radical right whose members *Time* magazine labeled the ultras. In 1961 Americans worried about the problems of the cold war – Cuba, Berlin, Laos, and the H-bomb – but those problems seemed so distant and massive to individual citizens that they despaired of being able to do anything about them. Those

---

4 Philip Horton, "Revivalism on the Far Right," *Reporter,* July 20, 1961.
5 Kenneth R. Loebel to Carlisle P. Runge, Asst. Sec. of Defense, Apr. 19, 1961, Series 4:19, Box 33:4, SPF.
6 Willard Hawkins to JWF, Apr. 21, 1961, Series 4:19, Box 26:1, SPF.
7 Pryor to Yingling, Aug. 9, 1961, Series 4:19, Box 26:1, JWF Papers. Trimble dismissed the incident with a joke, but Fulbright and his staff were infuriated and alarmed. J. W. Trimble to Leland F. Leatherman, May 8, 1961, Series 4:19, Box 26:1, SPF.

frustrations provided the breeding ground for the ultra movement whose leaders offered ready-made solutions to apparently insoluble problems. Like fundamentalists who promise to make a remote, transcendent God immanent, leaders of the radical right promised to make communism a tangible problem with which the average American could come to grips. As did the McCarthyites of the previous decade, they argued vehemently that the real threat to the nation's security resided not so much in Sino–Soviet imperialism overseas but in communist subversion at home. Appealing to the American penchant for action, they urged citizens to fight this subversion by keeping a close eye on their fellow citizens, scrutinizing voting records, writing letters, and generally raising a hue and cry across the land. If they could not fight the communists in Cuba or Laos, at least they could smite the ones alleged to be at their elbow. "Don't worry about the atomic bombs or H-bombs," said former Federal Bureau of Investigation (FBI) counterspy Matthew Cvetic. "It's right here we'll lose the fight."

Above all, the ultras were extremists – "true believers," Fulbright called them. They brooked no compromise. "You're either for us or against us," insisted a California electronics company executive. "There's no room in the middle any more." Indeed, these fanatics of the right saw those who would compromise – liberals – as perhaps the greatest danger to American society. Declared TV commercial producer Marvin Bryan. "We don't want to coexist with these people. We don't want our children to play with their children."[8] Like other reform movements, the radical right of the 1960s produced and thrived on a group of colorful and eccentric demagogues who, while attracting their own cult following, continued to emphasize themes common to the ultra movement as a whole.

Early in 1959 Robert H. W. Welch, Jr., a fudge-and-candy manufacturer from Massachusetts, gathered eleven of his friends in an Indianapolis hotel where, in due course, they founded the John Birch Society. The organization, which spread like wildfire for two years, was a semisecret network of "Americanists" dedicated to fighting communists by deliberately adopting some of communism's own clandestine and ruthless tactics, including the deliberate destruction of democracy, which Welch contemptuously described as government by "mobocracy." For Welch and the Birchites, Barry Goldwater was at least two shades too liberal. Most domestic programs, in the Welch view, were socialistic "welfarism" and a communist plot to destroy the Republic. He railed against Earl Warren, telling his followers that their campaign to impeach the chief justice would deliver a crippling blow to international communism. In that same vein, the *Brown* decision was portrayed as a product of the "radicalism" that dominated the Court and that

8 "The Ultras: Ultraconservative Anti-Communism," *Time,* Dec. 8, 1961, 22–5.

would lead to absorption by Russia without a struggle. To his devoted followers the "Stranger" was a strong man who had sounded the tocsin just in time and was bravely rallying the true believers for the decisive battle against communism.[9]

Meanwhile, from Tulsa, Oklahoma, the Reverend Billy James Hargis launched the Christian Crusade ("America's largest anti-Communist organization"). The pink-faced, jowly evangelist specialized in coast-to-coast revivalist meetings, during which he delivered fundamentalist, anticommunist sermons, and in organizing Christian youth to combat the Red Menace. Joining Hargis on the stump was Dr. Fred C. Schwarz, a medical doctor from Australia, whose Christian Anti-Communism Crusade took in a million dollars in 1960. In his traveling "schools" and "seminars" Schwarz predicted a total communist victory in the United States by 1973. It was clear from his research, he told his followers, that Lavrenti Beria and other victims of various Kremlin purges had ordered their own deaths to help promote world communism. He promised Americans a lurid end if they were not ever vigilant: "When they come for you, as they have for many others, and on a dark night, in a dank cellar, they take a wide bore revolver with a soft nose bullet, and they place it at the nape of your neck."[10] Virtually every radical right movement of the postwar era was bankrolled by Texas oil money, and the ultras were no exception. The most colorful of the right's deep pockets was Haroldson Layfayette Hunt, an eccentric billionaire who lived in secluded splendor in a Dallas replica of Mount Vernon. His tax-exempt Lifeline Foundation, Inc. broadcast his right-wing views over three hundred radio and TV stations.[11]

Racism was a sometimes implicit, sometimes explicit feature of the radical right of the 1960s. The Arkansas Minute-Men Association denounced *The Diary of Anne Frank* as a Jewish conspiracy to whitewash Joseph Stalin.[12] Before the decade was out, most members of the radical right claimed to see a link between the civil rights movement and international communism.[13] The degree to which the ultra movement and white supremacy had become intertwined was highlighted when *The Citizen,* the national publication of the white supremacist Citizens' Councils of America, featured J. William Fulbright on the cover of its first issue. The publication did not laud Fulbright for his segregationist voting record but rather denounced him as one of the nation's most dangerous liberals.[14]

9 George Barrett, "Close-up of the Birchers' 'Founder,' " *New York Times Magazine,* May 14, 1961, 13, 89, 91–2.
10 Horton, "Revivalism on the Far Right."
11 Jack Anderson, "Oil-Rich Hunt Sees Self as Nation Saver," *Washington Post,* June 30, 1963.
12 Arkansas Minute-Men Association to Associated Press, May 27, 1959, BCN 147, F66, SPF.
13 *Congressional Record,* House, Feb. 17, 1959, 2317–20.
14 "Racist Magazine Scores Fulbright," *New York Times,* Nov. 11, 1961.

From the outset Fulbright was a favorite target of the new right. His sophistication and Oxford education made him anathema to a movement that featured fundamentalist religion and appealed strongly to members of the working and lower middle class. To these xenophobes, Fulbright's advocacy of cultural and educational interchange threatened to expose young Americans to dangerous foreign ideas, to open the nation's doors to aliens who would subvert its institutions and mores, and even to mongrelize the pure American race. He preached the ultimate heresies – peaceful coexistence and toleration of foreign ideologies. Right-wingers like Dan Smoot, the former FBI agent who harangued the nation on the dangers of communism on his weekly radio and television program, saw Fulbright as part of an internationalist conspiracy that began with Colonel Edward House, the headmaster of "the eager young socialist intellectuals around Wilson," and that blossomed during the regime of Franklin D. Roosevelt. The objective of "the great cabal" of which Fulbright was a part, Smoot told his listeners, was the same as the objective of international communism: "to socialize the economy of the United States and make this republic a dependent unit in a one-world socialist system." It was clear to Smoot and his followers that "Fulbright wants the President free from constitutional restraints so that he can surrender the sovereignty of the United States to a world government."[15]

For Michael Bernstein – minority counsel of the Senate Committee on Labor and Public Welfare, an ultra, and one of the driving intellectual forces behind Strom Thurmond and Barry Goldwater – Fulbright was a traitor, not in the sense of being a communist but in the sense of being loyal to something other than the United States. The Arkansan had pledged his allegiance to internationalism rather than to American nationalism, Bernstein insisted. The former Rhodes scholar was a snob, an intellectual who despised the clods who made up the mass of Americans. Clearly, he was one of Welch's "compromisers," a leading spokesman for H. L. Hunt's "the Mistaken." "I don't say the phone rings in Fulbright's office," declared Colonel Fred A. Kibbe of the Florida Minutemen, "and a voice says, 'This is Khrushchev,' and tells him what to do, but I do say Fulbright helps the Communist cause."[16]

When in 1961 Fulbright set about exposing the military's involvement in the ultra movement, full-scale war erupted between him and the radical right. The Arkansan was convinced that it was not communists who had penetrated the federal government and were subverting American institutions but, rather, fascists masquerading as conservatives. And in fact, although many of the crusaders attacked the usefulness of the national defense program, some of their most ardent collaborators were high-ranking members of the officer corps.

In the wake of the Fort Smith Strategy for Survival conference, Fulbright

15 *The Dan Smoot Report,* June 18, 1962.
16 Fletcher Knebel, "Who's on the Far Right?" *Look,* Mar. 13, 1962.

asked Jack Yingling, who had transferred from the senator's personal staff to the SFRC, to investigate. Were members of the active military involved in organizing the meeting? Did speakers equate liberalism with socialism and socialism with communism? Was the thrust of the program that America's greatest threat came from communist penetration of domestic institutions and the federal government? Were Trimble and other members of the Arkansas delegation slandered? Yingling discovered not only that all of these things were true but that the Fort Smith, Little Rock, and Fayetteville meetings were part of a burgeoning national movement. "I was always kind of anti-military and Fulbright was too," Yingling recalled. "I began to read more and more. The fellow that worked for [Democratic Senator] Joe Clark brought me some clippings about meetings in Pennsylvania. Come to find out this was an organized thing that derived from a directive that Eisenhower put out. It said that the military should educate people about the evils of communism."[17] In fact, in 1958 the National Security Council (NSC) had entrusted the military with the task of educating not only troops but the American people concerning the dangers posed to the nation by international communism and Soviet imperialism.

Following a month of study, Yingling prepared a lengthy memorandum that listed eleven instances in which Strategy for Survival programs sponsored by military personnel "made use of extremely radical right-wing speakers and/or materials, with the probable net result of condemning foreign and domestic policies of the administration in the public mind." The thrust of many of these conferences was that "much of the administration's domestic legislative program, including continuation of the graduated income tax, expansion of social security . . . federal aid to education . . . would be characterized as steps toward communism."

The memo confirmed Fulbright's worst fears: The radical right had penetrated the military and was using it to expound "the thesis of right-wing radicalism."[18] Noting that civilian control of the military was one of the most hallowed and jealously guarded principles of the Republic, Fulbright recommended in a postscript to the document that the Department of Defense revise the 1958 directive to forbid political or ideological activities by military personnel acting in their official capacities.[19]

In mid-June President and Mrs. Kennedy asked the Fulbrights to join the official party that was to welcome President Mohammed Ayub Kahn of Pakistan. The evening of June 11 was relatively mild by summertime Washington standards, and the Kennedys, Fulbrights, Ayub Kahns, and other members of the official party were comfortable in their evening clothes as they boarded

17 Interview with Jack Yingling, Oct. 12, 1988, Savannah, Ga.
18 JWF to JFK, June 28, 1961, Box 639, WHOF, Kennedy Papers.
19 "Memorandum Submitted to Department of Defense," Aug. 2, 1961, Series 4:19, Box 26:
   1, SPF.

the presidential yacht for a cruise down the Potomac to Mt. Vernon. Aboard ship Fulbright encountered Robert McNamara and decided to seize the moment. "I've got a memo on my desk concerning something that happened in my state," he told the former Ford executive. "In Fort Smith, Little Rock and Fayetteville, my home town, there have been so-called defense seminars, conducted by the Chambers of Commerce, but apparently sponsored by high-ranking military officers. I'd like to call it to your attention if you're interested."[20]

McNamara was indeed interested. The Bay of Pigs fiasco had reinforced the Kennedy administration's commitment to the principle of civilian control of the military. Shortly after they took over at the DOD, McNamara and his deputy, Roswell Gilpatric, let it be known that on their watch there would be no interservice squabbling, civilian authority would rule the military, and policy statements would be delivered by civilians rather than military officials. Unaware of the 1958 Eisenhower directive, McNamara in May ordered all officials of the Defense Department to limit themselves to defense matters in their public statements. His worry, however, was about DOD encroachment on State Department turf, not that Defense would become a mouthpiece for the radical right.[21]

Both Kennedy and McNamara gave the Fulbright memo a careful and sympathetic reading, but before the DOD chief could prepare a directive incorporating Fulbright's recommendations, ultra officers in the Pentagon alerted Strom Thurmond, a major general in the Army Reserve and a leading spokesperson for the new right, to what was happening. Thurmond immediately stormed down to Fulbright's Senate office. He encountered legislative assistant Lee Williams and demanded to see Fulbright at once. When told that the senator was out of the office, he insisted on being given a copy of the infamous memo. He would have to check with his boss, Williams replied, and managed to persuade the indignant Thurmond to leave. When Fulbright returned to the office an hour later, Williams asked what he should tell Thurmond. "Tell him to go to hell," Fulbright answered.[22]

Unfortunately for Fulbright, the *Washington Post* and the *New York Times* obtained synopses of the memo and ran stories on it on the twenty-first. That afternoon, Thurmond, unwilling to risk a second rebuff by one of Fulbright's staffers, sent the Arkansan a note demanding a copy of the memo within the hour. The memo on the military was part of his private correspondence, Fulbright replied. It did not have the sanction of the SFRC; indeed, committee members were not aware of its existence. "Since it is a private communi-

20 Holmes Alexander, "Sen. Fulbright's Aide Wrote Controversial Memo," *Washington Star,* Aug. 14, 1961.
21 Department of Defense Directive, May 31, 1961, Series 4:19, Box 26:5, SPF.
22 Yingling interview.

cation to the Secretary of Defense, I have not felt that it is necessary to make it available to anyone else. Where it [the press] obtained the memorandum is a mystery to me."[23]

On July 29 Strom Thurmond decided that he could wait no longer. He took to the floor of the Senate to announce "that there is a concerted attack under way against the anti-Communist indoctrination of the American people and our troops in uniform and particularly against participation in this effort by our military officers." The attack, he said, was begun by the Communist Party, USA in its official organ, the *Worker,* and was now being carried forward by "innumerable sources." He then quoted an article in the *Worker* praising the Fulbright memorandum. Karl Mundt, Thomas Dodd (D–Connecticut), and other professional anticommunists leapt gleefully into the fray.[24]

On August 2 Fulbright inserted a copy of his memo and recommendations to McNamara in the *Congressional Record.* He was doing so, he said, not because he recognized the right of senators to demand access to the private correspondence of their colleagues but because, apparently, some of his fellow senators believed that the principle of civilian control of the military was still debatable.[25]

Two days later Senator Styles Bridges of New Hampshire, the ranking Republican on the Armed Services Committee, declared that he found the contents of the Fulbright memo "shocking." He was going to ask Armed Services to launch a thorough investigation. In the House, Representative Robert Sikes (D–Florida) deplored any and all efforts to "muzzle the military." From that time forward Fulbright and Yingling's creation was known as the "muzzling the military memo."[26]

As Thurmond and his contacts had hoped, Fulbright became the target for ultra attacks all across the nation. Among the milder denunciations was that of the Southern States Industrial Council, whose vice-president blasted Fulbright as a liberal who had no confidence in the people. The notion that the average American did not need to be educated concerning the communist menace was "the most incredible statement to be made by a prominent American in recent years."[27] Robert Welch urged Birchites everywhere to deluge their representatives and senators with letters and telegrams in an effort to head off "Operation FIB (The Fulbright Intimidation Binge)."[28] In his weekly broadcasts Billy James Hargis began referring to Fulbright as "the

23 JWF to Thurmond and Thurmond to JWF, July 21, 1961, Series 4:19, Box 26:4, SPF.
24 *Congressional Record,* Senate, July 29, 1961, 13998–9.
25 "Memorandum Submitted to Department of Defense," Aug. 2, 1961, Series 4:19, Box 26:1, SPF.
26 "Investigation Urged on Fulbright Memo," *Arkansas Gazette,* Aug. 4, 1961.
27 Thurman Sensing, "Government by the People," Aug. 13, 1961, Series 4:19, Box 29:6, SPF.
28 John Birch Society, *Bulletin for October,* Oct. 2, 1961, Series 4:19, Box 26:6, SPF.

red-wing Senator from Arkansas,''[29] while Dan Smoot declared that the muzzling the military memo proved beyond a shadow of a doubt that Fulbright was *"the* darling of the one-world-welfare-state conspirators" who sought to make America just another province of bolshevik Russia.[30] "Piltdown Clique Stalks Fulbright," declared the *Pittsburgh Post–Gazette.*[31]

Despite the ever-present risk of being labeled soft on communism, John F. Kennedy and Robert McNamara did not hesitate in defending Fulbright's warning and recommendations publicly. At his press conference the first week in August, Kennedy told reporters that Fulbright had performed a useful service in sending the Department of Defense a memorandum on political activities of the military. In fact, Kennedy said, McNamara had asked the junior senator from Arkansas for his observations and recommendations. It was manifestly in the interests of the military that its officers not be exploited for political purposes.[32] Indeed, on July 20 the DOD had issued a new set of directives laying down strict guidelines governing military participation in public programs.[33]

Meanwhile, the Senate on September 20 approved Thurmond's resolution authorizing the Armed Services Committee to investigate reports of censorship in the DOD. The Democratic majority on the committee, which included John Stennis and Richard Russell, was not enthusiastic about criticizing Fulbright and had no desire to take on the Kennedy administration, but a coalition of Russophobes and Republicans had forced its hand. To Thurmond's chagrin, however, the committee insisted on styling their exercise a "study and appraisal" rather than an investigation.[34] Richard Russell, chairman of Armed Services, then appointed a subcommittee headed by Stennis and including Thurmond and Stuart Symington to hold hearings.

Styles Bridges and Strom Thurmond, for both political and ideological reasons, were content to let their ultra allies smear Fulbright. They believed that the muzzling the military memo and the Armed Services Committee inquiry presented an opportunity to indict the entire Kennedy administration of which Fulbright was just a part.[35]

For two days during the first week in September, McNamara testified on the muzzling the military memo. The committee room was packed and the atmosphere tense. Several members of a women's ultra organization spat on the secretary of defense as he strode in. With John Stennis in the chair, the

29 Fred Michel to JWF, Sept. 26, 1961, Series 4:19, Box 31:3, SPF.
30 *The Dan Smoot Report,* June 18, 1962.
31 "Piltdown Clique Stalks Fulbright," *Pittsburgh Post–Gazette,* Oct. 22, 1961.
32 Statement on Fulbright Memorandum, undated, Box 29a, President's Office File, Kennedy Papers.
33 *Congressional Record,* Senate, Aug. 11, 1961, 15544–5; and McNamara to Sec. of Army et al., Oct. 5, 1961, Series 4:19, Box 26:5, SPF.
34 "Muzzling Probe Set," *Arkansas Democrat,* Sept. 20, 1961.
35 Interview with Robert McNamara, Aug. 2, 1991, Washington, D.C.

committee grilled McNamara for two days, demanding that he give them the names of the DOD review committee. With names, Thurmond and the ultras believed, they could utilize the intimidation tactics that had been employed so successfully by that heroic anticommunist of yesteryear, Joe McCarthy. But McNamara refused to comply with the committee's insistent requests. To do so would violate the principles of "sound management," he said.[36] At that point McNamara pulled out a letter from President Kennedy invoking executive privilege.

Fulbright's tête-à-tête with the radical right sent the Arkansan's stock with American liberals soaring. The *Advance*, the official publication of the Amalgamated Clothing Workers, praised Fulbright for saving the United States from takeover by a military junta. Southern liberal par excellence Ralph McGill praised him in his *Atlanta Constitution* column.[37] The Religious Freedom Committee, composed of Jewish, Catholic, and Protestant clerics of every denomination, denounced the political activities of certain military officers. "The United States government, in effect," the committee declared, "has been taking sides in a religious controversy – the attack by certain fundamentalist religious groups on liberal elements in the Protestant churches." It went on to praise Fulbright for the "courageous stand" he had taken.[38] To the right, however, he had become public enemy number one. "You are a stinking communist infiltrator," one superpatriot wrote in September 1961. "I call for your execution."[39]

By the midpoint of his first year in office, John F. Kennedy was under intense pressure from the radical right and the unscrupulous politicians who were waiting in the wings to reap the political whirlwind their more extremist brethren were sowing. "We need a man on horseback to lead this nation," E. M. Dealy, chairman of the board of the *Dallas Morning News*, told the president, "and many people in Texas and the southwest think that you are riding Caroline's bicycle."[40] Late in 1961 a man stepped forward to offer himself as America's Napoleon, Boulanger, and de Gaulle all wrapped into one – Barry M. Goldwater, Arizona's Republican junior senator. Arthur Schlesinger, the White House's resident intellectual, attempted to damn Goldwater and the ultras with faint praise, but Kennedy and his advisers realized that this union of traditional conservatives and the radical right posed a gen-

36 "McNamara Backs Review of Military Leaders' Speeches," *Arkansas Democrat,* Sept. 7, 1961.

37 Max Awner to JWF, Oct. 17, 1961, Series 4:19, Box 31:2, SPF; and Ralph McGill, "The Incredible Generals," *Atlanta Constitution,* Oct. 13, 1961.

38 Rev. William Howard McLish to JWF, Oct. 12, 1961, Series 4:19, Box 31:3, SPF.

39 Hoover to SAC, Chicago, Sept. 25, 1961, "Hoover's Official and Confidential File," FBI Files.

40 Quoted in Arthur M. Schlesinger, Jr., *A Thousand Days* (Boston, 1965), 752.

uine menace that had to be confronted.[41] The man who stepped forward to challenge Goldwater was J. William Fulbright. Indeed, the muzzling the military memo touched off a major debate over foreign policy, democratic ideology, and national purpose, a debate that established the boundaries of political dialogue for the remainder of the Kennedy administration.

Fulbright's sweeping survey of American foreign policy, delivered in late June of 1961, infuriated Goldwater. He had urged the administration to continue to align itself with the forces of social progress in developing nations, to pursue a course of competitive coexistence with Communist China and the Soviet Union, to adopt a stance of toleration/isolation toward Castro's Cuba, and to avoid military intervention in peripheral areas of the world. Air Force Reserves General Goldwater already had his sights set on the 1964 presidential election, and he decided that Fulbright would make the perfect foil. Two weeks after Fulbright delivered his address, Goldwater rose in the well of the Senate and heaped ridicule on his colleague's remarks. He was "surprised, amazed, and alarmed" by Fulbright's views. It was an argument for "continued drifting in the wrong direction." Those who thought that America could wipe out communism by wiping out poverty were naive – or worse. Fulbright, who he said was clearly speaking for the Kennedy administration, was foolishly preoccupied with a world opinion that seemed to prefer communism over democracy. The right course to follow, the only course to follow, Goldwater told the Senate, was for the president to declare "total victory as our fundamental purpose."[42]

Two days later Fulbright made his classic reply. In an age of ideological conflict and nuclear weapons, what exactly did Goldwater mean, he asked sarcastically, by "total victory"? Was he recommending that the United States stage a preemptive nuclear strike, "which at the very least would cost the lives of tens of millions of people on both sides, devastate most or all of our great cities, and mutilate or utterly destroy a civilization which has been built over thousands of years?" What price victory! Or did he mean that he had developed some brilliant stroke of diplomacy or compelling argument of logic that would cause the communists to admit the error of their ways and voluntarily embrace capitalism? Should the United States invade Cuba, thus alienating all of Latin America and acquiring a new, ungovernable dependency? The arena of world politics was not like a college football game or medieval joust where there were clear winners and clear losers, the Arkansan declared.

In his contempt for global opinion, Fulbright continued, Goldwater did a great injustice to the peoples of the world. It was not communism that at-

---

41 Arthur M. Schlesinger, Jr., "The 'Threat' of the Radical Right," *New York Times Magazine,* June 17, 1962, 10, 55, 58.

42 Robert S. Boyd, "Senate Argues Foreign Policy," *Memphis Commercial Appeal,* Aug. 29, 1961.

tracted them. The emergent peoples of Asia, Africa, and Latin America hoped for peace, a decent material life, and national self-determination. Only to the extent that communism was able to identify itself with these aspirations did it earn prestige, allegiance, and respect.

He was not, as Goldwater charged, a noninterventionist but, rather, an advocate of "long-range intervention in depth," using all the instruments of foreign policy to identify the United States with social and political progress. "Our proper objective," Fulbright concluded, "is a continuing effort to limit the world struggle for power and to bring it under civilized rules." Total victory would consist of the triumph of "a world-wide regime of law and order and peaceful procedures for the redress of legitimate grievances."[43]

The Fulbright–Goldwater debate gained front-page headlines and spawned numerous editorials during late 1961 and 1962. "Fulbright Becomes a National Issue" was the title of a feature article by E. W. Kenworthy in the *New York Times Magazine*.[44] "Clash of Irreconcilable Philosophies Involved" proclaimed Holmes Alexander in a column on the Fulbright–Goldwater encounter. "The forces of the left and right have joined battle on the deep-going principles expressed and implied in the Fulbright memo," producing "a clash that will be resounding throughout the sixties," he declared.[45] Conservative broadcaster Paul Harvey told his listeners that the debate could very well define the national purpose for an entire generation of Americans. Walter Lippmann, who had spent most of his life trying, futilely, to generate a national debate on one issue or another, defended Fulbright in his battle with the radical right, terming him a true conservative, "liberal in temper and progressive in policy."[46]

Lippmann, Kenworthy, Reston, and others' defense of Fulbright stemmed in part from the fact that the new right had targeted Fulbright for defeat in his 1962 bid for reelection. There was virtually no chance that a Republican could win in Arkansas, but Barry Goldwater and Styles Bridges believed that Orval Faubus would be a far less irritating thorn in their side than J. William Fulbright. Indeed, his election would provide a double benefit, removing an articulate critic of the GOP from the Senate and elevating to the national scene a living symbol of the racist traditions of the southern wing of the Democratic Party.

There is no doubt that Faubus could have beaten Fulbright in 1959, 1960,

43 *Congressional Record,* Senate, July 24, 1961, 13246–7.
44 E. W. Kenworthy, "Fulbright Becomes a National Issue," *New York Times Magazine,* Oct. 1, 1961, 21, 89, 92, 96–7.
45 Holmes Alexander, "Clash of Irreconcilable Philosophies Involved," undated, Series 4:19, Box 27:2, SPF.
46 Walter Lippmann, "Fulbright Great Conservative," *Washington Post,* Oct. 13, 1961.

or 1961. The governor and his principal adviser, William J. "Bill" Smith, commissioned polls throughout this period. During the three-year span in question, these surveys indicated that Faubus would take at least sixty percent of the vote in any head-to-head contest with Fulbright.[47]

In February 1962, however, Fulbright was notified by several reliable sources that Faubus would seek another term as governor rather than run for the Senate in 1962.[48] Indeed, so comfortable did Fulbright feel that at the last minute he reversed a decision to miss the Inter-parliamentary Union meeting scheduled for Bermuda. He and Betty left on the fifteenth for a few days of golf and sun in the Caribbean.

During the years following the Little Rock crisis of 1957–8, J. William Fulbright was careful to stay to Orval Faubus's right on the major civil rights issues of the day. Following passage of the 1957 act, the Commission on Civil Rights held hearings on black voting in several cities, North and South, and discovered, to few people's surprise, that blacks were being regularly denied the right to vote by certain white registrars in the South. As part of an effort to afford added protection, the Eisenhower administration had submitted to Congress the Voting Rights Act of 1960. The measure empowered federal courts to appoint referees to examine state voting-qualification laws and practices whenever a petitioner had been deprived of the right to register or vote because of race or color. The referees could issue certificates entitling the aggrieved to vote in federal elections.[49]

On February 15 Richard Russell, having divided his colleagues into three teams of six senators each, launched what became known as the "filibuster of reason." Serving on the team of Senator Allen Ellender of Louisiana with eight hours' duty every three days, the Arkansan delivered four major speeches during 125 hours of consecutive debate.[50] On March 1, he made a detailed review and analysis of federal and Arkansas law demonstrating that there was more than enough legislation in place to protect the voting rights of all citizens. "The Negroes of my State vote freely and without coercion," he declared. He accused the North of attempting to force its cultural will on the South, a situation that "could well be taken advantage of by the Communists."[51]

The junior senator from Arkansas may have been the picture of logic and reason when it came to foreign policy, but to all appearances, he continued

47 Interview with Orval Faubus, May 31, 1991, Conway, Ark:, and interview with William J. Smith, May 23, 1990, Little Rock, Ark.
48 Marcy to Holt, Feb. 13, 1962, Box 4, Folder Jan.–May, Marcy Papers, SFRC, RG 46, NA.
49 John Hope Franklin, *From Slavery to Freedom: A History of Negro Americans,* 5th ed. (New York, 1980), 440; and Legislative Meeting Notes, Box 6, WHOF–OSS, Eisenhower Papers.
50 Elizabeth Carpenter, "Fulbright Symbol of 'New' Filibuster Technique of 1960," *Arkansas Gazette,* Apr. 17, 1960.
51 Leslie Carpenter, "Filibuster's Wee Hours Drag for Weary Senators," *Arkansas Gazette,* Mar. 6, 1960.

to buy into the southern myth of Reconstruction. On April 5 Fulbright told the Senate that many of the proposals in the so-called civil rights bill were virtually identical to the punitive measures offered during the original Reconstruction period following the Civil War, a decade that historians had labeled "one of the darkest and most unhappy eras since the founding of the nation." Federal intervention in, and control of, elections would not only violate the Constitution but set off a backlash that would erode rather than promote the rights of black Americans.[52]

Despite Fulbright and the filibuster of reason, the Senate moved inexorably toward a vote. The eighteen irreconcilables who gathered around Richard Russell found themselves increasingly isolated. With his sights set squarely on the Democratic presidential nomination, Lyndon Johnson was relentless in pressuring for passage. In the end, the Senate voted to approve the Civil Rights Act of 1960 by a vote of 82 to 18.[53]

Ignoring his eloquence, the liberal press blasted Fulbright during the course of the 1960 civil rights debate. "No Colossus of Rhodes" ran the title of a *Washington Post* editorial. The criticism, indeed the controversy, bored and annoyed rather than distressed Fulbright. "I am sure you have noticed from the press that the Senate is tied up in a very wearisome controversy over civil rights again which seriously interferes with the ordinary conduct of the government," he wrote a friend in Puerto Rico.[54]

Meanwhile, the cold war refused to wait on anyone. Soviet and American acquisition of nuclear weapons and intercontinental delivery systems had given a new meaning to the term "crisis management." Images of Hiroshima and Nagasaki continued to haunt Fulbright, and they became more vivid as the nuclear arms race intensified in the early stages of the Kennedy administration. While continuing to hope and work for European integration and an Atlantic Union, the chairman of the SFRC turned his attention to a more immediate and pressing problem – the avoidance of Armageddon.

In the spring of 1961 President Kennedy and his advisers decided to implement a policy of peace through strength, that is, to ensure by establishing overwhelming American superiority in number and quality of nuclear weapons that the communists would never launch a nuclear strike. In the wake of the Bay of Pigs fiasco, consequently, the president asked for and received from Congress a multi-billion-dollar addition to the defense budget. The result by mid-1964 was an increase of 150 percent in the number of nuclear weapons available, a 200-percent boost in deliverable megatonnage, the construction of ten additional Polaris submarines (for a total of twenty-nine) and

52 *Congressional Record,* Senate, Apr. 5, 1960, 7321–6; and ibid., Apr. 8, 1960, 7728–30.
53 "Senate Vote Rejects Congress' Support of '54 School Ruling," *Arkansas Gazette,* Apr. 5, 1960.
54 JWF to Horace E. Thompson, Mar. 7, 1960, BCN 105, F67, SPF.

four hundred additional Minuteman missiles (for a total of eight hundred) above what the previous administration had scheduled.[55]

At the most, Khrushchev and his advisers believed, the United States intended to wage a preemptive war and, at the least, to use its advantage to overturn governments friendly to international communism. Determined to demonstrate that he could not be intimidated, Khrushchev at his meeting with Kennedy in Vienna in June 1961 revived the Berlin crisis by repeating his demands of 1958 and setting a new deadline of six months for a settlement of the status of the city. It was upon his return from this meeting that the president, egged on by Dean Acheson, asked Congress for $3 billion for defense and mobilized the reserves.[56] The new Berlin crisis loosed a flood of East German immigrants into West Berlin. By late July 1961, two thousand refugees a day were flooding into the enclave.

The deterioration in Soviet–American relations during that first, hopeful year of the Kennedy administration was intensely disappointing to J. William Fulbright. As tensions mounted over Berlin, the chairman of the SFRC searched desperately for a solution that would break the logjam and nip the spiraling arms race in the bud. After consulting with Walter Lippmann, he proposed to Dean Rusk that the West counter Khrushchev's ultimatum with a proposal to convert West Berlin into a "free city" under United Nations supervision. In return for the "neutralization of Berlin," that is, a promise by the West not to position nuclear weapons there, token forces from NATO and the UN could remain in the city, and the West would be guaranteed continued free access. Lippmann argued, and Fulbright agreed, that East and West Germany were political, diplomatic, and strategic realities. It was folly for Washington to expose the world to nuclear war out of a stubborn determination not to sign an agreement that recognized the sovereignty of the German Democratic Republic.[57]

When the State Department did not respond, Fulbright went public with his suggestion. "We should have conferences at the ministerial level to avoid a showdown leading to nuclear war," he told a group of reporters. "I believe in negotiation and discussion as opposed to ultimatums and showdowns." At the close of the news conference in an offhand remark, Fulbright wondered out loud why East Germany had not staunched the outflow of refugees from East to West Berlin and why Western authorities had not cooperated. The immigrants constituted a tremendous burden on the resources of West Berlin, were a continuing source of embarrassment to the

55 John Lewis Gaddis, *Strategies of Containment: A Critical Appraisal of Postwar American National Security Policy* (New York, 1982), 207–8.

56 Memorandum of discussion in the National Security Council on July 13, 1961, National Security Files [hereinafter referred to as NSF], Box 313–14, Kennedy Papers.

57 Walter Lippmann, memorandum on Berlin, June 7, 1961, and JWF to Dean Rusk, July 3, 1961, Series 48:16, Box 42:1, SPF.

communists, and could be stopped by the East Germans at anytime, anyway.[58]

Fulbright's remarks, as he should have anticipated, placed him at once at the center of a storm of controversy. "Two of the best German correspondents, old friends of mine from Berlin, called me this morning," Pierre Salinger's assistant reported to him. "Their editors kept them up all night with bulletins and requests regarding Senator Fulbright's statement. . . . [H]e occupies a special position, and the West Germans, particularly Berliners, are very uneasy about the matter."[59] The status of Berlin was not negotiable, Rusk subsequently announced, and the United States would never sign a treaty recognizing the existence of a government – the GDR – imposed on the German people against their will. West Berlin mayor Willy Brandt declared that the chairman of the SFRC must have been misquoted.[60] On August 13 Soviet and East German troops began sealing off the border between East and West Berlin. They started with barbed wire and ended with a concrete block wall twenty-eight miles long.

The White House let its spokespeople in the press know of the president's displeasure at Fulbright's lack of "diplomacy" and reiterated Kennedy's determination not to negotiate in the face of "ultimata and threats." To underscore his and America's commitment to Berlin, Kennedy flew to the beleaguered city in June 1963 to declare, "Ich bin ein Berliner." Whether or not J. William Fulbright's statements in the summer of 1961 encouraged the East Germans and Russians to erect the Berlin Wall is still a matter of conjecture, but they would continue to be a source of ammunition for his enemies.

Actually, the president believed that the wall was a sure sign that Khrushchev did not intend to take West Berlin by force. He agreed that a halt to the outflow of refugees was in everybody's interests except, perhaps, prospective refugees. "It's not a very nice solution," he told his aides, "but a wall is a hell of a lot better than a war." But he dare not say such things in public: Cold warriors in America and Western Europe would accuse him of appeasing the Soviet Union.[61]

Indeed, despite the hard line he took in public over Berlin, Jack Kennedy and his advisers did not believe that the fact that the Soviet Union was a communist state was, in itself, cause for overt conflict; rather, the United States should acknowledge the USSR's position as a great power and hold out to it the prospect of "constructive participation" in world affairs. "This

---

58 "Fulbright Calls on U.S. to Take Lead in Dispute over Berlin," *Arkansas Gazette,* July 30, 1961.
59 Memorandum to Mr. Salinger, Feb. 20, 1963, Fulbright Name File, Kennedy Papers.
60 "Fulbright Quote Creates Storm," *Arkansas Gazette,* Aug. 3, 1961.
61 Michael R. Beschloss, *The Crisis Years: Kennedy and Khrushchev, 1960–63* (New York, 1991), 278.

will not change the basic policy of Soviet leaders now in power,'' Walt Rostow contended, ''but it may have some moderating effects on their conduct, or that of their successors.''[62] If the administration was not willing to negotiate a halt to the arms race in which it enjoyed such a distinct advantage, it did prove willing to reach agreement on a test ban treaty. On September 1, 1961, Russia broke the informal moratorium on nuclear tests that had been in place since 1958 with an explosion over central Asia. Before completing their tests in November, the Soviets set off some fifty explosions that increased radioactive contamination of the atmosphere by one-half. This two-month series, moreover, included detonation of a fifty-eight-megaton bomb three thousand times as powerful as that which destroyed Hiroshima. Denouncing the Soviet action as ''atomic blackmail,'' Kennedy resumed American testing by authorizing several underground explosions in Nevada.

62 Gaddis, *Strategies of Containment,* 228.

4

Of Myths and Realities

In his desperate search for a gesture that would reverse the downward spiral of Soviet–American relations, Fulbright embraced the notion of a comprehensive test ban treaty. He was convinced that such a pact was both technically and politically feasible. An easing of the arms race was manifestly in Khrushchev and the Soviet Union's interests.[1] Even assuming that Khrushchev and his fellows in the Kremlin were the paranoid, xenophobic creatures that many Kremlinologists portrayed them as, Fulbright reasoned, the best method for dealing with them was to build trust, not engage in confrontation.

In the wake of the Cuban missile crisis, Kennedy and his advisers sensed a slight thaw in Soviet–American relations. The Russians had made good on their promise to allow the U.S. Navy to inspect ships carrying dismantled missiles out of the Ever Faithful Isle. In 1963, as a result of the Cuban confrontation, Kennedy and Khrushchev agreed to an emergency phone and teletype, or "hot line," connection between Washington and Moscow. It provided instant communication between the heads of the two superpowers when one or the other feared miscalculation in a crisis. Walt Rostow and Jerome Weisner, Kennedy's science adviser, both of whom had been American delegates to the 1960 Pugwash Conference, a privately funded international meeting designed to reduce the chances of nuclear war, urged the president to make a test ban treaty part of détente. In March 1963 Kennedy authorized his arms control representatives in Geneva to begin discussions in earnest on a treaty and in June announced that the United States would no longer test nuclear arms in the atmosphere "so long as other states do not do so."

In late July 1963 British, American, and Soviet representatives initialed a test ban treaty. Signatories promised not to conduct nuclear tests in the atmosphere, outer space, or underwater and not to abet tests by others. The new

---

1 Neither Fulbright nor Marcy, however, was naive concerning Soviet motives, and they were not going to support an agreement that allowed the Soviet Union to gain a strategic edge over the West. Marcy to Kuchel, Apr. 18, 1958, Box 2, Folder Apr.–Dec., Marcy Papers.

accord permitted underground testing and stipulated that inspection was to be carried out through listening stations rather than on-site visits. Immediately upon his return from the meeting in Moscow, special negotiator Averell Harriman briefed Fulbright and the rest of the SFRC in a closed-door meeting. At its conclusion, the chairman emerged arm in arm with Harriman and announced to reporters that the pact had his full support.[2] A week later Fulbright departed Washington for Moscow as part of the American delegation to the official signing.

Fulbright anticipated a difficult ratification struggle. In negotiating the test ban treaty, Kennedy, Rostow, McNamara, and Rusk had largely bypassed the Joint Chiefs of Staff.[3] Permanent senatorial representatives of the military such as Richard Russell and John Stennis might possibly ally with the know-nothings and succeed in blocking two-thirds approval.

For ten days a variety of administration officials from Dean Rusk to the scientists who had advised Kennedy on the technical aspects of the treaty paraded before the SFRC, assuring Fulbright and his colleagues that the ban was enforceable, that it would drastically reduce atmospheric fallout, and that it would not jeopardize the security of the United States. The principal naysayer was nuclear physicist Edward M. Teller, the "father of the H-bomb." A refugee from communist Hungary, Teller who resembled the proverbial "mad scientist," railed against the ban. It was full of technical holes. The perfidious Soviets could – and would – cheat. The treaty was an exercise in appeasement such as the world had not witnessed since the 1930s. Fulbright was not impressed. "Teller's an educated fool, you know," he would later recall. "I've never seen anybody quite as crazy as he is."[4] The committee voted 16 to 1 to recommend passage to the full Senate. It attached one reservation: Nothing in the test ban agreement should be construed as barring the United States from employing nuclear weapons in time of war.

The nation's attention was riveted on the Senate when Fulbright opened the debate on the test ban treaty on September 9. National polls indicated only a bare majority in favor of the pact, while Fulbright's mail ran 4 to 1 against.[5] The Arkansan was at the height of his powers. A laudatory biography entitled *Fulbright of Arkansas* had reached number three on the *New York Times* best-seller list in March.[6] In reviewing the reasons why the test ban was manifestly in the interests of both the United States and the Soviet Union, he ranged from the technical to the historical to the philosophical. He sensed, he said, the same atmosphere in international relations that existed prior to the Great War when a mindless arms race propelled unwilling nations

2 "Fulbright Endorses Pact After Briefing," *Arkansas Gazette,* July 30, 1963.
3 Memorandum of Conference with the President, July 18, 1963, NSF, Box 66, Kennedy Papers.
4 Interview with J. William Fulbright, Oct. 11–18, 1988, Washington, D.C.
5 Williams to JWF, Aug. 10, 1963, Series 48:4, Box 20:2, SPF.
6 "What Washington Is Reading," *Washington Post,* Mar. 10, 1963.

into a global conflict. The public wanted an end to the constant threat of annihilation, of sending their children off to school not knowing whether mass destruction raining down from the skies would separate them forever. The test ban was a small first step to relieving that anxiety. "Extreme nationalism and dogmatic ideology are luxuries that the human race can no longer afford," he concluded. "It must turn its energies now to the politics of survival."[7]

When Russell proposed a number of "reservations" to the treaty, à la Henry Cabot Lodge and the Treaty of Versailles, and declared that the pact was a first step toward "unilateral disarmament," Fulbright lashed out on the NBC *Today* show. Any reservation would require renegotiation and kill the treaty, he told Dave Garroway. The Joint Chiefs had been privately lobbying against the treaty, he revealed. The chairman and all of the service heads had testified before his committee; each had signified their approval. If they felt otherwise, they should say so publicly or stop undercutting their commander-in-chief.[8]

Fulbright's management of the test ban treaty, and particularly his eloquence in its behalf, helped pave the way for its ratification. Indeed, it was Fulbright's skill and eloquence that contained the hawks and turned public opinion around.[9] In the wake of the Berlin and Cuban missile crises, the American people had built their fallout shelters and more and more assumed a bunker mentality. The test ban treaty, as Fulbright repeatedly emphasized, offered a glimmer of hope, a ray of sunshine. Perhaps the holocaust was not inevitable. From mid-August to mid-September the percentage of Americans favoring the treaty rose from fifty-two percent to eighty-one percent.[10]

J. William Fulbright was in a buoyant mood as the fall of 1963 approached. The great desiderata of American foreign policy – avoidance of nuclear war and détente with the Soviet Union, its corollary – seemed at last within reach. After four years as chairman of the SFRC, the Arkansan was hitting his stride. Working through Carl Marcy, he had managed to put together what Richard Moose would later call the Fulbright majority, a bipartisan coalition on the committee that trusted the chairman on all procedural and most substantive matters and that could be counted on to follow his lead. His prestige at home and abroad was reaching an all-time high. True, the radical right had come to view him as the archenemy, but liberal intellectuals in academia and in the press chose for the most part to ignore his position on civil rights and focus on his "enlightened" stance on foreign affairs. Finally, although it had

---

7 *Congressional Record*, Senate, Sept. 9, 1963, 16525–40.
8 UPI41, Sept. 12, 1991, Series 48:1, Box 5:3, SPF.
9 Marcy to Hickenlooper, Sept. 12, 1963, Box 4, Folder June–Sept., Marcy Papers.
10 *Congressional Record*, Senate, Sept. 16, 1963, 17050.

had its ups and downs, Fulbright's relationship with the White House was sound. The junior senator looked forward to 1964 and beyond, to four more years of competitive but peaceful coexistence with the communist bloc, and to cooperation with the executive branch.

During the fall of 1963 President Kennedy and his advisers seemed to be devoting more attention than usual to politics. In September the president toured eleven western states and then followed up with a series of major speaking engagements on the East Coast. Given the fallout from the administration's efforts in the field of civil rights, Ted Sorensen and Bobby Kennedy were particularly worried about Democratic prospects in the South. In the 1964 presidential election Texas would be crucial, and Lyndon Johnson's presence on the ticket was no guarantee that the Lone Star state would remain loyal. Exactly four weeks before, Adlai Stevenson had gone to Dallas to attend a meeting on United Nations Day. The radical right decided to counter this visit by holding a "United States Day" just prior to Stevenson's arrival, with General Edwin A. Walker as the main speaker. The day following Walker's appearance, handbills with photographs of the president of the United States – full-face and profile – appeared on the streets of Dallas. "Wanted for Treason" read the caption.

In early November, Kennedy flew to Arkansas to dedicate the newly completed Greers Ferry dam near Heber Springs and to throw a few political bouquets in the direction of the junior senator. When Fulbright learned of the president's planned campaign swing through Texas, he begged him to avoid Dallas. "Dallas is a very dangerous place," he told Kennedy as the two drove from Little Rock to Heber Springs. "I wouldn't go there and don't you go."[11]

The morning of November 22 Fulbright attended a routine executive session of the SFRC devoted to amending the Foreign Assistance Act of 1961. He met his close friend Eugene Black, head of the World Bank, at the F Street Club. There, during lunch, they learned of Kennedy's assassination. Later that afternoon, the White House notified Fulbright that the new president wanted him to be at the executive mansion at six o'clock. Lyndon Johnson arrived there at 6:45 to begin conferring with the Capitol's movers and shakers. The first person he saw was his old acquaintance from Arkansas.[12]

Tall, powerfully built, simultaneously as ugly and handsome as the hound dogs he raised on his Texas ranch, Lyndon Baines Johnson stood in marked contrast to John F. Kennedy. His rural, southwestern background, teachers' college education, drawling speech, and backslapping demeanor seemed the antithesis of Kennedy's northeastern, metropolitan youthfulness, his Harvard

11 Fred Livingston to Robert S. McCord, Mar. 31, 1969, Series 48:1, Box 9:3, SPF.
12 Fulbright interview.

training, eloquence, and urbanity. The latter's tragic death seemed to erase in the public mind memories of Kennedy's working-class, Boston–Irish, ward-heeling ancestry. Johnson lacked his predecessor's graceful style on the speaker's platform, and his crude language and penchant for hyperbole dismayed many intellectuals. When warned by a staff member that in bringing a certain political figure into his administration the new president was hiring a chronic troublemaker, Johnson retorted (one of his favorites): "I'd rather have him inside the tent pissing out instead of outside the tent pissing in." But Johnson had a flair for the dramatic, and he was a man of enormous energy, drive, and determination.

Personally, Lyndon Johnson was a bundle of conflicting insecurities and ambitions. Like a number of other white southerners, he understood and empathized with the black revolution long before many northern politicians did. A man of self-made and conjugal wealth, Johnson understood poverty and all its implications and was determined to wipe it out. A product of a rural political oligarchy, Johnson preached the politics of populism minus its nativism. Although he would win the 1964 election by the largest margin of any presidential candidate in American history, the Texan felt unloved and even ridiculed. He was candid and deceitful, considerate and cruel, coarse and subtle, intelligent but capable of stubbornness to the point of stupidity. Despite his statement that he was but the trustee of the Kennedy legacy and his oft-repeated promises to enact the Kennedy program, the man from Johnson City was determined to be his own president.

Fulbright was more excited about the prospect of working with Johnson than with any of his predecessors. The apprehensions of the past were nowhere in evidence during the first days of the new administration. The goodwill the president enjoyed in Congress and his unparalleled achievements as legislative manager seemed to Fulbright to augur an end to the divided government he had so long lamented. The Texan was a man who could get the country moving in the direction in which Kennedy and Fulbright wanted it to go. On a personal level, the Fulbright–Johnson relationship had never been better. Johnson conferred with the chair of the SFRC throughout December. Just after Christmas the president sent Fulbright a picture of the two having breakfast aboard Air Force One. The inscription read: "To J. William Fulbright, than whom there is no better. Lyndon B. Johnson."

Allen Matusow has written that Lyndon B. Johnson was a "complex man notorious for his ideological insincerity."[13] If by that Matusow meant that Johnson was nonideological or that he wielded ideological justifications for pragmatically based policies already decided upon, he was right. He also shared that trait with most other successful presidents, notably the two Roosevelts. Lyndon Johnson was in basic agreement with the foreign policies of

13 Allen J. Matusow, *The Unraveling of America: A History of Liberalism in the 1960s* (New York, 1984), 94.

the Kennedy administration; indeed, as vice-president he had helped to shape them. Military preparedness and realistic diplomacy would contain communism within its existing bounds. In order to keep up morale among America's allies and satisfy hard-line anticommunists at home, the United States must continue to hold fast to Berlin, oppose the admission of Communist China to the United Nations, and continue to confront and blockade Cuba. He was aware of the Sino–Soviet split and the possibilities inherent in it for dividing the communist world. He also took a flexible, even hopeful view of the Soviet Union and Nikita Khrushchev. It was just possible, he believed, that Russia was becoming a status quo power and as such would be a force for stability rather than chaos in the world. The United States must continue its "flexible response" of military aid, economic assistance, and technical/political advice to the threat of communism in the developing world, but there was nothing wrong with negotiating with the Soviets at the same time in an effort to reduce tensions. Insofar as Latin America was concerned, Johnson was an enthusiastic supporter of the Alliance for Progress; as a progressive Democrat he was drawn to the Schlesinger–Goodwin philosophy of seeking openings to the democratic left. At the outset of his administration, it appeared that the new president did not buy into the myth of a monolithic communist threat. He was a staunch supporter of trade with Yugoslavia and Poland. Above all, he seemed a flexible, pragmatic cold war warrior, a position very congenial to J. William Fulbright.[14]

One evening in late March, in the midst of the Senate filibuster of the 1964 Civil Rights Bill, Lyndon Johnson invited Fulbright to dinner at the White House.[15] The discussion ranged over many topics. The president urged Fulbright, who was actively participating in the filibuster, to think about voting against cloture. He knew it was impossible for the Arkansan to support the final bill, Johnson said, but a vote for cloture would be of tremendous value. It would also help dispel the myth in foreign chanceries that Fulbright was a racist. The two talked of Vietnam where some twenty thousand American military advisers were trying to shore up the struggling Nguyen Khanh government against Vietcong attacks and North Vietnamese incursions and where the Agency for International Development (AID) was working to build an economically viable society. Johnson expressed his desire to win an overwhelming victory over the probable Republican candidate in 1964, Barry Goldwater. He wanted to unify the country behind his domestic programs, Johnson said, and discredit the radical right once and for all. Fulbright promised to do all in his power to help.

14 See *Congressional Record,* Senate, Jan. 21, 1964, 893.
15 Rowland Evans and Robert Novak, "Fulbright's Opportunity," *Washington Post,* Apr. 14, 1964.

When Fulbright rose in the Senate chamber on the afternoon of March 25 to take his turn speaking against the pending civil rights bill, the hall was virtually empty. Morse was there and so was Sam Ervin, but only a handful of others bothered to attend. In a low monotone Fulbright delivered one of the most important foreign policy speeches of his career. It would attract national and international attention and launch the 1964 presidential election campaign.

In their dealings with the communist world, Fulbright declared, Americans must abandon old myths and adapt themselves to new realities. The character of Soviet–American relations had changed. Washington had demonstrated clearly to Moscow in the Cuban missile crisis that "aggression and adventure" involved unacceptable risks. Khrushchev had retreated from his dream of world conquest, and in signing the test ban agreement, the two nations had tacitly relinquished their quest for "total victory." In this new era of "peaceful coexistence" it was imperative that Americans adopt a more flexible, sophisticated approach to their former adversaries. "We must dare to think about 'unthinkable things,' because when things become 'unthinkable,' thinking stops and action becomes mindless."

The tendency to view the communist world as a monolith bent on military destruction of the free world was an anachronistic, if understandable, holdover from the Stalinist era. The Sino–Soviet split and the growing independence of Poland, Yugoslavia, and Hungary were a clear indication that the formerly homogenous communist bloc was maturing into a diverse collection of nation-states with each of whom the United States must develop a separate, distinct relationship.

Too many Americans, Fulbright declared, returning to another favorite theme, confused means with ends. They tended to equate freedom and democracy with capitalism, federalism, and the two-party system. The latter were merely the mechanisms Americans preferred for achieving the former. It was quite possible for freedom and democracy to exist in a socialist or communist country, the Arkansan pointed out. What mattered was not the principles around which a society organized its economy but that society's aggressive intent. "Insofar as a great nation mobilizes its power and resources for aggressive purposes," Fulbright declared, "that nation, regardless of ideology, makes itself our enemy. Insofar as a nation is content to practice its doctrines within its own frontiers, that nation, however repugnant its ideology, is one with which we have no proper quarrel." If the United States continued to view all communist regimes as equally hostile and equally threatening, it would impose a degree of unity on the communist bloc that the Soviet Union had proved quite incapable of imposing. What, then, should American policy be toward the communist nations and those vulnerable to Sino–Soviet penetration?

The United States was going to have to come to grips with the fact that Castro and Castroism were not going to disappear in a season. Efforts to bring Cuba down through a policy of political and economic boycott had failed. Cuba, Fulbright declared, repeating a point he had made during and after the abortive Bay of Pigs invasion, was a thorn in the side but not a dagger at the heart. Certainly Castro was attempting to export his revolution, but he was failing. Through a combination of military and economic aid, the United States had enabled states such as Venezuela to defeat communist-led domestic insurrections.

In the long run, Fulbright concluded, the United States was going to have to abandon the notion that meaningful social change could take place in Latin America without violence. Long-established ruling oligarchies were so deeply entrenched and so repressive that in some cases armed insurrection was the only path to democratization and socioeconomic reform. Such uprisings were not by definition communist inspired or communist led. He was not advocating violent revolutions, he said, but the United States must confront socioeconomic change in the developing world with an open mind.

In the "old myths and new realities" speech, Fulbright did not go so far as to call for the admission of Red China to the United Nations, but he did reiterate his belief that there was only one China, mainland, Communist China, and that the United States should deal with it and it alone. America could not tolerate Chinese expansion, but it should act with patience and flexibility in dealing with Peking. If Mao and Chou should ever forswear their intention to reconquer Formosa, then Washington should consider normalizing relations.

Vietnam, Fulbright continued in his sweeping review of the nation's foreign policy, was perhaps the most complicated and pressing problem facing the Johnson administration. "Other than withdrawal, which I do not think can be realistically considered under present circumstances, three options are open to us," the Arkansan declared. The United States could continue the antiguerrilla campaign then under way, stepping up military and economic aid to the South Vietnamese. It could immediately seek a negotiated settlement looking toward the neutralization of all of South Vietnam. Or finally, it could widen the war through the introduction of American troops or sponsorship of a South Vietnamese attack on the North. Fulbright ruled out negotiations. "It is extremely difficult for a party to a negotiation to achieve by diplomacy objectives which it has conspicuously failed to win by warfare." The American–South Vietnamese position was then too weak to expose it at a peace conference. The only two realistic options were to step up American aid to Saigon to enable it to prosecute more effectively the counterinsurgency then under way or to widen the war. Surprisingly, Fulbright did not indicate a preference. Whatever the Johnson administration's decision, he concluded, "it should be clear to all concerned that the United States will continue to meet its obligations and fulfill its commitments with respect to Vietnam."[16]

Although the Senate was virtually empty when Fulbright delivered old

---

16 *Congressional Record,* Senate, Mar. 25, 1964, 6227–31.

myths and new realities, the wire services reported it verbatim on the twenty-sixth, and the national press gave it extensive and immediate coverage. By the end of the week, virtually every press pundit of note had written at least one column on the speech. "Fulbright Shows His Skill Again," proclaimed Drew Pearson in "The Washington Merry-go-Round." "The significant thing about the recent Fulbright full-dress speech . . . is that its author has an almost perfect score on foreign affairs," Pearson proclaimed. "It was one of the most important foreign policy statements made by any Senator in this decade."[17] The junior senator from Arkansas had launched a much-needed and long-delayed national debate, declared Arthur Krock in the *New York Times*. That postwar American foreign policy had been rigidly moralistic and punctuated by glaring failures was undeniable.[18] By the second week in April, Fulbright had received six thousand letters and telegrams, with those approving outstripping those criticizing by 4 to 1.

To the delight of the radical right, *Pravda* called Fulbright's speech a "light which has lit up a new realistic tendency in Washington's political thinking." *Izvestia,* the official newspaper of the Soviet government, devoted nearly three columns to a glowing appraisal.[19] Cuba's unofficial minister in charge of revolution, Che Guevara, thanked Fulbright for recognizing that "Cuba is here to stay."[20]

Convinced that Fulbright had led the Democratic Party into the "soft on communism" trap that had been set ever since the fall of China in 1949, Republican politicians and conservative columnists lined up to attack the "old myths and new realities" speech. Strom Thurmond, William Miller, chairman of the GOP national committee, and Senator John Tower (R–Texas) all charged Fulbright with "appeasement." The diminutive Texan accused the chairman of the SFRC of urging "an even softer line towards international communism than we now have."[21] Thurmond inserted in the *Congressional Record* an article on the Fulbright speech by labor leader George Meany entitled "A Return to Appeasement."[22] Declared Miller:

> This is a trial balloon which the Johnson administration is sending up to prepare public opinion for the acceptance of a foreign policy that could lead only to disaster for the United States and other free nations. The course Senator Fulbright advocates is the same road which Neville Chamberlain traveled in the 1930s.[23]

17 Drew Pearson, "Fulbright Shows His Skill Again," *Washington Post,* Apr. 1, 1964.
18 Arthur Krock, "Fulbright Has Started the Debate He Wanted," *New York Times,* Apr. 1, 1964.
19 "Fulbright Speech Praised in Pravda," *New York Times,* Mar. 29, 1964.
20 "Guevara Says Fulbright Talk Set Right Attitude," *Washington Evening Star,* Mar. 31, 1964.
21 "Tower Says Fulbright Urges 'Even Softer Line' on Reds," *New York Tribune,* Apr. 5, 1964.
22 *Congressional Record,* Senate, May 8, 1964, 10438–9.
23 Ned Curran, "Critics Claim Fulbright Hit at LBJ Policy," *Arkansas Gazette,* Mar. 26, 1964.

Response from the noncommunist world was sharp and mixed. The British were appreciative. The *Times* praised Fulbright's speech as "a landmark in the evolution of American policy," and Karl Meyer wrote in *The New States-man* that Fulbright had created an atmosphere in which Rusk and Johnson would have much greater room for maneuver.[24] Although most of their governments were anti-Castro, Latin American diplomats generally approved Fulbright's analysis of the Cuban situation. They did not believe that current American policies would bring down the Cuban regime. They were even more outspoken in praise of Fulbright's suggestion that the United States could afford to be more generous in its treatment of Panama.[25] Jiang Jie-shi, in a speech addressed to the youth of Taiwan on March 29, declared that his government would not tolerate the illusion of "international appeasement." The Fulbright speech, he subsequently told a reporter, would only encourage the communists "to hate and insult your country more."[26]

The Johnson administration's public reaction to "old myths and new realities" was guarded. Secretary of State Rusk told a news conference that he agreed with many of the points made by Fulbright, particularly about rapid changes in the communist and noncommunist worlds, but in regard to Cuba, Rusk insisted that Castro was "more than a nuisance" and that the economic boycott must continue. He denied that the speech was a trial balloon, as Miller had charged, but he welcomed Fulbright's efforts to stimulate a debate.[27] Some in the press and among the Democratic leadership, most notably the knee-jerk anticommunist Speaker of the House, John McCormack, accused Fulbright of attacking not only American foreign policy but his old friend Lyndon Johnson.[28]

In reality, while Johnson, Rusk, and McNamara were a bit apprehensive lest the public fall victim once again to the GOP's efforts to portray the Democratic Party as weak on communism, they were generally pleased. Fulbright had in effect carved out the middle ground that the Democrats could hopefully occupy during the forthcoming presidential election campaign. Liberals could rally around the call for flexibility, but the speech had really given away nothing. It rejected recognition of Red China, allowed room for a stepped-up commitment in Vietnam, and urged a diplomacy that had as its objective the breakup of the Soviet empire. Moreover, the administration was free to dissociate itself from various aspects of the speech, which Rusk did in regard to Cuba. Fulbright's speech would definitely aid the Johnson campaign in its efforts to portray Goldwater, almost certain to be the Republican

24 "U.S. Foreign Policy – The Feeling in Four Major Capitals," *New York Times,* Apr. 11, 1964.

25 "U.N. Diplomats Praise Fulbright," *St. Louis Post–Dispatch,* Apr. 8, 1964.

26 Thomas Hughes to Acting Secretary, Apr. 10, 1964, NSF, Box 3, Papers of Lyndon B. Johnson, Johnson Library, Austin, Tex. [hereinafter referred to as Johnson Papers].

27 "Fulbright's Stand on Cuban Policy Rejected by Rusk," *Arkansas Gazette,* Mar. 28, 1964.

28 See Marianne Means, "LBJ 'Friends' Helping GOP," *Washington Post,* Mar. 29, 1964.

candidate, as a go-for-broke cold warrior dedicated to total military victory over the forces of international communism.[29]

The "old myths and new realities" address launched what columnist Max Frankel referred to as the "Fulbright phenomenon." In early April, more than seventeen hundred students, teachers, and townspeople turned out on a rainy Sunday night at the University of North Carolina to hear the Arkansan appeal for a more rational division of resources between military and human welfare programs. The *Daily Tar Heel* praised him as a "man of political guts" and referring to his position on civil rights, lamented the fact that he was one of a number of southern legislators "chained to a role they must act out."[30] John Fitzgerald Kennedy's death had left a vacuum, especially among the idealistic youth that the Kennedy family had politicized, and despite his record on civil rights, Fulbright seemed to many liberals to be the man who could fill it. But Fulbright's appeal was not limited to college students. Arthur Schlesinger, Jr., would later speculate about the historical mind and the assassinated president. He would argue that Kennedy was attuned to the complexity of human existence, its tensions, contradictions, and shadings. He had not looked for morals, made sweeping judgments, and tried to come up with final solutions. This quality, Schlesinger would insist, was the essence of the historical and liberal mind. He could not have described J. William Fulbright more aptly, and that attribute was in large part what made the Arkansan appealing to liberal intellectuals as well as to so many young people.

To all appearances the Fulbright–Johnson relationship continued to flourish as the new president settled into his duties. During the early weeks of the transition, Johnson was on the phone with Fulbright regularly. Indeed, Fulbright at times felt overconsulted. After Johnson called him at home at eleven o'clock in the evening, he complained to Pat Holt: "Geez, he just won't hang up, and you can't hang up on him!" The two families saw a good deal of each other. The Christmas following the assassination, Betty did the president's shopping for Lady Bird, Lynda, and Luci.[31] In mid-April Johnson sent Fulbright an advance copy of a major address he was scheduled to deliver, asking for his advice.[32]

---

29 See Evans and Novak, "Fulbright's Opportunity."
30 Max Frankel, "Arkansas's Fulbright a New Hero to Youth," *New York Times,* Apr. 6, 1964.
31 Donald M. Ritchie, interviewer, *Oral History Interviews: Pat M. Holt* (Senate Historical Office: Washington, D.C., 1981), 165–6.
32 Bundy to Lyndon Baines Johnson, Apr. 18, 1964, NSF, Memos to President, Bundy, Box 1, Papers of Lyndon Baines Johnson, Johnson Library, Austin, Texas [hereinafter referred to as Johnson Papers].

5

Avoiding Armageddon

From 1882 until 1941, Laos, Cambodia, and Vietnam comprised French Indochina, France's richest and most important colony. Forced to relinquish control to the Japanese following their surrender to Germany in 1941, the French returned to Southeast Asia in 1946, determined to regain their profitable possessions. The war in the Pacific gave a strong fillip to anticolonial movements throughout the area, and Indochina was no exception. Shortly after Japan's surrender, Ho Chi Minh – leader of the Vietminh, a broad-based but communist-led resistance movement – proclaimed from Hanoi the existence of a new nation, the Democratic Republic of Vietnam (DRV). Over the next year and a half, however, the French, with the help of the British in the South and the Chinese Nationalists in the North, managed to reestablish themselves firmly in the South and tentatively in the North. In November 1946 a bitter colonial war erupted between the French and the Vietminh, culminating in 1954 with France's defeat at the battle of Dien Bien Phu. A subsequent peace conference at Geneva provided for the temporary division of the country at the seventeenth parallel. The French withdrew from the peninsula but left an anticommunist regime in place in the South – the Republic of Vietnam (RVN) – under Emperor Bao Dai and his prime minister, Ngo Dinh Diem. Within a year Diem had ousted Bao Dai and instituted a presidential system with himself as chief executive. Meanwhile, in the North, Ho consolidated his power as head of the DRV.

There was no doubt that Ho, one of the original members of the French Communist Party, was a Marxist–Leninist or that the DRV was a totalitarian regime. After both Moscow and Beijing recognized Ho's government as the legitimate ruler of all of Vietnam in 1950, the United States concluded that the DRV was a Sino–Soviet satellite and that Ho was a puppet of Stalin and Mao Zedong. Throughout the 1950s the Eisenhower administration poured economic and military aid into Vietnam. Diem, a principled, patriotic man, briefly attempted land and constitutional reform, but he proved unsuited to the task of building a social democracy. A devout Catholic and traditional mandarin by temperament and philosophy, he distrusted the masses and had contempt for the give-and-take of democratic politics. Increasingly, he relied on his family and loyal Catholics in the military and civil service to rule a country in which ninety percent of the population was Buddhist. His brother Ngo Dinh Nhu used the Can Lao Party, the press, and the state police to persecute and suppress opponents to the regime. As corruption increased and democracy all but disappeared, a rebellion broke out in the South against the Diem regime. In 1960 the DRV decided to give formal aid to the newly formed National Liberation Front, as the anti-Diemist revolutionaries called themselves.

A variety of factors combined to ensure that President Kennedy would attempt to hold the line in Southeast Asia. He viewed the conflict in South Vietnam as one of Khrushchev's wars of national liberation, a test of his administration's resolve just as much as Berlin or Cuba. Kennedy and his advisers fully accepted the "domino theory," whereby it was assumed that the fall of one government in a particular region threatened by communism would lead to the fall of all noncommunist governments in the area. His agreement in 1961 to the neutralization of Laos, a landlocked nation wracked by communist insurgency, further strengthened his resolve to ensure that South Vietnam remained a "free world bastion." The number of American uniformed personnel grew from several hundred when Kennedy assumed office to sixteen thousand by 1963.

Despite American aid, the Diem regime became increasingly isolated from the masses. Bribes and intimidation by civil servants and military officials alienated peasant and urban dweller alike. Law 10/59, which the government pushed through the rubber-stamp national assembly, gave Nhu's police and special forces the power to arrest and execute South Vietnamese citizens for a wide variety of crimes including black marketeering and spreading seditious rumors about the government. By 1963 the nation teetered on the brink of chaos with the Vietcong (VC) (the military branch of the National Liberation Front [NLF]) in control of the countryside, students and intellectuals demonstrating in Saigon and Hué, Buddhist monks burning themselves in protest, and high-ranking military officers hatching a variety of coup plots.

Shortly before his own assassination in November 1963, Kennedy tacitly approved a military coup in Saigon that led to the deaths of both Diem and Nhu. The president sensed that the United States was on the verge of plunging into a morass from which it could not extricate itself. Only the South Vietnamese themselves could establish a broad-based, noncommunist government and make the sacrifices necessary to sustain it. Without that commitment, all the American aid in the world would be for naught. And yet he was unwilling, for both political and strategic reasons, to stand by and see Vietnam fall to the communists.

Lyndon Johnson was no more ready than his predecessor to unilaterally withdraw from South Vietnam or seek a negotiated settlement that would lead to neutralization of the area south of the seventeenth parallel. First of all, he was, as McGeorge Bundy has noted, "a hawk."[1] Like so many other Americans of his generation, Lyndon Johnson had learned the lessons of Munich. He would not reward "aggression" with "appeasement" in Southeast Asia or anywhere else. In a typically vulgar analogy, he declared: "If you let a bully come into your yard one day, the next day he'll be up on your porch, and the day after that he'll rape your wife in your own bed." In addition, in 1961 as vice-president, Johnson had made a personal commitment to the survival of an independent, noncommunist government in South Vietnam. He seemed smitten with Diem and with the determination of the "brave people of Vietnam" to resist a communist takeover.[2] As the nation and the world would learn, Lyndon Johnson was that variety of southerner for whom compassion was an all-consuming obsession.

In addition, the Texan felt duty-bound to carry out the policies of his predecessor. He was acutely sensitive to the fact that he had not been elected in his own right.[3] It was impossible for the American people to put their trust in him instantly, he realized. It would have made them seem disloyal to Kennedy. Moreover, Johnson felt constrained to demonstrate to the world, allies and antagonists alike, that America's period of grief and self-searching would not diminish its strength or weaken its commitment to its allies. Thus it was that in his first message to Congress and the nation on November 27, 1963, Lyndon Johnson assured his audience that he would uphold American commitments "from South Vietnam to West Berlin."[4]

An even more potent factor in the Indochinese equation was the president's fear that right-wing adversaries would prevail over him, should South Vietnam fall to communism, just as Harry Truman had been hounded and his policies circumscribed by Joe McCarthy after the fall of China. Even though, as he indicated in his conversations with Fulbright, he may have wanted to question the assumptions that underlay the original containment policy – including the monolithic communist threat and the domino theory – he dare not, lest the debate fracture the domestic consensus he so desperately desired. In a word, Lyndon Johnson had no intention of allowing the charge that he was soft on communism to be used to destroy the programs of the Great Society.

On November 24, 1963, President Johnson instructed Ambassador Henry Cabot Lodge, Jr., to assure the generals who had overthrown Ngo Dinh Diem that they had the full support of the U.S. government. Two days later the NSC incorporated his pledge into policy, affirming that it was "the central objective of the United States" to assist the "people and Government of

1 Interview with McGeorge Bundy, Aug. 1, 1991, New York.
2 Quoted in Kathleen J. Turner, *Lyndon Johnson's Dual War: Vietnam and the Press* (Chicago, 1985), 53.
3 Doris Kearns [Goodwin], *Lyndon Johnson and the American Dream* (New York, 1976), 177.
4 Quoted in Turner, *Lyndon Johnson's Dual War,* 54.

South Vietnam to win their contest against the externally directed and supported communist conspiracy.''

Lyndon Johnson was well aware of his inexperience in foreign affairs. As
a consequence, he retained Kennedy's top advisers and relied heavily on
them. Rusk in State, McNamara in Defense, and National Security Adviser
McGeorge Bundy had all played prominent roles in shaping Kennedy's Vietnam policy, and as George Herring and others have pointed out, they had a
deep personal stake in upholding that policy. The new president assumed that
J. William Fulbright, as a longtime exponent of executive prerogatives in
foreign affairs, was part of his team and, if the ''old myths and new realities''
speech was any guide, shared his assumptions concerning Vietnam.

Indeed, if there had been constants in the Fulbright philosophy of diplomacy, they were that the chief executive should have the broadest possible
authority in the conduct of foreign affairs and that the president use that
authority. ''The American people have a long tradition of looking at the
world in terms of absolute good and absolute evil,'' he told a college audience
in 1963. ''But in a world of power politics the statesmen must often think
in terms of relative values, in terms of power and the struggle for power, in
terms of what is possible as well as what is desirable.'' Echoing Dean Acheson and George Kennan, he declared that he favored open policies but not
open negotiations. Diplomats should be allowed to bargain in secret; they
could then be held accountable for the results at election time. If negotiations
were the subject of public scrutiny, failure was all but certain.[5]

At the outset, Johnson and his civilian advisers were absolutely opposed to
a massive commitment of land forces on the Asian mainland. Infusion of
U.S. combat troops, they reasoned, would undercut South Vietnam's prospects for self-reliance, provoke hostile propaganda throughout the developing
world, and generate domestic dissent that would threaten the Great Society
programs and Johnson's chances for reelection. What course, then, should
the United States follow?

He was strongly leaning, the president told Fulbright in a telephone conversation on March 2, 1964, toward doing what the United States had been
doing – only better. When the Arkansan asked him if there were any hope
of getting ''that damn Vietnam straightened out,'' Johnson outlined the options available. American support for neutralization would lead to the same
result as unilateral withdrawal, he declared. He could send marines and U.S.
forces in ''à la Goldwater,'' but that would involve American boys in a war
''100,000 miles from home,'' possibly against masses of Chinese communist
troops. The current policy of providing technical and economic aid had not
yet failed, and he intended to keep it up until it did. Fulbright agreed: ''I

5 ''Diplomats Backed by Fulbright,'' *Washington Post*, Mar. 10, 1963.

think that's right. . . . [T]hat's exactly what I'd arrive at under these circumstances at least for the foreseeable future.'' He was sending McNamara on a fact-finding trip to Vietnam, Johnson continued. If he found that the United States and its ally were losing, ''we've got to decide whether to send them in or whether to come out and let the dominoes fall. That's where the tough one is going to be. And you do some heavy thinking and let's decide what we do.''[6]

On March 15, the day following McNamara's return from Saigon, Fulbright went to lunch at the White House. He, Johnson, and Rusk heard from the secretary of defense that the situation had deteriorated since September. In twenty-two of the forty-four provinces the Vietcong controlled fifty percent or more of the land area. There were widespread signs of apathy and indifference. Desertion rates in the South Vietnamese army (AVRN) were on the rise, and draftdodging was pervasive. Morale among the hamlet militia and the Self Defense Corps was failing. General Nguyen Khanh, head of the ruling Military Revolutionary Council, ''though a very able man,'' lacked broad-based political support and was unsure of the military. After reiterating his belief that unless the United States could maintain an independent, noncommunist South Vietnam, all of Southeast Asia would fall into enemy hands, the DOD chief reviewed the objectives with his typical machine-gun delivery. He came down where Johnson wanted him to: The administration should postpone a graduated program of pressure against North Vietnam, including bombing, until needed; the president ought to commit American troops only as a last resort. Through the utilization of military advisers, AID workers, and the latest techniques and equipment, both military and civilian, American personnel should continue to act on the ''oil spot'' theory, helping the South Vietnamese to work outward from areas they already controlled to provide physical and economic security to contiguous territory.[7]

As the Vietnam section of the ''old myths and new realities'' speech indicated, Fulbright fully supported these recommendations. ''I sincerely hope we can keep the situation from collapsing,'' the Arkansan wrote Will Clayton in early April. A communist takeover in Indochina ''would have serious repercussions at home, as well as in Asia.''[8]

The dire consequence Fulbright feared at home was the triumph of Barry Goldwater. Although public opinion polls taken after the presidential nominating conventions showed Johnson with a commanding lead over his Republican challenger, Goldwater still alarmed J. William Fulbright. In

6 Quoted in Kearns, *Johnson and the American Dream,* 204–5.
7 McNamara to LBJ, Mar. 13, 1964, NSF, Memos to President, Box 1, Johnson Papers.
8 JWF to Clayton, Apr. 6, 1964, Alpha File, Folder FU, Clayton Papers.

Goldwater's person and candidacy, Fulbright believed, were concentrated all of the ignorance, chauvinism, and absolutism against which he had been struggling throughout his political life. Above all, he was worried that Goldwater was fully capable, under the proper circumstances, of touching off World War III. The Republican candidate had earlier urged that NATO commanders be given control of tactical nuclear weapons and, when asked about the situation in Southeast Asia, had said, "I'd drop a low-yield atomic bomb on the Chinese supply lines in North Vietnam or maybe shell 'em with the Seventh Fleet."[9] Thus it was that when the Johnson administration came to Fulbright in early August 1964 and asked him to punch through the Senate a resolution authorizing the president to use military force to contain the spread of communism in Indochina, he readily agreed.

As part of his effort to do more of the same and do it more efficiently, Lyndon Johnson appointed General William Westmoreland to command American forces in Vietnam. Tall, erect, handsome, "Westy" was a fifty-year-old veteran of World War II and Korea with a chest full of medals. Westmoreland was a corporate executive in uniform, a diligent, disciplined organization man who would obey orders. Like his superior Robert McNamara, the general saw the war as basically an exercise in management. At the same time he appointed Westmoreland, Johnson named General Maxwell Taylor to replace Lodge, who had allowed the U.S. country team in Vietnam to degenerate into warring factions. A former chairman of the Joint Chiefs of Staff under Kennedy, Taylor, a combat veteran who spoke several languages, was seen as a tough-minded, sophisticated individual who, together with his new deputy, career diplomat U. Alexis Johnson, would blend AID, the CIA, the Military Assistance Command, Vietnam (MAACV), and embassy personnel into an efficient nation-building machine. Within weeks, the new leadership had put together the most formidable American presence in a foreign country ever assembled. American experts in the provinces were teaching Vietnamese peasants to dig wells, breed pigs, build houses, and kill communists. The United States underwrote all of these activities as well as imports of milk, gasoline, fertilizer, and other products with a huge supplemental appropriation – $50 million for military aid and $76 million for nonmilitary – pushed through Congress in mid-1964.[10]

Still the situation in the South continued to deteriorate. As of mid-1964 the Vietcong controlled more than forty percent of the territory and fifty percent of the population of South Vietnam. Where it could function freely, the government was hampered by a shortage of skilled officials and a lack of clear-cut goals. High desertion rates persisted, with the result that the

9 Quoted in ibid., 258.
10 Bundy to LBJ, May 15, 1964, NSF, Memos to President, Bundy, Box 1, Johnson Papers.

ARVN remained well below authorized troop levels.[11] All the while, North Vietnam was becoming more deeply involved in the struggle in the South. In mid-1964 Hanoi launched a program to convert the Ho Chi Minh Trail, which ran southward from North Vietnam through Laos and Cambodia, entering South Vietnam at various points, from a network of jungle trails to a modern transportation system. This, coupled with the decision taken earlier in the year to introduce regular North Vietnamese Army (NVA) units into the South, meant that by summer's end hundreds and then thousands of veteran North Vietnamese soldiers were taking up positions below the seventeenth parallel.

In response to this worsening picture, a number of Johnson's advisers urged him to authorize the use of "selected and carefully graduated military force against North Vietnam."[12] Precisely orchestrated attacks on the North would serve several purposes. "We should strike to hurt but not to destroy," McGeorge Bundy told Johnson, "and strike for the purpose of changing the North Vietnamese decision on intervention in the south."[13] Johnson's experts also portrayed an attack on the North as the one thing that could save the Khanh government and bring political stability to the South. Bundy and company somehow believed that one major military triumph would suddenly end Buddhist-Catholic infighting, alleviate corruption, raise up a pluralistic democracy, and transform Khanh into a South Vietnamese version of Franklin D. Roosevelt.

Virtually everyone in Johnson's inner circle agreed that it would be necessary to go to Congress for a resolution of approval prior to raining blows on North Vietnam.[14] From May through July, Bundy and the NSC staff worked on the content of a congressional resolution and a strategy for passing it. All agreed that the administration should not go to Congress unless and until it was sure of overwhelming support. To this end, it was imperative to wait until the civil rights bill was passed. It would also be necessary to cultivate individual representatives and senators and to convince them that the United States had made every effort to solve the Vietnamese problem through the United Nations and other diplomatic channels. The resolution would permit "selective use of force" but would not be a blank check. Administration spokespeople would assure doubters that "hostilities on a larger scale are not envisaged."[15]

According to Robert McNamara, Johnson needed no convincing. Uppermost in the president's mind was the memory of the criticism Harry Truman

---

11 NSF Meeting, May 15, 1964, NSC Meeting Notes, Box 1, Johnson Papers.
12 McGeorge Bundy to LBJ, May 25, 1964, NSF, Memos to President, Box 1, Johnson Papers.
13 Bundy to LBJ, May 22, 1964, NSF, Memos to President, Box 1, Johnson Papers.
14 Bundy to LBJ, May 25, 1964, NSF, Memos to President, Box 1, Johnson Papers.
15 Bundy Memo for Discussion, June 10, 1964, NSC File, Memos to President, Box 2, Johnson Papers.

had sustained for not securing congressional approval for the introduction of troops into Korea. "By God, I'm going to be damn sure those guys are with me when we begin this thing," McNamara remembered Johnson as saying. "They may try to desert me once we get in there!" He was not planning an escalation, McNamara insisted, but he was shrewd enough to realize that events might outrun his ability to control them.[16]

On the evening of July 26 Fulbright had dinner with the president at the White House. The Arkansan sensed that something was about to happen in Indochina. The Khanh regime was in serious trouble, and it might be necessary to employ additional American force to save it, Johnson confided. He would soon go to Congress and ask for a resolution of support.[17] There was no intention to widen the war, Johnson insisted. The object was to demonstrate American unity to Hanoi and to pressure the communists not to overrun South Vietnam and Laos. The president assured him that if for any reason the American mission changed character, he would seek fresh authority from Congress. And there was Goldwater, a man who represented everything Fulbright detested. He was determined, the president said, to take the "soft on communism" issue away from the Republicans. Fulbright sympathized completely. "I didn't suspect that he [Johnson] was misleading us," he later recalled. "This was in the beginning of the contest between Johnson and Goldwater. I was just overpersuaded, I guess you'd say, in my feeling that I ought to support the president, that he was right and he was not going to escalate the war."[18]

When early in 1964 North Vietnam began to step up its infiltration into the South, the Johnson administration had issued a series of not-so-veiled threats of retaliation. To help counter any possible moves that the Americans and South Vietnamese might make, Hanoi persuaded the Russians to install modern antiaircraft missiles and radar stations around North Vietnam's main cities and along the broken coastline of bays and islands on the Tonkin Gulf. As contingency planning for possible bombardment, blockade, or invasion of North Vietnam got under way in Washington, military intelligence began gathering information on this protective network. U-2 flights were able to photograph inland sites, but they were incapable of mapping the coastal installations. For this task, intelligence enlisted South Vietnamese commandos to harass the enemy radar transmitters, thereby activating them so that American electronic intelligence vessels cruising in the Tonkin Gulf could chart their locations. In addition to these operations, code-named DeSoto missions, a State Department–CIA task force under McGeorge Bundy was

16 Interview with Robert McNamara, Aug. 2, 1991, Washington, D.C.
17 William C. Berman, *William Fulbright and the Vietnam War: The Dissent of a Political Realist* (Kent, Ohio, 1988), 22.
18 Charles Morrissey interview with J. William Fulbright, "Modern Congress in American History" (Library of Congress: Washington, D.C.), 22.

coordinating OPLAN-34, a topsecret program of infiltration and harassment of North Vietnam by South Vietnamese covert operatives. As 1964 progressed, then, North Vietnamese positions along the gulf coast were subjected to repeated attacks by the high-speed, heavily armed Norwegian speedboats used in the DeSoto program and to landings by OPLAN-34 operatives.

In July, Admiral Ulysses Grant Sharp, Jr., commanding U.S. forces in the Pacific, ordered the aircraft carrier *Ticonderoga* to the entrance to the Tonkin Gulf and instructed the destroyer *Maddox* to engage in DeSoto-type patrols off the North Vietnamese coast.

On the night of July 30–31 South Vietnamese commandos in four patrol boats assaulted North Vietnamese positions on the islands of Hon Me and Hon Ngu, three and four miles, respectively, from the North Vietnamese mainland. Hon Ngu was only about three miles from Vinh, one of North Vietnam's busiest ports. The crackle of North Vietnamese radar signals and radio traffic triggered by the attacks was monitored aboard the *Maddox* and transmitted to a special American intelligence center in the Philippines.

At eleven o'clock on the morning of August 2 the *Maddox* was situated some ten miles out to sea, adjacent to the Red River delta, the northernmost point of its circuit. Suddenly from behind the island of Hon Me, three North Vietnamese patrol boats attacked. As the trio fired their torpedoes, missing, the *Maddox* opened fire and signaled for air support from the *Ticonderoga*. The skirmish, which lasted a bare twenty minutes, ended in a clear-cut American victory. A single bullet struck the *Maddox* harmlessly, while U.S. fire sank one hostile craft and crippled the other two.[19]

Reports of the incident reached Lyndon Johnson on the morning of the same day, Sunday, August 2. Because no American had been hurt, he told his staff, further action was unnecessary; he specifically rejected suggestions from the military for reprisals against North Vietnamese targets. The president instructed his spokespeople to play down the matter, and as a consequence, the initial Pentagon press release on the subject did not even identify the North Vietnamese as antagonists. At the same time, however, Johnson directed the *Maddox* and another destroyer, the *C. Turner Joy*, as well as protective aircraft, to return to the gulf. The commanders bore with them orders to "attack any force that attacks them."[20] Meanwhile, the JCS and their commanders in the Pacific placed U.S. forces in South Vietnam and Thailand on alert. They pinpointed such targets as harbor installations and oil depots for retaliatory raids. The commander of the *Ticonderoga* task force radioed Herrick that the North Vietnamese had "thrown down the gauntlet"

19 CINCPAC Communiqué, Aug. 3, 1964, Meeting Notes File, Box 2, Johnson Papers.
20 Quoted in Stanley Karnow, *Vietnam: A History* (New York, 1984), 369.

and should be "treated as belligerents from first detection."[21] Finally, on the third, Rusk, McNamara, and Earle Wheeler, chairman of the Joint Chiefs, briefed a combined meeting of the SFRC and Armed Services Committee in executive session. They described the attack on the *Maddox* and the generally deteriorating situation in South Vietnam. Wayne Morse, among others, came out of the meeting convinced that the administration was determined to go to war with North Vietnam. Speaking years later, Fulbright declared that Johnson had missed the significance of the August 2 attack and, realizing that this was just the situation he had been waiting for, maneuvered quickly to create a second one;[22] but if the Arkansan had any such suspicions at the time, he did not voice them.

The night of the fourth was a stormy, moonless one. Around eight o'clock, Captain John J. Herrick of the *Maddox* intercepted radio messages that seemed to indicate that communist patrol boats were bracing for an assault. Sonar began picking up bleeps on this night that one sailor later described as "darker than the hubs of hell."[23] An hour later the two destroyers started firing in all directions and taking evasive action to avoid North Vietnamese torpedoes. Their officers reported sinking two or perhaps three communist craft during the raid.

The battle report and traffic between the *Maddox* and Honolulu were monitored directly in the situation room in the basement of the White House. Duty officers summoned the president at once. Although his information was still sketchy, Johnson called the congressional leadership, including Fulbright, to the White House on the morning of the fourth and announced that there had been a second, unprovoked, deliberate attack on the *Maddox* and *Turner Joy*. This time, he said, the United States had no choice but to retaliate, and he intended to ask for a resolution of support. After huddling briefly with Fulbright, Aiken, and Hickenlooper, Mansfield "read a paper expressing general opposition." Richard Russell supported retaliation in principle but voiced concern about whether or not the United States had enough manpower and equipment in the area to do the job. Should the United States continue to allow the North Vietnamese "to murder us from bases of safety?" McNamara asked incredulously. "I think I know what the reaction would be if we tucked our tails."[24] At this point, Johnson chimed in: "Some of our boys are floating around in the water," he said. The Republican leadership – Saltonstall, Halleck, and Dirksen – all expressed support and promised to vote for a congressional resolution. Fulbright came away from the meeting convinced that both attacks had occurred, that they were part of a communist

---

21 Ibid., 370.
22 Berman, *Fulbright and the Vietnam War,* 23.
23 Quoted in George C. Herring, *America's Longest War: The United States and Vietnam, 1950–1975,* 2d ed. (New York, 1986), 120.
24 Summary of Leadership Meeting, Aug. 4, 1964, Meeting Notes File, Box 1, Johnson Papers.

test of American resolve, as Rusk put it, and that the assaults would continue unless the United States responded.[25]

Johnson strolled back to the Oval Office from the meeting with Kenneth O'Donnell, a former Kennedy aide who had stayed on at the White House. Speculating on the potential political effect of the crisis, they agreed that Johnson was "being tested" and would have to respond firmly to defend himself, not against the North Vietnamese but against Barry Goldwater and the Republican right wing. As O'Donnell later wrote, they felt that Johnson "must not allow them to accuse him of vacillating or being an indecisive leader."[26]

Still, Lyndon Johnson, despite his later claims that he did not really need a resolution from Congress to employ additional force in Vietnam or that retaliation against the North in that instance preordained escalation in the future, sensed that he was about to take a momentous step. He ordered McNamara to obtain verification of the second North Vietnamese strike. Unfortunately, Captain Herrick had begun to have second thoughts about whether or not an actual attack had occurred. On the afternoon of the fourth, he cabled CINCPAC, Sharp's headquarters. The entire action had left many doubts, he reported, and he was conducting an immediate investigation. Several hours later he cabled: "Review of action makes many reported contacts and torpedoes fired appear very doubtful. . . . Freak weather effects and overeager sonarmen may have accounted for many reports. No actual sightings by *Maddox*. Suggest complete evaluation before any further action."[27]

Meanwhile, however, the White House believed that it had obtained independent verification that the second attack had occurred. Naval intelligence provided McNamara with a batch of intercepts of North Vietnamese radio flashes that seemed to be ordering their patrol boats into action. Although he was in Martha's Vineyard at the time and was not summoned back to Washington until the afternoon of the fourth, Assistant Secretary of State William Bundy recalled that the intercepts – "get ready, go, we are attacking" – were compelling. "These intercepts were certainly taken by all concerned to prove beyond a shadow of a doubt that there had been a second attack."[28] According to McNamara, he and others were not so certain:

> My first reaction was that the first attack might not have occurred, because we'd been wrong on so many damn things – the Cuban missile crisis. So many times we'd gotten erroneous information. . . . We made extensive efforts to insure that we found out what happened inclusive

25 Notes Taken at Leadership Meeting, Aug. 4, 1964, Meeting Notes File, Box 1, Johnson Papers.
26 Quoted in Karnow, *Vietnam: A History,* 371.
27 George McT. Kahin, *Intervention: How America Became Involved in Vietnam* (Garden City, N.Y., 1987), 221.
28 Interview with William Bundy, July 5, 1990, Princeton, N.J.

of obtaining fragments of the shells off the deck of the *Maddox*. And actually we had them flown to Washington to be sure that it was the goddamn case. Because the sonar and other evidence is very difficult to interpret. The second attack – to this day I doubted it ever occurred. I think the people who reported it were not trying to deceive. They were reporting their judgment about the sonar evidence. Then, finally we had intercepts of North Vietnamese transmissions indicating that they were saying that the attack had occurred.[29]

Although the Command and Control study of the Tonkin Gulf incident that the Pentagon completed in early 1965 assumed that it did, in all probability the second attack did not occur. But in the minds of Johnson and his colleagues the August 4 assault really did not matter.[30] The first had occurred, and to their thinking, it was an unprovoked North Vietnamese assault on American craft in international waters. McNamara later recalled:

It never entered my mind that they might have been responding to what they considered to be our attack – the covert operations – because they were so unimportant. They were pinpricks; they were accomplishing nothing. I don't believe Bill Bundy or I ever believed they were worth a damn. It never occurred to me that we should check and see whether one of those things was underway at the time.[31]

Johnson accepted his brain trust's conclusions without question and in the late afternoon authorized retaliatory air strikes against North Vietnamese torpedo boat bases and nearby oil storage dumps. The strikes destroyed or damaged twenty-five patrol boats and ninety percent of the oil storage facilities at Vinh. As American jets lifted off the *Ticonderoga* and *Constellation*, Lyndon Johnson appeared on television to report to the nation that an unprovoked attack had taken place against American vessels on the high seas. "Repeated acts of violence against the armed forces of the United States must be met not only with alert defense, but with positive reply. That reply is being given as I speak to you tonight."[32]

On August 5 Fulbright went to the White House, where he agreed to manage the congressional resolution that Johnson would submit to Congress that day. It was clear that the chairman of the SFRC never knew

---

29 McNamara interview. Indeed, in my interview with him, McNamara admitted that the intercepts probably were delayed broadcasts relating to the first attack. When confronted with McNamara's admission, William Bundy responded: "Mr. McNamara, if I may say so, is an extraordinarily unreliable witness on this and all other matters relating to Vietnam." W. Bundy interview.

30 Office of the Director of Defense Research, Critical Incident Report No. 7, Command and Control of the Tonkin Gulf Incident, Feb. 26, 1965. Document provided to the author by Professor Edwin E. Moise, Clemson University.

31 His testimony is belied by other portions of the historical record. See Kalin, *Intervention*, 221.

32 Quoted in Karnow, *Vietnam: A History*, 372.

about the DeSoto patrols. While Fulbright was closeted with Johnson and McGeorge Bundy on the fifth, the national security adviser assured him that there was no connection between the 34-A missions and the presence of the American destroyers in the gulf. Bundy knew better. At the NSC meeting on August 4, when Johnson had asked if Hanoi wanted a war by attacking U.S. ships in the gulf, CIA Director McCone had replied, "No. The North Vietnamese are reacting defensively to our attacks on their off-shore islands."[33] Most important, the chairman of the SFRC was not informed about the communiqué from Captain John Herrick of the *Maddox* suggesting that the second North Vietnamese attack may not really have occurred. According to Fred Dutton, Fulbright alone among the members of the Democratic leadership had been kept in the dark regarding contingency planning for a military escalation in Vietnam during the spring and summer of 1964. McGeorge Bundy remembered that Johnson already considered Fulbright "a leaker," a man who could not be trusted with sensitive information.[34] Nevertheless, by his own admission, Fulbright knew as a result of his July 26 dinner with the president that the administration was planning some new move in Southeast Asia. He was not surprised by the retaliation against the North Vietnamese patrol boats. What he was ignorant of was the bombing campaign against the North then being considered and that the congressional resolution he was being asked to support would be used as justification for a wider war. In the end, Fulbright, who had opposed the 1957 Middle East Resolution, agreed to support and manage a Vietnam resolution. In 1957 he had not trusted the man in the White House; in 1964 he did. Given the fact that he believed Johnson when he said he would not escalate, and needed to demonstrate to the country that he could be tough with North Vietnam in order to fend off Goldwater, it would not have mattered if Fulbright had had the full picture, including Herrick's reservations. What subsequently infuriated him was that he was not given all of the pertinent information. J. William Fulbright did not like to be deceived, and he did not like to be used.

On the morning of August 6, George Ball met in Majority Leader Mansfield's offices with him, Fulbright, Russell, Saltonstall, and Aiken. Both Pat Holt, then acting director of the SFRC, and his counterpart for Armed Services, William Darden, were there as well. There was no discussion of substance. It was decided that Fulbright would introduce the resolution as soon as possible with Russell, Hickenlooper, and Saltonstall cosponsoring. The SFRC and Armed Services committees would hold perfunctory hearings on the morning of the seventh; passage, they anticipated, would come easily that afternoon. Holt and Darden listened with growing incredulity. They remem-

33 Summary Notes of 538 NSC Meeting, Aug. 4, 1964, NSC Meeting File, Box 1, Johnson
   Papers.
34 McG. Bundy interview.

bered the endless debate and soul-searching that had taken place over similar resolutions pertaining to Formosa and the Middle East.[35]

That afternoon Fulbright introduced the Gulf of Tonkin Resolution, which authorized the president to take ''all necessary measures to repel any armed attacks against the forces of the United States and to prevent further aggression.''[36] On the sixth, McNamara appeared before a joint session of the SFRC and Armed Services to testify on the resolution. It was plain from the beginning that he would face little opposition. Opinion polls showed that eighty-five percent of the American people stood behind the administration; most newspaper editorials reflected this support. Nothing was said about the covert raids. Official reports indicated that the *Maddox* was engaged in routine patrols in international waters. The incidents were portrayed as ''deliberate attacks'' and ''open aggression on the high seas.''[37] That morning, however, a Pentagon officer had telephoned Wayne Morse with a tip: The *Maddox* had been intimately involved with South Vietnamese raids north of the seventeenth parallel, he confided. When the lean, humorless Morse confronted McNamara, however, the defense secretary flatly denied any relationship. By that point, Morse was regarded by many as part of the lunatic fringe, and his insinuations were brushed aside.[38] Indeed, Fulbright and others congratulated the administration on its restraint in dealing with North Vietnam.

Congress responded to the administration's request with amazing alacrity. Senator Ernest Gruening of Alaska attacked the resolution as ''a predated declaration of war,'' and Senator Gaylord Nelson of Wisconsin pointed out that the resolution amounted to a sweeping grant of authority to the executive. Morse demanded to know why American war vessels were menacing the coast of North Vietnam. George McGovern of South Dakota asked incredulously why a tiny nation like North Vietnam would want to provoke a war with the greatest superpower in the history of the world. One by one Fulbright responded to the questions and criticisms. The *Maddox* had been attacked without provocation, and the American reaction was entirely justified as an act of self-defense under article 45 of the UN Charter. ''It would be a great mistake,'' he declared, ''to allow our optimism about promising developments in our relations with the Soviet Union and Eastern Europe to lead us to any illusions about the aggressive designs of North Vietnam and its Chinese Communist sponsor.'' He did not know what the limits on the president's power to take action in Vietnam were under the terms of the resolution, he told Nelson. ''I personally feel it would be very unwise under any circumstances to put a large land army on the Asian Continent,'' he said, but

---

35 Donald A. Ritchie, interviewer, *Pat M. Holt: Oral History Interviews* (Senate Historical Office: Washington, D.C., 1980), 177–8.
36 Quoted in Herring, *America's Longest War,* 122.
37 Quoted in ibid.
38 Karnow, *Vietnam: A History,* 375.

that decision was one for the executive to make. It could be trusted. What was needed at that point was national unity and proof of resolve, and that is precisely what the resolution provided.[39] Behind the scenes Fulbright gave his personal assurances to McGovern and other doubters.[40]

The Senate debated the Gulf of Tonkin Resolution less than ten hours; for much of the time the chamber was less than one-third full. Fulbright carefully guided the resolution through, choking off debate and amendments. In the Senate only Morse and Gruening dissented; the final vote was 88 to 2. Consideration in the House was even more perfunctory, passage taking a mere forty minutes. With the Gulf of Tonkin Resolution out of the way, Fulbright could turn his attention to the final stages of the 1964 campaign.

When the Democratic delegates to the national convention met in Atlantic City in mid-August, Johnson's nomination was a foregone conclusion. The gathering divided its time between tributes to the Texan, who was nominated on his fifty-sixth birthday, and attacks on the trigger-happy conservative from Arizona. With Betty and Lady Bird watching together from the galleries, Fulbright stood before the assembled delegates to deliver the second nominating speech:

> I know him well. He has a genius for reconciling the irreconcilable, for resolving differences among many of deep conviction. The same understanding of human nature which enabled him to lead the Senate so effectively during a difficult period in our history will enable him to find a way to resolve differences which exist among nations. . . . I commend Lyndon Johnson to this convention and to all our people as a man of understanding with the wisdom to use the great power of our nation in the cause of peace.[41]

With Johnson's pro forma nomination wrapped up, Fulbright hit the campaign trail with a vengeance:

> The foreign policy issue in this campaign is as profound as any that has ever arisen between the two great American political parties. The Goldwater Republicans propose a radical new policy of relentless ideological conflict aimed at the elimination of Communism and the imposition of American concepts of freedom on the entire world. The Democrats under President Johnson propose a conservative policy of opposing and preventing Communist expansion while working for limited agreements that will reduce the danger of nuclear war.[42]

39 *Congressional Record,* Senate, Aug. 6, 1964, 18399–407.
40 Interview with George McGovern, June 27, 1991, Washington, D.C.
41 Ned Curran, ''Fulbright Seconds Nomination of LBJ with High Praise,'' *Arkansas Gazette,* Aug. 27, 1964.
42 *Congressional Record,* Senate, Aug. 15, 1964, 19786.

In a speech dripping with sarcasm, Fulbright compared Goldwater's view of Soviet–American relations with a Gary Cooper movie: "Who ever heard of cowboys coexisting with Indians? Who ever heard of Wyatt Earp coexisting with Jesse James?"[43] In early October he delivered two speeches in Phoenix, Goldwater's hometown. "I'm just returning his visit," a grinning Fulbright told reporters.[44] As the campaign progressed, the Democrats hammered away at "Goldwater the Trigger Happy."[45] The Republicans thought that they might turn the campaign around when in October longtime Johnson aid Walter Jenkins was caught in a compromising position in a YMCA men's room in Washington; but alas for the GOP, the people were not interested.

The election returns on November 3 confirmed the opinion polls' forecast of a Democratic landslide. The Johnson–Humphrey ticket received a total of 43.1 million popular votes to 27.1 million for Goldwater and Miller. The Democrats carried forty-four states with a record 486 electoral votes. Only an unusual amount of ticket splitting saved the Republicans from being annihilated in the congressional races. Still, the Democrats added to their existing majorities by gaining thirty-eight seats in the House and two in the Senate.

Some have speculated that Fulbright's enthusiasm for Johnson – indeed, his support of the Gulf of Tonkin Resolution – stemmed from his desire to replace Dean Rusk as secretary of state. There is no doubt some truth in the argument. A number of people had been touting the Arkansan. "I have never talked with you about Bill Fulbright," John Kenneth Galbraith wrote Johnson. "It has always been my feeling that Kennedy's most serious mistake was in not following his first instincts and making Bill Secretary of State."[46] But there was never any chance that Johnson would have chosen Fulbright. The Texan demanded absolute loyalty from his team: Once a decision had been made, there must be no dissent, no hanging back, and certainly no public discussion. The Arkansan, Johnson and Bundy perceived, could not be counted on. If he felt that the administration was headed in the wrong direction, he would "leak," a term that Johnson applied to those who voiced their misgivings in public.[47]

Fulbright would deny that he wanted to be Johnson's secretary of state, just as he rejected the notion that he would have accepted the job from John F. Kennedy. Whatever his innermost ambitions, he would have supported Johnson and the Gulf of Tonkin Resolution, anyway. The Texan's shortcomings, his tendency to equate process with substance, means with ends, his

43 Ibid.
44 Curran, "Fulbright Seconds Nomination."
45 Quoted in Allen J. Matusow, *The Unraveling of America: A History of Liberalism in the 1960s* (New York, 1984), 147.
46 Galbraith to LBJ, Feb. 21, 1964, Conference File, Box 139, SPF.
47 McG. Bundy interview.

willfulness and impetuosity, his personal insecurity, his penchant for blurring ideological and policy lines for the sake of consensus – these paled in contrast to Goldwater. As cold war warriors were wont to say about ''democracy'' and ''communism,'' all things were possible with Johnson, Fulbright was convinced, whereas with Goldwater, disaster was a certainty.

6

Escalation

John Newhouse, the SFRC's designated Southeast Asia expert, recalled that he experienced considerable difficulty in persuading Fulbright to focus on Vietnam during the Kennedy administration and the first stages of the Johnson presidency. He seemed more interested in Europe, in foreign aid, and in the exchange program. Several times when Newhouse brought up the Indochinese situation, Fulbright accused him of trying to make a mountain out of a molehill.[1] Then, in May of 1964, a horrifying picture in the *Washington Post* caught Pat Holt's attention. A prostrate Vietcong guerrilla, clad only in his undershorts, was being chained to an armored personnel carrier on a riverbank by South Vietnamese soldiers. They would drag him back and forth through the stream in an effort to get him to talk. Revolted and angered by the scene, Holt took the picture to Fulbright, who reacted similarly. "I want to know if this is the kind of advice the numerous American advisers are giving the Vietnamese," Fulbright subsequently wrote Robert McNamara. Aside from the fact that torture was morally repugnant, he declared, it was counterproductive as well. If the struggle in Vietnam was basically political, that is, one for the hearts and minds of the Vietnamese people, then such abuses would play into the hands of the communists, especially in view of the fact that they came hard on the heels of reports of "napalm bombing of innocent villagers simply because the presence of Viet Cong is suspected." Even without reports of torture and indiscriminate bombing, Fulbright told McNamara, he had become "gravely concerned" over the situation in Vietnam.[2]

In fact, Newhouse's warnings concerning the deteriorating situation in Vietnam had not, as he first thought, fallen on deaf ears. One of his best friends and most reliable contacts in East Asia, *Time–Life* correspondent Stanley Karnow, had been providing Newhouse with detailed reports on the situation in Indochina. "Militarily we may be dropping more napalm than

1 Interview with John Newhouse, June 27, 1991, Washington, D.C.
2 JWF to McNamara, Box 2, JWF Papers, Papers of the Senate Foreign Relations Committee, RG 46, National Archives, Washington, D.C. [hereinafter referred to as SFRC, RG46, NA].

ever," he wrote in one, "but this is a political situation, and the heart of the matter is that we're trying to help a regime that can't help itself."[3] Fulbright, and more important perhaps, Marcy and Holt, read those reports. In December Fulbright played golf with David Ness, a foreign service officer with extensive experience in Vietnam. "In selecting Vietnam to demonstrate that we can meet successfully the challenge of 'wars of liberation'," he told the Arkansan, "we could not, in my opinion, have chosen more disastrously."[4]

By the end of November 1964 the movement within the JCS, the Pentagon, and certain levels of the State Department in support of what Maxwell Taylor described as a "carefully orchestrated bombing attack" against North Vietnam was cresting. A variety of justifications in behalf of air warfare emerged: Bombing would force Ho and his colleagues to halt infiltration into the South, it would reassure Saigon of America's commitment, and it might even force an end to the fighting in South Vietnam. For many in the military, there merely seemed to be a job to do and they were anxious to do it.[5]

Despite Lyndon Johnson's obsession with secrecy, reports that the administration was considering a bombing campaign against North Vietnam began appearing in the press in early December. Hints of an impending escalation coupled with reports of a deteriorating political and military situation in Vietnam prompted Carl Marcy to write a comprehensive analysis for his boss. In the first place, he insisted, the assumptions underlying escalation were erroneous. As proved to be the case in Europe during World War II and then in Korea, destruction of the enemy's industrial base by air had very little impact on their will or ability to fight. In the second, it was absurd and contrary to historical precedent to believe that once Americans became directly involved in carrying out combat missions, the country would permit defeat. Escalation could very well lead to a protracted, bloody conflict. Moreover, Marcy inquired, was there a political and cultural entity south of the seventeenth parallel to defend? In its effort to build a nation, the Johnson administration was relying on a military dictatorship and, in the process, offending the democratic sensibilities of both Vietnamese and Americans. It was probably an ironic truth that only a totalitarian regime would be strong enough to fight a war against the communists and keep the peace in South Vietnam. But in the end, such a regime would prove incapable of winning the hearts and minds of the people and so incapable of ruling. In addition, without the quick knockout on which the administration was clearly counting, the American people would begin to question the ideological justification for the war and

3 Newhouse to JWF, Dec. 25, 1964, Series 48:1, Box 35:1, SPF.
4 Ness to JWF, Dec. 16, 1964, Series 48:11, Box 35:1, SPF.
5 Quoted in George C. Herring, *America's Longest War: The United States and Vietnam, 1950–1975,* 2d ed. (New York, 1986), 124.

ultimately ask whether their interests were really tied up with those of Southeast Asia. As it became apparent that they were not, "the American public would object vigorously."

Echoing earlier administration papers on the subject, Marcy asserted that the United States had three options available to it in Vietnam: It could continue on its present course, expand its military role, or initiate "a planned, phased contraction of United States military assistance" ending with "neutralization and ultimate withdrawal." It was the third course that the chief of staff recommended. Withdrawal and neutralization would not have the dire consequences American hawks predicted. "The 'domino theory' has never been proven in history," he pointed out. "Faced by foreign domination of a great power, coalitions have always emerged to challenge that power." The specter of Chinese imperialism had only served to stimulate Japanese, Filipino, Indonesian, Indian, and Pakistani nationalism. The United States and the Soviet Union, Marcy concluded, had become the world's most important status quo powers. There was every possibility that the two could cooperate in fostering an independent, unified and truly nonaligned Vietnam.[6] Thus, in a single memo, did the chief of staff explode the myths that underlay American involvement in Vietnam and foreshadow the disaster that was in store for the nation.

Fulbright conveyed his and Marcy's concerns over Vietnam to Johnson during various conversations, but the president and his advisers attributed the Arkansan's warnings to personal pique rather than to any true insight into the problem. The first week in December, McGeorge Bundy told Johnson:

> Carl Marcy called me this morning to say that Fulbright is in a rather difficult mood at the moment because he fears war in Vietnam and is at odds with us also on the organization of the AID program. Finally, his nose is out of joint over the Cultural Center, where he thinks Eisenhower has been given too much credit and he too little. I relate it not to add to your troubles, but simply to mark it down as an objective report in case you happen to want to give Fulbright a coat of butter.[7]

If Johnson subjected Fulbright to "the treatment," it apparently did not take, and the chairman began to air his concerns in public. Stepping up the war in Vietnam would be "senseless," Fulbright told students at Southern Methodist University in December 1964, and declared America's involvement to have been a mistake in the first place. He agreed with Douglas MacArthur, he told a press conference that followed. The United States should never become bogged down in a land war in Asia.[8] Surprisingly,

---

6 Memorandum on Vietnam, Dec. 22, 1964, Box 4, Folder Oct.–Dec., Marcy Papers.
7 Bundy to LBJ, Dec. 9, 1964, NSF, Memos to President, Bundy, Box 2, Johnson Papers.
8 UPI 27, Dec. 9, 1964, Series 48:1, Box 6:3, SPF.

Fulbright's Dallas speech received almost no attention in the national press, and Marcy's efforts to peddle it to *Foreign Affairs* fell flat.[9]

Fulbright was not alone among Democratic congressional leaders in his misgivings and warnings. Mike Mansfield, a Pacific veteran and self-appointed expert on Asia and the Pacific, had never forgiven Kennedy's advisers for their complicity in the demise of the Ngo brothers. He told Johnson that escalation would involve the United States in a prolonged, costly conflict and saddle the country with a permanent dependency.[10] In mid-December Senator Frank Church (D–Idaho) called for a congressional debate on Southeast Asia. In a survey of eighty-three senators the Associated Press (AP) reported that only seven favored the dispatching of troops or the bombing of North Vietnam, whereas a substantial number supported negotiations either then or whenever the military balance would permit.[11] But given the administration's commitment to maintain an independent, noncommunist South Vietnam, there was nothing to negotiate.

In vain did Johnson, Rusk, the Bundy brothers, and McNamara wait for a Vietnamese Winston Churchill to emerge from the political morass in Saigon. In late 1964 Nguyen Khanh sacked his civilian cabinet and instituted military rule in South Vietnam. Buddhist-led demonstrations swept the country, and in late January five thousand students rampaged through the United States Information Service library in Hué, destroying everything in their path.

On the very day that Khanh ousted his civilian government, McGeorge Bundy and Robert McNamara met with Lyndon Johnson to have "a very private discussion of the basic situation in Vietnam." The policy of the United States, they observed, had been just to sit around and wait for a stable government to emerge in the South. That, it was obvious, was not going to happen by itself. The United States was going to have to take a more active role – not politically or economically but militarily.[12] Instead of attributing the instability in Vietnam to the absence of experienced political parties, a tradition of democracy, sectarian hatreds, or military domination of the political system, Bundy and McNamara told their chief that lack of physical security in the provinces and the United States' refusal to do anything about it were to blame.

Despite the fact that their recommendations made absolutely no sense, except in the context of the "good doctor" analogy, and that Dean Rusk,

9 Marcy to Hamilton Fish Armstrong, Dec. 18, 1964, Box 4, Folder Oct.–Dec., Marcy Papers.
10 Bundy to LBJ, Dec. 16, 1964, NSC File, Memos to President, Box 2, Johnson Papers.
11 William C. Berman, *William Fulbright and the Vietnam War: The Dissent of a Political Realist* (Kent, Ohio, 1988), 33.
12 Bundy to LBJ, Jan. 27, 1965, NSC File, Memos to President, Box 2, Johnson Papers.

who was out of town at the time, disagreed with them, Johnson bit. Suddenly the patient who was too sick to fight seemed in danger of being murdered. No formal decision was taken, but by the end of January, most administration officials agreed that the United States should seize the first opportunity to launch air strikes and then build that initiative into a sustained bombing campaign against North Vietnam.

By early 1965 Americans were so deeply involved in every aspect of the war in Vietnam that an incident that could be used to justify a bombing campaign occurred virtually every week. On February 6, Vietcong units attacked a U.S. Army barracks in Pleiku and a nearby helicopter base, killing nine Americans and destroying five aircraft. Following a brief evening meeting with his advisers, Johnson ordered retaliatory strikes. In accordance with Flaming Dart, a plan of reprisal already drawn up by the JCS, American aircraft struck North Vietnamese military installations just across the seventeenth parallel.

On February 8 Johnson met with congressional leaders, including Fulbright, to brief them. He cited the Gulf of Tonkin Resolution and "the legal power of the Presidency" as justifications for his action. His intent, he said, was "to carry out at a manageable level an effort to deter, destroy and diminish the strength of the North Vietnamese aggressors and to try to convince them to leave South Vietnam alone." The views of a few senators would not be allowed to control his actions, he warned.[13] Fulbright's only response was to express misgivings about bombing the North while Alexsei Kosygin, who at the time was paying an official visit to Ho Chi Minh in Hanoi, was in the vicinity.[14] There was little danger of a break with the Soviets, administration spokespeople declared, because the bombing was a specific retaliation for the attack on the American barracks at Pleiku.

Sensing disaster, George McGovern, then a young, first-term senator from South Dakota, screwed up his courage and made an appointment with the president. The Oval Office with Johnson's persona inhabiting it was more than a little intimidating, McGovern recalled. Well aware that his guest was opposed to escalation, the president began: "Well, George," he said, "you know, we're dealing with a bunch of communist bastards here. John McCone [head of the CIA] was in here the other day. He reported that the communists are moving in Central America. The Chinese are moving into Africa. You know that they want to take over Asia." McGovern dared to point out that the Chinese and Vietnamese had been fighting each other for a thousand years. "It's hard for me to believe that Ho Chi Minh is a stooge of the Chinese." The Texan exploded: "Goddamn it, George, you and Ful-

---

13 Summary Notes of 547th NSC Meeting with Cong. Leaders, Feb. 8, 1965, NSC Meeting Notes, Box 1, Johnson Papers.
14 Berman, *Fulbright and the Vietnam War,* 34.

bright and all you history teachers down there. I haven't got time to fuck around with history. I've got boys on the line out there. I can't be worried about history when there are boys out there who might die before morning."[15]

When the Vietcong on February 10 attacked an American enlisted men's quarters at Qui Nhon, the president ordered another, even heavier series of air strikes. In April, American and South Vietnamese pilots flew a total of thirty-six hundred sorties against North Vietnamese targets. The White House approved the use of napalm, and pilots were given the authority to strike alternative targets without prior authorization if the original targets were inaccessible.

In explaining the bombing campaign to Congress and the American people, Johnson was, to use George Herring's phrase, "less than candid."[16] Clearly, Rolling Thunder was a turning point in the eyes of the administration. "We face the choice of going for war or running," the president had told his advisers on February 8. "We have chosen the first alternative."[17] But Johnson and his spokespeople justified the air strikes as a response to the attacks on Pleiku and Qui Nhon and emphatically denied implementing any basic change of policy.[18] "Those dirty rotten bastards sneaked up on them [the American soldiers at Pleiku] in the middle of the night and plugged them right in their beds," Johnson told George McGovern.[19]

In the days following the decision to bomb, pressure mounted on the administration from both the right and left to justify its actions publicly. National Security Adviser McGeorge Bundy urged his chief to resist that pressure and avoid mobilizing public opinion. The task ahead was to make it absolutely clear to the foreign affairs establishment and the military that a "major watershed decision" had been taken while concealing from the American public that the United States had assumed direct responsibility for the war.[20] The president acceded. Johnson, in fact, seemed not nearly as worried about congressional and public opinion – he could control those, he was sure – as he was about future investigations and his place in history. Throughout the decision-making process, Johnson insisted on a full and free debate – for the record at least. "At some time in the future a brutal prosecutor like Tom Dewey might be asking how we got into these troubles," he

15 Interview with George McGovern, June 27, 1991, Washington, D.C.
16 Herring, *America's Longest War,* 131.
17 Partial Record of Feb. 8, 1965, Meeting with President by group that met before NSC Meeting, Feb. 8, 1965, NSC Meeting Notes, Box 1, Johnson Papers.
18 "At an appropriate time, we could publicly announce that we had turned a corner and changed our policy," Bundy had advised Johnson, "but . . . no mention should be made now of such a decision." Summary Record of NSC Meeting No. 548, Feb. 10, 1965, NSC Meeting Notes, Box 1, Johnson Papers.
19 McGovern interview.
20 Bundy to LBJ, Feb. 16, 1965, NSC File, Memos to President, Box 2, Johnson Papers.

confided to his advisers, "and he wanted to be sure that the answers would be good."[21]

Fulbright was present at the various briefings on Vietnam and spoke with Johnson personally on both February 8 and 14. The president convinced him that the bombing of the North was necessary to get the negotiating process started:

> We face several bad alternatives. The thing is to find one resulting in the least evil. The raids in North Vietnam are intended to create conditions that will make the Communists want to negotiate. As of now, there is no one to negotiate with and nothing to negotiate about, so we have to build up pressure for negotiation.[22]

Convinced that the bombing was only a tactical maneuver designed to avoid a much larger war, the Arkansan promised Johnson his continued public support. In mid-March on *Meet the Press* Fulbright again expressed his conviction that the air raids were necessary and declared that the situation in Vietnam was then so critical that a public debate either by the SFRC or by the Congress as a whole would be dangerous.[23] Like most other Americans, Fulbright did not realize that a most important corner had been turned, that the administration was assuming direct responsibility for winning the war.

Anticipating Vietcong attacks against U.S. air bases in retaliation for the bombing of the North, General Westmoreland in late February urgently requested two marine landing teams to protect the air base at Danang. Although Maxwell Taylor objected and pointed out some of the long-term implications, Johnson and his advisers agreed almost routinely. On March 8 two battalions of marines, clad in full battle dress complete with tanks and eight-inch howitzers, splashed ashore near Danang, where they were welcomed by the mayor and a bevy of local beauties who adorned the soldiers with leis.

As Taylor had predicted, once troops were introduced, it proved very difficult to control the escalation process. At a summit conference in Honolulu in late April, McNamara, Taylor, and the Joint Chiefs put aside their differences and agreed on a strategy whose object was to "break the will of the DRV/VC by depriving them of victory."[24] They decided to dispatch to Vietnam some forty thousand additional combat troops. Rather than being used without restriction to help the ARVN defeat the communists, as Westmoreland wanted, however, they stipulated that the additional soldiers were to be employed in an "enclave strategy." Positioned around major American military installations, the troops would restrict their operations to a fifty-mile radius of their base. The administration hoped that this limited commitment

21 Memorandum for the Record, NSC File, Memos to President, Box 2, Johnson Papers.
22 Quoted in Berman, *Fulbright and the Vietnam War,* 35.
23 *Meet the Press,* transcript, Mar. 14, 1965, Vol. 9, No. 9, Merkle Press.
24 Quoted in Herring, *America's Longest War,* 132.

of forces would be adequate to prevent the enemy from delivering a knockout blow, thus allowing time for the South Vietnamese to establish a viable government and to build an effective fighting force.

News that the administration had introduced ground combat troops into Vietnam and that Westmoreland was asking for a gradual buildup to three hundred thousand, coupled with the international outcry over the bombing of the North, caused Fulbright increasing anxiety. The second week in March, Lee Williams attended a cocktail party at the Bulgarian embassy and reported that "the Russians are terribly disturbed about our aggressive actions in Viet Nam." That report was confirmed when Fulbright subsequently spent two hours with Ambassador Anatoly Dobrynin at the Soviet embassy. The strikes on North Vietnam were "causing deep embarrassment and concern" to the Kremlin, Fulbright's Russian friend told him, and it would be necessary at the very least for the Soviet Union to step up arms aid. For Fulbright the central issue of the age continued to be peace and détente with the Soviet Union. He was terrified that the conflict in Southeast Asia would lead to a Great Power confrontation.

In Fulbright's view, it was the duty of the Democratic leadership to present the president with alternatives, and that is what the chairman of the SFRC, in consultation with Lippmann and Marcy, set out to do in the spring of 1965. Following his conversations with Dobrynin, the Arkansan proposed a halt in the bombing in return for Russian pressure on North Vietnam to staunch the flow of men and material into the South. According to the scenario that he developed, as hostilities ground to a halt in Indochina, the USSR and the United Kingdom would reconvene the Geneva Conference, with all parties agreeing to abide by the results of free, nationwide elections in Vietnam. He was convinced, he said, that overtures toward negotiations would be "received with rejoicing" in Moscow.[25] The United States must be willing to accept the legitimacy of an independent, nationalist, and united Vietnam. By strengthening its ties to the Soviet Union, this Yugoslav-style entity could serve as a counterweight to China. At all costs, the United States must avoid committing a large land army to the war in Vietnam because such a move would inevitably involve the country in a "bloody and interminable conflict in which the advantage would lie with the enemy." A major war in Asia, Fulbright predicted, "could be expected to poison the political life of the United States, undoing the beneficial results of the election of 1964 and reviving the influence of irresponsible and extremist political movements."[26]

Fulbright voiced his criticism of America's course in Vietnam privately, but others were not so discreet. Although the administration had attempted to conceal the direction of its policy, the obvious expansion of the war, particularly the bombing, had created widespread misgivings and provoked

25 JWF to Rusk, Mar. 12, 1965, Series 2:1, Box 4:2, SPF.
26 Quoted in Berman, *Fulbright and the Vietnam War,* 36.

isolated outcries. White House mail ran heavily against the aerial assault. A few newspapers had joined with the *New York Times* in warning of the cost of "lives lost, blood spilt and treasure wasted, of fighting a war on a jungle front 7,000 miles from the coast of California."[27] Faculty members at Harvard, Michigan, and Syracuse conducted all-night "teach-ins," students on various campuses held small protest meetings and distributed petitions against the bombing, and in April, twenty thousand young people gathered in Washington to march in protest against the war. Congressional doubters such as Frank Church, Wayne Morse, and George McGovern echoed Charles De-Gaulle's call for a negotiated settlement. The White House responded by organizing "Target: College Campuses." White House staffers and State Department personnel fanned out across the country to spread the gospel of a holy war against communism. Morse and company suddenly found their control over federal patronage threatened.

Meanwhile, Fulbright had come to the conclusion that North Vietnam had been "softened up" enough and that negotiations could never start without a bombing halt. He did not relish differing with the administration in public, Fulbright told reporters, but the bombing was only causing the North Vietnamese to "dig in" and the Russians to refuse to talk. What harm, he asked, would there be to stopping the aerial assault temporarily in an effort to get talks started?[28] When Dean Rusk brushed off the chairman's proposal publicly, Carl Marcy blew his top. "I think the time has come for Mr. Rusk to go," he told Fulbright. He had been all right under Kennedy, who was able to act as his own secretary of state, but Lyndon Johnson was "a babe in the woods in the field of foreign policy."[29]

Fulbright's pleas for a bombing halt struck a chord with the public. While Joseph Alsop, America's most hawkish commentator, berated him, the Arkansan's mail ran strongly in favor of a bombing suspension. Marcy released the figures to reporters, which in turn led to direct pressure on the White House.[30] In early May, reluctantly, indeed resentfully, Johnson approved a five-day suspension of American air raids. In reality, he accepted the idea only because the administration could then tell "Mansfield, Fulbright and the *New York Times*" that the administration had held out the olive branch, and Hanoi had "spit in our face." Even then, the Texan thought it all a waste of time. Increasingly influenced by Dean Acheson, he declared, "I'm afraid if we play along with this group, we will wind up with no one on our side. My judgment is that the public has never wanted us to stop the bombing."[31]

---

27 Quoted in Herring, *America's Longest War,* 133.
28 "Stopping Raids Might Pay Off, Fulbright Says," *Arkansas Gazette,* Apr. 19, 1965.
29 Marcy to JWF, Apr. 20, 1965, Box 5, Folder Apr., Marcy Papers.
30 Joseph Alsop, "Pompous Ignorance," *Washington Post,* Apr. 21, 1965; and Norvill Jones to JWF, Apr. 23, 1965, Series 48:11, Box 35:2, SPF.
31 Meeting with Foreign Policy Advisors on Vietnam, May 16, 1965, NSC Meeting Notes, Box 1, Johnson Papers.

During the pause, the State Department informed Hanoi that if and when NVA and VC military activity decreased, air attacks would be permanently scaled down. Ho Chi Minh denounced the bombing pause as a "worn-out trick of deceit and threat," and refused to curb military operations.

In March the SFRC added an important new member to its staff. The previous fall, John Newhouse had resigned to take a position in the private sector. As part of a round-the-world fact-finding trip in 1963, Marcy had stopped in Yugoslavia to survey the situation in the Balkans. Ambassador George Kennan had assigned his young political officer, James Lowenstein, to be Marcy's control officer. The two men became fast friends. At the time of Newhouse's departure, Lowenstein was in Washington working in the State Department, bored to death. Although it meant leaving the foreign service with no guarantee of return, Lowenstein responded enthusiastically to Marcy's invitation to apply for the vacant staff position. Following an interview with Fulbright and the committee, he got the job. Fluent in French and a veteran of a dozen years in the navy, the Ivy League–educated Lowenstein inherited Newhouse's job as Southeast Asia expert.[32]

As of the spring of 1965 Fulbright still believed that Lyndon Johnson was the main advocate of restraint in an administration of hard-liners. "I am doing all that I can to influence the president not to expand this war and to find a way to the Conference table," he wrote a constituent. "You must remember he inherited the involvement and it is not easy to overcome past mistakes."[33] Carl Marcy was not so sure; it seemed to him that Johnson had already sold out to hard-liners inside and outside his administration. Moreover, his anxiety over the diminution of the prerogatives of the SFRC and its chairman was becoming intense. The chief of staff was far less willing to give Johnson the benefit of the doubt, and he worked assiduously throughout the summer of 1965 to generate some skepticism in his boss. Marcy had come to suspect that in his obsession with "consensus" Lyndon Johnson was bending over backward to appease the radical right.

Fulbright took Marcy's views seriously, but he continued to resist an open break with the Texan. He still believed that mild public opposition to the administration's policies, coupled with repeated statements of support for the president personally, would have the desired effect. He continued to treasure what he believed to be his close relationship with Johnson. When the president sent him a series of pictures showing the two in rapt conversation in the Oval Office – inscribed, "To, Bill, I can see I haven't been very persuasive" and "To Betty Fulbright, Delightful wife of an eloquent husband" – Fulbright hung them on his office wall.

32 Interview with James Lowenstein, Oct. 3, 1991, Washington, D.C.
33 JWF to Rev. Daniel H. Evans, July 29, 1965, Series 48:1, Box 7:3, SPF.

In fact, Marcy's aphorism that all presidents and all foreign policy establishments come to view Congress in general and the Senate in particular as either a nuisance to be circumvented or an asset to be manipulated was at no time truer than during the Johnson administration. Neither Rusk, Bundy, nor McNamara had ever held elective office. Like George Kennan and Dean Acheson, they believed that the executive should be free to make foreign policy decisions that would be judged by the general electorate every four years. Bundy in particular, the Ivy League academic come to Washington, was contemptuous of Congress. Senators were a collection of uninformed yahoos, he insisted. Like everyone and everything else, they should be cajoled and coerced into supporting the policies that the executive branch in its wisdom had devised. The uncooperative should be cast out into the darkness. "They [congressional opponents] are quite free to oppose you if they choose," Bundy wrote the president, "but they are not free to make statements that you regard as damaging and pretend that they are speaking as your friends and supporters."[34]

Indeed, instead of opening up the decision-making process, as Fulbright and Marcy wanted him to, Johnson was gradually circumscribing it. He came to distrust National Security Council meetings: They were too large and too often the source of the hated leak. Most important decisions were made at the famous Tuesday luncheon meetings at which only the president, Bundy, McNamara, Rusk, and one aide each were present. The conclusions reached there were carefully presented in a stage-managed fashion, first to the NSC, then to the congressional leadership, and subsequently to the nation as a whole. Although Marcy and Fulbright did not yet realize it, they were going to be able to affect policy not by being part of the "team," not by forcing access through legislation, but through open and relentless opposition designed to erode the consensus that Lyndon Johnson so treasured.

In the middle of June 1965, Johnson called Fulbright to the White House and asked him to make a public statement in support of administration policies in Vietnam. He needed help, he told the Arkansan, in fighting off the hard-liners and getting negotiations on track. The following day Fulbright rose on the Senate floor to proclaim that president Johnson was showing "steadfastness and statesmanship" in his handling of the Southeast Asia situation. On the one hand, military victory, though possible, was not worth the cost; on the other, withdrawal from South Vietnam would "betray our obligation to people we have promised to defend." The only answer was a compromise settlement based on major concessions by both sides:

34 Bundy to LBJ, Mar. 15, 1965, NSC File, Memos to President, Box 3, SPF.

> In the months ahead we must try to do two things in South Vietnam. First we must sustain the South Vietnamese Army so as to persuade the Communists that Saigon cannot be crushed and that the United States will not be driven from South Vietnam by force; second, we must continue to offer the Communists a reasonable and attractive alternative to military victory.[35]

He was convinced, he said, that the Vietcong believed that the rainy conditions of the current monsoon season gave them a military advantage and therefore would not respond to invitations to talk. Consequently, he concluded, "I approve of the president's efforts to strengthen South Vietnam and to maintain its security through . . . November or December."[36] The chairman had delivered his message of support, but it was conditional and terminable.

Indeed, even at this early date, Fulbright believed that any settlement in Indochina ought to include a political role for the communists. When, on the morning following his Senate speech, Fulbright was asked by Sander Vanocur on the *Today* show whether the Vietcong ought to be allowed to participate in negotiations, Fulbright responded with an unqualified yes. Legalities were irrelevant. The VC were major players in the game. Republicans immediately screamed sellout. If the administration sanctioned any negotiations that "would include Communist elements in a coalition government," it could forget bipartisan support, Dirksen and company warned.[37] Johnson quickly disassociated himself from Fulbright's TV remarks, but at the same time, the president expressed satisfaction with his old colleague's Senate remarks and chose to interpret them as an endorsement of a massive troop buildup.

Throughout May, June, and July, despite the bombing, continued increases in U.S. aid, and the small infusion of American ground forces, the military situation in South Vietnam continued to deteriorate. Following a whirlwind tour of South Vietnam the last week in June, McNamara returned to report that the situation was desperate. The United States must escalate before it was "too late to do any good." There were great risks involved in increasing the national commitment, but decisive and immediate action might "stave off defeat in the short run and offer a good chance of producing a favorable settlement in the longer run." Most important, General Westmoreland must be given the authority to use American troops and firepower whenever, however, and wherever he chose. JCS Chairman Earle Wheeler's advice – "You must take the fight to the enemy. . . . No one ever won a battle sitting on his ass" – seemed compelling.[38] Accordingly, Johnson delegated to Westmore-

---

35 *Congressional Record,* Senate, June 15, 1965, 13657.
36 Ibid.
37 Quoted in Berman, *Fulbright and the Vietnam War,* 43.
38 Quoted in Herring, *America's Longest War,* 138, 137.

land, in consultation with the Khanh's Military Revolutionary Council (MRC), the authority to move beyond the enclave strategy and do whatever was necessary to win the war. Johnson promised his field commander all the logistical and troop support that he needed. At this point the war had cost America 420 combat dead, surpassing the total of the Spanish–American conflict (385).[39]

On June 28 Johnson once again asked the chairman of the SFRC to the White House. During a stroll through the Rose Garden, the president outlined the desperate situation in Vietnam and told Fulbright he was going to have to send more troops and equipment to hold the line until the United States and its ally could establish a firm negotiating position. The Republicans and their ultra allies were waiting in the wings like so many vultures, ready to pounce, should the administration falter. Fulbright was sympathetic. He subsequently told *Newsweek*'s Samuel Shaffer:

> As the Republicans see it, the President is damned if he does and damned if he doesn't. If there are a lot of American casualties, they'll talk about the "Johnson War" the way they talked about "Truman's War" in Korea. If the war is settled by negotiation, they'll claim we "lost" Vietnam the way we "lost" China.[40]

Carl Marcy's contacts and sensors within the executive branch were extensive. Leaks from these sources and information provided by Ned Kenworthy of the *New York Times* convinced him that something more significant than just "holding the line" was taking place. Marcy tried to warn Fulbright: "We seem to be on the verge of another important decision regarding Vietnam," he told his superior, "one on which the views of the Senate will not be sought until after the decision. There is now a last chance to do something that may halt this constant progression toward war."[41]

Urged on by the SFRC chief of staff, Fulbright met with Walter Lippmann throughout early July. The journalist's estimation of the situation matched Marcy's. He convinced Fulbright to join him in putting forward a strategy that they believed would lead to a negotiated settlement without a provocative escalation. As the president was telling Westmoreland to go ahead and use his troops in offensive operations throughout Vietnam, Fulbright and Lippmann suggested an enclave strategy whereby American troops would pull back to strong points, with their backs to the sea. While avoiding a general or even "Korea-sized" war, this strategy, they insisted, would deny North Vietnam and the Vietcong control over all of Vietnam. Rather than exhaust themselves attacking impregnable strongholds, the communists would eventually sit down at the negotiating ta-

---

39 "The Road Past North C Pier . . ." *Newsweek,* June 28, 1965.
40 Ibid.
41 Marcy to JWF, July 12, 1965, Box 5, Folder July, Marcy Papers.

ble.[42] This, of course, was the very strategy that Johnson had imposed on Westmoreland in April and that was in the process of being scrapped. That Marcy, Fulbright, and Lippmann regarded it as an imaginative new initiative demonstrated just how isolated they were from the decision-making process and how out of touch they were with what was really transpiring in Vietnam.

Although he found lobbying his colleagues extremely distasteful, Fulbright on the afternoon of July 27 met with the Senate's foreign policy heavyweights in Mansfield's office.[43] Fulbright picked the Montanan's suite not only because he was majority leader but also because up to that point he had been the most consistent, thorough, and – so his colleagues believed – credible critic of U.S. involvement in Vietnam. As a professor of political science at the University of Montana, he had specialized in East Asia. He had taken innumerable trips to Indochina and had been personal friends with the Diems before their demise, with Norodom Sihanouk of Cambodia, and with Ne Win of Burma. Throughout 1964 and early 1965, Mansfield had periodically dispatched to the White House long, turgid memos, prepared by his chief aide, Frank Valeo, another China–Burma–India (CBI) theatre veteran, decrying American involvement in Vietnam. He pressed his dissent with what Mc-George Bundy called "mousy stubbornness," but his lack of personality and his unwillingness to confront the president publicly would make him a largely ineffective dissenter.[44]

Indeed, on the morning before Fulbright and the others gathered in his office, Mansfield attended a legislative leadership meeting on Vietnam at the White House. "We owe this government nothing," he declared, "no pledge of any kind. We are going deeper into war. Escalation begets escalation. The best hope for salvation is quick stalemate and negotiations." Having indicted the war in Vietnam and the assumptions that underlay it, he then declared he would support the president "as a Senator and Majority Leader," whatever course he chose to follow.[45]

Fulbright found a surprising, gratifying degree of consensus in the group that gathered in Mansfield's office – Russell, Sparkman, Aiken, and John Sherman Cooper (R–Kentucky). There was full agreement that "insofar as Viet Nam is concerned we are deeply enmeshed in a place where we ought not to be; that the situation is rapidly going out of control; and that every effort should be made to extricate ourselves." Russell and Stennis, both southerners and both members of the Armed Services Committee, had been arguing for all-out bombing of the North, but they readily agreed at the

42 "Two Alternatives in Vietnam War," *Arkansas Gazette,* July 14, 1965.
43 Vietnam Chronology, July 24 and 27, 1965, Box 5, Folder July, Marcy Papers.
44 Bundy to LBJ, May 31, 1965, and Mansfield to LBJ, June 5, 9, and 14, 1965, NSC File, Memos to President, Box 3, Johnson Papers.
45 Cong. Leadership Meeting, July 27, 1965, Meeting Notes File, Box 1, Johnson Papers.

meeting that the bombing should never have been started in the first place. The war, the group lamented, was threatening relations with the Soviet Union, which was aiding the North Vietnamese only because of its rivalry with Communist China. And finally, they agreed that Vietnam was of only marginal strategic importance to the United States. The five drafted a letter embodying their views and sent it to Johnson post haste. Most people backing the president on Vietnam did so primarily because he was president, the group told the Texan, and not out of any understanding or sympathy with administration policies.[46]

Fulbright was most hopeful that the meeting and resulting letter would halt what he considered to be a descent into full-scale war. The signers did not include Morse, McCarthy, McGovern, Church, or Joseph Clark, the liberal Democratic senator from Pennsylvania, men whom he and Marcy knew the White House regarded as dangerous visionaries or political opportunists. No one could ever accuse Richard Russell or John Sparkman of being soft on communism or of being unwilling to take their country into war to defend its interests. In short, the chairman and his chief of staff were sure that they had assembled a group that Johnson could not afford to ignore. They were wrong.

The day following receipt of the Mansfield letter, Johnson called the dissidents to the White House. After outlining the deteriorating military and political situation in Vietnam, he told Fulbright and company that there was no turning back. America was in for the duration. The war could well last six or seven more years.[47]

Johnson's frank review of the situation stunned and then infuriated Fulbright. He had supported the president and his escalation of the war to that point out of a belief that limited bombing and introduction of troops were necessary to placate American hard-liners and get all sides to the negotiating table. Now it turned out that the administration was committed to winning a battlefield victory, to securing all of South Vietnam physically and then bombing North Vietnam to the peace table. Could it be, he asked himself, that Carl Marcy was right, that in his desire to appease the hawks Lyndon Johnson was selling out to them?

46 Mansfield to LBJ, July 27, 1965, NSF, Name File, Box 6, Johnson Papers.
47 Berman, *Fulbright and the Vietnam War*, 44.

7

Texas Hyperbole

At 4:40 on the afternoon of April 28, 1965, Lyndon Johnson sat down with Rusk, McNamara, Ball, Bundy, and presidential aide Bill Moyers to discuss the perilous situation in Vietnam. An hour into the meeting President Johnson was handed a cable marked "critic" (critical) from Ambassador W. Tapley Bennett in Santo Domingo. The Dominican military had spilt into at least two factions, and one was arming the populace in an effort to seize power. "Regret report situation deteriorating rapidly," it stated. "[C]ountry team unanimously of opinion that time has come to land the marines .... American lives are in danger." After conferring with his advisers, all of whom approved intervention, President Johnson ordered four hundred marines to proceed to the Dominican capital at once. Rusk rushed off to inform all the Latin American embassies in Washington, and Moyers left to set up a briefing session in the Cabinet Room for congressional leaders later that evening.[1]

When Johnson and his advisers closeted themselves with the congressional leadership, Rusk stressed that the administration's decision to intervene had been based on the need to protect American lives. Newly named head of the CIA Admiral William "Red" Raborn declared that there had been "positive identification of three ring-leaders of the Rebels as Castro-trained agents." Everett Dirksen and John McCormack immediately warned of the danger of allowing another Castroite regime to emerge in the hemisphere and declared their support for armed intervention. Fulbright's only contribution to the council of war was to recommend that the OAS be involved. When asked whether American troops, soon to number some twenty-four thousand, would be pulled out immediately or allowed to remain there, Johnson answered that that bridge had not yet been crossed.[2]

The causes of the Dominican Republic's many troubles were varied, but most were rooted in the thirty-year dictatorship of Rafael Leónidas Trujillo

---

1 Chronology of Pertinent Events in the Dominican Republic Situation, undated, NSF, Box 8, Johnson Papers.
2 Meeting with Congressional Leadership on Dominican Republic, Apr. 28, 1965, Meeting Notes File, Box 1, Johnson Papers.

Molina. That villian had brutally suppressed all opposition, turned the army into his personal palace guard, and ravaged his country's fragile economy. Then, in the summer of 1961, assassins shot him through the head. His family tried to perpetuate his tyranny but failed and fled into exile. In December 1962 the Dominicans elected the liberal intellectual Juan Bosch president. Seven months later a military coup overthrew him, its leaders charging that he was too tolerant of communists and communism. Despite support from the Johnson administration for the new government of Donald Reid Cabral and the presence of some twenty-five hundred Americans on that island of some 3.5 million souls, stability eluded the Dominicans. Drought, widespread unemployment, strikes, sabotage, and continuing opposition from dissidents kept the country in constant turmoil. From exile in Puerto Rico where he was employed as a college professor, Juan Bosch directed the disruptive activities of the Dominican Revolutionary Party (PRD).

The spring of 1965 found the Dominican military deeply divided. A minority were devoted to Bosch's return, but the majority regarded him as a dangerous revolutionary who would "open the door to the communists" and, not coincidentally, do away with the military's privileges.[3] When officers loyal to Reid Cabral had attempted to arrest some of their fellows for plotting against the government in behalf of Juan Bosch, the PRD, with the support of some military officers, had declared a general uprising and seized the presidential palace. At this point, the anti-Bosch military, led by the pious and thoroughly reactionary General Elias Wessin y Wessin, issued an ultimatum to the PRD demanding that it turn over power to the army. Wessin had become convinced that Bosch and the PRD were encouraging the Castroite Fourteenth of June Movement.[4] When the rebels ignored his demand, air force planes began bombing and strafing the palace, as well as the slums of Santo Domingo, which were Bosch strongholds and, in the minds of the military, seedbeds of communist agitation. The brutal attacks inflamed the population, which flooded into the streets in response to calls from the PRD. At this point Santo Domingo teetered on the edge of chaos. Under the auspices of Tapley Bennett, who now decided that the embassy could no longer remain aloof, the anti-Bosch military put together a junta headed by Colonel Pedro Bartolome Benoit. The sole purpose of this government was to request armed intervention by the United States.

On the afternoon of April 28, while President Johnson met with his ad-

---

3 There were as of that year three communist factions present in the Dominican Republic: the Dominican Popular Movement (MPD), illegal since 1963, which was Maoist and claimed some five hundred hard-core supporters; the Dominican Popular Socialist Party (PSPD), Moscow oriented and between seven hundred and a thousand strong; and the Fourteenth of June Movement (PACJ), which was financed by and loyal to Fidel Castro. U.S. Senate, Committee on Foreign Relations, Executive Sessions of the SFRC, Vol. 17, 1965 (Washington, D.C., 1990), 805.

4 SFRC, Executive Sessions, Vol. 17, 1965, 491.

visers on Vietnam, Undersecretary Thomas Mann, the State Department's leading expert on Latin America, and Bennett exchanged a flurry of telegrams. Bennett managed to convince the State Department that given General Wessin and Colonel Benoit's inability to control the situation in Santo Domingo, there was a very real danger of a communist, Castro-controlled takeover in the Dominican Republic. All "responsible" elements agreed that U.S. Marines should be dispatched at once, and he agreed with them, Bennett declared. Mann then advised the ambassador that he must compel Benoit to base his request for American intervention on the need to protect American lives. "We did instruct our Ambassador to go back to Benoit . . . and in order to improve our juridical base asked him to specifically say that he could not protect the lives of American citizens," Mann subsequently admitted to the SFRC.[5] In his later cables, as a result, Bennett insisted that the large number of Americans residing at the Hotel Embajador were in danger of being killed or wounded.

The first week in May, reporters flooded into the Dominican Republic determined to check out the administration's version of events. They quickly discovered that no American civilian had been killed or even wounded at the Ambassador Hotel or anywhere else on the island. When pressed, anonymous sources in the American embassy declared that they had in their possession the names of fifty-eight card-carrying communists who had led the uprising against Reid Cabral. Editorials in the *New York Times*, the *New York Herald-Tribune,* and the *Washington Post* began to question the administration's reasoning and veracity. The notion that fifty-eight communists posed a massive threat in any Latin American country, even one as small as the Dominican Republic, seemed ludicrous.[6]

The ever-sensitive Johnson overreacted. He began exaggerating. He described scenes that never took place, misquoted cables for dramatic effect, and ridiculed his detractors. Throughout Sunday, May 2, the president briefed various congressional leaders and railed against his critics. More troops were going into Santo Domingo; the issue was now greater even than the loss of American lives, he proclaimed. Now the Dominican Republic must be saved from "other evil forces."[7]

The next afternoon at a union convention in Washington, he told how he had received Bennett's urgent cable. "You must land troops immediately," he quoted it as saying, "or blood will run in the streets, American blood will run in the streets." Then, in a veiled reference to John F. Kennedy's handling of the Bay of Pigs, he declared: What is important . . . in this hemi-

5 Ibid., 827.
6 See Tad Szulc, Dominican Diary (New York, 1965), for a critical contemporary account of the intervention.
7 Bundy to LBJ, May 2, 1965, NSC File, Memos to President, Box 3, Johnson Papers.

sphere ... [is] that we know, and that they know, and that everybody knows, that we don't propose to sit here in our rocking chair with our hands folded and let the Communists set up any government in the Western Hemisphere."[8]

At this point, Fulbright's attention was focused on Vietnam. It remained to others on the SFRC to look behind the president's rhetoric and challenge his justifications. Wayne Morse, the SFRC's Latin American expert, and Pennsylvania liberal Joe Clark were profoundly disturbed at the administration's bypassing of the OAS. They were convinced that the State Department had overreacted. Thomas Mann and Tapley Bennett, in their view, were throwbacks to the days of Big Stick diplomacy, men determined to work with and support only Latin leaders who were "good-suited" and pro–United States. Clark was convinced that Johnson had been captured by McNamara, Bundy, and other of his hard-nosed advisers and was being misled by "McCarthyite–CIA" reports. Both Morse and Clark were as yet afraid to break with Johnson publicly, but they did persuade Fulbright and the rest of the committee to request Johnson to have Mann and others brief the committee in executive session.[9]

By June 17 a shaky peace prevailed in the Dominican Republic, but public criticism had not abated. On that date Johnson gave an unforgettable performance at a nontelevised press conference. Away from the glare of the television lights, he shouted and snapped his fingers under the noses of reporters, thumped the desk, and brandished what he said were top secret documents. He gave a new version of the scene that had allegedly prompted Tap Bennett to ask him to intervene. "In this particular instance, a fact that has been emphasized all too little [is that] some 1500 innocent people were murdered and shot and their heads cut off." In that same press conference, he also told reporters that Bennett "was talking to us from under a desk while bullets were going through his windows and he had a thousand American men, women, and children assembled in the hotel who were pleading with their President for help to preserve their lives."[10] To Johnson his statements concerning heads rolling in the streets of Santo Domingo and Tap Bennett hiding under his desk while bullets whizzed overhead were not fabrications but embellishments of a basic truth. "Those weren't lies," McGeorge Bundy would later insist. "He was building up, 'argufying'; he was certainly going

---

8 Quoted in Haynes Johnson and Bernard M. Gwertzman, *Fulbright: The Dissenter* (New York, 1968), 248.

9 Bundy to LBJ, May 5, 1965, NSC File, Memos to President, Johnson Papers; and JWF to Rusk, June 2, 1965, Box 5, Folder June, Marcy Papers.

10 Quoted in Johnson and Gwertzman, *Fulbright: The Dissenter,* 249.

beyond the truth, but that's not the same as lying. In his mind he was 'trying to make the whole situation totally clear.' " He had a terrible time, Bundy recalled, trying to keep some sort of limit on the president's "unfettered exposition."[11]

J. William Fulbright did not appreciate Texas hyperbole. Johnson's description of events seemed at odds even with the version presented to the SFRC by the president's aides. He set about proving to himself whether or not the administration was lying to the American people. From mid-July through mid-August 1965, Mann, Bennett, Raborn, Assistant Secretary of Defense Cyrus Vance, and Assistant Secretary of State Jack Hood Vaughn testified at length before the SFRC. The committee was still split, but this time Fulbright took charge. He was every inch the trial lawyer, questioning, probing, careful not to antagonize the Republican members or pro-administration Democrats. He asked for and received virtually all of the cable traffic that passed between Santo Domingo and the State Department. Pat Holt conducted his own investigation, and Seth Tillman interviewed Tad Szulc, who was shortly to publish his firsthand and very critical version of the intervention, entitled *Dominican Diary*. From all of this evidence Fulbright was finally able to piece together an accurate picture.

Bennett and his staff first refused to act, allowing chaos to reign, and then overreacted to the threat of a communist takeover. Fulbright forced Mann to admit that Washington had instructed Benoit to alter his appeal to emphasize the need to preserve American lives. He demonstrated not only that there had been no American civilian casualties, but that any threat to U.S. citizens had been greatly exaggerated.[12] Behind the scenes Pat Holt argued that Johnson and Tom Mann had set their faces against a return to power by Juan Bosch, in their eyes a weak and vacillating man who would open the door to the Castroites. It was to prevent this eventuality, and not to save American lives, that the marines had been landed.[13]

During the course of the investigation, Holt learned that Johnson not only had lied to Congress and the American people but had attempted to compromise the CIA whose operatives had delivered accurate intelligence reports on the crisis. When the Dominican affair erupted, CIA director Raborn had been in office for only a few days. Shortly after American troops landed, Johnson asked Raborn to produce evidence of communist involvement in the unrest on the island. The admiral returned to Langley and appealed for help, but the Latin American experts in the agency told him that they could not come up with any communists for the president. Infuriated, Johnson called in J.

11 Interview with McGeorge Bundy, Aug. 1, 1991, New York.
12 SFRC, Executive Sessions, Vol. 17, 1965, 737–95, 841–937, 1111–17.
13 Donald A. Ritchie, interviewer, *Pat M. Holt: Oral History Interviews* (Senate Historical Office: Washington, D. C.: 1980) 185, and Memo of Conversation between Peter H. Freeman and Holt, July 26, 1965, Series 48:14, Box 38:5, SPF.

Edgar Hoover. "Find me some Communists in the Dominican Republic," he commanded. The FBI Director secretly flooded the country with FBI agents, who generated the list of fifty-three that Szulc and Kurzman subsequently discredited.[14]

On September 14 McGeorge Bundy was tipped off by "friendly newspapermen" that Fulbright was going to deliver a major address the next day indicting the administration for mishandling the Dominican situation and then intervening to no good purpose. He went to Johnson at once. Bundy did not have a copy, but he understood, he said, that the speech would be particularly hard on Bennett.[15]

The Dominican address was indeed a devastating indictment. After laying out the chronology, Fulbright blasted Bennett for underreacting and then overreacting. The embassy was paranoid concerning the threat that Castro and communism posed to the hemisphere, he said. Bennett had solicited armed intervention only after it appeared that the PRD and its allies might win, and the sole purpose of that intervention was to create and then maintain an anticommunist, pro-U.S. regime. The threat to American lives, greatly exaggerated, was a mere pretext, Fulbright declared. "In their apprehension lest the Dominican Republic become another Cuba, some of our officials seem to have forgotten that virtually all reform movements attract some Communist support."[16]

There is no doubt that Fulbright's speech on the Dominican Republic destroyed his relationship with Lyndon Johnson. The president was willing to listen to dissenting views – indeed, he at times demanded them of his subordinates – but once a decision was made, he expected his lieutenants to close ranks. "From Lyndon Johnson's point of view, anything less than 100% support was rank desertion," McGeorge Bundy remembered.[17] His was not an unreasonable expectation of members of the executive branch. The trouble was that Lyndon Johnson extended that criterion to virtually everyone in America, including Democratic members of Congress and Fulbright in particular. Like Woodrow Wilson, Franklin D. Roosevelt, and any number of lesser political figures, Johnson believed that he personified the country, was the receptacle of its hopes and the font of its wisdom. It was not surprising that the Texan was wont to convert differences over policy into personal feuds. Fulbright was part of his "team," and Johnson expected the Arkansan to manage the SFRC so as to facilitate and not obstruct administration policy. As he so often did when someone challenged him in public, Johnson felt "betrayed." He wanted to be loved, expected to be loved, and was deeply disappointed when he believed he was not.

14 Richie, *Holt: Interviews,* 187.
15 Bundy to LBJ, Sept. 14, 1965, NSF, Memos to President, Bundy, Box 4, Johnson Papers.
16 *Congressional Record,* Senate, Sept. 15, 1965, 23855–63.
17 McG. Bundy interview.

Even among those who differed with him, Johnson singled Fulbright out for special treatment. The second week in December, no fewer than three state dinners were held at the White House, one a gala affair for Chancellor Ludwig Erhard of West Germany; the chairman of the SFRC was excluded from all of them.[18] In November the White House denied Fulbright the use of a government jet to transport him and a senatorial delegation to Wellington, New Zealand, to attend a meeting of the British Commonwealth Parliamentarians' Association. To the chairman's chagrin, he and his party had to make the trip, which stretched halfway round the world, in a lumbering, prop-driven C-118. In addition, Fulbright would be banned from all official functions at the White House for more than a year. Johnson would curse and ridicule the Arkansan to his staff and visiting dignitaries alike. All the while, the Texan continued to "consult" with Mansfield and Morse, both publicly and privately. "I spoke publicly the fifteenth of September . . . in '65," Fulbright later recalled, "and Johnson never after that had another private conversation with me" (which was not true).[19]

The break with Fulbright seemed to unleash resentments that had long been festering within Lyndon Johnson. Above all, there was the Texan's educational inferiority complex. "The Johnsons were as close to the Fulbrights as to any other couple in Washington," William Bundy recalled, "and at the same time there was that subtle difference deriving from what George Ball eloquently described as not LBJ's inferior education but his belief that he had had an inferior education."[20] Although he liked having Rhodes scholars like Rostow and Rusk on his team, Johnson was ambivalent toward people with gold-plated academic credentials and "intellectuals." He resented them and at the same time longed to please them. Johnson hated the Kennedys, and the Kennedys had gone to Harvard. He detested Arthur Schlesinger, the ultimate Ivy League professor, because he was the most loyal of Kennedy loyalists. In the aftermath of the Dominican Republic speech, the president began to lump Fulbright and Schlesinger together. Although the Arkansan had no particular tie to the Kennedys, he was an intellectual and he shared their contempt for him, Johnson believed.

The image of Fulbright that formed in Johnson's mind, then, was that of a traitor and a coward. He was a traitor in the sense of putting his doubts above the interests of his country and his president. Unlike Morse, who would "whack him in the open," Fulbright would sneak around behind his back. He was not a "stand up kind of guy," McGeorge Bundy remembered Johnson as saying.[21]

---

18 "Unbecoming a President," *Detroit News*, Dec. 22, 1965.
19 Charles Morrissey interview with J. William Fulbright, "Modern Congress in American History" (Library of Congress: Washington, D.C.), 21.
20 Interview with William Bundy, July 5, 1990, Princeton, N.J.
21 McG. Bundy interview.

What in fact lay behind the Arkansan's momentous decision to break with Lyndon Johnson? Some attributed Fulbright's broadside to "moodiness" and "oversensitivity." He was in many ways a typical youngest child (the twins were an afterthought as far as Jay, Roberta, and the older siblings were concerned). The only one of the Fulbright children close to both of his parents, Bill became adept at pleasing both. As he had shown throughout his life, he was driven to live beyond reproach, to be the perfect child and husband, if not father (reflecting, in part, his own father's aloofness), and the ideal citizen. Fulbright took life very seriously, and he had been taught to take responsibility for his social environment. He brooded over personal slights, aspirations cast on his native region, imperfections in the nation's foreign policy, and flaws in those whom he had helped elevate to power. Wayne Morse, who gloried in public combat, shrewdly commented on the differences between himself and Fulbright. In the fall of 1965 Morse went to the White House for a ceremonial function. Johnson, who was then doing bitter battle with the burgeoning antiwar movement of which Morse was a prominent member, greeted the Oregonian cordially: "Wayne, I've never seen you looking so fit. How do you do it?" Morse replied: "Well, Mr. President, I'll tell you. Every time I read in the papers what you're doing about Vietnam, it makes my blood boil. That purges me; it keeps me fit." But Fulbright was different, Morse later observed. "Bill's a bleeder. He keeps agonizing over it."[22]

In addition, Fulbright's natural, rather mild arrogance had been sharpened by association with Seth Tillman. A native of Massachusetts and a graduate of Tufts, Tillman considered himself a member of the intellectual and cultural elite. (He had, in fact, come from a middle-class background, attended Syracuse as an undergraduate, and even taught public school for awhile.) Tillman was a gifted speechwriter, "as good as Sorensen, better than Goodwin," according to James Lowenstein. He had published his dissertation, and he could not help but feel superior to the "Arkansas Mafia" and other staffers on the hill. Tillman believed that the combination of his prose and Fulbright's vision could change the world, that the Fulbright persona was an island of rationality and insight in a sea of know-nothingness. The interaction between the two men produced a combination of voice and vision that made Fulbright far more formidable than he would have been alone. But Tillman's personality also fed an already deep-seated intellectual arrogance and self-righteousness in Fulbright. To the speechwriter and his boss, Lyndon Johnson was an unlettered Texan desperately in need of enlightened guidance in matters of foreign policy. That he would not take it from the best available source – Fulbright and Tillman – was infuriating. It was Tillman's advice Fulbright was taking when he asked Carl Marcy if the Dominican speech were correct and then told him that he would take care of the political consequences.

22 Quoted in Johnson and Gwertzman, *Fulbright: The Dissenter*, 260.

Finally, there was Carl Marcy. By 1965 his determination to preserve congressional prerogatives in the area of foreign policy had become an obsession. Over the years the executive branch's unfailing habit of ignoring, circumventing, or manipulating the Senate in general and the SFRC in particular had created a smoldering resentment in the Oregonian. He believed that his committee under Fulbright was fully as competent to judge the national interest as the State or Defense departments. He had long ago identified his not-inconsiderable ego with the SFRC. Indeed, his reservations about the Dominican speech concerned the probable loss of influence and status that would ensue for both Fulbright and the Committee rather than any questions about the correctness of the chairman's position.

What is puzzling about the whole Dominican episode was Fulbright's surprise and dismay at the intensity of the Johnson counterattack. After all, what did he expect? His staff had warned him. He had known Lyndon Johnson for years. "If you took issue publicly with President Johnson," he later declared, "that's the end of you from his point of view. You're on his team or you're not."[23] Johnson's claims that heads were rolling in the streets of Santo Domingo were absurd, but he had been expostulating thusly in public life for thirty years. What startled him, Bundy later declared, was that Fulbright was so distressed: "He must have known this about him. If I could get used to it in my cold-roast New England way, why couldn't Fulbright?"[24]

As was true of so many people with a minimum of imagination and a maximum of security, Fulbright frequently found it difficult to identify with others. The same inability to empathize with poor black sharecroppers in the Arkansas delta made him a very poor handler of presidents. Perceived ignorance or deceit rendered him caustic, sarcastic, condescending; having roasted Johnson, the object of his scorn, he subsequently expressed shock and hurt at the cutting response his scathing remarks elicited. But Fulbright's response was typical. Whether he was deriding a family member for his or her ignorance or dressing down public figures like John Foster Dulles or Lyndon Johnson for their errors, he always subsequently claimed to have been misinterpreted, not to have meant his remarks personally. What amazing ignorance of human nature not to have realized that people invest their egos in their vocations!

If J. William Fulbright misunderstood the implications of the Dominican speech and the break with the White House for his career, so too did Lyndon Johnson underestimate the impact of Fulbright's alienation on his presidency and the course of American foreign policy. One snowy afternoon in November, several weeks before the New Zealand trip, Fulbright, Holt, Marcy, and Lowenstein were sitting around the office, discussing the war in Vietnam. Fulbright had just read *Street without Joy* by Bernard Fall. Intrigued, he asked

23 Morrissey interview with Fulbright, "Modern Congress," 21.
24 McG. Bundy interview.

if anyone knew Fall, who was then teaching at Howard University in Washington. Lowenstein said that he did. When Fulbright asked him to set up a meeting, Lowenstein got in a cab, went immediately to Fall's Georgetown home, and persuaded the journalist-scholar to agree to come to lunch the following Monday.[25]

A French-born expert on Southeast Asia, Fall interspersed long trips to Vietnam during the 1950s and 1960s, where he absorbed the warp and woof of village life and flew on combat missions with both the French and Americans, with teaching stints in Europe and America. Until he was killed in 1967 by a Vietcong land mine, he would spend much of his time warning the United States of the complexities of the Vietnam conflict. He repeatedly urged Washington to treat the encounter as "a revolutionary war, that is, a military operation with heavy political overtones. To win the military battle but lose the political war could well become the U.S. fate in Vietnam."[26] Marcy's opinion carried great weight with Fulbright, but Fall was a scholar and combat journalist. The break with Johnson over the Dominican intervention created in the Arkansan alienation sufficient to prepare him emotionally for open conflict with the administration over Vietnam. The lunch with Fall marked the beginning of Fulbright's effort to educate himself on every aspect of the war in Southeast Asia.

As part of his effort to inform himself concerning the complexities of East Asia, Fulbright brought along *The Crippled Tree* by Chinese–Belgian author Han Suyin on the long trip to New Zealand.[27] The book was a personal and vivid account of China's ill-treatment at the hands of the West. More important, among the senators on the trip was Republican Hiram Fong of Hawaii. As the two engaged in long conversations on the culture and politics of the East, Fulbright began to realize for the first time that his country had undertaken a task that it could not accomplish, that it was attempting to "save" a culture that it did not understand, and that, in fact, in its obsession with the cold war, America had interjected itself into a conflict whose roots were largely indigenous.

25 Interview with Pat Holt, Oct. 7, 1988, Washington, D.C.; and interview with James Lowenstein, Oct. 3, 1991, Washington, D.C.
26 Quoted in Charles DeBenedetti with Charles Chatfield, *An American Ordeal: The Antiwar Movement of the Vietnam Era* (Syracuse, 1990), 84.
27 Johnson and Gwertzman, *Fulbright: The Dissenter,* 265.

8

The Hearings

"The war is not only not going well," Clyde Petit wrote Lee Williams from Bangkok in January 1966; "the situation is worse than is reported in the press and worse, I believe, than is indicated in intelligence reports." Petit, a lawyer-turned-journalist who had just finished interviewing some two hundred military personnel for the Arkansas radio network, instructed his friend to show the letter to Fulbright but otherwise to keep it confidential. That communication, a devastating account of the political and military situation in Southeast Asia, would become the existential basis for Fulbright, Marcy, and Williams' already deeply rooted philosophical and historical dissent from the war.

For the most part, the American military buildup was having little effect on the war because most troops "are literally confined in closely-guarded compounds, protected by moat-like defenses of concertina-wire and incessant barrages of U.S. artillery," Petit wrote. Among American enlisted personnel and lower- and middle-ranking officers, particularly in combat areas, morale was unbelievably high. This gung-ho attitude made U.S. soldiers vigorous and effective fighters but, ironically, rendered them useless in the battle for the hearts and minds of the South Vietnamese. Their "messianic attitude of anger" made pacification most difficult.[1] One erudite officer had told him, "If there is a God, and he is very kind to us, and given a million men and five years and a miracle in making the South Vietnamese people like us, we stand an outside chance of a stalemate."[2]

As Fulbright and Williams sensed immediately, Petit and his cynical officer were not exaggerating. Americans had repeatedly identified themselves with a French colonial regime that had denied the Vietnamese an education, a decent living, and a sense of independence and that "insulted a national dignity in countless ways." American officers, Petit reported, insisted on inhabiting the old French colonial mansions that served as constant reminders to the Vietnamese of their past exploitation. "We are Westerners, the out-

1 Petit to Williams, Jan. 13, 1966, Series 48:17, Box 43:1, SPF.
2 Ibid.

106

sider, the alien,'' Williams's friend observed. "To the leftists, we are villains; to the rightists we are fools."[3] Petit's reports were confirmed by Bernard Fall, Stanley Karnow, and a host of other sources.

In brief, in early 1966 the books that Fulbright was reading and the people to whom he was talking convinced him that the war in Vietnam was a civil conflict in two senses. On one level the struggle was between the people of North Vietnam and the inhabitants of South Vietnam. On another it was a battle within South Vietnam between the forces of democracy and pluralism, on the one hand, and the "Saigonese," to use George Kahin's term – the corrupt and dictatorial MRC and their hangers-on – on the other. The opponents of the regime in Saigon, both communist and noncommunist, had seized the banner of nationalism, whereas the generals in charge of the South Vietnamese government and their American sponsors were identified in the popular mind with colonialism. "It is fundamental in the affairs of men," Petit concluded in his report, "that when you see the imminent and inevitable death of an ancient regime, that you go to the funeral, but you are amiable to the heirs and do not sit forever holding hands with the corpse in necrophilial devotion."[4]

Fulbright was not alone in his growing alienation. If they were not as privy to the deteriorating situation in Vietnam as Fulbright, Morse, and Mansfield, a number of Americans had, nonetheless, come out into open opposition to the war by 1966. Traditional pacifists such as A. J. Muste and the organizations they headed, the Fellowship of Reconciliation and the War Resisters League, spoke out against the carnage in South Vietnam because they were against all wars. The taking of human life, no matter what the reason, was immoral. Antinuclear activists who had organized the Committee for a Sane Nuclear Policy (SANE) in the mid-1950s opposed the war in Vietnam because they feared it would lead to a nuclear confrontation between the United States and the communist superpowers. Student activists who, energized by the civil rights movement, formed the Students for a Democratic Society (SDS) in 1962, enlisted in the antiwar movement as part of a larger campaign to alter American society fundamentally. SDS members and their academic mentors formed what came to be known in intellectual circles as the New Left. They espoused the radical critique of American foreign policy that William Appleman Williams had put forward in his famous 1959 book, *The Tragedy of American Diplomacy*. Building on the economic determinist interpretations of Charles Beard and Fred Harrington, Williams and the New Leftists insisted that because it was a capitalist society, America was dominated by financiers and manufacturers who, having subdued the American proletariat and exploited the nation's resources in the nineteenth century, set out to establish their economic hegemony throughout the rest of the world

3 Ibid.
4 Ibid.

in the twentieth. Because politics always follows economics, the government and military were permanently and primarily committed to Wall Street's cause. Liberals of a more moderate stripe, concentrated in one wing of the Americans for Democratic Action (ADA), had become convinced by the end of 1965 that the war in Southeast Asia was a perversion of the liberal internationalism that they had espoused since the end of World War II. In its quest to protect democracy and liberty from communist totalitarianism, the United States was allying itself with brutal military dictatorships and facilitating the murder of thousands of innocent people. Finally, the Quakers and elements within the other major religious denominations began denouncing the war in Vietnam, some because they thought the whole enterprise unjust, some because they deplored the indiscriminate and brutal taking of civilian life, and some because they were appalled at the spectacle of the richest, most powerful nation in the world attempting to bomb into submission a tiny, fifth-rate power situated halfway around the world. In October 1965 the Reverend Richard Neuhaus, Rabbi Abraham Heschel, and Father Daniel Berrigan formed Clergy Concerned about Vietnam.[5]

During a marine search-and-destroy mission in Cam Ne in August 1965 American troops rousted the villagers, suspected of collaborating with the VC, from their huts, which they then set on fire with cigarette lighters. CBS newsman Morley Safer and his camera crew taped the scene, which included anguished, pleading villagers. Despite the outraged protests of the White House, the tapes were shown during the six o'clock news in homes all across America.[6] In October antiwar activists sponsored the International Days of Protest. Nearly a hundred thousand people in eighty cities and several nations participated.[7]

Far more troubling to the president than these public displays, however, was the discomfiture of those "liberals" in Congress who were increasingly uneasy about the bombing and escalation. Following testimony on the Hill, McNamara reported that support in the House and Senate was "broad" but "thin." "There is a feeling of uneasiness and frustration. There is criticism of our allies for not helping more in Vietnam," he reported.[8]

In December, Bundy, Ball, Rusk, and others began to urge Johnson to consider a Christmas bombing halt. What was needed, as presidential aide Jack Valenti put it, was something that would "de-fang the leftists, and comfort the moderates."[9] On Christmas Eve 1965, the constant pounding of NVA positions between the seventeenth and twentieth parallels that had been going

---

5 Charles DeBenedetti with Charles Chatfield, *An American Ordeal: The Antiwar Movement of the Vietnam Era* (Syracuse, 1990), 144.

6 Harriman to Rusk, Aug. 28, 1965, Box 499, Papers of W. Averell Harriman, Library of Congress, Washington, D.C. [hereinafter referred to as Harriman Papers].

7 DeBenedetti and Chatfield, *American Ordeal,* 125.

8 Notes of 554th NSC Meeting, Aug. 5, 1965, NSC Meeting Notes File, Johnson Papers.

9 Valenti to LBJ, Dec. 6, 1965, WHCF, Nat'l. Sec./Def., Box 218, Johnson Papers.

on continuously since May suddenly stopped. Immediately, a small army of diplomats headed by ambassador-at-large Averell Harriman departed for various European and Asian capitals with much-publicized instructions to leave no stone unturned in their search for a negotiated settlement. Before he left, Johnson told Harriman that the object of the trip was to enable the envoy "to testify [before Congress] . . . that he had sent me to go the last mile in trying to come to a settlement."[10]

From the beginning Carl Marcy sensed that the bombing halt was a ploy by the administration to undercut and divide congressional opposition to the war. He felt the country moving inexorably toward massive intervention into Vietnam, and he was desperate to stop the drift. "The present bombing pause and negotiation initiative offer the last clear chance to stop short of unlimited escalation," he warned Fulbright.

The third week in January the SFRC, with some difficulty, persuaded the secretary of state to testify on a supplemental appropriations bill for Vietnam. The bombing pause had been accompanied by the most intense congressional debate on Vietnam to date. When Rusk entered the Foreign Relations hearing room, he found it unusually full. In addition to the regulars – Fulbright, Mansfield, Symington, Hickenlooper, and Aiken – Clifford Case (R–New Jersey), Eugene McCarthy (D–Minnesota), Lausche, Mundt, Williams, Clark, and Claiborne Pell (D–Rhode Island) were on hand as well. He would be frank with the committee, Rusk said. The Soviet Union was willing to accept a Korea-like settlement in Vietnam, to interpret the Geneva conventions in such a way as to allow separate elections below and above the seventeenth parallel. But because of "their contest with Peiping" they had "given their proxy to Hanoi"; thus, the road to a negotiated settlement had reached a dead end. Meanwhile, the North Vietnamese were using the bombing pause to pour men and equipment into the South. The administration's goal was to convince the other side it could not win. If the United States and its allies remained firm, the communists would eventually give up in Vietnam.

Had the administration offered to negotiate with the NLF or the Vietcong, Fulbright asked? No, Rusk replied. Both were creatures of the government of North Vietnam. "Hanoi organized the VC, the NLF, in Hanoi in 1960," he declared, "and immediately started the infiltration of men and arms into South Vietnam." Had not the VC, NLF, and Vietminh originally been part of the same movement, a nationalist movement that, following World War II, had been spurned by the United States and only then had turned to Moscow and Peiping for help, the chairman queried?

Rusk squirmed; his eyes flashed. Frank Lausche tried to run interference. What gallant composure under fire Rusk was showing, the Ohio Democrat

---

10 Harriman to Rusk, Dec. 28, 1965, Box 499, Harriman Papers.

interjected. Upon seeing the secretary's strained, beleaguered face on television (Rusk had appeared on a network news program to discuss Vietnam) the night before, Lausche declared, "I pretty nearly wept." Rusk and Fulbright ignored him.

Fulbright then proceeded to read from testimony given by then CIA Chief John McCone in October 1963 to the effect that the Diem regime was a dictatorship operating under the facade of a democracy, and then from Rusk's statement given a month later assuring the committee that Diem's regime was a constitutional government chosen by the people. The secretary of state, Fulbright seemed to be saying, did not know what he was talking about. "Never criticize a man out of his own mouth," Lyndon Johnson once advised McGeorge Bundy. It was a sure way to make a lifelong enemy. Rusk was furious. His eyes narrowed and his austere face drawn into a hard mask, he murmured to Fulbright that he was sure South Vietnam would choose "something that is not communism" over communism if there were free elections.

"I do want to say that there is one subject on which I am extremely sensitive, and that is the question of credibility and integrity," Rusk declared with all the gravity he could muster. "When I came into this job I made a firm resolution . . . that I would never lie to the press." Silently, Rusk promised himself that he would never again be forthcoming with Fulbright or Marcy.[11] One way to keep from being caught in a lie was not to provide any information.[12]

The clash between Fulbright and Rusk, between the State Department and the SFRC, had been building a long time. In August 1965 Marcy had written an impassioned assessment of American foreign policy for Fulbright. What had happened to "turn the liberal supporters of President Kennedy into opponents of the policies of President Johnson?" The answer was obvious, Marcy declaimed. "We have tried to force upon the rest of the world a righteous American point of view which we maintain is the consensus that others must accept. Most of the tragedies of the world have come from such righteousness."[13] The chief purveyor of American exceptionalism, Marcy believed, was Dean Rusk. No longer the impotent bureaucrat of his earlier imaginings, Rusk had assumed the role of chief villain in the escalation drama. At the close of World War II the United States was thrust into a position of international leadership. Very quickly it defined its mission as

---

11 Interview with Dean Rusk, Oct. 14, 1988, Athens, Ga.

12 Fulbright began by notifying Rusk that the committee had voted not to allow transcripts of closed hearings to leave its offices under any circumstances. The previous fall, following George Ball's testimony on Vietnam in executive session, Rusk had asked for a copy of the transcript. Fulbright had agreed but with an "eyes only" stipulation. In an effort to prove that the committee was deeply divided over Vietnam, State had leaked various senatorial statements to the press.

13 Briefing by Secretary Rusk on His Recent Visits Abroad, Jan. 24, 1966, Executive Sessions, SFRC, RG 46, NA.

saving the world from the scourge of communism. Rusk grew up in, and was part of, that national conversion to a secular religion.[14] Neither Marcy nor Fulbright could ever forget that Rusk's chief backer for the secretary of state's position had been Henry Luce.[15]

In fact, Dean Rusk was both an impotent bureaucrat and a naive missionary. Born on a farm in Cherokee, County Georgia, Rusk moved with his family to Atlanta, where his father had secured a job as a mail carrier. An excellent student, he earned a scholarship to Davidson and subsequently a Rhodes to Oxford. During World War II Rusk served in the China–Burma–India theater and subsequently secured a position in the State Department working under George Marshall, whom he worshipped. During the Eisenhower years, Rusk taught briefly and then became head of the Rockefeller Foundation, the position he abandoned for the secretary of state's job in 1961.[16]

The Georgian was a gracious, self-effacing, driven man: driven to serve his country, to prove himself in battle, whether for George Marshall in Southeast Asia during World War II or for Lyndon Johnson before the klieg lights in the SFRC hearing room. Rusk's intellect was nondiscriminating and much of his intelligence derivative. He absorbed the ideas and assumptions of the authority figures he found himself serving. Thus, his views on foreign policy became fixated during the late 1940s and early 1950s, when international communism was directed from the Kremlin and the domino theory gained currency. His justifications for the Vietnam War sounded anachronistic even to his colleagues in the State Department in the 1960s. But Rusk was no hypocrite – he believed them.

Dean Rusk came to have questions about the war, to doubt the efficacy of bombing, to wonder if there was any chance of winning with the nation only half mobilized; but, incredibly, he did not believe that it was his duty to express those doubts. Kennedy had selected Rusk because the president wanted to control foreign affairs personally. He soon discovered that he only had time to focus on the most pressing issues and most important crises, and he became frustrated with the Georgian. ''I can't get Rusk to take any responsibility,'' the president once complained to Douglas Dillon. ''He sends cables – every paragraph – over here and wants me to sign.'' Dillon recalled that during the Cuban missile crisis the secretary of state sometimes had not attended the meetings of the Executive Committee of the National Security Council, and when he had, he'd rarely spoken.[17] Matters did not change under Johnson. Rusk insisted that it was not his job to give advice to the president

14 Marcy to JWF, Aug. 17, 1965, Series 48:1, Box 16:2, SPF.
15 Donald A. Ritchie, interviewer, *Carl A. Marcy: Oral History Interviews* (Senate Historical Office: Washington, D.C., 1983), 187–8.
16 Dean Rusk as told to Richard Rusk, *As I Saw It* (New York, 1990), 27–32, 93–8, 193–200.
17 Interview with Douglas Dillon, May 5, 1993, New York.

in a cabinet meeting or in front of the NSC; that must be left to one-on-one conversations with his boss. McNamara, for one, doubted that Dean Rusk ever gave Lyndon Johnson any advice, even when they were alone.[18]

Rusk's January 24 testimony before the SFRC seemed to Fulbright to demonstrate beyond a shadow of a doubt that the administration was locked into its blind anticommunist assumptions and that it would not meet the minimum conditions for beginning negotiations, namely, recognition of the NLF.[19] Fulbright hoped against hope that Johnson would continue the pause, but in his heart, he knew that Carl Marcy was right: The president and his men had already set their course. Before Rusk left the Hill, Fulbright asked that at the very least the committee be consulted before a decision on resumption was taken.

Lyndon Johnson was eager to resume bombing North Vietnam as soon as the New Year began, and he only became more anxious and determined as time wore on. When the Joint Chiefs were able to produce statistics showing a dramatic increase in infiltration, McNamara pointed out that it was the dry season and this was to be expected. The CIA continued to insist that bombing had had no impact on the North's willingness or ability to infiltrate and that the assault from the air would continue to be ineffective.[20] They argued in vain. From Saigon, Cabot Lodge, under intense pressure from Westmoreland, railed against the pause. On Christmas Day alone, he reported to Johnson, "1,000 North Vietnamese soldiers were reliably observed entering South Vietnam."[21] "Every day increases their capability in the South," Earle Wheeler insisted to Johnson, and he called for a full-scale air assault on Hanoi.[22]

By January 20 Johnson had made the decision to resume bombing. He could not bear the thought that he was letting America's fighting men down. The president's friend, Jack Valenti, the Houston public relations expert and campaign aide whom Johnson had brought to the White House with him, advised Johnson to resist Fulbright, Lippmann, and the other "Lyndliners."[23] Former Governor John Connally bombarded Johnson with hawkish advice throughout the pause. He told the president to remember that there

18 Rusk, *As I Saw It,* 16; and interview with Robert McNamara, Aug. 2, 1991, Washington, D.C.

19 "Continue Bombing Lull, Fulbright Urges U.S.," *Washington Star,* Jan. 24, 1966.

20 Meeting between President, Rusk, Bundy, McNamara, Ball, Moyers, Valenti, Jan. 3, 1966, and Meeting between President, Rusk, Helms, McNamara, Harriman, Taylor, Ball, Raborn, Thompson, Goldberg, Bundy, and Valenti, Jan. 22, 1966, NSF, Meeting Notes File, Box 1, Johnson Papers.

21 Lodge to LBJ, Jan. 5, 1966, NSF, Memos to President, Box 6, Johnson Papers.

22 Cabinet Meeting, Jan. 10, 1966, Meeting Notes File, Box 2, Johnson Papers.

23 Historian and peace activist Staughton Lynd had gone to Hanoi in early January to try to start negotiations himself. As the administration well knew, he was in touch with Fulbright during and after his trip. Marcy to JWF, Jan. 17, 1966, Box 6, Folder Jan., Marcy Papers.

were only two hundred thousand boys in Vietnam and they had only four hundred thousand parents. Their one advocate was Lyndon Johnson.

Although he had been wounded by his confrontation with Fulbright on the twenty-fourth, Dean Rusk persuaded Johnson to meet with the chairman. "The committee would have no serious problem if you see Fulbright," he advised.[24] The president agreed, but only on condition that the Arkansan be bracketed by hawks. On the evening of the twenty-fifth Johnson met with the entire congressional leadership. Dirksen, Russell, McCormack, Hickenlooper, Carl Albert, and others urged the president to resume and even expand the bombing; only Mansfield and Fulbright spoke out for a continuation of the pause.[25]

On January 31, 1966, American fighters and fighter-bombers took off once again and struck bridges and staging areas north of the seventeenth parallel. Resumption would, Johnson hoped, compel the North Vietnamese to "show their ass before we showed ours."[26]

With Lyndon Johnson's decision to resume the bombing of North Vietnam, J. William Fulbright's pent-up anger and frustration burst forth. On the evening the bombing resumed, he appeared on a CBS national television hookup to declare the war morally wrong and counterproductive to the interests of his country. The world's largest, richest, most powerful nation had no business, he told Martin Agronsky and Eric Sevareid, laying waste to a small, desperately impoverished, weak, and divided state like Vietnam. No matter how the conflict ended, the United States had lost stature by participating in a struggle beneath its dignity and even its notice. The administration, the chairman of the SFRC declared, was still a prisoner of the Munich analogy, a comparison that was totally inapplicable to Southeast Asia. As visualized by its architects, containment was designed to prevent the spread of Soviet aggression. As it had evolved under Johnson, it was an attempt to contain a worldwide movement toward self-government and self-expression by peoples formerly yoked to European empires. This misreading of reality and a failure to distinguish between "big C" communist revolutions and "little c" communist revolutions lay at the very heart of the Vietnam misadventure. He ended by expressing deep regret at the role he had played in ushering the Gulf of Tonkin Resolution through the Senate.[27]

---

24 Meeting of Foreign Policy Advisors, Jan. 24, 1966, Meeting Notes File, Box 1, Johnson Papers. A number of senators had spoken to him privately, Rusk said, complaining about the fact that the chairman of the SFRC was not included in White House meetings with the congressional leadership. Rusk to Johnson, Jan. 24, 1966, NSF–NSC History, Box 44, Johnson Papers.

25 Bipartisan Congressional Meeting, Jan. 25, 1966, Meeting Notes File, Box 1, Johnson Papers.

26 Meeting with Foreign Policy Advisors on Vietnam, Jan. 20, 1966, Meeting Notes File, Box 1, Johnson Papers.

27 William C. Berman, *William Fulbright and the Vietnam War: The Dissent of a Political Realist* (Kent, Ohio, 1988), 55.

With the end of the Christmas bombing halt, Fulbright and Marcy proceeded with plans to hold public hearings on the war in Southeast Asia. It was now more than ever necessary to generate a congressional and public debate over Vietnam, to start a controversy over a very controversial subject, they believed. Fulbright had learned, to his deep dismay, during the Dominican crisis that an articulate, thoughtful, and provocative speech was not sufficient to arouse the nation. That tactic had left him isolated, "dangling in the wind," to anticipate a phrase. Public hearings with establishment figures in which he and other doubters questioned both the assumptions underlying the war in Vietnam and the tactics being employed to fight it might just do the trick – especially if they were televised. On February 3 the SFRC met in executive session; Fulbright, Gore, Morse, and Aiken persuaded the others to authorize hearings not just on the pending $415 million supplemental aid bill for Vietnam but on the war in its broadest sense. The hearings were to be public, and Carl Marcy was directed to obtain the widest possible exposure.

By early 1966 a majority of the SFRC were either deeply disturbed by U.S. involvement in Southeast Asia or overtly opposed. Those who had previously been willing to give the administration the benefit of the doubt had run out of patience. A number, including John Sparkman (D–Alabama), had lost confidence in the administration because of its overly optimistic and consistently wrong predictions in the past – we are winning in Vietnam, light at the end of the tunnel–type statements. Moreover, several members feared that Vietnam had brought the United States and China to the brink of a major war. A consensus existed on the SFRC that John Stennis, second-ranking member of Armed Services, was plugged into the decision-making process in the White House. The Mississippi hawk had correctly and accurately predicted the troop buildup that took place in the fall of 1965. On January 27, 1966, he stated in a speech to the Mississippi legislature that by the end of the year there would be six hundred thousand men in Vietnam and that if the United States went to war with China, he favored the use of tactical nuclear weapons. Fulbright and the majority of SFRC members believed that Stennis was accurately foretelling the future, and they were frightened. The only dissenters from what one staffer referred to as "the Fulbright majority" were Lausche, Dodd, Symington, and Hickenlooper.[28]

Fulbright and Marcy were realistic about what precisely the televised hearings could accomplish. To listen to the "armed services boys," the chairman wrote Marriner Eccles, it would seem that "although we ought to get out, it is actually impossible, and it even discredits one to suggest that we do so."

28 Hearings on S. Res. 217, Authorizing and Directing the Committee on Foreign Relations to Conduct a Full and Complete Investigation of All Aspects of United States Policies in Vietnam, Executive Sessions, Feb. 3, 1965, SFRC, RG 46, NA; and Henry H. Wilson to LBJ, Feb. 18, 1966, WHCF, Subject File, Box 342, Johnson Papers.

Given this mind-set, "the most favorable thing the hearings can possibly accomplish is to prevent the enormous escalation of this war."[29]

As soon as the SFRC decided on public hearings and the meeting broke up, Marcy got on the phone with executives from the major television networks. He described the scope of the hearings and ticked off the impressive list of witnesses scheduled to appear.[30] On January 28 Dean Rusk had testified in public session on the supplemental appropriations bill. He and Fulbright had taken up where they had left off on the twenty-fourth. Both the CBS and NBC nightly news had carried clips of the clashes between the two Rhodes scholars. The networks realized that this was the stuff of real-life television drama.[31] Thus, when Marcy called with news of the wider hearings and list of witnesses, CBS and NBC ordered their crews to be prepared to occupy the Hill.

Mike Mansfield, as he would do throughout the remainder of the Johnson administration, immediately briefed the White House as to what was afoot. In turn, Johnson ordered his aides to spare no effort to sabotage the "Fulbright hearings." When Fulbright requested permission from the Senate as a whole to hold hearings during the regular session of the Senate, Senate Minority Leader Everett Dirksen, at Johnson's behest, blocked him.[32] Fulbright and Marcy forced Dirksen to back down by threatening to hold the Vietnam inquiry in the evenings, during prime time.[33] Then, on the night of February 3, without telling any of his aides, Johnson decided to hold an impromptu summit meeting with South Vietnamese Prime Minister Nguyen Cao Ky in Honolulu. The meeting would take place during Fulbright's show.

The Honolulu conference was, to use McGeorge Bundy's description, "a big farrago, meant to take the spotlight off the hearings."[34] The first Bundy or any of Johnson's other aides heard of the trip was when the president announced it at a press conference on Friday the fourth.[35] The meeting opened with neither adequate preparation nor even a precise agenda. Johnson used the occasion to give a pep talk and to exhort the American and Vietnamese military to renew their efforts. He wanted "coonskins on the wall," he told them. When Ky finished his speech, an optimistic set piece that promised not only victory but a new era of political stability, Johnson leaned over and whispered to him, "Boy, you talk just like an American." And no won-

29 JWF to Marriner Eccles, Mar. 1, 1966, Series 48:18, Box 47:7, SPF.
30 Donald A. Ritchie, interviewer, *Pat M. Holt: Oral History Interviews* (Senate Historical Office: Washington, D.C., 1980), 204.
31 Melvin Small, *Johnson, Nixon, and the Doves* (New Brunswick, N.J., 1988), 78.
32 "Senate Nears Vietnam Inquiry," *Los Angeles Times,* Feb. 3, 1966.
33 Godfrey Sperling, Jr., "Backstage at Senate's Great Debate," *Christian Science Monitor,* Feb. 14, 1966.
34 Interview with McGeorge Bundy, Aug. 1, 1991, New York.
35 Note (anonymous), 1966, NSF, NSC History, Box 44, Johnson Papers.

der: Ky's speech had been prepared by the American embassy. Johnson could not leave Honolulu without a blast at Fulbright, Morse, and his congressional detractors. He warned America that the war effort was being hampered by "special pleaders who counsel retreat in Vietnam."[36]

Fulbright and Marcy had intended to mix administration figures with prominent dissidents during the open hearings, but the administration had no intention of cooperating. To Fulbright's chagrin, Johnson took both Maxwell Taylor and Alexis Johnson, then deputy undersecretary of state, with him to Hawaii.[37] Both McNamara and Rusk refused to appear in open hearing. Not all were able to escape, however. On the morning of the fourth, with Lyndon Johnson watching on television, David Bell testified before the SFRC on the aid program in Vietnam and was subjected to withering cross-examination.

At stake in the 1966 SFRC hearings was control of the television airways and, through them, American public opinion. Fulbright and Marcy had become acutely aware of the executive's ability to dominate the media and especially television. Since the time of Franklin D. Roosevelt, powerful presidential personalities had co-opted and manipulated print and broadcast newspeople. The White House was easier and simpler to cover, and the president's press secretaries ensured that reporters were furnished with an abundance of interesting stories and photo opportunities. Most shared the executive's contempt for Congress, a complex, perverse place very difficult to squeeze into a thirty-second sound bite. One who was different was Fred Friendly, head of CBS news and protégé of Edward R. Murrow. Throughout his career, Friendly had been pressing television to devote more space and money to news, particularly to live coverage. The Fulbright hearings offered him his opportunity. After persuading his superiors to agree to thirty-minute coverage for the Fulbright hearings, Friendly took personal charge and kept the hearings on throughout the morning and into the afternoon. Captain Kangaroo and various soap operas were preempted, and Friendly's superiors were furious.[38]

When the committee met again in public session and on television, it heard testimony from General James Gavin, who presented the case for the enclave strategy that Fulbright and Lippmann had earlier advocated and that the Johnson administration had already discarded. Fulbright was able to persuade Korean War hero Matthew Ridgway to submit a letter to the committee endorsing this approach. On February 11, Fulbright and Marcy pulled out their big gun – George Kennan. No individual in or out of government had more prestige as a foreign policy analyst. As the father of containment policy, he was hardly subject to the criticism that he was soft on communism; at the

36 Bryce Nelson, "Fulbright Sees Active Congress Role in Vietnam," *Washington Post,* Feb. 8, 1966.
37 JWF to John B. Oakes, Feb. 5, 1966, Series 438:18, Box 49:4, SPF.
38 David Halberstam, *The Powers That Be* (New York, 1979), 504.

same time, he had endeared himself to cold war liberals by his calls for a defense policy that matched means with ends, his attacks on massive retaliation and brinkmanship, and his advocacy of patience in dealing with the Soviets. A distinguished scholar, the former ambassador to Yugoslavia and the Soviet Union was a model of decorum, precisely the establishment figure Fulbright needed to question Johnson's policy. Kennan agreed with Gavin that it was essential to avoid further escalation, and he urged also that the war be liquidated "as soon as this could be done without inordinate damage to our prestige or stability in the area." If the United States sought to resolve the problem of Vietnam by winning a clear-cut military victory over Ho and DRV cofounder General Vo Nguyen Giap, there was every chance that full-scale war with China would ensue.[39]

Like the Kefauver crime investigations of 1951 and the army–McCarthy encounters of 1954, the Vietnam hearings impinged on the lives of virtually all Americans. If they did not watch directly, they saw excerpts on the six o'clock and ten o'clock news. Fulbright, the questioner, and Gavin, Kennan, and the other witnesses were not irresponsible students or wild-eyed radicals but conservative, establishment figures. Maybe, some Americans began to think, Vietnam was not analogous to World War II or Korea. Even more began to suspect that the country had become involved in a situation that it did not truly understand.

Worried by the attention the hearings were receiving, Lyndon Johnson called Frank Stanton of CBS and demanded that he cease coverage. On February 10, the network abandoned the hearings and ran its normal daytime fare, including reruns of the *I Love Lucy* show. Only after respected news director Fred W. Friendly resigned over the incident did CBS resume coverage. NBC carried the entire proceeding, however, including Kennan's telling testimony.[40]

With each day the hearings continued, Johnson became more and more distraught. His public relations people were maddeningly candid. Do not worry about the effect that the hearings were having on Beijing and Hanoi, presidential adviser George Reedy told him, worry about their impact on the American people. Fulbright's show, he said, was deeply divisive; it was doing nothing less than polarizing the electorate. "At the present time, the debate is being conducted in the tone of a 'hawks' and 'doves' clash with the 'hawks' convinced that anyone outside of their ranks is a 'chicken' and the 'doves' convinced that anyone outside of their ranks is a 'vulture.' " Moreover, whenever the doves held center stage, the administration came off as hawkish, and when the hawks grabbed the microphone, it was made to appear dovish. The end result was a divided country and the appearance of a vac-

---

39 "Fulbright Fears U.S. Eliminating Chance for Peace," *Arkansas Gazette,* Feb. 11, 1966.
40 "Hearings Coverage Draw Heavy Fire," *Washington Star,* Apr. 4, 1966; and Small, *Johnson, Nixon, and the Doves,* 78.

illating government.[41] "Dick Goodwin called yesterday to say that every-
where he speaks, he runs into deep concern about the situation in Vietnam,"
Joseph Califano told the president on February 19. "He said he is personally
and firmly convinced that you are pursuing the correct course, but that the
Fulbright hearings particularly are doing a tremendous amount to confuse the
American people."[42]

At this point Dirksen, Symington, Russell Long, and Hickenlooper intervened with Johnson and persuaded him to allow Maxwell Taylor and Dean
Rusk to appear.[43] With "hostile" witnesses on the stand, Fulbright abandoned the sympathetic, solicitous manner he had used with Gavin and Kennan and adopted the prosecutorial style for which he was becoming famous.
For the first time the public was treated to images of the chairman, leaning
forward intently toward the witnesses, his eyes shielded by dark glasses from
the glare of the powerful television lights, questioning, probing, confronting
witnesses with history and logic. It was standing room only in the klieg-lit
hearing room as Taylor, bespectacled and civilian suited, took his seat. Conspicuously occupying a front-row chair was Mrs. Ethel Kennedy, Robert's
wife; the senator stood in the back of the room. (So fond of Taylor were the
Kennedys that they had named their one-year-old son after the general.) Was
not the American Revolution a "war of national liberation?" Fulbright asked
Maxwell Taylor. Wasn't it true that politically there was no such thing as
South Vietnam? Taylor, who had been carefully coached by Stuart Symington, could only defend administration policy as "the best that has been suggested."[44] Fulbright then read a letter from an "anonymous but articulate"
observer in Southeast Asia who declared that the United States was losing
the war. The countryside was insecure, the Army of the Republic of Vietnam
was well meaning but ineffectual, and the threat of terrorism ever present.
The author, of course, was Clyde Petit.[45] The hearings climaxed when Rusk
appeared on February 18. In what constituted a summation of the proceedings, the secretary of state articulated the case for continuation of the war in
Vietnam and Fulbright the case against:

> FULBRIGHT: I think there is something wrong with our approach. There
> must be something wrong with our diplomacy.

41 Reedy to LBJ, Feb. 17, 1966, WHCF, Nat'l Sec./Def., Box 219, Johnson Papers.
42 Califano to LBJ, Feb. 19, 1966, Box 219, WHCF, Nat'l Sec./Def., Johnson Papers.
43 Mike Manatos to LBJ, Feb. 16, 1966, WHCF, Subject File, Box 342, Johnson Papers. During
    the hearings, presidential aides were in constant contact with their friends on the committee,
    especially Dodd and Lausche, supplying them with questions and giving them encourage-
    ment. Manatos to LBJ, Feb. 17, 1966, Box 342, WHCF, Subject File, Johnson Papers.
44 "New Kind of War for Gen. Taylor," *New York Herald Tribune*, Feb. 18, 1966; and Mike
    Manatos to LBJ, Feb. 16, 1966, WHCF, Subject File, Box 342, Johnson Papers.
45 Ned Curran, "Fulbright Reveals Note from Vietnam Saying U.S. Losing," *Arkansas Gazette*,
    Feb. 19, 1966.

RUSK: Senator, is it just possible that there is something wrong with them [the North Vietnamese and NLF]?

FULBRIGHT: Yes. There is a lot wrong with them. They are very primitive, difficult, poor people who have been fighting for twenty years and I don't understand myself why they can continue to fight, but they can.

RUSK: And they want to take over South Vietnam by force.

FULBRIGHT: It is said the liberation front would like to take it over by election.[46]

So threatened did the president feel by the hearings that on February 19 he called J. Edgar Hoover and ordered him to have the FBI "cover Senate Foreign Relations Committee television presentation with a view toward determining whether Senator Fulbright and the other Senators were receiving information from Communists." The bureau obliged by drawing "parallels" between presentations made at the hearings and "documented Communist Party publications or statements of Communist leaders."[47] Shortly after the hearings ended, Johnson had Fulbright and several other Senate doves placed under strict FBI surveillance.[48] Perhaps the president hoped Hoover would expose some link between his critics and the international communist conspiracy. More likely, he anticipated that the director would be able to uncover an illicit love affair, a financial wrongdoing, or some other personal peccadillo that could be used to silence his tormentors. At the same time, the White House ordered the research division in State to ferret out Fulbright's public statements during the period when mainland China was being overrun by Mao. Johnson may have feared a revival of McCarthyism, but he was not above appropriating Tail Gunner Joe's techniques.[49] "The criticism from the Executive is becoming bitter and mean," Fulbright complained to a constituent.[50]

Unbeknownst to Fulbright, Johnson ordered J. Edgar Hoover to provide Everett Dirksen and Bourke Hickenlooper with "evidence" that the chairman of the SFRC was either a communist agent or a dupe of the communists. Given the frequent contacts between Fulbright and his staff and personnel from the Soviet and East European embassies, this was not difficult. The first week in March the director's assistant, C. D. DeLoach, visited the two Republicans. He indicated that he was coming at the president's specific request and asked that their conversations be held in the strictest confidence. Both were more than ready to believe that the Arkansan was "deeply involved and very much obligated to communist interests," as DeLoach subsequently

---

46 Quoted in Haynes Johnson and Bernard M. Gwertzman, *Fulbright: The Dissenter* (New York, 1968), 281.

47 Athan G. Theoharris, *From the Secret Files of J. Edgar Hoover* (Chicago, 1991), 237.

48 Berman, *Fulbright and the Vietnam War,* 68.

49 Marcy to JWF, Feb. 22, 1966, Box 6, Folder Feb. 66, JWF Papers, SFRC, RG 46, NA.

50 JWF to M. S. Craig, Feb. 11, 1966, Series 48:18, Box 47:5, SPF.

reported. According to the bureau, Hickenlooper observed that Fulbright's willingness to betray the interests of his country stemmed from his resentment at not being named secretary of state. Both promised to do everything in their power to counteract his baleful influence.[51]

It should be pointed out that Fulbright was not calling for unconditional withdrawal from Vietnam. What he advocated in early 1966 was an end to the bombing of the North, the withdrawal of American troops to enclaves around South Vietnam's major cities, the reconvening of the 1954 Geneva Conference looking toward national elections in Vietnam, and following a negotiated political settlement, the removal from Vietnam of all foreign troops. The Johnson administration was adamantly opposed to this strategy because it was certain that it would lead to the electoral triumph of Ho Chi Minh and the communization of all of Vietnam. That development, in turn, would represent a clear victory for the forces of international communism and tip the scales in favor of Moscow and Beijing. "I regard the analogy between the Cuban missile crisis and the Viet Nam war as legitimate," Walt Rostow, then head of the policy planning staff in the State Department, wrote Averell Harriman. "Both are conscious and purposeful Communist efforts to shift the balance of power against us at a decisive point."[52]

Fulbright was still unsure of Johnson's motives, of the sources of his erroneous policy in Southeast Asia. It was probably a combination of things, he guessed. In his obsession with consensus, the president was too ready to collaborate with the Goldwaterites. In his ignorance, he was too willing to rely on advisers who had a vested intellectual and bureaucratic stake in victory in Vietnam. In his altruism, he overestimated America's ability to save the world. Indeed, it was this latter tendency to see himself as "a combination of Santa Claus and God whose personal destiny it is to insure life, liberty, happiness, wealth, health, education, etc., not only for every person in the U.S. but to all the world" that was at the root of the problem[53] – which made it hard for Fulbright to harden his heart completely against his old Senate colleague. Young men were dying, however, and a foreign culture teetered on the brink of destruction because of Lyndon Johnson's tragic flaws.

Public and press reactions to the 1966 hearings were mixed. The national print media split, with critics headed by the *Washington Post* – intensely pro-Johnson since Ben Bradlee's transfer from *Newsweek* – and supporters spearheaded by the *New York Times*. For the most part, television news just reported; what editorial comment there was tended to be pro-Fulbright. Roger

---

51 DeLoach interview with Everett Dirksen, Mar. 7, 1966, and DeLoach interview with Bourke Hickenlooper, Mar. 8, 1966, "Hoover's Official and Confidential File," FBI Files.

52 W. Rostow to Harriman, Jan. 28, 1966, Box 499, Harriman Papers.

53 JWF to Jim Ballard, Series 48:18, Box 47:2, SPF.

Mudd, for example, praised the Arkansan for being able "to shed his American clothes and look at a situation objectively." His "disinterest" was good for the country, and it was in the national interest that "he continues to be elected."[54] Of 1,207 letters sent to the State Department, 1,028 were counted as approving Rusk's presentation. But the White House was soon chastising the State and Defense departments for exaggerating or distorting the contents of opinion mail. Of the 924 "pro" letters the DOD claimed it received from January 1 through February 14, 1966, only 30 were deemed reliable enough in the end to turn over to newspeople.[55] Marcy and the SFRC staff claimed that the committee's mail ran 30 to 1 against escalation in the wake of the hearings.

The hearings created almost as much attention abroad as they did at home. On February 14 the British Broadcasting Company (BBC) ran Kennan's testimony and Fulbright's cross-examination almost verbatim. Various members of the ruling Labour Party went on talk shows to voice their agreement with the doubts that had been expressed.[56]

At first glance, Fulbright and Marcy's media event seemed not to have had a significant impact on public opinion.[57] A Louis Harris poll taken a few days afterward revealed that only thirty-seven percent of those queried had heard about the committee's hearings, and a majority of those were college educated. Of people with opinions, fifty-five percent believed that the hearings had been helpful, whereas forty-five percent thought otherwise.[58] The vast majority of representatives and senators continued to support the war in Vietnam publicly, although to Johnson and Russell's enragement, a \$4.8 billion Vietnam appropriations bill stalled in the Senate for two weeks while thirty-five senators made speeches attacking the war or the tactics being used to fight it.[59] Antiwar activists certainly expected more; most agreed with George Ball, who found the hearings "disappointingly docile."[60] Jack Valenti assured his boss that the administration had sustained only minor damage, and John Connally told the president that the hearings did not change anyone's mind and that the "concerned people" with whom he had talked "are not questioning U.S. foreign policy."[61]

Valenti and Connally, two of Johnson's most hawkish advisers, were just telling him what they wanted him to hear. The fact that many people reacted negatively to the hearings did not mean that they did not adversely affect their attitude toward the president and his handling of the war. George Reedy

54 PW to JWF, 1966, Series 48:17, Box 43:3, SPF.
55 Larry Levinson to Joe Califano, Feb. 12, 1966, WHCF, Box 134, Johnson Papers.
56 Hilary A. Marquand to JWF, Feb. 15, 1966, Series 48:18, Box 49:3, SPF.
57 Small, *Johnson, Nixon, and the Doves,* 79.
58 Berman, *Fulbright and the Vietnam War,* 60–1.
59 "Fulbright Wants to Zero in on Humphrey," *New York Herald Tribune,* Feb. 17, 1966.
60 Marvin Watson to LBJ, Feb. 21, 1966, Meeting Notes File, Box 2, Johnson Papers.
61 Ibid.

was right: The administration was getting hit from both sides – and Lyndon Johnson knew it. In late February, Bill Moyers reported to the president that the approval rating for his handling of the war had in one month – from January 26 to February 26 – dropped from sixty-three percent to forty-nine percent.[62] "Never have I known Washington to be so full of dissonant voices as it is today," Moyers wrote to Theodore H. White.[63]

More important, perhaps, Kennan's and Gavin's testimonies and Fulbright's cross-examination made it respectable to question, if not oppose, the war. On February 26 Robert Komer, McGeorge Bundy's top aide, reported to Johnson that the New York business community was getting cold feet. If, as they suspected, the administration was going to spend $10 billion and then get out of Vietnam following the 1966 congressional elections, then it ought to get out at once.[64]

The February hearings, in short, opened a psychological door for the great American middle class. It was Fulbright's ability to relate to this group as well as his capacity for building bridges to conservative opponents of the war – figures like Russell, Sparkman, and Symington – rather than his being a symbol of, and a catalyst for, the political left that would make him important to the antiwar movement. As Lyndon Johnson correctly noted, the hawks were and would continue to constitute a majority in the country. It would be Fulbright rather than A. J. Muste, Staughton Lynd, or Tom Hayden who could speak to them. If the administration intended to wage the war in Vietnam from the political center in America, the 1966 hearings were indeed a blow to that effort.

Johnson could not help but note that Robert Kennedy took pains to associate himself with the SFRC and the hearings. Appealing as he always did to the president's worst instincts, John Connally told him that Bobby was "the motivating force behind the Senate hearings."[65] Fresh from a visit to the University of Chicago, George Reedy reported: "The students, though polite, are quite frank in their preference for President Kennedy [in comparison]. They state that somehow you do not 'come across' to them and that even though they like your domestic programs, they have some deep reservations."[66] As Tom Mann observed, if one did not understand the mutual hatred between the Kennedys and Johnson, one could not understand anything about the 1960s. By sticking in and saving Vietnam, Lyndon Johnson believed he could win a victory over the ghost of his assassinated predecessor. During the Bay of Pigs invasion, Kennedy's enemies charged, the president had lost his nerve, leaving Castroism free to infect the hemisphere. Just

62 Meeting in Cabinet Room, Feb. 26, 1966, Meeting Notes File, Box 2, Johnson Papers.
63 Moyers to White, Mar. 7, 1966, Box 219, WHCF, Nat'l Sec./Def., Johnson Papers.
64 Meeting in Cabinet Room, Feb. 26, 1966, Meeting Notes File, Box 2, Johnson Papers.
65 Marvin Watson to LBJ, Feb. 21, 1966, WHCF, Box 342, Johnson Papers.
66 Reedy to LBJ, Jan. 27, 1966, WHCF, Nat'l. Sec./Def., Box 219, Johnson Papers.

as Truman had in Korea, Johnson would hold the line in Vietnam. History would view the Texan as the man who had not only passed Kennedy's legislative program but fulfilled the nation's commitment to contain Sino–Soviet imperialism. Now here were the ex-president's brother and Fulbright joining forces to attack him for pursuing a policy that they had once fully supported. In May, Johnson joked bitterly at a public meeting, "You can say one thing about those hearings, but I don't think this is the place to say it."[67] Johnson invited J. Edgar Hoover and the national commander of the American Legion to the White House and instructed them to coordinate a letter-writing campaign to demonstrate to Fulbright that the nation was solidly behind the war in Vietnam.[68] "Those hearings were a declaration of war," McGeorge Bundy recalled, "and were so taken by the White House."[69]

67 Quoted in Small, *Johnson, Nixon, and the Doves,* 80.
68 Hoover to Tolson, Mar. 3, 1966, "Hoover's Official and Confidential File," FBI Files.
69 McG. Bundy interview.

9

The Politics of Dissent

The third week in March 1966 Fulbright traveled to Storrs, Connecticut, to deliver the Brien McMahon lecture. He was glad for the opportunity to honor his late friend and colleague. It was an appropriate occasion, Fulbright decided, to attempt to start a searching national self-examination. He told his audience:

> There are two Americas. One is the America of Lincoln and Adlai Stevenson; the other is the America of Teddy Roosevelt and General MacArthur. One is generous and humane, the other narrowly egotistical, one is modest and self-critical, the other arrogant and self-righteous; one is sensible, the other romantic; one is good-humored, the other solemn; one is inquiring, the other pontificating; one is moderate and restrained, the other filled with passionate intensity.[1]

After thirty years as a superpower, America stood at a crossroads, he told the students and faculty. The United States would have to decide which of the two sides of its character would prevail – "the humanism of Lincoln or the aggressive moralism of Theodore Roosevelt." He was, he said, afraid that America's better half was in eclipse. The nation's aggressive, militaristic spirit had in part been responsible for the Vietnam War, and that conflict was in turn reinforcing the dark side of the American character. The war would destroy Lyndon Johnson's vision of a better America just as surely as it would destroy Vietnam. "The President simply cannot think about implementing the Great Society at home while he is supervising bombing missions over North Vietnam," Fulbright insisted. Not only was the war consuming the nation's generous, humanitarian instincts; it was eating up the resources necessary to give substance to those instincts.

The fundamental dualism in the American character was reflected in the two dominant strains in postwar American foreign policy: opposition to communism and support for nationalism, Fulbright continued. "The tragedy of Vietnam is that a revolution against social injustice and foreign rule has

---

1 *Congressional Record*, Senate, Mar. 25, 1966, 6749.

become a contest between Asian communism and the United States," he said. Had it not been for Western colonialism and the unwillingness of the Great Powers to decolonize wisely, the oppressed of Asia would never have turned to communism. He then uttered the ultimate heresy: "American interests are better served by supporting nationalism than by opposing communism, and . . . when the two are encountered in the same country, it is in our interest to accept a Communist government rather than undertake the cruel and all but impossible task of suppressing a genuinely national movement."[2]

While the televised hearings and Fulbright's call for America to accept and even support communism under some circumstances unsettled some Americans, it infuriated others. In March 1966 a Missouri chapter of the Minutemen, a right-wing terrorist organization, developed plans to assassinate the chairman of the SFRC. After his arrest by the FBI, Jerry Milton Brooks testified in Kansas City that his orders to shoot Fulbright were called off at the very last minute. The assassination, he said, was part of a plan to intimidate certain members of Congress into "voting American."[3]

The McMahon Lecture was to be the first installment of a national speakng tour that Fulbright and Marcy planned for the spring of 1966. The SFRC had entered the fray, Marcy observed to Fulbright, and was actively competing with the president for the attention of the nation. They were under no illusion as to how easy their task would be; the White House would counterattack with an unprecedented propaganda blitz, a campaign as ferocious in its way as the aerial bombardment being visited on the Vietnamese. There was no way the SFRC could co-opt the mass media and reach the number of people that the executive could on a day-to-day basis, Marcy warned. "He can command radio, TV, the press, and he has his own publications." Speeches by the chairman and individual members would not suffice. Although such a course would be "politically dangerous," the chief of staff favored holding additional hearings on Vietnam, in order, he said, to control the public spotlight and to "keep the Committee in the midst of the crucial decisions relating to war and peace."[4] But Fulbright said no; it was too soon; people would tire of the subject and tune him and the committee out. It would be better to concentrate his efforts during the next few months on persuading and galvanizing the opinion-making elite.

During the last part of April and the first part of May, Fulbright delivered the Christian A. Herter Lectures at Johns Hopkins University. In late April he traveled to New York to address the Associated Press and the American Newspaper Publishers Association. In his speeches, he repeated earlier themes: that erroneous assumptions underlay America's Vietnam policy, that the United States must adopt a realistic policy toward China, and that the

2 Ibid., 6749–53.
3 "Talk of Killing Fulbright Laid to Minutemen," *Arkansas Gazette,* Apr. 8, 1966.
4 Marcy to JWF, Mar. 23, 1966, Series 48:3, Box 16:3, JPF.

war in Vietnam must be ended through negotiation. Throughout the tour, Fulbright worked under intense pressure – externally and internally. There was the smear campaign directed by the White House and snubs by the president. While addressing a congressional dinner in Washington in mid-May, Johnson looked directly at Fulbright and said, "I am delighted to be here tonight with so many of my very old friends as well as some members of the Foreign Relations Committee."[5] Not even Wayne Morse had been so singled out by Johnson. A visible shiver went through the crowd. The president, whose control over federal largesse could make or break senators and representatives, was labeling the Arkansan a pariah. Fulbright quickly came to realize that not only Johnson but the American people as well were angry with him – angry with him because he was telling them the truth and, in fact, foretelling their future.

In response to the pressure, Fulbright's speeches and public statements in March and April became more strident. His country was succumbing to "that arrogance of power which has afflicted, weakened and in some cases destroyed great nations in the past," and it must be saved from the error of its ways.[6] Three weeks later he told a group of reporters that America was killing what it would save in South Vietnam. If the United States did not stop, its AID programs, its money, and its massive military presence would destroy traditional Vietnamese society. Saigon, in fact, was well on its way to becoming "an American brothel" with thousands of Vietnamese, seduced by the almighty dollar, putting their wives and daughters to work as bargirls.[7] During one of his talks in New York he likened the United States in its "current imperial mode" to Nazi Germany.[8] Those who were openly protesting the war deserved the country's sympathy and respect, the Arkansan proclaimed, although he urged youthful demonstrators to abjure "direct dissent" like draft card burning. He quoted Albert Camus's "Letters to a German Friend": "This is what separated us from you: we made demands. You were satisfied to serve the power of your nation and we dreamed of giving ours her truth."[9]

More significant, in the wake of the 1966 hearings Fulbright abandoned his longtime advocacy of executive predominance in foreign policy. Since he had been first elected to Congress, the Arkansan had urged the nation to accept the need for an active presidency with maximum freedom to conduct diplomacy and contain communism through armed strength and foreign aid. His principal criticism of the Eisenhower administration had been that it was

---

5 Quoted in William C. Berman, *William Fulbright and the Vietnam War: The Dissent of a Political Realist* (Kent, Ohio, 1988), 67.
6 "Fulbright Mail Runs 30 to 1 for War Stand," *Arkansas Gazette,* Feb. 12, 1966.
7 "Fulbright Calls Saigon 'An American Brothel,' " *Saigon Post,* May 9, 1966.
8 "Views on Viet Nam Policy," *Rochester Times-Union,* Apr. 30, 1966.
9 "Fulbright Calls Saigon 'An American Brothel.' "

too passive. But over the years in response to crisis after crisis, the balance had shifted too far. He decried the transformation in his first Herter Lecture:

> Congress, inspired by patriotism, importuned by Presidents, and deterred by lack of information, has tended to fall in line behind the Executive. The result has been the unhinging of traditional constitutional relationships; the Senate's constitutional powers of advice and consent have atrophied into what is widely regarded . . . to be a duty to give prompt consent with a minimum of advice.[10]

Fulbright's primary loyalty was not to a particular interpretation of the Constitution in regard to foreign affairs but to his country's interests economically, strategically, and culturally defined. He was a true internationalist, committed to the notion of cultural pluralism and convinced that economic interdependence advanced the interests of all peoples. In the aftermath of World War II, with the tide of isolationism still running strong and deep in the United States, an assertive, active executive was needed to advance the cause of internationalism and keep the peace. Over the years, however, the stresses and strains of fighting the cold war under the shadow of a nuclear holocaust had taken their toll. The executive, its actions at times circumscribed and at times dictated by fanatical anticommunist elements at home, had adopted a missionary posture that assumed that America had the duty and the power to make the world over in its own image. "America is showing some signs of that fatal presumption, that overextension of power and mission, which brought ruin to ancient Athens, to Napoleonic France and to Nazi Germany." The war in Vietnam was both a sign of that trend and an accelerator of it. If the war continued and America became "what it never has been, a seeker after unlimited power and empire, then Vietnam will have had a mighty and tragic fallout indeed." One of the answers to the problem of creeping imperialism, he declared, was "to find a way to restore the Constitutional balance, to find ways by which the Senate can discharge its duty of advice and consent in an era of permanent crisis."[11]

Fulbright's indictment of imperial America and the grasping, insensitive executive that served it was a reflection not only of his views but of those of Carl Marcy. The trend toward executive usurpation that had begun in the early stages of the cold war had culminated in the Johnson presidency, the chief of staff believed. Not only had the White House alternately ignored and manipulated the Senate; it was deliberately deceiving the American people.

In response to various evidences of administration fraud, Marcy began to develop plans for what could only be called an alternative State Department. What he proposed was a system whereby professional staff people would either assume permanent stations in Europe, Latin America, Southeast Asia,

10 Quoted in Berman, *Fulbright and the Vietnam War,* 64.
11 Quoted in ibid., 64, 66.

Africa, and other locations or be sent there on special assignment to report independently to the SFRC. He had considered the approach before, he told Fulbright, but had rejected it because it smacked of McCarthyism and would create doubt in the minds of other nations as to who was in charge of American foreign policy. But the administration could not be trusted; the information given the SFRC and the public was either slanted or false. In addition, it put the committee at a disadvantage to have to quote an unnamed source in AID, for example, or an article in the *New York Times*.[12] Fulbright pointed out, and Marcy agreed, that the committee members would have to be won over to this concept. Aside from their fear of Johnson, many viewed staffers as peons. But the chairman agreed to take the matter under advisement.

It should be noted that despite Johnson and Rusk's efforts to convince the American people otherwise Fulbright had not become an irresponsible radical. He still believed that the United States had a role to play as the major stabilizing force in world politics, and he continued to advocate the use of air and sea power to contain China. As Omar Bradley had said of MacArthur's proposal to invade North Korea, Vietnam to Fulbright was "the wrong war in the wrong place at the wrong time." It was one thing, the Arkansan believed, for his country to play the role of balancer of power and quite another for America to attempt to remake the world in its own image and to try to solve every problem that plagued the "global village," to use the Marshall McLuhan term then in vogue.

Although certainly not an isolationist in the strictest sense, Fulbright at times sounded like Charles Beard and Robert Taft. He declared:

> If America has a service to perform in the world – and I believe it has – it is in large part the service of its own example. In our excessive involvement in the affairs of other countries, we are not only living off our assets and denying our own people the proper enjoyment of their resources: we are also denying the world the example of a free society enjoying its freedom to the fullest.[13]

In September he joined with Mike Mansfield in cosponsoring a resolution calling for the withdrawal of a substantial number of American troops from Europe.

Within the imperatives Fulbright had outlined, the Johnson administration could not "win" in Vietnam. During 1965 and 1966 the United States struggled desperately to create a nation south of the seventeenth parallel it could defend. To a degree, the American war effort hinged on the ability of the U.S. country team to help establish a broad-based government capable of holding the allegiance of Buddhist and Catholic, student and worker, peasant and entrepreneur, and residents of both Saigon and the Mekong Delta. It had

12 Carl Marcy to JWF, May 16, 1966, Series 48:4, Box 19:1, SPF.
13 *Congressional Record,* Senate, May 17, 1966, 10808.

to reach out into the complex of villages, secure them, and create a life for which the average Vietnamese was willing to fight and die. To win, America would have to intervene in Vietnam on a massive scale, and the transposition of its values, institutions, and culture to that faraway land was inevitable; but what the Vietnamese wanted, Fulbright insisted, was simply the freedom to work out their own destiny. He refused to acknowledge that the Marxist–Leninist theories and the totalitarian techniques employed by Ho and Giap were as alien to Vietnam as the institutions and processes of the Great Society. When years later he was asked whether South Vietnam died of too much democracy, of the American insistence on elections and representative government, McGeorge Bundy agreed. What South Vietnam needed was "leadership": someone who would use noncommunist institutions and theories to dominate, galvanize, and mobilize the South as Ho had in the North. But Diem was dead, Washington could not resurrect him, and Fulbright would not have tolerated such a figure anyway. The only alternative, in his view, was a negotiated withdrawal.[14]

Insofar as a negotiated settlement in Vietnam was concerned, the key difference between Fulbright and the Johnson administration in 1966 was the inclusion of the NLF in a coalition government in South Vietnam. From June 1964 through August 1965, J. Blair Seaborn, the chief Canadian delegate to the International Control Commission on Indochina, made five trips to Hanoi with Washington's approval. His proposal to Ho was simple and straightforward: If Hanoi would stop its assistance to the Vietcong and withdraw its forces from South Vietnam, the United States would remove its troops from South Vietnam and extend economic assistance and diplomatic recognition to North Vietnam. Through the Canadian diplomat, Rusk warned the North Vietnamese that if they did not respond favorably, air and sea operations would commence north of the seventeenth parallel. Ho responded by demanding that American forces withdraw from Vietnam and that the NLF be included in a coalition government in Saigon.[15]

Although unaware of Seaborn's mission, Fulbright, joined by Robert and Edward Kennedy, George McGovern, and others, tacitly supported Hanoi's position, insisting that South Vietnamese communists would have to be admitted to any provisional government if there was to be a compromise settlement. The administration's position was, and would remain, that the NLF was simply an instrument of Hanoi and that it would use its position in a coalition government to subvert that regime, control elections, and facilitate communization of the entire country. There was no difference then, between Hungary in 1946, Czechoslovakia in 1948, or South Vietnam in 1966. When the administration declared during the peace initiative of 1965, "We have put everything into the basket of peace except the surrender of South Viet-

---

14 Interview with McGeorge Bundy, Aug. 1, 1991, New York.
15 Dean Rusk as told to Richard Rusk, *As I Saw It* (New York, 1990), 461.

nam," it included in the term "surrender" NLF participation in a coalition government.[16] In vain did Fulbright, Albert Gore (D–Tennessee), McCarthy, and Mansfield point out to the administration that to refuse to negotiate with the Vietcong – which, as of the spring of 1966, controlled three-fourths of the territory of South Vietnam and comprised eighty percent of the military force with which the United States was contending – was to refuse to negotiate at all.[17]

In the McMahon Lecture, Fulbright had appealed to his fellow citizens to respond to a "higher patriotism," one that conceived of America as a nation of principles and ideals rather as than one that was rooted in blood-and-soil nationalism. In so doing he had clearly and unequivocally embraced the role of dissenter and in the process had put himself at emotional and psychological odds with his president and a substantial majority of his countrymen. Lyndon Johnson was committed to consensus; Fulbright was not. The president had a visceral dislike of conflict and discord. He was a reconciler. Like so many academics, Fulbright was uneasy with consensus, and he thought his country's obsession with it a great flaw. In "A Higher Patriotism," he observed with distaste that intolerance of dissent was a typically American characteristic. He insisted that what de Tocqueville had said of the United States 150 years earlier was still true: "I know of no country in which there is so little independence of mind and real freedom of discussion." Fulbright realized that his was a society that was unnerved by dissent because it had experienced so little of it, but he insisted nonetheless that unanimity was tantamount to complacency. In the absence of debate and dissension, errors were likely to be made. "Freedom of thought and discussion gives a democracy two concrete advantages over a dictatorship in the making of foreign policy," he declared; "it diminishes the danger of an irretrievable mistake and it introduces ideas and opportunities that otherwise would not come to light."[18]

Much has been made of Fulbright's aversion to the protest movement, to the fact that his establishment credentials prevented him from being embraced by the SDS or the New Left, much less the yippies. It was true that he was much too conventional in his personal life to march or demonstrate, and he rejected draft card burnings, sit-ins, and other "symbolic" and frequently illegal forms of dissent. "We are, for better or worse, essentially a conservative society," he told the protesters. Symbolic acts inflamed passions, closed ears, blocked channels. Ignoring the fact that extremists have consti-

16 Ibid., 465.
17 Discussion with Vice-President Humphrey, Mar. 2, 1966, Executive Sessions, SFRC, RG 46, NA.
18 *Congressional Record,* Senate, Apr. 25, 1966, 8869–72.

tuted the vanguard of every effective reform movement, Fulbright insisted that the object of dissent was to change society. Forms that were counterproductive of that goal, that is, that alienated moderates, should be rejected. Nevertheless, Fulbright not only endorsed the antiwar movement but over time gradually came to embrace it – intellectually if not philosophically and culturally. Indeed, during his spring 1966 speaking tour, he went out of his way to identify himself with those who were demonstrating. "The wisdom and productivity of the protest movement of students, professors, clergy and others may well be questioned, but their courage, decency, and patriotism cannot be doubted," he declared. The mass uprising against the war that developed in the mid-1960s was "a moral and intellectual improvement on the panty raids of the 1950s," he told the students at Johns Hopkins. The new radicalism was not shallow and sophomoric, and opposition to the war was not "hypocritical," as the superpatriots were charging. Critics of the war were rebelling against a "corrupt vision of society," he insisted, and only a fool would refuse to make moral distinctions between wars for fear of being called inconsistent or unpatriotic.[19]

Nevertheless, as his family and his staff frequently observed, Fulbright was a pragmatist, not an ideologue or a zealot. To him, his critique of the war was logical, sensible, and correct, but he had no desire to go down in history as a Cassandra or an Old Testament prophet who gloried in the approval of the Almighty as his people trod the path of destruction. Moreover, despite his public outbursts of early May, Fulbright and his staff, Lee Williams recalled, were afraid of appearing to be extremists. If the public began to lump the chairman with people like Wayne Morse, notorious for his negativism, he would lose his credibility and effectiveness.

Further tempering Fulbright's public statements if not his views was the fact that it was very difficult for him to give up on Lyndon Johnson – personally and politically. He wanted to believe that Johnson would do nothing to endanger Democratic prospects either in the midterm elections or the 1968 presidential campaign.[20]

During a speech before the National Press Club on May 17, Fulbright expressed regret for calling Saigon a whorehouse and comparing the United States to the Third Reich. At the same time, he wrote Johnson complaining that his statements had been misconstrued. The president's reply was surprisingly conciliatory. He agreed that "statements can be taken out of context and interpretations can draw a different meaning than you mean from your words. It's happened to me!" While defending his policies, Johnson seemed to invite reconciliation: "I cannot believe our differences over policy have erased the friendship we have shared for so long. I have a fondness for you and Betty that is real. . . . I am sorry that careless people have appeared to

19 Ibid., 8871.
20 JWF to Arthur Schlesinger, Mar. 15, 1966, Series 48:8, Box 50:1, SPF.

paint another picture.''[21] When Fulbright failed to show up at the White House signing of a bill creating an Asian Development Bank to which he had been invited, Johnson had one of his aides call to tell him he had been missed.[22] Indeed, in late April Johnson had invited Bill and Betty to fly to Houston with him and Lady Bird.[23] Fulbright's New York speech forced him to turn down the invitation, but he thanked Johnson profusely. When, a couple of weeks later, Johnson complained about Fulbright's use of the term ''arrogance of power'' in relation to the administration, the Arkansan wrote him: ''Never at any time have I spoken, or even thought, of you in connection with arrogance.''[24]

The temporary thaw in the Johnson–Fulbright relationship led to several face-to-face meetings between the two during the first half of June; but Fulbright soon learned that Johnson's apparently softening attitude toward him did not indicate a change of heart concerning the war. By the time Nguyen Cao Ky returned to Vietnam from the Honolulu conference in February, Vietnamese Buddhists were demonstrating in behalf of a return to democratic rule and the end of foreign, that is, American, domination of their country. An angry mob set fire to the U.S. consulate in Huế, and firefighters refused to put out the blaze. The American country team labored mightily but unsuccessfully to reconcile the dissenters to the Saigon regime. As the crisis worsened, some administration officials proposed abandoning Ky, whereas others had begun to develop plans for yet another escalation of the war.[25]

In light of the deteriorating situation in Vietnam, Robert McNamara had come to the conclusion by the summer of 1966 that the United States should abandon its crusade in South Vietnam. According to Averell Harriman, McNamara told him on May 14 that Washington should ''get in touch direct with the NLF, also the North Vietnamese, but particularly the NLF, and begin to try to work up a deal for a coalition government.''[26]

Counteracting naysayers inside the administration and outside, however, was the U.S. embassy in Saigon, which explained that Vietnamese were not like Americans and that South Vietnam could achieve military security and realize the fruits of pacification without a stable, broad-based government. In a remarkable cable sent to Johnson in late April, Henry Cabot Lodge observed that Vietnam ''was not going to be stable in our meaning of the word

21 LBJ to JWF, May 27, 1966, NSF, Memos to President, Box 7, Johnson Papers.
22 Mike Manatos to LBJ, Mar. 17, 1966, WHCF, Subject File, Box 18, Johnson Papers.
23 Lee Williams to JWF, Apr. 25, 1966, Series 1:1, Box 3:5, Johnson Papers.
24 JWF to LBJ, May 9, 1966, Series 1:1, Box 3:5, SPF.
25 Meeting of Foreign Policy Advisors on Vietnam, Apr. 4, 1966, Meeting Notes File, Box 1, Johnson Papers.
26 Memorandum of Conversation with Secretary McNamara, May 14, 1966, Box 486, Harriman Papers.

for a long, long time.'' But it did not matter, Lodge insisted. The United States could still succeed: Vietnam could ''evolve.''[27]

Walt Whitman Rostow, who had succeeded Bundy as national security adviser on April Fool's Day 1966, was even more unrealistic than Lodge. In a conversation with Averell Harriman in early 1966, Rostow outlined the course America must follow. The head of the policy planning staff wanted to fight a war of attrition against the enemy in the South and blast the North. He wanted to bomb not only oil storage facilities, but also electric power plants and to mine Haiphong harbor. ''I would use our air power as our equivalent to guerrilla warfare.''[28] Four days after he became national security adviser, Rostow repeated these arguments to Johnson, and even recommended using B-52s to bomb the Mu Gia pass on the Laotian border. He supported pacification, he said, but it would not win the war. Only punishment of North Vietnam and defeat of its main force units would do that.[29]

Thus, in spite of clear evidence of political and military paralysis in South Vietnam, Lyndon Johnson decided to press ahead. To their credit, Dean Rusk and Averell Harriman argued that it would be unwise to escalate bombing of the North with political chaos threatening the South, but Johnson swept their objections aside.[30] They had spent too much time considering new proposals and changes in policy, he told his more hesitant advisers in mid-May:

> Our strategy has been the same for three years. There are island hoppers who jump from issue to issue and there are those who would put a bag of cement on the back of the man running the race. We are committed, and we will not be deterred. We must accept the fact that some will always oppose, dissent and criticize.[31]

In mid-June when the JCS reported that the number of NVA trucks on the Ho Chi Minh Trail had jumped from sixty-nine hundred to ten thousand per month and that the North Vietnamese were preparing for a major push into northern South Vietnam, Johnson authorized the bombing of petroleum storage facilities in Hanoi and Haiphong.[32]

Shortly before this onslaught, Johnson summoned Fulbright to the White House. He must strike at the North, he told the Arkansan, in order to stop the NVA buildup in the South. With communist staging areas and supply lines destroyed or disrupted, Westmoreland would be able to smash the main

---

27 Lodge to LBJ, Apr. 29, 1966, NSF, Memos to President, Box 7, Johnson Papers.
28 Rostow to Harriman, Jan. 28, 1966, Box 499, Harriman Papers.
29 Rostow to LBJ, Apr. 5, 1966, NSF, Memos to President, Box 7, Johnson Papers.
30 Harriman to Rusk, May 10, 1966, Box 499, Harriman Papers.
31 Summary Notes of 557th NSC Meeting, May 10, 1966, NSC Meeting Notes, Box 2, Johnson Papers.
32 Summary Notes of 559th NSC Meeting, June 17, 1966, NSC Meeting Notes File, Box 2, Johnson Papers.

units of the North Vietnamese Army in pitched battles along the demilitarized zone (DMZ) during the monsoon season. Hanoi would then be receptive to another peace offensive he was planning for the winter.[33] Fulbright listened, then repeated his arguments in behalf of disengagement. They fell on deaf ears. On June 29 and 30 at Johnson's direction, American planes struck oil refineries and tanks in and around Hanoi.

On July 1 Fulbright rose in the Senate to denounce the attacks on Hanoi and Haiphong. He described the escalation as a long step toward "ultimate war" and proof that once more the administration had been mesmerized by the vision of total military victory in Vietnam.[34] What gave a particular sharpness and urgency to his comments, however, was his belief that the renewed aerial assaults were not meant to be a prelude to negotiations and ultimate American withdrawal, but, rather, were an indication of the administration's determination to play a larger, permanent role in Asia.

At the same time Fulbright was decrying America's foreign policy overreach, he embarked on a crusade to expose and discredit the administration's vast propaganda campaign in behalf of the war in Vietnam. In April 1966 Carl Marcy informed his boss that the lead article in the spring issue of the prestigious journal *Foreign Affairs* had been written by George A. Carver, who was then a full-time CIA analyst. His piece, "The Faceless Vietcong," was a compilation of the evidence supporting the administration's contention that the NLF was a "contrived political mechanism" of North Vietnam. The article itself seemed contrived, but that was not what angered Fulbright. Carver was not even identified as an employee of the federal government, much less the CIA.[35] Fulbright complained to Admiral William F. "Red" Raborn, Jr., who headed the agency, but he refused to do anything about the article or to promise that his employees would not again engage in such activities. To Raborn's and Johnson's enragement, Marcy leaked the contents of their letters to Martin Agronsky, who went into the issue on his CBS morning news broadcast.[36]

Over the years Fulbright had become increasingly alarmed at the growth of the CIA and the fog of secrecy in which it insisted on operating. Like many others, he believed it had been primarily responsible for the Bay of Pigs fiasco, and he suspected that the agency had had a hand in sabotaging the 1960 summit meeting between Eisenhower and Khrushchev. He was also irritated by the CIA's habit of using American embassies abroad as "cover"

---

33 James Reston, "Prognosis in Vietnam Is More of the Same," *Arkansas Gazette,* June 20, 1966.
34 "Fulbright Fears New Raids Step to 'Ultimate War,' " *Arkansas Gazette,* July 1, 1966.
35 UPI 61, Mar. 7, 1962, Box 1, Miscellaneous 1961–62 Folder, Marcy Papers.
36 Russell to JWF, Apr. 30, 1966, Series 48:3, Box 16:3, SPF.

for its activities.[37] Most important, Fulbright recognized that the CIA was intimately involved in the making and implementation of American foreign policy and as such should be made responsible to the SFRC as well as to Armed Services.

The agency reported to a special subcommittee of the Senate Armed Services Committee – the "secret seven," as it was dubbed by the *New York Times* – chaired by Richard Russell.[38] In 1954 Mike Mansfield, seconded by Fulbright, had attempted to expand the membership of the committee, making it a joint committee of the House and Senate. Russell, ever jealous of his prerogatives, beat back the attempt.[39] Although Fulbright and the SFRC's attitude toward the CIA improved somewhat under Kennedy's appointee, John McCone, Russell continued to insist that the SFRC and its chief be kept in the dark concerning America's intelligence operations. In 1962 when Francis Gary Powers and John McCone testified on the U-2 incident, the SFRC was the last committee to hear their comments, although it had been the first to request them.[40] The 1966 Carver article convinced Fulbright that not only was the CIA making and implementing foreign policy; it was propagandizing the American people in behalf of those policies.

Throughout April Fulbright attempted to persuade Richard Russell to add three members of the SFRC to the secret seven voluntarily, but he consistently refused. Armed Services had originated the legislation in 1946 creating the CIA as well as the NSC, and it would retain oversight, the Georgian declared.[41] Frustrated, in mid-May 1966, Fulbright, Mansfield, and McCarthy persuaded the SFRC to report out a measure that would transform the secret seven subcommittee into the Full Committee on Intelligence Operations.[42] The proposed new body, consisting of three members each from Foreign Relations, Armed Services, and Appropriations, would oversee the intelligence activities of all government agencies, including the CIA.

In the midst of his tête-à-tête with Russell, Fulbright received disturbing reports that the CIA had penetrated the exchange program and was using Fulbrighters abroad to gather information. Although spokespeople for the agency promised that their operatives were not exploiting the exchange program, or that if it had, they would stop, Fulbright ordered Marcy to investigate.[43] When, shortly thereafter, the chief of staff reported that not only had

---

37 Moose to JWF, May 19, 1966, Series 48:3, Box 16:3, SPF.
38 Gilbert C. Fite, *Richard B. Russell, Jr., Senator from Georgia* (Chapel Hill, 1991), 391.
39 *Congressional Record,* Senate, Mar. 10, 1954, 2986–7.
40 UPI 61, Mar. 7, 1962, Box 1, Miscellaneous 1961–62 Folder, Marcy Papers.
41 Russell to JWF, Apr. 30, 1966, Series 48:3, Box 16:3, SPF.
42 Although Eugene McCarthy was the official sponsor of the resolution, Marcy had drafted it. Marcy to McCarthy, Oct. 8, 1965, Box 5, Folder Oct., Marcy Papers.
43 Richard Helms to Marcy, Dec. 7, 1966, and Marcy, Memorandum of Conversation, Dec. 15, 1966, Box 2, JWF Papers, RG 46, NA.

the CIA penetrated Fulbright's creation, but it was subsidizing such diverse organizations as the National Student Association, the American Newspaper Guild, and the Retail Clerks International Association, the chairman called for a special investigation. The extent of the CIA's activities "was much greater than I had ever imagined," he declared on ABC's *Issues and Answers*.[44]

Richard Russell was still one of Lyndon Johnson's closest friends – he could be depended on not to leak – and he had no intention of allowing Fulbright to "muscle in" on his territory.[45] He, Johnson, and Raborn were convinced that if Fulbright penetrated the oversight committee, he would deliberately sabotage the agency's operations by revealing its sources and methods. Indeed, the CIA director pleaded with both Johnson and Russell to go to any lengths to block the measure.[46] At a going-away party for Thomas Mann, Raborn, Johnson, and J. Edgar Hoover agreed that Fulbright was engaged in a conspiracy to "disrupt intelligence operations" throughout the executive branch.[47] Prior to Senate consideration of the CIA bill, Russell and various White House staffers did their best to convince other senators and the press that the SFRC under Fulbright and Marcy had consistently leaked information affecting the national security during both the Dominican crisis and the Vietnam escalation.[48] After hours of debate, the full Senate in mid-July turned back Fulbright and the SFRC by a vote of 61 to 28.[49] Thus did the secret seven remain in control, and the CIA continued to play an active role in the administration's propaganda campaign.[50]

Marcy and Fulbright had long recognized that their struggle with the administration was essentially a competition for the attention of the press – that to change American foreign policy, they would have to have massive exposure and gain the support of a significant number of public opinion makers. During the Vietnam War a fundamental change took place in the relationship between the press and the political power structure in America. During World War II and the Korean conflict, American news reporters had become an extension of the war effort. With some grumbling the press had accepted the

44 "Fulbright Urges Special Probe of CIA's Funding Operations," *Washington Post,* Feb. 20, 1967.
45 McG. Bundy interview; and Fite, *Russell,* 391.
46 Rostow to LBJ, June 1, 1966, NSF, Memos to President, Box 8, Johnson Papers.
47 Hoover to Tolson, July 1, 1966, "Hoover's Official and Confidential File," FBI Files.
48 The chairman and his chief of staff did not deny they had leaked but insisted that none of the information released affected the national security. Memorandum for Possible Use during Debate on CIA Resolution, June 29, 1966, Series 48:3, Box 16:3, SPF.
49 Fite, *Russell,* 390–1.
50 "CIA Chief Rebuked for Letter Praising Attack on Fulbright," *Arkansas Gazette,* July 29, 1966.

dichotomy that Franklin Roosevelt posed during World War II between the civilian realm and the military, between war and peace, and his insistence, in effect, that they join the military and help fight the war. Ernie Pyle was the embodiment of the patriotic "combat correspondent." That marriage was shattered by the Vietnam War. Reporters such as Malcolm Browne, Stanley Karnow, Neil Sheehan, Morley Safer, and David Halberstam were alienated by the discrepancy that existed between the view of the war presented by embassy personnel in Saigon and what they saw with their own eyes and heard with their own ears. They rebelled, and by 1966 their reports in many instances were contradicting the official version of the war. This new breed, moreover, came to think of themselves as actors in the drama, players in the game. Safer's August 1965 telecast of the marine burning of Cam Ne was quite calculated. Harrison Salisbury went so far as to report from North Vietnam on the effects of U.S. bombing on the civilian population. In 1966 two of Fulbright's closest friends in the press, Harry Ashmore and William Baggs of the *Miami News,* undertook their own private peace mission to Hanoi.[51] The independence of the press was accelerated by the activities in the mid-1950s of a group of self-styled foreign policy pundits like Walter Lippmann and Joseph Alsop (who criticized from the right) who believed that only they could provide long-term perspective, and hence proper guidance, to U.S. diplomacy.

As Kathleen Turner and others have pointed out, Vietnam-era presidents in general and Lyndon Johnson in particular mishandled the press and contributed to the alienation of the media. Johnson viewed the Washington press corps as "one hundred enemies and one good reporter named Bill [William S.] White," as McGeorge Bundy put it.[52] The president might leak stories to favored reporters, but he was determined that no one else would. More important, Johnson's refusal to publicize his escalation in Vietnam, his hyperbole, and the efforts of U.S. military and embassy spokespeople to put the best face on the war in Vietnam had by 1966 created a huge "credibility gap."

Fulbright and Marcy cultivated their ties with independent reporters and did their best to widen that gap. In early August, Fulbright notified Leonard Marks, head of the United States Information Agency (USIA), that he was going to hold hearings on the information agency's activities in Vietnam, specifically, its practice of providing free trips to Southeast Asia to selected journalists. The USIA chief knew perfectly well what Fulbright intended to do. He tried frantically to arrange for a private meeting with the chairman to plead with him not to question too closely or to demand to know the names of the junketeers, lest he give the communists "propaganda leverage." Unfortunately for the administration, Fulbright's schedule was "too full" to

51 William C. Baggs to JWF, Dec. 27, 1965, Series 48:1, Box 8:1, SPF.
52 McG. Bundy interview.

permit a conference with Marks.[53] No sooner had the hearings opened than Fulbright gained the floor. Why, he asked Marks, was the USIA using tax-payers' money to fund media trips to Vietnam when he knew that it would bias reporting on the war. Marks insisted that his agency's motives were pure, and he refused to reveal the names of his press guests.[54] Nevertheless, the blow had been struck. The national press carried the story on its front pages; "Fulbright Hints Junkets Used to Manage News" ran a typical head-line.[55]

From mid-1966 on, the administration attempted to portray its congressional opponents, and especially Fulbright, as men who were cowards and who would not only welch on their promises but have their country betray its commitments as well. For Dean Rusk, the ultimate rationale for the war in Vietnam was the American "commitment" under the Southeast Asia Treaty Organization (SEATO) treaty. Although the signatories to that document pledged only to "counter armed attack" against the nations of Southeast Asia and to do so in accordance with their "constitutional processes," the secre-tary regarded it as "the law of the land" that "linked South Vietnam to the general structure of collective security,"[56] Because Congress had ratified the SEATO treaty and passed the Gulf of Tonkin Resolution, all "constitutional processes" had been satisfied to his way of thinking.[57] Some like Rusk and Rostow actually believed that. (Whether or not they knew that the govern-ment of South Vietnam had never officially requested troops from the United States is unclear.) "Taking it all in all, the conclusion is quite simple from the full range of his [Fulbright's] speechmaking," Rostow told Johnson. "He is unwilling to acknowledge that the role of force is a legitimate element in U.S. foreign policy."[58] Fulbright had signed on, Rusk later wrote, and then gotten cold feet. In the spring of 1966 White House staffers dredged up Fulbright's speeches and votes on the treaty and resolution and gave them to friendly senators and journalists.[59] The president's intent was to condemn the Arkansan out of his own mouth.

53 Kinter to Johnson, Aug. 15, 1966, Box 13, Confidential File, CO 312, Johnson Papers.
54 Frank Starzel, retired president of AP; Frank Stanton of CBS; and Palmer Hoyt of the *Denver Post.*
55 "Fulbright Hints Junkets Used to Manage News," *Arkansas Gazette,* Aug. 17, 1966. After checking with LBJ, Marks scheduled a new round of trips. Kinter to President, Aug. 15, 1966, Box 13, Confidential File, CO 312, Johnson Papers.
56 George McT. Kahin, *Intervention: How America Became Involved in Vietnam* (Garden City, N.Y., 1987), 74; and Dean Rusk in, *As I Saw It,* 427.
57 Rusk, *As I Saw It,* 445; and Summary Notes of 557th NSC Meeting, May 10, 1966, NSC Meeting Notes, Box 2, Johnson Papers.
58 Rostow to LBJ, May 24, 1966, NSF, Memos to President, Box 7, Johnson Papers.
59 Alexis Johnson to White House, Feb. 11, 1966, NSF, Memos to President, Box 6, Johnson Papers.

The White House's counteroffensive did nothing to close the credibility gap. By the summer of 1966 Johnson's "peace offensive" had come to be widely viewed as the staged affair that it was. The administration frequently declared that it would "negotiate anywhere at any time without reservations," but in fact it continued to refuse to negotiate with the Vietcong. Even Walt Rostow noted that although there were good reasons for the latter, it was "not consistent with the former." The administration's unwavering habit of hailing every change of government in Saigon as a "good" change had made it seem either stupid or devious.[60] Moreover, it lied about casualties. Not only did the Pentagon exaggerate VC and NVA dead and wounded; it misled Congress and the public concerning the number of North Vietnamese civilians killed by the bombing. At the same time the military was telling Fulbright and the SFRC that only six civilians had been killed in Vietnam as a result of all American military action during the first two months of the war, the First Cavalry Division alone was reporting 131 deaths – this in South Vietnam only.[61] In June, Rostow admitted to Johnson that "we may have killed in the first year of bombing the North three to four thousand civilians."[62]

Further contributing to the credibility gap among college students, the press, and certain members of Congress was the growing rift within the administration itself. McNamara continued to argue that the bombing of the North was counterproductive. Despite Henry Cabot Lodge's laboriously optimistic reports from Saigon, it was plain for all to see that "South Vietnam" as a viable political entity did not exist. There was increasing doubt as to the willingness of the citizens of that contrived republic to fight in their own behalf. As Richard Russell privately admitted, "[T]he South Vietnamese just can't hack it."[63] Nicholas Katzenbach, who would become undersecretary of state in December 1966, recalled that he never had any problem with the rationale for America's presence in Vietnam. "The notion of trying to keep the North Vietnamese from taking over South Vietnam seemed to me to be a perfectly reasonable thing to do," he later observed. "The problem was that there was no government there to do it."[64] In the absence of one, the United States would have to do the job itself. If that was the case, then what, in fact, was the country fighting for in Southeast Asia? Katzenbach was forced to ask himself. Johnson, Rostow, and the White House public relations experts liked to think that dissent was limited to the spoiled and irresponsible children of America's upper middle class and to a liberal–intellectual coalition spearheaded by Fulbright, Reston, and Lippmann and made up of college

60 Rostow to LBJ, June 10, 1966, NSF, Memos to President, Box 8, Johnson Papers.
61 JWF to McNamara, Mar. 21, 1966, Box 2, Fulbright Papers, SFRC, RG 46, NA.
62 Rostow to LBJ, June 16, 1966, NSF, Memos to President, Box 8, Johnson Papers.
63 Interview with William Bundy, July 5, 1990, Princeton, N.J.
64 Interview with Nicholas deB. Katzenbach, July 5, 1990, Princeton, N.J.

professors, professional liberals, pretentious senators, and the *New York Times*.[65] The cancer had spread to the president's inner circle, however, and McNamara, Moyers, presidential speechwriter Harry McPherson, and East Asian specialist Roger Hilsman's loss of faith in America's mission in Vietnam both reflected and accelerated a similar loss of faith among the general citizenry.

To the consternation of the White House, Fulbright managed to make war on the conflict in Vietnam and at the same time avoid being labeled part of the lunatic fringe by the national press and the great American middle class. "There still is no doubt that once his name is attached to a particular position," Brock Brower wrote in *Life*, "even his boldest detractors are forced into a grudging respect for it. . . . Senator Fulbright belongs at this critical moment not to Arkansas but to world opinion."[66] He managed to convey the impression that he was genuinely interested in the welfare of all parties concerned, that he was a disinterested observer, a man of goodwill who did not have all the answers but who wanted nothing so much as to see the peoples of the world enjoy peace and self-determination; this, despite his civil rights record. His staff, all of whom deplored his public posture toward the rights of African Americans, never doubted his sincerity. When Jim Cash suggested that his boss throw in the towel over Vietnam in order to save his political neck, Lee Williams rebuked him. In addition to the fact that Fulbright was right and Johnson wrong, he declared that

> a capitulation by the Senator would have incalculable effect upon our adversaries, primarily the Russians, but also the bloc nations who look to Fulbright and those of his persuasion as the voice of reason in the U.S. Government. If Fulbright gives up, I think their tendency would be to abandon all hope for a rational settlement of the conflict.[67]

65 See Robert Kintner to LBJ, July 1 and 5, 1966, WHCF, Confidential File, Box 83, Johnson Papers.
66 Brock Brower, "The Roots of the Arkansas Questioner," *Life*, May 13, 1966, 92–115.
67 Williams to Cash, July 1, 1966, Papers of Lee Williams, Mullins Library, University of Arkansas.

10

Widening the Credibility Gap

Throughout the early weeks of 1967, American newspapers were filled with pictures of wounded GIs and screaming Vietnamese children, their clothes burned off by napalm. Stories of American atrocities began to mount. Letters from GIs sickened by the war poured into Fulbright's office. He read them all.[1] One of the most poignant was written by a battle-hardened second lieutenant serving near Tuy Hoa:

> I have been meaning to write this letter to you for a long while. This evening the pressures are too great to be ignored, even though they are the result of several small occurrences rather than one large disaster. Although, in one sense, the large disaster surrounds me. Adding fresh dimensions of madness daily.
>
> It is just that, in the past few months as an advisor to the VN Coastal Force, I have seen too often the real casualties of this conflict – the farmers and their families in the Delta mangled by air strikes, and the villagers here killed and burned out by our friendly Korean mercenaries.
>
> Of course, I do my share in the lunatic ward. I have even been reprimanded for over-enthusiastic pursuit of VC. Part of it is just compensation – it is refreshing, after seeing so many innocent people suffer, to meet real, live hostile forces capable of striking back.
>
> This evening they showed the JFK documentary film here in the MACV compound. I could not help but feel a great sense of loss as I listened to the richly rolling phrases – what ever has become of our dream? Where is that America that opposed tyrannies at every turn, without inquiring first whether some particular forms of tyranny might be of use to us? Of the three rights which men have, the first, as I recall, was the right to life. How then have we come to be killing so many in such a dubious cause?
>
> As you are probably aware, I am possibly violating seventeen thousand directives in writing to you. But it is not possible to keep silent, as you so amply demonstrate. You remind me of Kent, in *Lear*, who in the face of dire threats from his king replied: ''Whilst my tongue can

---

1 See, e.g., Capt. James E. Terrell to JWF, July 21, 1967, Series 48:18, Box 53:4, SPF.

yet give vent to clamour, I'll tell thee thou doest evil!'' I pray that you
fare better than Kent. . . . Good night sir. God keep you well and safe.''[2]

Fulbright was overwhelmed. ''I agree with everything you have written,''
he replied to the author, Lieutenant Karl Phaler, ''and am ashamed of the
fact that I have been unable to persuade this Administration to make a reasonable and timely offer of negotiations so that we might bring this tragic
conflict to an end.''[3]

No one would ever characterize J. William Fulbright as a brooder or a
dreamer. He was not cursed with an overactive imagination; indeed, Paul
Greenberg, one of the senator's most relentless critics, once observed that
Fulbright feared prophets who claimed to hear the voice of God whispering
in their ear. Fulbright was a man much closer to Henry V than Hamlet;[4] yet,
by 1967, Vietnam had begun to haunt him.

Indeed, had the war not changed Fulbright, he would never have been
able to change it. By 1967 for him the issue was not just strategic or constitutional or political but moral as well. He was not really sure what that
meant, as his halting approaches to theologian Reinhold Niebuhr indicated.
Throughout his life, he had had little time for moral philosophy, much less
theology. But the more the Vietnam War impinged on his consciousness, the
more time he had for both. In the summer of 1967 he wrote an introduction
and commentary to a life of Mahatma Ghandi. In the master's spiritualism,
if not in his tactic of nonviolent disobedience, were to be found the tocsins
that would call the American people back to their fundamental humanity and
decency, he declared.[5] However, as Fulbright realized better than anyone,
combat with Lyndon Baines Johnson required more than morality and spiritualism.

The administration gave General William Westmoreland broad discretion in
developing a strategy to defeat the enemy on the ground in South Vietnam
(in contrast to the air war, over which it retained tight control). Westmoreland's ''search and destroy'' strategy demanded more and more men. In June
1966 the president had approved a force level of four hundred thirty-one
thousand to be reached by mid-1967. As this buildup was taking place, Westmoreland put in a new request for an increase to five hundred forty-two
thousand troops by the end of 1967.

The massive infusion of American uniformed personnel between 1965 and
1967 may have forestalled a military collapse in South Vietnam, but West-

2 LTJG Karl J. Phaler, May 17, 1967, Series 48:18, Box 53:1, SPF.
3 JWF to Phaler, May 17, 1967, Series 48:18, Box 53:1, SPF.
4 Interview with Paul Greenberg, June 9, 1989, Pine Bluff, Ark.
5 Thomas C. Mulholland to JWF, Aug. 1, 1967, and JWF to Mulholland, Aug. 4, 1967, Series
   48:1, Box 8:5, SPF.

moreland's approach was based on a number of erroneous assumptions. Inherent in any attrition strategy was the notion that one could inflict intolerable losses on the enemy while keeping one's own losses within acceptable bounds. In Vietnam that proved not to be the case. Because an estimated two hundred thousand North Vietnamese reached draft age each year, Hanoi was able to replace its losses, counter each American escalation, and frustrate Johnson's hopes for a quick victory. General Vo Nguyen Giap, commander of North Vietnamese forces, understood quite precisely what it would take to win the Second Indochina War, and he took full advantage of the special opportunities available to military men in a totalitarian society. Not having to worry about public opinion and elections, he and Ho could mobilize North Vietnam down to the last person and sacrifice life on the battlefield on a scale unheard of in a democracy. To North Vietnam's strategic advantage, Giap proved absolutely ruthless. Consequently, the United States was able to achieve only temporary military advantage. The North Vietnamese and Vietcong had been hurt, in some cases badly, but their main forces survived. Able to choose the time and conditions of battle, and free of time constraints, they retained the strategic initiative. In an effort to force the South Vietnamese to assume responsibility for defending their country, Johnson and McNamara deliberately held U.S. troop levels to one-half million; but as a result, Westmoreland did not have sufficient forces to wage war against the enemy's regular units and to control the countryside.

Throughout late 1966 Fulbright's detractors had demanded that he either stop criticizing the administration or offer a concrete alternative for ending the war, an alternative that was politically and strategically viable. In December, Random House published *The Arrogance of Power,* a compilation of Fulbright's Johns Hopkins speeches topped off with his eight-point plan for negotiation, American withdrawal, and eventual neutralization of all of Southeast Asia. As with all of Fulbright's books, *The Arrogance of Power* was an amalgam of ideas worked out by Fulbright and his staff and then skillfully edited by Seth Tillman. Combining the Gavin enclave strategy with his own call for the neutralization of Southeast Asia, his eight-point program prescribed an end to the bombing of the North, recognition of the NLF as a party to negotiations, and concentration of American troops in defensible enclaves as a prelude to withdrawal. Hanoi's continuing unwillingness to give assurances that it would halt infiltration and cease hostilities in return for a suspension of the American bombing campaign, coupled with Johnson and Rostow's hostility to a negotiating role for the NLF, made Fulbright's plan unworkable.

Nonetheless, Fulbright's reputation as America's most articulate and influential dove continued to grow. *The Arrogance of Power* made the *New York Times* best-seller list, and by June 1967, Random House had sold one hundred thousand copies. Italian, Spanish, German, Japanese, and Swedish editions followed. One Japanese journalist recalled that the book became virtually required reading for graduate students in his country. "Since leaving the United States I have visited other countries," an English M.P. wrote Fulbright, "and . . . when the word 'Vietnam' is mentioned, invariably your name comes into the conversation. . . . The fact that you are risking your political neck in differing from the views of your Administration is one of the things that will serve the United States in good stead in the future."[6] Ultimately, *The Arrogance of Power* sold over four hundred thousand copies, making it one of the most widely known works of its time.

The notoriety of *The Arrogance of Power* hinged far more on Fulbright's analysis of the role of the nation-state in international affairs and his critique of American foreign policy than it did on his eight-point program to end the war. Max Frankel noted in the *New York Times Book Review* that while Fulbright's book was "an invaluable antidote to the official rhetoric of the government," it was "not a satisfying prescription for alternatives to the policies it condemns." Writing in the *Washington Post,* Ronald Steel grasped the larger point when he observed that *"The Arrogance of Power* marks the passage of Senator Fulbright from a relatively orthodox supporter of the liberal line on foreign policy to a spokesman for the post-cold-war generation."[7]

Fulbright and Marcy understood more clearly than ever in early 1967 that the key to eroding congressional and public support for the war was alienation of the hawks. At the same time he was participating in the burgeoning New Left critique of American society, the chairman of the SFRC searched for arguments that would appeal to Russell, Sparkman, Symington, and conservative Republicans. He could not very well take overt advantage of their frustration over Johnson's determination to fight a limited war, but he could exploit their traditional commitment to a strict construction of the Constitution and their opposition to a powerful, activist executive. Many of the congressional hawks were, after all, either founders or political heirs of the old conservative coalition that had battled Harry Truman over the Fair Deal and that had managed to stymie John F. Kennedy's New Frontier. In late February, Senator Joseph Clark offered an amendment to a $4.5 billion supplementary appropriations bill for Vietnam. Fulbright used the debate over the Clark amendment, which would bar the use of funds for military operations in or over North Vietnam or forbid an increase in U.S. military personnel above five hundred thousand without a declaration of war, to provoke Richard

---

6 A.J. Levin to JWF, Apr. 12, 1967, Series 48:18, Box 52:4, SPF.
7 Quoted in William C. Berman, *William Fulbright and the Vietnam War: The Dissent of a Political Realist* (Kent, Ohio, 1988), 78.

Russell into breaking with the administration.[8] Did he not recall that the framers of the Constitution initially reserved to Congress the right not only to declare but to conduct war? he asked the Georgian. Only with great reluctance did they allocate to the executive the power to oversee military operations. Was not the Johnson administration conducting military operations without a declaration of war? How many troops would Russell countenance in Vietnam without a declaration? One million? Two million? They had been allies in disciplining the executive over "domestic" (civil rights) matters, Fulbright reminded his colleague; why could they not act in harness over foreign policy as well?[9]

Russell refused to be entrapped, at least for the moment. He readily admitted that he was a longtime defender of congressional prerogatives, but in the case of Vietnam the legislative branch had been consulted, he argued. All it had to do if it did not like the war in Vietnam was to pass a concurrent resolution, which was not subject to presidential veto, terminating the Gulf of Tonkin Resolution.[10]

As Russell well knew, Fulbright was walking a tightrope. He did not, in fact, want a formal declaration of war. Nor did he wish for a congressional vote on the Gulf of Tonkin Resolution. Historically, no representative or senator had ever voted to withhold support from American troops once they were in the field and not suffered politically as a result. In 1967 Lyndon Johnson was sure to win any vote on the war decisively.

Yet, as Fulbright sensed, the hawks were becoming restive. Russell had not supported intervention in 1954, and he had opposed the introduction of American troops under Kennedy. He chafed under the restrictions Johnson had imposed on the JCS. "Our great difficulty is that we are fighting the kind of war our enemy wants and not using all of the resources that are available to us," he complained to a constituent.[11] The influential Stuart Symington, a former secretary of the air force who sat on both Armed Services and Foreign Relations, was intensely angry with the DOD for what he considered its "arrogance" in not heeding his demands for an all-out air war. Privately he admitted to Carl Marcy that his conviction that the United States ought to be in Vietnam was crumbling under Fulbright's onslaughts.[12] Both men were alienated by Johnson's unabashed use of such mindless flag-wavers as Frank Lausche and Thomas Dodd.

Fulbright also sensed mounting support for his position from the liberal, internationalist wing of the Republican Party. In the spring of 1967 Clifford

8 John Herbers, "Fulbright Backs Vietnam Limit of 500,000 G.I.'s," *New York Times*, Mar. 1, 1967.
9 *Congressional Record*, Senate, Mar. 13, 1967, 6427–9.
10 Ibid., Feb. 28, 1967, 4714–17.
11 Russell to General L. O. Grice, Mar. 21, 1967, Dictation Series, Box I.J. 34e., Vietnam Folder, Russell Papers.
12 Marcy to Bader, Mar. 4, 1967, Box 7, Folder Jan.–Mar., Marcy Papers.

Case (R–New Jersey) and John Sherman Cooper (R–Kentucky) toured Vietnam and returned filled with apprehension over the political situation and the pace of pacification.[13] The immensely popular young mayor of New York, John Lindsay, denounced the war for diverting funds that were desperately needed to rebuild the inner cities' rotting ghettos and crumbling infrastructures.[14]

Finally, traditional Republican isolationists began to find Fulbright's critique congenial to their views. After all, the notion that the United States ought not to fight a land war in Asia and that it should defend its interests in the Pacific by means of a ring of naval and air bases was the essence of the "unilateralist" approach propounded by Robert Taft and Herbert Hoover in 1950. In fact, in early 1967 Fulbright had struck up an admiring correspondence with FDR's old isolationist bête noir, Burton K. Wheeler.[15] Vermont's venerable George Aiken had never been enthusiastic about Vietnam, and in the late spring of 1967, he took to the floor of the Senate, armed with a speech prepared by Carl Marcy, calling for an "Asian" settlement to the war. If the countries of the region, who had the most to lose by a communist triumph, did not agree to shoulder their fair share of the burden in Vietnam, the United States should gradually withdraw.[16]

Fulbright, as one family member put it, had the constitution of a horse. Throughout his life, he had proved amazingly resistant to stress. His health problems had been largely limited to the aftereffects of his lacrosse injuries. In May, however, he came down with a cold that soon turned into bronchitis. His fever skyrocketed, and he was forced to check himself into Walter Reed Hospital for a week.[17]

Fully recovered, Fulbright, together with Joe Clark, Claiborne Pell, and several other legislators, traveled to Geneva the last week in May to attend the Pacem in Terris conference, an international gathering of parliamentarians, businesspeople, and scientists who had been meeting intermittently since the 1950s to try and figure out a foolproof way to avert nuclear war. Fulbright was one of the keynote speakers.

By the time he addressed the Pacem in Terris gathering, Fulbright was being labeled by many in the United States as a "neo-isolationist." The application of that term to the Arkansan was an indication of how deeply the globalist assumptions in NSC-68 had become embedded in the popular mind. Shortly before the Geneva meeting Carl Marcy reread Admiral Alfred Thayer

13 Clifford P. Case to JWF, Feb. 27, 1967, Series 48:1, Box 8:4, SPF.
14 Jack Files to JWF, Mar. 13, 1967, Series 48:17, Box 4:1, SPF.
15 JWF to Burton K. Wheeler, Oct. 30, 1967, Series 48:18, Box 53:5, SPF.
16 Marcy to Aiken, May 8, 1967, Box 7, Folder Jan.–Mar., Marcy Papers.
17 Lee Williams to Theodore Matoff, May 13, 1967, Series 39:2, Box 14, SPF.

Mahan and prepared a new American foreign policy statement for Southeast Asia, a statement that summarized Fulbright's views. The goal of the United States should not be to defend and promote "freedom" and "democracy" – those were culturally relative values – but "to maintain such base facilities there [in the Pacific] as will protect the sea and air routes of the area from domination by hostile forces, and to do so without involving American manpower in combat with the manpower of Asia."[18] Surely, that position smacked of Theodore Roosevelt and, more recently, of Robert Taft and Herbert Hoover, men whom Democratic globalists like Dean Acheson (and J. William Fulbright) had labeled as neo-isolationists. It should be pointed out, however, that neither they nor Fulbright favored an American withdrawal from world affairs; what the Arkansan advocated was a narrower definition of the national mission than that espoused by those who had been "present at the creation."

Fulbright coupled this scaled-down definition of America's strategic goals and responsibilities, dubbed the "new realism" by University of Chicago political scientist Hans Morgenthau, with a return to the internationalism of his first years in Congress. Since the birth of the nation-state system, Fulbright told the gathering in Geneva, extended periods of peace had been the result of a balance of power. When, as had been the case during the Napoleonic era, one nation, through overweening ambition and the acquisition of unlimited power, had destroyed the balance, the victims of that imperial impulse had attempted to form a permanent community to regulate competition and mediate conflicts. The Concert of Europe, formed in the wake of Waterloo, had collapsed in 1914, and the United Nations had fallen victim to the exigencies of the cold war. Initially it was Stalinist Russia that threatened the balance of power, but now a different hegemonic power sought to force its will on the rest of the world, albeit for seemingly noble purposes. That nation was the United States. For his country's sake as well as for the good of the rest of the world, the United Nations was going to have to mediate international disputes, and multinational organizations such as the World Bank were going to have to attend to the socioeconomic problems of developing areas. America needed to be saved from itself.[19]

Reflecting his new interest in education, mass psychology, anthropology, and moral philosophy, Fulbright insisted that international community was the only alternative to nationalism, aggression, empire, and ultimately holocaust. It was the nature of humankind to deny its base origins:

18 Summary Proposal for Disengagement in Vietnam, May 18, 1967, Box 7, Folder Apr.–June, Marcy Papers.
19 Throughout the remainder of 1967 Fulbright would suggest that the Security Council be asked to assume responsibility for mediating the Vietnam War. Specifically, the council should pass a resolution calling for a cease-fire and then reconvene the Geneva Conference. "Fulbright Wants UN to Rule on Vietnam," *Christian Science Monitor,* Sept. 25, 1967.

We pay lip service to Darwin, but, in our heart of hearts, how many of us really believe that we are not fallen gods but unusually precocious apes? Not many, I dare say. And why should we? Who wants to associate with chimpanzees when he has the words and the ideas which enable him to believe that he is only slightly lower than the angels?[20]

But humanity erred in denying his baser nature. The need for an international community that would restrain unbridled nationalism and thereby ensure the survival of the species was greater than ever.

The mainstays of Fulbright's political thought in 1967 were limited national commitment, international cooperation, and educational exchange. As the communist world diversified and Stalinism receded into history, there was no longer any need for an American crusade or symmetrical containment – if there ever had been. In seeking to fulfill its cold war mission, in acting as if the bipolar political system that emerged from World War II continued to exist, the United States was threatening to become the hegemonic power it had frequently decried and occasionally taken up arms against. Vietnam was the mirror that would reflect the perversion of America's values and traditional policies, and Fulbright was determined to hold it before the nation's face.

What gave Fulbright's critique of American foreign policy special sharpness and poignancy was that he had been one of the principal architects of the very cold war liberalism he was now decrying. Indeed, his disillusionment both paralleled and accelerated disillusionment within the nation's preeminent liberal organization, the Americans for Democratic Action.

Because of Fulbright's record on civil rights, his numerous antiunion votes, and his intermittent attacks on American Zionists, the ADA did not, indeed could not, explicitly embrace him. Nonetheless, the moderate and reform wings of the organization were vastly influenced by the SFRC hearings and by the chairman's humane and intelligent criticism of the war. Fulbright bridged the gap between people like Arthur Schlesinger and Chester Bowles, on the one hand, and Curtis Gans and Allard Lowenstein, on the other. In so doing he dealt the Vietnam consensus a serious blow. He also further damned himself in Lyndon Johnson's eyes.

Beginning in 1966, Lowenstein – a former student activist at the University of North Carolina at Chapel Hill, a past head of the National Student Association, and a leader of the reform wing of the ADA – launched a campaign to persuade the organization to support someone other than Lyndon Johnson for president in 1968. Although Lowenstein did not succeed, the National Board at its annual meeting in Washington in the spring of 1967 did denounce the war in Vietnam. At the same time, a group of antiwar enthusiasts in New York opened the "Citizens for Kennedy–Fulbright" headquarters in prepa-

20 *Congressional Record*, Senate, June 7, 1967, 15018.

ration for the 1968 presidential election.[21] In July the group organized some fifty former delegates to the Democratic National Convention and had them send a public letter to the president urging him not to run in 1968. Because of deep divisions over foreign affairs, they declared, "millions of Democrats will be unable to support Democratic candidates in local, state or national elections."[22]

From that time on, Lyndon Johnson viewed the ADA as nothing less than a "Kennedy-in-exile" government. The dump-Johnson organization also served to further identify Fulbright in Johnson's mind with the hated Bobby. Although he publicly repudiated the movement to draft him for the 1968 Democratic vice-presidential nomination, Fulbright continued to cultivate members of both the moderate and reform groups within the ADA. If the Texan heeded the antiwar consensus emerging among American liberals, he could save his presidency; if he did not, he would have to go down with his ship of war. Like Lowenstein, Fulbright believed that ending the war in Vietnam was far more important than saving Lyndon Johnson's presidency.

21 RFK–Fulbright Group to Ignore Objections, Run in New Hampshire," *Arkansas Gazette,* May 5, 1967.
22 " 'Help Party, Don't Run,' Dissenters Tell Johnson," *Washington Evening Star*, July 31, 1967.

11

The Price of Empire

In early February, David Ness, deputy chief of the American mission in Cairo and an old acquaintance of Fulbright's, wrote the chairman warning him that the Middle East was teetering on the edge of an abyss, ready to plunge into war at a moment's notice. Arab nationalism, inflamed by the suffering of exiled Palestinians and fueled by Egyptian President Gamal Abdel Nasser's ambition, was reaching a fever pitch. Ambassador Lucius Battle (former head of cultural affairs in State and another acquaintance of Fulbright's) was scheduled to leave in March, and Washington had not even thought of a replacement. The region was ready to explode, and the Johnson administration did not have a clue as to what was going on. Ness pled with Fulbright to help. "I will try to get the word through [to the White House and State Department] in the best way I can," the chairman replied. "I need not tell you that things are testy here in Washington these days, and one has to watch his step."[1]

Throughout the late 1950s and early 1960s, Egypt, Syria, and Jordan offered their territory as staging grounds for Palestinian guerrilla attacks into Israel. In 1964 Nasser, who still aspired to head a pan-Arab union, persuaded other Arab leaders to join him in creating the Palestine Liberation Organization (PLO) and financing a guerrilla army whose purpose it would be to wrest Palestine from Israel. Al Fatah ("conquest") began raiding Israel from Syria and Jordan. When Israel responded with devastating reprisal attacks against its two Arab neighbors, the Soviet Union declared its support for the Palestinian movement and began shipping large quantities of tanks and planes to Syria.

On May 22, 1967, Nasser, in an effort to exert pressure on Israel, closed the Straits of Tiran, the entrance to the Gulf of ʿAqaba, which separated the Sinai Peninsula from Arabia. The gulf was Israel's only opening to the south, and that nation operated a major oil terminal at its head. President Johnson denounced the closing on May 23. He then simultaneously appealed to Egypt

---

1 JWF to David G. Ness, Feb. 3, 1967, Series 48:11, Box 35:5, SPF, and "U.S. Ignored Crisis Signs in Mideast," *Baltimore Sun,* June 11, 1967.

to reopen the waterway and asked Israel to refrain from retaliation. He promised, moreover, to work out an international guarantee of free passage.

Days passed and the Strait of Tiran remained closed. Meanwhile, Egypt, Syria, and Jordan massed troops along Israel's borders. On June 5 the Israeli military attacked. An air strike caught most of Egypt's planes on the ground, where they were obliterated, while the army raced across the Sinai Peninsula. Within a week the Israelis had driven the Egyptians back to the west side of the Suez; the Star of David flew over the entire Sinai. Somewhat to their surprise, the Israelis were able in addition to conquer the West Bank of the Jordan – including all of Jerusalem, the putative capital of eretz Israel – and to occupy the Golan Heights, strategic high ground just inside Syria. In the process, the Israelis became reluctant caretakers of some eight hundred thousand Palestinian refugees.[2] On June 10 the fighting stopped when all belligerents accepted the UN cease-fire proposal.

Once Fulbright and Marcy became convinced that the Johnson administration was not going to intervene unilaterally in the Six-Day War, they began to view the Middle East crisis through the prism of the conflict in Vietnam. Incredibly, they saw in the weeklong conflagration an opportunity to hammer out a great-power rapprochement that would in turn make possible an end to the fighting in Indochina.

As soon as he received word of the closing of the Straits of Tiran, Rusk called Fulbright and other congressional leaders to the State Department for an extended meeting. He assured them that Johnson was determined to avoid a Soviet–American conflict and to see the crisis resolved peacefully.[3] Two days later Fulbright told reporters that it was "hypocritical" for the president to appeal to the Israelis to show restraint when he was attempting to bomb North Vietnam back to the Stone Age. Well aware that the vast majority of the American people were pro-Israeli, Fulbright and Stuart Symington declared that the United States was unprepared to mediate in the Middle East and to protect its "vital interests" – a euphemism for Israeli security – because it was bogged down in Vietnam. Johnson, Rusk, and McNamara were furious. What an irony, Rusk remarked bitterly; the dove was sprouting talons.[4]

In the aftermath of the 1967 war, which left Israel in control of the Golan Heights, Gaza, and the West Bank, Fulbright and Marcy claimed to see a certain symmetry in the Soviet and American positions in world affairs. Both had underestimated the power of nationalism in developing regions of the world. Both had found their modern weaponry incapable of determining the

---

2 Johnson to Truman, August 3, 1967, Box 15, Post-Presidential Files, Papers of Harry S. Truman, Independence, Mo. [hereinafter referred to as Truman Papers].

3 JWF to Irma Jennings, May 22, 1967, Series 48:18, Box 52:2, SPF; and *Congressional Record,* Senate, May 24, 1967, 13788.

4 Memorandum for the Record, May 24, 1967, NSC Meeting Notes, Box 2, Johnson Papers.

outcome of regional conflicts; and both, as a result, had suffered a significant loss of prestige and influence. The opportunity was ripe, Fulbright asserted repeatedly, for Soviet–American cooperation in the context of the United Nations. In the Middle East, the two superpowers could defuse the situation by guaranteeing free international access to the Gulf of ʿAqaba in return for an Israeli withdrawal from the occupied territories. In Southeast Asia, the Soviet Union could use its good offices to bring Hanoi to the negotiating table.[5] What the chairman and his chief of staff hoped was that the Soviet Union's humiliation in the Middle East would blunt Russophobia in the United States and create enough political room for the president to accept a mediated settlement in Vietnam. They were, of course, wrong.

Deciding that two could play the Zionist card in regard to Vietnam, Johnson told Israeli foreign minister Abba Eban that traditional isolationism was on the loose in Congress. "We are almost back to the Gerald Nye days when the monstrous munitions maker was on every school child's tongue." Everyone with any sense knew that Israel was the free world's front line against communism in the Middle East and that the struggle there was part and parcel of the war in Vietnam. The growing sentiment against foreign commitments boded ill for Israel as well as South Vietnam, the president warned Eban. The same senators who opposed the war in Vietnam would abandon Israel in a twinkling of an eye. Putting words in Fulbright's mouth, Johnson told Eban that "one Senator" had told him that "we should abandon Southeast Asia because they are not our kind of people." If that was to be the basis of American foreign policy, he told Eban, "you've done had it." The message was clear: If Israel wanted continued help from the United States, it had better mobilize American Zionists in behalf of the war in Vietnam.[6]

The Six-Day War had only momentarily diverted Fulbright from his campaign to unify hawks and doves around the issue of executive usurpation of the congressional prerogatives in the field of foreign policy. Fulbright and Marcy focused increasingly on the idea of a national commitments resolution. Throughout June and the first part of July, Marcy, Don Newhouse, and the SFRC staff labored over a document that would, in Marcy's words "unite the hawks and the doves, the North and the South, and the liberals and conservatives – all acting in glorious defense of the Constitution."[7]

Meanwhile, a series of events in the Congo had persuaded Richard Russell, the powerful chairman of Armed Services, that the administration had to be

---

5 *Congressional Record*, Senate, May 24, 1967, 13788, and Possible Security Council Resolution, June 9, 1967, Box 7, Folder Apr.–June, Marcy Papers.
6 Notes on the President's Meeting with Abba Eban et al., Oct. 24, 1967, Meeting Notes File, Box 2, Johnson Papers.
7 Marcy to Morse, July 24, 1967, Box 7, Folder July–Sept., Marcy Papers.

confronted lest America become involved in one Vietnam after another. Throughout the Congo's bloody struggle for independence from Belgium and the civil strife that followed, the United States had acted to shore up the pro-Western, anticommunist government of President Joseph Mobutu. In June, President Johnson dispatched three C-130 cargo planes and 150 military personnel to the central African republic. The American presence was necessary, Mobutu claimed, to help him suppress a major rebellion against his government. On July 8, shortly before the planes left, Rusk called Russell and Fulbright to inform them of the enterprise. In his telephone conversation, he gave the impression that the purpose of the expedition was to rescue Americans about to be butchered in the jungle. The following day, however, Rusk called again and said that the planes would be used to move Mobutu's troops "around the Congo to deal with revolutionary elements."[8]

On July 10 Russell seized the floor in the Senate to criticize the administration sharply. The situation in the Congo, he said, was purely an internal conflict and one in which the United States should not become involved. Americans must not become bogged down in "local rebellions and local wars" where the nation had "no stake and where we have no legal or moral commitment to intervene."[9] He had protested privately to the administration, he said, but his objections had gone unheeded.

Fulbright moved quickly to take advantage of the opening. During a long lunch in the Senate dining room, the Arkansan broached the subject of a national commitments resolution to his old friend from Georgia and urged him to introduce a bill embodying it. The document that Marcy and his staff had produced was a masterpiece, the chairman observed, one that "seems to me to come pretty close to expressing what I would guess is a nearly universal Senate view." It provided that a national commitment by the United States to a foreign power "necessarily and exclusively results from affirmative action taken by the executive and legislative branches of the United States Government through means of a treaty, convention, or other legislative instrumentality specifically intended to give effect to such a commitment."[10] Thus was planted the seed that would flower into the Hatfield–McGovern and Cooper–Church resolutions as well as the War Powers Act. The long, bitter struggle against the imperial presidency had begun.

After testifying before the newly formed Subcommittee on the Separation of Powers headed by Senator Sam Ervin (D–North Carolina), Fulbright met with the Capitol Hill press corps. He detected, he told them, a growing desire by the Senate to reclaim its prerogatives. He then departed for Idaho and a float trip down the middle fork of the Salmon River with James H. Doolittle

---

8 Quoted in Gilbert C. Fite, *Richard B. Russell, Jr., Senator from Georgia* (Chapel Hill, 1991), 451.
9 Quoted in ibid.
10 JWF to Richard Russell, July 14, 1967, Series 48:3, Box 16:4, SPF.

of Tokyo air raid fame and executives of the Potlatch Forests Company. It was a fruitless attempt at diversion. In the middle of the trip, he had the canoes put ashore and ordered the guide to radio for a helicopter. Young men were dying, a congressional revolt was brewing, and he needed to get back to the scene of action. By the twenty-second Fulbright was once again in the capital ready to do battle.[11]

On July 25 Lyndon Johnson convened what he expected to be a routine gathering of Senate committee chairs. The group included Scoop Jackson, Allen Ellender, James Eastland, Mike Monroney (D–Oklahoma), Warren Magnuson (D–Washington) – all committed party-liners on the war – as well as Mansfield and Fulbright. The president thanked the group for their ''experience, friendship and judgment'' and invited comments. ''Mr. President,'' Fulbright began, ''what you really need to do is to stop the war. That will solve all your problems.'' Johnson's face reddened. He sensed a change in the attitude of his colleagues toward the conflict in Vietnam, Fulbright declared. Even Frank Lausche had called for an end to the bombing of the North. Senator Russell was very upset about being lied to on the Congo. ''Vietnam is ruining our domestic and our foreign policy. I will not support it any longer.'' By now Johnson's steely gaze was fixed on the Arkansan. The group was absolutely still. ''I expect that for the first time in 20 years I may vote against foreign assistance and may try to bottle the whole bill up in the Committee,'' Fulbright warned.

Johnson exploded. If Congress wanted to tell the rest of the world to go to hell, that was its prerogative. ''Maybe you don't want to help the children of India, but I can't hold back.'' He understood that, ''according to Bill Fulbright at least,'' all of them felt under the gun when they came to the White House. He then dared the leaders to defeat foreign aid.

Fulbright refused to be intimidated. ''Vietnam is central to the whole problem,'' he declared. It was unbalancing the budget and undermining the nation's foreign policy.

''Bill,'' Johnson responded, ''everybody doesn't have a blind spot like you do. You say don't bomb North Vietnam on just about everything. I don't have the simple solution you have.''

Turning to the group, the president said bitterly, ''If you want me to get out of Vietnam, then you have the prerogative of taking out the resolution under which we are out there now. You can repeal it tomorrow. You can tell the troops to come home. You can tell General Westmoreland that he doesn't know what he is doing.''[12] Mansfield interrupted to say that perhaps the group ought to move on to a discussion of governmental operations.

Six days after his explosive encounter with the president, Fulbright was

11 ''Fulbright Cuts Float Trip Short,'' *Arkansas Democrat,* July 22, 1967.
12 Meeting of the President with Senate Committee Chairman, July 25, 1967, Tom Johnson Notes, Box 1, Johnson Papers.

ready to move on the national commitments resolution. "This could be a pretty important statement," Marcy told another staff member with vast understatement. "[T]he break between JWF and LBJ openeth again."[13] On the thirty-first Fulbright introduced his "sense of Congress" proposal. It was, he told his colleagues, a simple reaffirmation of the constitutional truth that a national commitment could be made only through formal executive and legislative action. Immediately Richard Russell rose to his feet. "I know of nothing that is more in need of clarification than the present state of the alleged commitment of the United States all over the world." Conservative North Carolinian Sam Ervin followed. "The Senator from Arkansas has rendered a real, a lasting, and a most significant service to the country in proposing the resolution which he has offered today," proclaimed the self-styled "country lawyer." A host of others followed – doves, hawks, northerners, southerners, liberals, conservatives.[14] At last Fulbright had in his fingers the thread that would unwind the congressional consensus in behalf of the Vietnam War. He had no intention of forcing an early vote, however. With the resolution pending, there would be a continual focal point for anti-Vietnam debate.

But the national commitments resolution was, in addition, a frontal assault on NSC-68 and the globalist assumptions that underlay it. Fulbright let newspeople know that he was drawing up a "diplomatic catechism" for Rusk to answer during his next appearance before the SFRC. These questions would force the secretary to define precisely American responsibilities under the forty-two bilateral and multilateral aid agreements the United States had concluded around the world. No one noted the irony of the fact that the sponsor of the national commitments resolution was the same person who had proved instrumental in defeating the Bricker amendment more than a decade earlier.

By the late summer of 1967, the antiwar movement had become a major force in American politics and culture. On April 4 Martin Luther King, Jr., had told the ritzy congregation at New York's Riverside Church: "I could never again raise my voice against the violence of the oppressed in the ghettos without having first spoken clearly to the greatest purveyor of violence in the world today – my own government."[15] The decision by the 1964 Nobel Prize winner to join the antiwar movement gave it a sudden infusion of much-needed prestige. King endorsed Fulbright's eight-point program for ending the war but, like Fulbright, explicitly rejected civil disobedience and draft evasion. In July, King joined Benjamin Spock, whom Fulbright had publicly

13 Marcy to Newhouse, July 27, 1967, Box 7, Folder July–Sept., Marcy Papers.
14 "Bid to Curb Executive's Role Gains," *Baltimore Sun,* Aug. 1, 1967.
15 Quoted in Charles DeBenedetti with Charles Chatfield, *An American Ordeal: The Antiwar Movement of the Vietnam Era* (Syracuse, 1990), 172.

praised, and others in cofounding Vietnam Summer, an ambitious effort to organize liberals and radicals into local antiwar chapters. Following a December 1966 "We Won't Go" conference in Chicago, students at Chicago, Wisconsin, and Queens College independently announced in 1967 that they would not fight in Vietnam. In March Fulbright inserted into the *Congressional Record* a letter protesting the war signed by eight hundred former Peace Corps volunteers.[16] Only a February snowstorm prevented two thousand members of Women's Strike for Peace from demonstrating in Washington.[17] By July popular approval of the president's handling of the war had dropped to thirty-three percent.[18]

The White House had reason to fear the antiwar movement, not because it was a threat by alien and radical factions to destabilize the nation but because it was an increasingly mainstream movement whose objective was to conserve American institutions and living standards. Support for the war among middle- and working-class Americans dropped sharply during 1967. By the summer of that year, draft calls exceeded thirty thousand per month, and more than thirteen thousand Americans had died in Vietnam. In early August, the president recommended a ten percent surtax to cover the steadily increasing costs of the war.[19] Polls taken shortly after the tax increase was announced indicated that for the first time a majority of Americans felt the United States had been mistaken in intervening in Vietnam. Public approval of Johnson's handling of the war plummeted to twenty-eight percent by October.[20] A number of major metropolitan dailies shifted from support of the war to opposition in 1967, and the influential *Time–Life* publications, fervently hawkish at the outset, began to raise serious questions about the administration's policies.

Lyndon Johnson was a stubborn, controlling man, however. Had he accepted defeat easily, he would have been neither the Senate's youngest majority leader nor president of the United States. Johnson's definition of victory in Vietnam, despite what Fulbright thought or said, did not include the conquest, or even military defeat, of North Vietnam. It did call for the protection and sustenance of a noncommunist South Vietnam. But that was the problem. Called on to describe the political and cultural entity it was fighting to protect, the administration was hard-pressed to come up with a convincing answer. Since the formation of nation-states, the willingness of citizens to bear arms in behalf of their country had been both a badge of their citizenship and a sign of the viability of their country. By that standard, as well as other political and cultural guidelines, South Vietnam did not exist. In July, while

16 *Congressional Record,* Mar. 7, 1967, 5635.
17 WSP to JWF, Feb. 9, 1967, Series 48:17, Box 44:1, SPF.
18 DeBenedetti and Chatfield, *American Ordeal,* 179.
19 George C. Herring, *America's Longest War: The United States and Vietnam, 1950–1975,* 2d ed. (New York, 1986), 174.
20 Sherwin Markman to Barefoot Sanders, July 11–14 and 20, 1967, and DeVier Pierson to Barefoot Sanders, Aug. 3, 1967, WHCF, Box 324, Johnson Papers.

calling for additional American troops, President Nguyen Van Thieu rejected the notion of a general mobilization of his countrymen.[21]

Through sheer willpower, the Johnson administration had brought into being a South Vietnamese constitution in the spring of 1967 and persuaded Thieu and his vice-president, Nguyen Cao Ky, to schedule elections for the following September. The process was flawed from beginning to end, however. The American embassy carefully "monitored" elections to a constituent assembly to ensure that "anti-Americanism" did not crop up and that NLF members and fellow-travelers were excluded.[22] The problem was that in seeking to keep anti-Americanism out of the election the embassy virtually guaranteed that the Buddhists would not participate.

With members of the NLF excluded and the Buddhists boycotting, participants in the constituent elections were limited largely to members of the government and their clients. Fulbright, who had been following events closely, was disgusted. "If they had an honest election in South Vietnam they would tell us to go home," he wrote a constituent, "but there is not a chance to have an honest election when we control all modes of transportation . . . and for all practical purposes dominate the country."[23]

Assisted by John Roche, the same White House staffer who wanted to jail draft card burners and other dissenters, the constituent assembly drafted a constitution that called for a two-house legislature and a powerful president. Fulbright was not impressed. Noting that the president could suspend the constitution for reasons of "security, national defense . . . national interest . . . public safety," he warned the Senate that the ballyhooed document was an invitation to tyranny.[24] When, subsequently, 1 of the 117 members of the assembly who dared support negotiations with the NLF was murdered, Fulbright, appearing on *Meet the Press*, accused the Ky government of being responsible.[25] The charge infuriated Ky. The South Vietnamese ambassador delivered an official protest, and militant Roman Catholic youths burned effigies of Fulbright in Saigon.[26]

Although not flagrantly fraudulent by Ngo Dinh Nhu standards, the September elections were hardly fair and impartial. Only NLF members or sympathizers were excluded. The vast majority of Buddhists wound up voting – indeed, they had little choice. The Vietcong had called for a boycott of the elections, and the government warned that all Vietnamese who did not par-

21 Baggs to JWF, July 14, 1967, Series 48:18, Box 51:2, SPF.
22 Principles Governing U.S. Operations Concerning Elections and Constitutional Assembly in South Vietnam, May 12, 1966, NSF, Memos to President, Box 7, Johnson Papers.
23 JWF to Oscar Fendler, May 14, 1966, Series 48:18, Box 48:1, SPF.
24 *Congressional Record,* Senate, June 6, 1967, 14758.
25 Notes on Senator Fulbright *Meet the Press* Interview, Jan. 24, 1967, Box 462, Harriman Papers.
26 JWF to Tran Van Do, Mar. 3, 1967, Series 48:18, Box 53:4, SPF; and "Fulbright, Others Burned in Effigy at Rally in Saigon," *Arkansas Gazette,* Feb. 26, 1967.

ticipate would be prosecuted. The ambitious Thieu forced Ky to change places with him on the ticket, then prepared for a landslide victory. He was sadly disappointed. The Thieu–Ky ticket polled barely thirty-five percent of the vote. Of further embarrassment to the government was the strong showing of Truong Dinh Dzu, an unsavory lawyer who had once put his wife up as collateral for a loan. Concealing his neutralist tendencies, Dzu slipped through the screening process and then campaigned as a dove. Immediately following the election, President Thieu, whose thirty-five percent still represented a plurality, had Dzu arrested and jailed.[27]

"These are our elections," Fulbright told reporters, "not the kind anticipated under the Geneva accords."[28] It was all one big farce, he said; the American-financed pacification program in Vietnam stemmed not from any commitment to the welfare of the people but from a determination to bribe them into voting for a pro-American government. In view of the "unsatisfactory political situation" in South Vietnam, Fulbright called on Johnson for "a major reassessment of our position."[29]

The administration, including Johnson and Lodge, was not so naive as to believe that Western-style democracy could be exported to Vietnam, a land that had stubbornly resisted Westernization for four hundred years. Many within the administration feared that a completely open government would lead to chaos. Indeed, by 1967 the Johnson administration had recast its definition of "victory" in Vietnam. Perhaps the best that could be hoped for, Lodge told Johnson, was a reduction in the level of terrorism, an open stretch of road from Camau (Quan Long) in the South to Quang Tri in the North along which civilians could travel safely. Victory, in the final analysis, could be defined as the absence of defeat.[30]

Unable to establish a government that would either satisfy its own publicly stated standards for democracy and viability or to compel the Vietnamese to fight for a political edifice that was acceptable to Washington and the Vietnamese military, Johnson, Rostow, Lodge, and the Joint Chiefs turned once again, inevitably it seemed, to the issue of physical security. If the North Vietnamese could be bombed into halting their infiltration of the South and if the South Vietnamese countryside could be pacified, then perhaps, they hoped, there would emerge a South Vietnam for which its citizens would be willing to fight.

By the late summer of 1967, so stubborn had Robert McNamara's opposition to the bombing of the North become that Lyndon Johnson had to either

27 Stanley Karnow, *Vietnam: A History* (New York, 1984), 449–50.
28 Carolyn Lewis, "Fulbright Calls Vietnam Pacification 'Political,' " *Washington Post,* May 19, 1967.
29 JWF to LBJ, June 30, 1967, Box 2, RG 46, SPF.
30 Lodge to LBJ, Aug. 10, 1966, NSF, Memos to President, Box 9, Johnson Papers.

order a stand-down or part company with his secretary of defense. The DOD chief was sick of the war, sick of being ignored by the president, and sick of war protesters, several of whom had burned down his condominium in Aspen. In December, at McNamara's request, Johnson recommended him to head the World Bank. He officially departed in February 1968.

Although he pared Westmoreland's troop request from two hundred thousand down to fifty-five thousand, Johnson, on the recommendation of McNamara's successor Clark Clifford, significantly expanded the list of aerial targets in North Vietnam. In the fall of 1967 troop staging areas, rail yards, and munitions depots within the greater Hanoi–Haiphong area, as well as previously restricted supply routes along the Chinese border, came under attack.[31] The Johnson administration's decision to bomb so close to Chinese territory frightened and angered Fulbright. ''I think it's very dangerous and extremely stupid,'' he told reporters.[32] Observers noted ominously that the decision to widen the bombing war came just as the Senate was preparing to debate the 1967 foreign aid bill.

No sooner had Johnson submitted his $3.2 billion aid measure than Fulbright and the SFRC immediately began hacking away at it. After some $200 million had been cut, both Rusk and McNamara suddenly found time to testify before the committee. For over a year Fulbright had been waiting to get the two in open session. The United States was running a negative balance of payments, the national debt was growing at a rate of $30 billion a year, the inner cities were suffering from neglect, and the president was thinking of imposing new taxes. How could it justify a multi-billion-dollar aid program? Fulbright asked. The United States must seek ''to build a peace,'' Rusk replied. ''When you talk about building a peace, do you consider the 12,000 deaths in Vietnam and the 70,000 wounded?'' Fulbright asked. ''That doesn't seem to be a typical figure of building a peace.''[33]

By the time Fulbright ''reluctantly'' presented the foreign aid bill to the Senate as a whole, the SFRC had cut nearly three-quarters of a billion dollars from it. An amendment by Frank Church prohibited arms aid to countries where economic development would suffer as a result of excessive military spending. The administration had been warned time and time again, Fulbright declared, and ignored the signals. Now it was time to pay the price.[34] In the end, the Senate cut another $100 million from the aid measure, approved the Church amendment, and passed the revised bill by a vote of 60 to 26.[35] While the national press trumpeted Fulbright's victory, Johnson fumed.

31 Notes of President's Meeting with Clifford and Taylor, Aug. 5, 1967, Box 3, T. Johnson Meeting Notes, Johnson Papers.
32 ''Fulbright Calls Raid Widening a Great Risk,'' *Washington Star,* Sept. 10, 1967.
33 ''Senate's Cuts in Aid Irk Rusk,'' *Chicago Tribune,* July 15, 1967.
34 *Congressional Record,* Senate, Aug. 14, 1967, 22549–51.
35 Manatos to LBJ, Aug. 16, 1967, WHCF–Leg., Box 57, Johnson Papers; and ''Senate Supports Fulbright, Passes a Reduced Aid Bill,'' *Arkansas Gazette,* Aug. 18, 1967.

12

Denouement

As the series of cease-fires in honor of Christmas and Tet, the Vietnamese lunar New Year, got under way in the last days of 1967, Ambassador Ellsworth Bunker threw a New Year's Eve party, inviting everyone to come "see the light at the end of the tunnel."[1] That light turned out to be fire in the hole. On the evening of January 31, 1968, Americans turned on their television sets to view the nightly news. They had become somewhat inured to film clips depicting American combat teams combing the countryside for the ever elusive enemy and Vietcong rockets exploding among supposedly secure villages and troop compounds. But the war had seemed to be going better during the winter of 1967–8, and amid optimistic prognostications by Westmoreland and others, hope that the long nightmare might soon be over began to rise in the collective bosom. What the nation saw that January evening withered that hope and blasted any chance Lyndon Johnson had of maintaining his much-coveted consensus.

The previous night, nearly seventy thousand communist soldiers had launched a surprise offensive of extraordinary intensity and astonishing scope. Violating a truce that they themselves had pledged to observe during the Tet season, they surged into more than a hundred cities and towns, including Saigon, audaciously shifting the war for the first time from its rural setting to a new arena – South Vietnam's supposedly impregnable urban areas. "War Hits Saigon" screamed the front-page headline of Washington's afternoon tabloid *The News*. But print accounts paled beside the television images. Fifty million Americans saw the dead bodies lying amid the rubble, heard the rattle of automatic gunfire as dazed American soldiers and civilians ran back and forth, trying to flush out the guerrillas.[2]

Once they recovered from their initial surprise, U.S. and South Vietnamese troops struck back quickly and effectively. Within days, they had cleared Saigon and the other provincial capitals of enemy troops. In the process, they killed and captured tens of thousands of Vietcong cadre and seized valuable

1 Quoted in Marilyn B. Young, *The Vietnam Wars, 1945–1990* (New York, 1991), 216.
2 Stanley Karnow, *Vietnam: A History* (New York, 1984), 526.

160

caches of arms. The ARVN, perhaps because in many cases it was literally defending its homes and families, fought with vigor and tenacity. Only in Hué were the communists able to hold out for an appreciable time. The liberation of that city took nearly three weeks and required heavy bombing and intensive artillery fire, which in the end left the beautiful old city, in the words of one observer, "a shattered, stinking hulk, its streets choked with rubble and rotting bodies." As allied troops moved into the city, they discovered the mass graves of twenty-eight hundred South Vietnamese murdered by VC and NVA troops.[3]

Tactically Tet was a devastating defeat for the North Vietnamese and Vietcong. The Thieu government did not collapse. The South Vietnamese people did not rise to welcome the attackers as liberators. Estimates of combined Vietcong and North Vietnamese losses ran as high as forty thousand. Indeed, Tet broke the back of the Vietcong, which had theretofore borne the brunt of the fighting in the Second Indochinese War. Superior American and ARVN firepower destroyed many of its main units, and the fighting killed or wounded an irreplaceable political cadre.

Strategically, however, the lunar New Year offensive was a grand success for the communists. American and South Vietnamese losses amounted to eleven hundred and twenty-three hundred killed, respectively. An estimated twelve and a half thousand civilians died in the fighting, and the communist offensive created as many as one million new refugees. Most important, Tet was interpreted by American journalists and their followers not only as proof that the United States was not winning the war but as evidence that the Johnson administration was out of touch with reality. "What, indeed, is the U.S. trying to save" in Vietnam? asked the *Wall Street Journal*. "If the Saigon government . . . doesn't really have the support of most of the people or the ability to save them from nation-wide terror and murder, how good is it?"[4]

Westmoreland and Johnson's hawkish advisers pointed out to him that Tet presented the greatest military opportunity of the war. The enemy was on the run; if the United States was willing to apply the necessary force, the Vietcong could be destroyed once and for all. With the indigenous guerrilla war over, the U.S. military and ARVN could seal South Vietnam's borders, á la South Korea, and put an end to North Vietnamese infiltration. The United States did not follow up, however, because it could not. Tet constituted a devastating blow to Johnson's prowar consensus. Fulbright and others had so weakened it, so highlighted the Texan's lack of credibility, that it could not survive. In the days and weeks following Tet, it was J. William Fulbright, rather than William Westmoreland, who was able to press his advantage.

3 George C. Herring, *America's Longest War: The United States and Vietnam, 1950–1975,* 2d ed. (New York, 1986), 190.
4 "Vietnam: The American Dilemma," *Wall Street Journal,* Feb. 6, 1968.

To Fulbright's great irritation, Dean Rusk frequented *Meet the Press* and other national television talk shows to discuss Tet while steadfastly refusing to testify in open session before the committee.[5] "These are more or less controlled exhibitions," Fulbright complained to reporters. The administration "can do everything except say to [*Meet the Press* moderator Lawrence] Spivak what the questions will be." If he objected, Spivak "knows that he will be dropped from the list."[6] Should Rusk be replaced, David Brinkley asked Fulbright shortly thereafter? He did not want to make a "personal judgment," Fulbright said, but he had always believed that Secretary Rusk had never wanted any peace terms except the unconditional surrender of North Vietnam.[7] "We have gotten our Committee in a perfectly untenable position," he told the SFRC, "where it is assumed by the public . . . that we as Senators and members of the Foreign Relations Committee have less self-restraint and less responsibility than a bunch of newspaper people."[8]

The prospect of attacking the secretary of state in public, however, while the battle for Hué was raging continued to be an intimidating one for the SFRC. "I am not going to contribute to the continued disruption of our military operations and our military effort," Hickenlooper told Fulbright and his colleagues. Even the aggressively dovish Joseph Clark was dubious. He doubted, he said, whether "it is wise to put on a public show even if we could get him to come, until this present offensive is blunted." The administration was "at bay" and dangerous, he said. But Fulbright, supported by Albert Gore, held his ground. The most effective time to act was during a crisis, the chairman argued, when the country's attention was focused on the problem. When several suggested that Fulbright request a face-to-face meeting between the president and the SFRC similar to the one Henry Cabot Lodge had arranged with Woodrow Wilson in 1919, Fulbright resisted. "The more traditional and time-proven way is public hearings," he insisted. The public was entitled to know what was going on. After all, "it is their boys who are being killed, it is their money that is being spent, it is their country that is being ruined and they ought to be given an opportunity to judge about the course of it." Following an 8 to 4 vote, Fulbright drafted a formal letter to the president asking him to direct Rusk to appear in public session.[9]

5 Marcy to Gore, Feb. 5, 1968, Box 8, Folder Jan.–Mar., Marcy Papers.

6 "Fulbright Hits 'Show,' " *Washington Post,* Feb. 7, 1968.

7 In a follow-up to the interview, Brinkley told his audience that Fulbright was particularly incensed that though he had just recently appeared on *Meet the Press,* Rusk still refused to testify before the SFRC in open session. Bob Fleming to LBJ, Feb. 16, 1968, WHCF, Box 287, Johnson Papers.

8 Discussion on Secretary Rusk's Appearance before the Committee, Feb. 7, 1968, Executive Sessions, SFRC, RG 46, NA.

9 Ibid.

In the days that followed, Mike Mansfield worked frantically to hammer out a compromise. Perhaps Rusk would agree to appear in public session to discuss the foreign aid bill, he told Fulbright. You tell the president, Fulbright retorted, that if Rusk did not get his butt up to the Hill, there would not be a foreign aid bill to discuss.[10]

Reluctantly, Johnson called Rusk in and told him he would have to go before the SFRC and the television cameras again and take his punishment. Everyone must do his duty to help maintain public support for the war. The Georgian agreed, but he was bitter at Fulbright, at Marcy, and at Johnson.[11] During a backgrounder with the press on February 26, he lashed out. "There gets to be a point when the question is, whose side are you on?" he responded to a hostile questioner. "Now I'm Secretary of State of the United States and I'm on our side. . . . [N]one of your papers or your broadcasting apparatuses are worth a damn unless the United States succeeds."[12]

While Fulbright, Marcy, and the rest of the SFRC prepared for Rusk, the Johnson administration was facing a turning point in the war. Since 1967 Westmoreland and the JCS had fought against suggestions by Fulbright and others that the United States revive the enclave strategy. To do so, argued Westmoreland and Wheeler, would be "to abandon a large portion of Vietnam to the control of the enemy and would preclude further significant broadening of the GVN's [Government of Vietnam] influence throughout the countryside."[13] The enemy's strategy depended on the establishment of prestocked bases in secure areas. These bases, in turn, were necessary to support the activities of regular NVA and main-force VC units, Westy insisted. Only by striking at these bases through search-and-destroy missions could "Free World Forces" divorce the enemy's various echelons from each other and defeat them. An enclave strategy would allow the NVA and VC to grow stronger and stronger.[14]

Confident that he could exploit the enemy's defeat at Tet, and buoyed by the president's dispatch of ten and a half thousand additional men to Khe Sanh, Westmoreland devised a "two-fisted" strategy designed to take advantage of the enemy's weakened condition. During a late February visit to Saigon by JCS chief Wheeler, he and Westmoreland decided to propose an "amphibious hook" designed to take out North Vietnamese bases and staging

10 Even though the State Department's legal adviser told him that Congress could not require an officer of the executive branch to appear, and if he did, that officer could impose whatever limitations he chose, LBJ gave in. Larry Temple to LBJ, Feb. 8, 1968, WHCF, Box 342; Manatos to LBJ, Feb. 15, 1968, WHCF, Box 287; and Mansfield to LBJ, Feb. 19, 1968, Box 102, NSF, Country File – Vietnam, Johnson Papers.

11 Harry McPherson to LBJ, Feb. 26, 1968, WHCF, Confidential File, Box 34, Johnson Papers.

12 "Rusk Is Identified as Critics' Critic," *New York Times,* Feb. 24, 1968.

13 Wheeler to LBJ, Feb. 3, 1968, Box 102, NSF, Country File – Vietnam, Johnson Papers.

14 Harold K. Johnson to LBJ, Feb. 1, 1968, NSF, Country File – Vietnam, Box 102, Johnson Papers.

areas across the demilitarized zone, attacks on the communist sanctuaries in Laos and Cambodia, and an intensified bombing campaign directed against North Vietnam. Wheeler was to return to Washington and ask for two hundred and six thousand additional men, a number sufficient to meet any contingency in Vietnam and an increase that would force the president to call up the reserves.[15]

Fulbright learned of the request for over two hundred thousand additional troops and permission to expand the war almost as soon as Wheeler returned to Washington. His source could have been any one of a number of people. Clark Clifford, the new secretary of defense and a staunch opponent of lifting the administration's self-imposed limit of five hundred and twenty-five thousand men, had every reason to tell the chairman. Some of the president's defenders would later claim that Johnson himself leaked the information in order to contain the hawkish Wheeler and Westmoreland. Whatever the case, Fulbright rose on the floor of the Senate on March 7 and called for a full-fledged congressional debate on the rumored troop buildup. The administration was responding to "our recent defeats and difficulties" not by pulling back but by putting in two hundred thousand more soldiers and expanding the war beyond the South, a reference to Westmoreland's two-fisted strategy. He had not, he told his colleagues, urged the Senate to adopt the Gulf of Tonkin Resolution out of the belief that it gave the president the authority to wage all-out war in Southeast Asia. Indeed, the administration had presented the resolution as congressional authorization to respond to the torpedo boat attacks and nothing more. Reminding the Senate that Johnson had promised the American people during the 1964 campaign not to send American boys to fight an Asian war, Fulbright declared that the resolution "like any contract based on misrepresentation . . . is null and void."[16]

Fulbright's speech fell like a spark on dry tinder. A dozen senators vied for the floor; Robert Kennedy, Jacob Javits, Frank Church, and Gaylord Nelson rose to applaud Fulbright's speech and to call for a full-scale debate on the rumored expansion of the war. "If the Senator from Arkansas had stood on the floor of the Senate, in the middle of that debate in 1964," Nelson declared, "and had said that the resolution authorizes a ground commitment of an unlimited number of troops . . . he would have been soundly defeated." Only diehard hawks such as John Tower of Texas dared argue that the issue was none of Congress's business.

Meanwhile, the long-awaited day of the second televised confrontation between Dean Rusk and the SFRC had arrived. When the kleig lights went on Monday morning the cameras revealed a packed committee room and a tight-lipped witness peering apprehensively over his half-glasses at the members. They were, Rusk had to admit, more imposing than he remembered.

15 Herring, *America's Longest War,* 193–4.
16 *Congressional Record,* Senate, Mar. 7, 1968, 5644–54.

There was George Aiken, his ancient head crowned with wisps of white hair; the square-jawed Sparkman; the mustachioed Wayne Morse, his brows perpetually arched; the dour-faced Mike Mansfield; and at the center of the inquisitory board, Fulbright. Without makeup, tortoise-shelled dark glasses perched atop his nose, the chairman looked like a gargoyle in a three-piece suit.

"I am more than ever convinced that [U.S. strategy] is wrong and that our present policies in Vietnam have had and will have effects both abroad and at home that are nothing short of disastrous," Fulbright declared in his opening statement. When asked whether reports that the administration was going to send two hundred thousand additional troops to Vietnam were true, Rusk declared that the president was considering all options, and "it was not right to speculate on new numbers." Would Congress be consulted before any decision on escalation was taken? Fulbright inquired. The secretary replied that Lyndon Johnson had consulted Congress more than any president in the twentieth century.[17] And so it went.

The 1968 Rusk hearings were not the public relations event that the 1966 hearings were. Polls showed opinion about evenly divided between Rusk and the committee's position. Still, the secretary of state's obfuscation, his vagueness, and his self-righteousness coming as it did hard on the heels of Tet did not sit well with the public. Moreover, the hearings revealed that the antiwar majority on the SFRC had expanded to include former hawks like Mundt and Sparkman.[18]

Much more important in undermining the administration's position than the televised confrontation with Rusk was Fulbright's decision, made during the height of the Tet offensive, to reopen the whole Gulf of Tonkin debate. This time the chairman was prepared to go beyond his argument that the administration had misrepresented its intentions and exceeded its authority. This time he would insist that Johnson, McNamara, and Rusk had lied to Congress about the circumstances surrounding the attacks on the *Turner Joy* and the *Maddox* – and, in fact, that the second foray had never taken place.

Momentum toward a confrontation with the administration over the Gulf of Tonkin Resolution had been building for almost two years. The first hint that things were not as they had seemed on the nights of August 2 and 4, 1964, came during the Senate's consideration of the original Gulf of Tonkin Resolution. One of Wayne Morse's contacts in the Pentagon had called him and told him to ask McNamara for the *Turner Joy*'s and *Maddox*'s logbooks.

17 "Troop Issue Still Open, Rusk Says," *Washington Evening Star,* Mar. 11, 1968.
18 Bob Fleming to LBJ, Mar. 11, 1968, and Ernest K. Lindley to Rostow, Mar. 29, 1968, WHCF, Subject File, Box 342, Johnson Papers.

McNamara had told Morse at the time that they were unavailable – still on board ship (In fact, they had been flown back to Washington.) Whether the Department of Defense wanted to suppress the books because they indicated that the ships were running cover for South Vietnamese DeSoto patrols or because they indicated that the second attack did not occur is unclear – probably both. Whatever the case, in August 1964, Fulbright was a strong administration partisan, and he viewed Wayne Morse as a humorless Don Quixote who was obstructing his efforts to help the president defeat Barry Goldwater.

As Fulbright's doubts about the administration's veracity grew, particularly in the aftermath of the Dominican crisis, and the administration continually beat him about the head and shoulders with his sponsorship of the Tonkin resolution, the chairman began to recall the missing logbooks. Then in March 1966, he received a letter from retired Admiral Arnold True, a distinguished veteran of World War II, who wrote that the administration's account of the August 4 attack "sounds unrealistic."[19] Knowing that George Ball had been present throughout the 1964 crisis, Fulbright asked him whether the second attack had really occurred. "I'll tell you what the President told me," Ball said. "He said, 'Those goddamn admirals; they see a bunch of flying fish and they think they're ships. They don't know how to run the goddamn navy.' "[20] Ball did not, however, tell Fulbright that the CIA and the South Vietnamese had been running a covert operation in conjunction with the destroyer patrols. He did not because he had not been informed. Then, in mid-December 1967, Lieutenant. (j.g.) John White told the Associated Press that no North Vietnamese torpedoes had been fired during the second attack. He had been on duty aboard the *Pine Island,* the first ship into the war zone on August 4 after suspected enemy action had been reported. The sonarman aboard the *Maddox* reported throughout the incident that no torpedoes had been fired into the water.[21]

Still, Fulbright was loath to charge the administration publicly with fabricating the whole incident. It would be difficult to prove, and while an investigation had the potential of destroying the president, it could also backfire and deflate the antiwar movement in Congress. What apparently changed Fulbright's mind was Nicholas Katzenbach's testimony in August 1967. When Fulbright castigated the administration for going to war without a declaration and insisted that the Tonkin resolution was limited to the incident in question, Katzenbach bristled. Why would the administration need a declaration of war? he asked rhetorically . . . "[D]idn't that Resolution authorize the President to use the armed forces of the United States in

19 Quoted in William C. Berman, *William Fulbright and the Vietnam War: The Dissent of a Political Realist* (Kent, Ohio, 1988), 69.
20 Interview with George Ball, July 6, 1990, Princeton, N.J.
21 "Red Boats Fired No Shots in Tonkin, Ex-officer Says," *Arkansas Gazette,* Dec. 10, 1967.

whatever way was necessary? Didn't it? ... You explained it, Mr. Chairman.''[22]

Several days later Fulbright asked William Bader, an SFRC staffer with a background in naval intelligence, to began an investigation quietly. In mid-December the chairman planted the first seeds of doubt in the public's mind when he released portions of Assistant Secretary William Bundy's testimony given in executive session over a year earlier. Bundy had let slip that the State Department had prepared the Gulf of Tonkin Resolution months before the actual incident occurred.[23] Clearly, the administration had planned to escalate the war; it had either seized on or fabricated the Gulf of Tonkin incident to justify a policy already decided on. Journalists and academics remembered FDR's duplicity over the USS *Greer* prior to America's entry into World War II. Finally, in early January 1968, with the national commitments resolution pending and the tide turning in Congress against both the war and Lyndon Johnson, Fulbright announced that the SFRC staff would conduct an official inquiry into the Gulf of Tonkin incident. Secretary McNamara and other relevant officials would be asked to testify in open hearing at the appropriate time.

On January 23, with Khe Sanh under siege and the Tet offensive just a week away, President Johnson was awakened at 2:24 in the morning. The duty officer informed him that the USS *Pueblo,* a highly sophisticated intelligence ship, had been surrounded and then seized by a North Korean flotilla of warships. The communists had captured the vessel fifteen and a half miles from the nearest land, outside the territorial limit, and had wounded four of the eighty-three-man crew, one mortally.[24] The consensus among Johnson's advisers was that the seizure was a diversionary tactic by the North Koreans designed to help Hanoi.[25] Fearful that the North Koreans might be willing to go so far as to ''open a second front,'' the president rushed the nuclear carrier *Enterprise* to the scene. The huge ship cruised twelve miles offshore, broadcasting demands for release of the *Pueblo*'s crew.[26] As the nation held its breath over the incident, the forthcoming hearings on the Gulf of Tonkin took on special meaning.

''An intelligence ship off your coast is very irritating,'' Fulbright told a Pine Bluff audience. ''People for some reason just don't like eavesdropping. ... I can tell you now that I don't think there will be any 24-hour resolution on this incident.''[27] A number of observers, including Arthur Schlesinger,

22 Quoted in Berman, *Fulbright and the Vietnam War,* 88.
23 ''War Resolution Drawn Up Early,'' *Arkansas Gazette,* Dec. 22, 1967.
24 Lyndon Baines Johnson, *The Vantage Point: Perspectives of the Presidency, 1963–1969* (New York, 1971), 533.
25 Notes of the President's Meeting with the NSC, Jan. 24, 1968, T. Johnson Meeting Notes, Box 2, Johnson Papers.
26 ''U.S. Stations Nuclear Carrier Near N. Korea,'' *Arkansas Gazette,* Jan. 25, 1968.
27 ''U.S. Ambitions Assailed,'' *Pine Bluff Commercial,* Jan. 26, 1968.

credited the pending investigation of the Gulf of Tonkin Resolution with preventing the administration from launching an immediate attack on North Korea and then coming to Congress for approval.[28] In turn, the *Pueblo* incident whetted the public's appetite for the true story behind the Gulf of Tonkin incident. "We feel that the country should have all the facts on what happened in the Tonkin Gulf in August, 1964," editorialized the hitherto staunchly pro-administration *Washington Post.*[29]

Fulbright's announcement that the SFRC was resuming its Gulf of Tonkin investigation was made on the day the Tet offensive began. He went to great lengths not to appear to accuse the administration of a conspiracy. All the committee wanted to know, he told reporters, was why the Commander-in-Chief, Pacific (CINCPAC) had dispatched two American destroyers on a sensitive mission off the coast of North Vietnam at the time that it had.[30]

Although he was determined to press ahead, Fulbright took no joy in his task. His country was in a terrible predicament, writhing in the coils of its own misguided altruism, reaching once again for the sword in its frustration. "There is literally a miasma of madness in the city, enveloping everyone in the administration and most of those in Congress," he wrote Erich Fromm. "I am at a loss for words to describe the idiocy of what we are doing."[31]

Robert McNamara, although he detested Fulbright and felt deep contempt for most of the rest of the members of the SFRC, agreed to run the gauntlet in order to try to cleanse his reputation before he left for the World Bank. From the beginning, it was clear that his intention was to manipulate the information at his command so as to prove decisively that the North Vietnamese had staged armed attacks on both August 2 and August 4, even though he knew full well that there had been no second assault.[32]

When McNamara met with the SFRC in executive session on February 20, the atmosphere was tense. The secretary, as always, was immaculately dressed, his straight hair slicked back, his lower lip protruding aggressively beneath his famous rimless glasses. Although he brought a large entourage with him, he refused to read from his prepared statement until the SFRC staff left the room. During the grueling seven-and-a-half-hour cross-examination, the secretary read testimony from an "unimpeachable" North Vietnamese source stating that an assault had in fact taken place on the fourth. When Fulbright asked for copies, McNamara quickly reclassified the document.[33]

28 Schlesinger to JWF, Jan. 25, 1968, Series 48:16, Box 42:1, SPF.
29 J. R. Wiggins, ed., "Midwife to History," *Washington Post,* Jan. 27, 1968.
30 "Senate Panel to Re-examine Tonkin Case," *Arkansas Gazette,* Jan. 31, 1968.
31 JWF to Fromm, Feb. 1, 1968, Series 48:18, Box 54:5, SPF.
32 Indeed, the Pentagon refused to provide any cable traffic or other information connected with the incident until Fulbright persuaded Richard Russell to intervene. The Armed Services chairman summoned Paul Nitze to his office and advised him to cooperate, but even then, the documentation was incomplete.
33 Gulf of Tonkin Hearing, Feb. 21, 1968, Executive Sessions, SFRC, RG 46, NA.

When the secretary of defense denied that there had been any connection between the destroyer patrols and the OPLAN-34 raids being conducted on two North Vietnamese islands in the gulf by the South Vietnamese, Fulbright produced a message sent by Captain John J. Herrick, commander of the destroyer task force, on August 3 to his superiors stating that the DRV considered the two connected and were determined to treat the *Turner Joy* and the *Maddox* as aggressor ships. He also produced a copy of the cable Herrick had sent to the Pentagon in the early afternoon of August 4: "Review of action makes many recorded contacts and torpedoes fired appear doubtful. Freak weather effects and over-eager sonarman may have accounted for many reports. No actual visual sightings by *Maddox*." McNamara could only reiterate that he had copies of intercepted NVA cable traffic indicating that the attack had occurred.[34]

Before the Tonkin Gulf hearing closed, both McNamara and Fulbright agreed that neither would say anything substantive to the phalanx of reporters who waited outside the committee room doors; but no sooner had the DOD chief made that commitment and exited his chamber of tribulation than he presented to the press a twenty-one-page document "proving" conclusively that both the *Maddox* and *Turner Joy* were attacked by North Vietnamese torpedo boats in international waters on August 4, 1964. He blasted Fulbright and the SFRC for impugning his and the president's integrity. Any suggestion that the United States induced the attack as part of an effort to find an excuse for its subsequent retaliation was "monstrous," he said.[35]

Infuriated at McNamara's duplicity, Fulbright tried to strike back. He called the committee into executive session on the twenty-first. Before he went in, he told reporters that it was "monstrous" to insinuate that members of the committee had accused the administration of a conspiracy. He then denounced the DOD chief for engaging in selective declassification designed to safeguard his reputation. "Security classification is intended to protect the nation from an enemy . . . not to protect the American people from knowledge of mistakes."[36]

The next day Fulbright showed his ace in the hole. Not only was the Johnson administration misleading the American people about the 1964 Gulf of Tonkin incident, an ambiguous event that had been used to justify a major escalation of the war, but it had locked up in a mental ward a navy commander who had volunteered to tell Congress what he knew of the affair.[37] The officer, a Commander Cowles who had worked in flag plot in the Pentagon at the time of the

---

34 John W. Finney, "McNamara Says Destroyers in Gulf of Tonkin Warned of Enemy," *New York Times,* Feb. 25, 1968.
35 "Fulbright Hints McNamara Version of Tonkin Attack Misleading," *Northwest Arkansas Times,* Feb. 21, 1968.
36 Fulbright press release, Feb. 21, 1968, Series 48:6, Box 28:3, SPF.
37 "Fulbright Says Public Misled About Vietnam," *Malvern Daily Record,* Feb. 22, 1968.

Tonkin incident, had indeed gone to see Fulbright in mid-November to express his reservations concerning the second attack. When, shortly thereafter, Cowles's commander had discovered the liaison, he had had the officer committed to the Walter Reed psychiatric ward for four weeks. In a public exchange of letters with Fulbright, McNamara insisted that Cowles had had a history of "neuroses" but had since been returned to active duty.[38]

On Sunday, February 25, Ned Kenworthy of the *New York Times* printed an accurate summary of the McNamara hearing transcripts. "McNamara Says Destroyers in Gulf of Tonkin Warned of Foe" and "9 on Fulbright Panel Feel U.S. Over Reacted to Tonkin Attack" ran the headlines. "McCarthyism" screamed pro-Johnson columnist William S. White. "The violently dovish chairman of the Senate Foreign Relations Committee, J. William Fulbright, is employing its apparatus for a masked attack upon American policy in Vietnam."[39] During the weeks that followed, enterprising reporters interviewed dozens of sailors who had served aboard the two American destroyers and published the results. The overwhelming consensus was that the *Turner Joy* and the *Maddox* had been on a secret mission in support of the South Vietnamese and that the second attack had never happened.[40]

The 1968 brouhaha struck a major and perhaps decisive blow at the president's credibility – and it did so at a crucial time. If he had misled Congress and the American people concerning the North Vietnamese attack on the two American destroyers in 1964, then the Gulf of Tonkin Resolution, which the administration had so often invoked as justification for the presence of American troops in Vietnam, was invalid. In the context of the Tet offensive, this meant not only that Johnson lacked the authority to expand the war and give Westmoreland the troops he wanted but also that he would have to withdraw the forces already in Vietnam.

Six weeks following the beginning of the Tet offensive, the gains made by the NVA and VC had been wiped out. Pressure on Khe Sanh eased as Giap transferred two of his three besieging divisions to other areas.[41] From various outlying districts, American intelligence reported that VC activity was ebbing sharply. The communists had suffered unprecedented losses, an estimated fifty-eight thousand killed.[42] Yet public opinion polls in the United States showed that both disillusionment and disapproval of the president's handling of the conflict were on the rise. Moreover, the man with whom Lyndon

---

38 "Uneasy Truce Descends on Tonkin Gulf Dispute," *Washington Post,* Feb. 2, 1968; Naval Inspector General to Secretary of the Navy, Feb. 24, 1968, Series 48:1, Box 9:1, SPF; and Marcy to Jones, Feb. 28, 1968, Box 8, Jan.–Mar. '68, RG 46, NA.

39 *Congressional Record,* Senate, Feb. 26, 1968, 4009.

40 Ibid., Mar. 14, 1968, 5201.

41 Memorandum for Record, Apr. 4, 1968, NSC Meeting Notes File, Box 2, Johnson Papers.

42 Clark Clifford, *Counsel to the President: A Memoir* (New York, 1991), 473.

Johnson had replaced Robert McNamara as secretary of defense was beginning to see the war in Vietnam as strategically hopeless and politically counterproductive.

Clark Clifford recalled in his memoirs that Lyndon Johnson had selected
him because he wanted a man who would support his position in Vietnam,
end the struggle between the secretary of defense and the JCS, and improve
relations with Congress.[43] Those three objectives were mutually incompatible.
It was perhaps crucial to the history of the war that Johnson appointed Clifford to succeed McNamara in 1968. While his longtime friend Bill Fulbright
was busily widening the credibility gap and eroding the domestic consensus
in behalf of the war, Clifford, the man who had acted as political adviser to
Democratic presidents since Harry Truman, was placed in a position to advise
Johnson on strategic matters. This coming together of the political and strategic in the person of Clifford forced Johnson to realize that he could not
win the war in Vietnam and that, having plunged the nation more deeply into
the quagmire than any of his predecessors, he could not retain the presidency.

Fulbright applauded Clifford's appointment as secretary of defense. He was
not publicly committed to a continuation of the war, the chairman told reporters, and would thus be able to persuade the president to stop the bombing
of the North "without embarrassment." Terming Clifford a personal friend,
Fulbright told reporters, "I feel that I could speak with him and have an
opportunity to try to persuade him. In any case, I think he would listen."[44]

As he surveyed the scene from his office in the Pentagon, Clifford decided
that the JCS, Westmoreland, and the American military did not know what
they were doing in Vietnam and that the war was a millstone that would drag
Lyndon Johnson and the Democratic Party down to defeat in 1968.[45] At a
meeting of the Tuesday luncheon group on March 4, Clifford laid his cards
on the table. Westmoreland and the Joint Chiefs had been overly optimistic,
Tet had been both a military and public relations defeat for the United States
and South Vietnam, and Westmoreland's troop request was just an invitation
to pour more money and troops down a rathole, he declared. North Vietnam
was showing an ongoing capacity to meet the United States man for man
and gun for gun. Where would it stop? the new DOD chief asked. More than
likely, two hundred and six thousand more men would not suffice. If the
president continued to heed Westmoreland and the JCS, there would be one
million American soldiers in Vietnam by the end of the year, with still no
end in sight. Johnson did not protest.[46]

---

43 Ibid., 465.
44 "Hanoi Desires End to War, Fulbright Feels 'Quite Sure,' " *Arkansas Gazette,* Jan. 22,
    1968.
45 Clifford, *Counsel to the President,* 473–5.
46 Notes of Press Meeting with Senior Foreign Policy Advisors, Mar. 4, 1968, T. Johnson
    Meeting Notes, Box 3, Johnson Papers.

Clifford's realistic appraisal broke the dike. Although Rusk and Rostow initially supported Wheeler and Westmoreland and insisted that the Thieu regime represented a viable state that deserved U.S. support, they quickly began to soften. During a mid-March meeting of the president and his top advisers, Rusk observed that the element of hope had been taken away from the American people by Tet, while Rostow acknowledged that Thieu would soon have to accept the NLF as part of the political system.[47]

By the time Johnson had to make his crucial decisions concerning an expansion of the war in Vietnam, he was already faced with a formal challenge to his presidency within the Democratic Party. In August 1967, during Nicholas Katzenbach's claim before the SFRC that Johnson had virtually unlimited constitutional authority to carry on the war in Vietnam, Senator Eugene McCarthy got up and stalked out of the committee room. Marcy and Ned Kenworthy followed him. "The Catholic Church has now abandoned the doctrine of Papal infallibility, but the Johnson administration has taken it up," McCarthy remarked when he reached the staff office. "Somebody's got to take these guys on and I'm going to do it even if I have to run for President."[48] By early 1968 McCarthy supporters had established campaign organizations in a dozen states and were preparing for the New Hampshire primary.

Although Eugene McCarthy had won the endorsement of the ADA, it was hard for Democratic Party leaders to take the Minnesota senator – a nonpartisan, soft-spoken, cerebral man – seriously. On March 12, however, McCarthy stunned the White House by making a strong showing in the New Hampshire primary. Although Johnson's name had not been on the ballot, the party organization had mounted a vigorous write-in campaign for him. Thus, when "Clean Gene" won 42.2 percent of the vote and twenty of twenty-four convention delegates, the media declared New Hampshire to be a major defeat for the president and his policies – despite the fact that most of those voting for McCarthy were disgruntled hawks. To make matters worse, on March 14 William Randolph Hearst, Jr., a longtime Johnson supporter, announced in his huge chain of papers that the Hearst Corporation was changing its stance on the war.[49] Two days later Robert Kennedy entered the race for the Democratic nomination. With his name, glamour, party connections, and money, Kennedy appeared to be a serious threat to the Texan's renomination. Indeed, although the ADA had officially endorsed McCarthy,

47 Meeting with Foreign Policy Advisors, Mar. 19, 1968, Meeting Notes File, Box 2, Johnson Papers.
48 Donald A. Ritchie, interviewer, *Carl A. Marcy: Oral History Interviews* (Senate Historical Office: Washington, D.C., 1983), 201–2.
49 Williams to JWF, Mar. 14, 1968, Series 48:18, Box 55:1, SPF.

it was clear that the rank and file, particularly the moderates like Schlesinger, would work for Bobby. Johnson's longtime friend and adviser Jim Rowe urged him to do "something exciting and dramatic to recapture the peace issue."[50]

In these circumstances, the president rejected Westmoreland's request for two hundred and six thousand additional men and agreed merely to deploy thirteen and a half thousand support troops to augment the emergency reinforcements sent in February. At the same time, he recalled his field commander to Washington to become army chief of staff. But Lyndon Johnson had more demotions in mind.

Fulbright was scheduled to deliver a speech on Vietnam in Cleveland the night of March 31. Shortly before he left Washington, Clark Clifford told him that the president was going to announce a bombing halt the same night he was scheduled to speak. Fulbright decided to keep his engagement, but he interrupted his talk so that he and his audience could watch the president.[51]

Johnson's image on television, even with makeup, was shocking. His eyes betraying the immense strain he was under, his face deeply lined, the commander in chief seemed at a crossroads. He announced that the bombing of North Vietnam would henceforth be limited to the area just north of the DMZ and that this would cease if there were evidence the enemy was scaling back its military activity. He named Averell Harriman his special representative, should peace talks materialize. He then dropped his bombshell: "I shall not seek, and I will not accept, the nomination of my party for another term as your President."[52]

The country was much impressed. For Johnson, the ultimate political animal, to relinquish the reins of the most powerful office in the world voluntarily was clearly a sacrifice of the first order. There were, of course, thousands of individual reactions to that abdication speech, but none was more dramatic than that of Wayne Morse. The Oregon maverick had jousted with Johnson over Vietnam but avidly supported his civil rights stand. That Wednesday evening, Morse was part of a crowd gathered around a radio in the U.S. embassy in Mexico City. As Johnson announced that he would not seek reelection, the group sat in stunned silence. Roy Reed, then a reporter for the *New York Times*, looked up at Morse. Tears were streaming down his face.[53]

Fulbright's and Marcy's initial reactions to Johnson's abdication speech were ones of relief and gratitude. At Lee Williams's urging, the chairman called the president to congratulate him and offered to do whatever he could

50 Quoted in Herring, *America's Longest War,* 202.
51 Berman, *Fulbright and the Vietnam War,* 97.
52 Quoted in Herring, *America's Longest War,* 206.
53 Interview with Roy Reed, Sept. 17, 1993, Fayetteville, Ark.

to get the peace process started in earnest. Johnson thanked the Arkansan and accepted his offer of help.[54] The next day, Marcy met with his contact in the Soviet embassy, Igor Bubnov, and told him that he was "absolutely certain" that the president was sincere in his stated desire for peace.[55] "I think this is a very useful move by the President," Fulbright told reporters. "I think the President's statement shows he is really determined to bring about peace, a liquidation of the war." The North Vietnamese would be "extremely foolish" if they did not respond immediately.[56]

Despite his initial optimism and the opening of preliminary peace talks in Paris on May 13, however, Fulbright soon began to have doubts about Johnson's willingness to change the substance of his position. Harry Ashmore, who had been in Hanoi the night of Johnson's speech, reported to the chairman that upon his return to Washington he had found the door just as firmly closed to compromise as it had been a year earlier. Rusk refused to budge from his position that Hanoi would have to de-escalate in return for a complete American bombing halt.[57] Fulbright began to suspect that Johnson was hoping somehow to produce a military victory or, at the very least, preserve a stalemate that the next president might resolve in America's favor. Yet, as Johnson's skyrocketing public approval ratings indicated, he and the doves were going to have to show restraint and give the peace process a chance. Silence seemed all the more important given the fact that Fulbright was seeking election to his fifth term in the Senate in 1968.

The last week in March, the junior senator flew to Little Rock to file for office formally. As reporters trailed after him, asking if he would support Lyndon Johnson in 1968, whether Arkansans would penalize him for his dissent on the war, and if the black vote that had proved so important to electing Governor Winthrop Rockefeller (Arkansas's first Republican governor since Reconstruction) would figure in his campaign, Fulbright had walked from his hotel first to the Democratic State Headquarters and then to the courthouse. His answers were amiable, and he appeared quietly confident of reelection.

Indeed, as the closing date for filing drew near, Lee Williams and other Fulbright aides relaxed in anticipation of a clear sail through to the general election. Then, on May 1, the last day to file, former State Supreme Court Justice Jim Johnson, Arkansas's most outspoken racist, paid his entry fee. "He is a man of no character, but with a considerable ability for inflammatory

---

54 Memo for the Files, Apr. 1, 1968, Williams Papers.
55 Marcy, memorandum of conversation, Apr. 2, 1968, Box 8, Folder Apr.–June, Marcy Papers.
56 "Fulbright Hails President Johnson's Vietnam Peace Proposal," *Fort Smith Southwest Times Record,* Apr. 2, 1968.
57 Ashmore to JWF, Apr. 17, 1968, Series 48:18, Box 54:1, SPF.

demagoguery,'' Fulbright wrote his wealthy benefactor, Cyrus Eaton. ''If there are riots this summer, as expected, he can be a dangerous opponent.''[58]

In fact, the violence that followed in the wake of Martin Luther King's assassination produced a white backlash of major proportions. In spite of the fact that there was not one case of looting or arson reported in Arkansas, the state's residents were as much agitated by the specter of urban violence as any New Yorker or Washingtonian. Footage showing entire city blocks in flames and rioters hindering firefighters which flickered nightly across the state's television screens, seemed to confirm Arkansas's worst fears about black retaliation for years of oppression – today Newark, tomorrow Forrest City.

Fulbright and his supporters considered Jim Johnson a threat not only because he was racist and anti-intellectual in his own right but because they viewed him as a stalking horse for George Wallace. The Alabama governor – famous among white supremacists for his theatrical stand in the schoolhouse door during efforts to integrate the state university – had formed a third party, the American Independent Party, and was planning to run in 1968 as its presidential nominee. He was still a nominal Democrat, however, and he hoped that a number of southern delegations, including Arkansas's, would support him at the Democratic National Convention in August.

As Fulbright moved back and forth between Washington and Arkansas during the tumultuous days of 1968, he kept one eye on state politics and the other on the Paris peace talks. His initial pessimism only grew with each passing day.

Soon after the Paris talks opened, the American delegation introduced a variant of the old San Antonio formula: The United States would stop the bombing ''on the assumption that'' North Vietnam would respect the demilitarized zone and refrain from further rocket attacks in the South and that ''prompt and serious'' talks would follow.[59] It seemed, however, that the closer peace approached, the more fearful of it Lyndon Johnson became. ''Some of you think we want resolution of this in an election year,'' he told his foreign policy advisers. ''I want it resolved, but not because of the election. Don't yield anything on that impression.''[60] Indeed, his instructions to the American negotiating team were to ''let the enemy do his own negotiating and hold to our basic positions.''[61]

The opening of the Paris peace talks placed tremendous pressure on the government of South Vietnam. The rivalry between Ky and Thieu intensified, fragmenting and paralyzing both civilian and military authorities. The Bud-

---

58 JWF to Cyrus Eaton, May 1, 1968, Series 2:1, Box 5:5, SPF.
59 Quoted in Herring, *America's Longest War,* 210.
60 Notes of the President's Meeting with Foreign Policy Advisers, May 6, 1968, Meeting Notes File, Box 3, Johnson Papers.
61 Rostow to LBJ, May 21, 1968, NSF, Country File – Vietnam, Box 101, Johnson Papers.

dhists remained more alienated than ever, openly demanding formation of a peace cabinet and urging ARVN troops to lay down their arms. Both the Buddhists and the newly active sects appeared to look forward to the collapse of the government. New political groups sprouted after the peace talks began, but they were dissension ridden and incapable of forming a meaningful opposition.

Lyndon Johnson's inability or unwillingness to get the peace talks off dead center loomed as a potentially mortal handicap to his heir apparent, Hubert Humphrey. The Happy Warrior's candidacy, announced on April 27, three weeks after Johnson's abdication, was initially buoyed by the Paris talks. Johnson's decision, and the simultaneous announcement of a partial bombing halt and new peace negotiations, had denied McCarthy and Kennedy their most compelling issue and forced them to resort to personalities. After the ADA endorsed McCarthy, the Democrats turned their attention to the important California primary scheduled for June 4. A poor showing in a televised debate convinced McCarthy and his aides that defeat was inevitable. As he watched Robert Kennedy make his victory speech, McCarthy reached to turn his hotel television off. He was frozen by the announcement that his rival had been shot by a deranged Jordanian, Sirhan Sirhan. Twenty-five hours later, without ever regaining consciousness, Bobby Kennedy died.

On June 7, shortly after Robert Kennedy's assassination, McCarthy called Carl Marcy and told him that despite losing the California primary he had decided not to withdraw. Now that Kennedy was dead, he was the only alternative to the policies of either Humphrey or Richard Nixon, who, it seemed, was sure to be the Republican candidate. What he needed, he said, was for one or two Democratic senators to announce support publicly.[62] The chief of staff was certainly supportive. Despite a directive he had written to his subordinates warning them to avoid political activity, Marcy had been writing campaign speeches for McCarthy and quietly plumping for him since December.[63] In fact, for Carl Marcy, Eugene McCarthy's candidacy marked the culmination of his crusade to bring the executive to heel and reestablish congressional influence on foreign policy.[64]

Fulbright certainly leaned toward McCarthy. He thought the Minnesotan somewhat ineffectual, but Humphrey too was frequently all sail and no anchor. Moreover, he and the vice-president had repeatedly clashed over Vietnam.[65] Finally, the Arkansan suspected that Humphrey might be a stalking horse for Johnson. Writing Martha Gelhorn, an old family acquaintance then

62 Marcy to JWF, June 7, 1968, Box 8, Folder Apr.–June, Marcy Papers.
63 Marcy to Staff, Mar. 22, 1968, Series 48:3, Box 16:5, SPF, and Marcy to McCarthy, Dec. 14, 1967, Box 7, Folder Oct.–Dec., Marcy Papers.
64 Marcy to Jean D. Andres, June 10, 1968, Box 8, Folder Apr.–June, Marcy Papers.
65 See, e.g., Summary Notes of 578th NSC Meeting, Nov. 8, 1967, NSC Meeting Notes, Box 2, Johnson Papers.

living in Kenya (and once married to Ernest Hemingway), he observed of Johnson's abdication speech, "[N]o one can say at this time whether it was a ploy or trick or whether he means it." There was a good chance that "Hubert will withdraw at the last moment in favor of Johnson, who will be nominated by acclamation."[66] Nevertheless, Fulbright felt that he could not endorse McCarthy publicly. It was unwise for any incumbent senator running for reelection to tout a particular national candidate when that candidate was an uncertain quantity with his constituents.

Meanwhile, in Arkansas, Fulbright was moving to shore up two of his shakiest constituencies – blacks and organized labor. At the state AFL–CIO (American Federation of Labor and Congress of Industrial Organizations) convention, president J. Bill Becker, a longtime Fulbright family friend and Democratic Party activist, urged his fellows to hold their noses and endorse the junior senator. With an eye to his other potential weak spot, Fulbright in mid-June named a Pine Bluff minister and black civil rights activist, Ben Grinage, to his campaign staff. Fulbright's record on civil rights was "indefensible," Grinage told reporters, but it was no worse than those of the other members of the Arkansas delegation.[67]

All the while, Jim Johnson was alienating most thinking Arkansans by the viciousness of his attacks. Terming Fulbright the "pin-up boy of Hanoi," Justice Jim toured the state telling all who would listen that the incumbent was giving aid and comfort to the enemy and that he was directly responsible for American casualties.[68]

As election day approached, the campaign staff was guardedly optimistic. The senator predicted a first-primary victory with sixty-five percent of the vote. Arkansas political pundits were not so sure; Johnson was indeed an accomplished demagogue, and like the nation, the state was in a very unsettled condition. "Fulbright Faces Most Serious Challenge of His . . . Career," ran a *Gazette* headline.[69]

The pundits were right. Although he led in sixty-eight of Arkansas's seventy-five counties, Fulbright garnered only fifty-three percent of the popular vote against candidates who consistently accused him of giving aid and comfort to the enemy. His victory was made possible by help from some unexpected quarters. Orval Faubus not only shunned Johnson but organized Madison County for Fulbright – or so he claimed.[70] According to Ben Grin-

66 JWF to Gelhorn, Apr. 25, 1968, Series 48:18, Box 54:5, SPF.
67 "Grinage to Be Aide to Senator Fulbright," *Arkansas Gazette,* June 12, 1968.
68 "Fulbright Calls 'Hanoi Pin-Up Boy' Label 'Utter Trash and Hogwash,' " *Pine Bluff Commercial,* July 26, 1968.
69 Bill Lewis, "Fulbright Faces Most Serious Challenge of His (24-Year) Career Tuesday," *Arkansas Gazette,* July 28, 1968.
70 Faubus to Darby, Aug. 1, 1968, Williams Papers.

age, the incumbent received nearly forty thousand votes, eighteen percent of his total, from Arkansas blacks.[71] Had the Man from Greasy Creek not remained neutral and had African Americans stayed home, Fulbright might have had to face a runoff.

To compensate for his abandonment of McCarthy, Fulbright flew to Washington on August 20 to testify before the platform committee of the Democratic National Committee. American involvement in Vietnam was a national tragedy, he told the committee in remarks that were given wide coverage by the national press. Intervention was the product of a rigid cold war mind-set that turned Ho Chi Minh "into another lunatic Hitler" and that posited the existence of a monolithic communist threat. As a result of that ill-advised crusade, old allies, like Britain and France, had abandoned the United States, the Great Society lay in shambles, and power had become centralized in the executive to the point where an "elective dictatorship" was ruling America. He then offered his model plank. With the ultimate goal of self-determination and neutralization of Southeast Asia, the United States should commit itself to an immediate bombing halt and cease-fire. He also asked the party to endorse his national commitments resolution.[72]

Hubert Humphrey did not want to repudiate the war in Vietnam, but he favored a plank that would promise to get the negotiating process in Paris off dead center. Lyndon Johnson would have none of it. He and Earle Wheeler agreed that there should be no "unilateral" concessions. He was determined, the president said, that the Democratic Party not be surrendered to the new isolationists.[73] Dean Rusk testified before the platform committee that it would be "neither wise or practicable" to spell out in detail the contents of an agreement with Hanoi. At the same time, the Texan summoned to the White House two of Humphrey's aides charged with drafting the Vietnam plank and told them he would not put up with any statement calling for an unconditional bombing halt. He also sent Charles Murphy, one of his chief troubleshooters, to Chicago to make sure that there was no slippage when the convention actually drafted the plank. There was none. Over the outraged protests of its dovish minority, the Democratic National Convention praised the administration for its efforts to halt aggression in South Vietnam and left the details of negotiation completely up to the executive.[74]

It was fortunate for Fulbright that he decided not to attend the Chicago

71 Grinage to Williams, Aug. 12, 1968, Williams Papers.
72 Berman, *Fulbright and the Vietnam War,* 101–2.
73 Bromley Smith to LBJ, Aug. 28, 1968, NSF, Country File – Vietnam, Box 102, Johnson Papers.
74 "Rusk Says Not to Dictate Terms of Vietnam Conflict," *El Dorado News,* Aug. 21, 1968; and John W. Finney, "How Johnson Got the Vietnam Plank He Wanted," *New York Times,* Aug. 27, 1968.

convention. Following the angry floor debate over the party's position on Vietnam, Humphrey was easily nominated on the first ballot. McCarthy's quest for delegates had been undermined by his own introspective and enigmatic personality, the image of his campaign as a "children's crusade," and the fact that most professional politicians distrusted him. Their candidate and their peace plank unceremoniously rejected, antiwar delegates decided to be as disruptive as possible and to demonstrate to the national television audience watching the convention that they had been steamrolled.

Confident of victory, the GOP convention meeting in Miami chose Richard M. Nixon on the first ballot. The "new Nixon" that won the New Hampshire primary was not the strident ideologue of old; the new Nixon was gracious, cool under fire, and imminently reasonable. Following his nomination in Miami, Nixon surprised most observers by selecting Governor Spiro T. Agnew of Maryland for second place on the ticket. The combative Agnew, although a national unknown, was the choice of ultraconservatives in the party like turncoat Democrat Strom Thurmond. Anticipating the politics of division advocated by Pat Buchanan and Kevin Phillips, the GOP platform promised an "all-out" campaign against crime, reform of the welfare laws, an end to inflation, and a stronger national defense. On Vietnam, the platform pledged to "de-Americanize" the war, to engage in "clear and purposeful negotiations," and not to accept "a camouflaged surrender."[75]

By early September the national campaign was well under way. The Republicans, confident that they would be able to smash the divided Democrats, unleashed the most elaborate and expensive presidential campaign in U.S. history. Nixon campaigned at a deliberate, dignified pace, seeking to dramatize the nation's decline at home and abroad under two Democratic administrations. The Democratic effort, by contrast, started very badly: The disastrous Chicago convention still hung like a pall over the party, and Humphrey and his running mate, Senator Edmund Muskie of Maine, also faced a serious challenge for control of the South and Midwest from the third-party candidacy of former Democrat George Wallace.

Nevertheless, from a rock-bottom beginning, Humphrey's campaign made steady progress. As was true in July, he needed to create some distance between himself and Johnson on Vietnam without seeming to repudiate the president. What he needed was some movement in the Paris peace talks themselves. In that way – and that way alone – it would be possible for Humphrey to have Johnson and the peace issue both.

Then, on October 11, Le Duc Tho indicated that if the United States agreed to stop the bombing of the North, his country would drop their objections to

---

75 Quoted in Dewey W. Grantham, *Recent America: The United States since 1945* (Arlington Heights, Ill., 1987), 307.

participation by the Thieu government in the Paris talks. At the same time, a major NVA–VC offensive launched in September collapsed. Rusk and Wheeler – after checking with Ellsworth Bunker and Creighton Abrams – decided that the communists, having been defeated on the battlefield, were ready to negotiate. At long last they assented to a bombing halt. Reluctantly, on November 1, just before the election, President Johnson called off aerial attacks over the North.[76] Unfortunately for the Democratic ticket, Nguyen Van Thieu denounced the bombing halt and refused to go to Paris.

Whether Thieu's refusal to negotiate led to Hubert Humphrey's defeat is unknowable. What is certain was that he fell short – by an agonizingly small margin. Nixon won 31,770,000 votes, or 43.4 percent of the total, compared with Humphrey's 31,270,000, or 42.7 percent. George Wallace finished a distant third with 13.5 percent.

More important, Richard Nixon's election in 1968 marked the end of eight years of Democratic rule and symbolized America's disillusionment with liberal reform both at home and overseas. Indeed, as the tumultuous decade approached its close, cold war liberals found themselves under attack from all sides. From the left, intellectuals, students, and minorities complained about liberal complicity in waging an immoral war in Vietnam and creating an indifferent bureaucracy that resisted change. Disillusioned black radicals rejected the concept of nonviolent civil disobedience and denounced civil rights evolutionists as Uncle Toms. From the right came slings and arrows unleashed by an emerging "silent majority" – working- and middle-class Americans who insisted that the nation reassert its commitment to patriotism, the work ethic, and "law and order."

Perhaps liberalism's bitterest critics were its disillusioned own. In his critique of postwar American foreign policy, J. William Fulbright revealed that in their efforts to reconcile the ideal with the real, American liberals had allowed their obsession with social justice to be welded to the anticommunist crusade that pervaded the nation during the 1950s and 1960s. As a result, American foreign policy had become a missionary campaign that blinded Americans to the political and cultural realities of Southeast Asia as well as other developing regions. Had liberals not permitted themselves to be intimidated by McCarthyism and its radical right offspring, then Vietnam could never have happened. The extension of the liberal impulse from the domestic to the international sphere made possible an unholy alliance between realpolitikers preoccupied with markets and bases, and emotionally committed to the domino theory, and idealists who wanted to spread the blessings of freedom, democracy, and a mixed economy to the less fortunate of the world. The foreign aid program with its dual emphasis on armaments and infrastructure symbolized the marriage between the two. Conservatives were willing to accept nonmilitary aid because they were convinced that it was essential

---

76 Marcy to John Rielly, Sept. 6, 1968, Box 8, Folder July-Sept., Marcy Papers.

to halting the rise of communism, whereas liberals could reconcile themselves to massive military assistance on the grounds that America was simply protecting the recipients of its global social experiment.

In Vietnam Fulbright saw the ultimate product of liberal internationalism, and he spoke. The United States was battling an enemy that had long since changed in form and substance. America, acting in part out of altruism, was trying to impose its culture and institutions on nations whose folkways and political processes far antedated its own. In their anxiety to be politically relevant, to play the anticommunist card, American liberals had embraced the military–industrial complex and had thereby placed the very things they worshipped – freedom, democracy, diversity – at risk. John F. Kennedy and Lyndon Johnson's agenda had not triumphed over that of Barry Goldwater; the two had become joined. What gave Fulbright's insights – stated so eloquently in *The Arrogance of Power* and ''The Price of Empire'' – such sharpness and poignance was that he more than any other figure had been responsible for convincing his fellow Americans to embrace liberal internationalism.

13

Nixon and Kissinger

Cheered by the thought of not having to campaign again for another six years, Arkansas's most famous son returned to Washington in January 1969 in a buoyant mood. Fulbright's reelection had elevated him to the top echelon of the Senate seniority system and earned him a spot on the Democratic Steering Committee. Despite the fact that Congress was in the hands of one party and the executive the other, Fulbright was cautiously optimistic concerning the prospects for a bipartisan foreign policy. The day following the election, Nixon had called Fulbright to exchange congratulations and to emphasize his intent to consult the SFRC every step of the way. Fulbright was delighted with Nixon's choice of his old friend William Rogers to be secretary of state. Rogers, an urbane New York lawyer, had handled his duties as point man for the Eisenhower administration's civil rights program with tact and skill. He had repeatedly demonstrated that he was neither a right-wing ideologue nor an inflexible cold warrior. Fulbright anticipated, somewhat naively, that, unlike the manipulation that had characterized bipartisanship under Dulles and Eisenhower, authentic cooperation would be the watchword under Rogers and Nixon. The fact that Nixon had consulted with him before naming a secretary of state pleased the chairman immensely. "A Sweet J. W. Fulbright," proclaimed Rowland Evans and Robert Novak in their bi-weekly column.[1]

Four days before Richard Nixon was inaugurated, the Senate bade farewell to Lyndon Johnson. Room S-207 was packed with senators and their staffs when the president, Lady Bird, Lucy, and Linda arrived. Johnson charged into the crowd with his accustomed enthusiasm. Encountering Frank Valeo, longtime secretary of the Senate and companion to Johnson on his 1961 trip to Vietnam, the president grabbed the much smaller man by the lapels, pulled him up to face level, and said with vehement sincerity, "I want to take

---

1 Rowland Evans and Robert Novak, "A Sweet J. W. Fulbright," *New York Times,* Jan. 28, 1969.

another trip with you!"[2] Fulbright came to the Johnson send-off, but he and his former adversary never spoke. Although Johnson had kept Fulbright posted on developments in Paris throughout January, the two men were too angry and too wary of each other for a true reconciliation.[3]

Richard Nixon nominated William Rogers to be secretary of state because he was convinced the New York lawyer would "make the little boys in the State Department" behave and because he knew next to nothing about foreign policy.[4] He was the perfect choice for a president who intended to run foreign affairs out of the White House. Typically, Henry Kissinger, Nixon's national security adviser, was both jealous and contemptuous of Rogers. He went out of his way to see that the State Department was kept in the dark during major negotiations. During both the Vietnam peace talks in Paris and the strategic arms limitations discussions in Vienna, Kissinger ordered negotiators to communicate directly with him through top secret, "backchannel" networks. Rogers complained to Nixon, and the president promised to correct the problem, but he never did. Nixon knew about the rivalry and rather enjoyed it.[5]

Although a novice at bureaucratic infighting and power consolidation, Henry Kissinger proved superb at it. The offices of national security adviser to the president and executive director of the National Security Council remained separate in name but not in fact. As national security adviser, Kissinger enjoyed direct, primary access to the president but also chaired every NSC committee meeting, approving or disapproving its recommendations. In short, under Nixon the foreign-policymaking process was centered in the NSC rather than the State Department, and Kissinger completely dominated the council.[6] The professor and the politician were well pleased with the setup. It would allow them, they believed, to bypass not only Foggy Bottom but Congress as well.

Richard Nixon wanted to end the war in Vietnam, but prompted by the JCS and his new military adviser, General Andrew Goodpaster, the president came to believe that he could do so by winning rather than losing. A week following his election, Nixon met with General Creighton Abrams, Goodpaster, and the JCS. Despite Thieu's resentment over the Paris peace talks, there had been no "breach between the United States and South Vietnam

---

2 Interview with Frank Valeo, Oct. 2, 1991, Washington, D.C.
3 Mansfield and Dirksen to JWF, Jan. 16, 1969, Series 48:18, Box 56:7, SPF.
4 Quoted in Stephen E. Ambrose, *Nixon*, vol. II, *The Triumph of a Politician, 1962–1972* (New York, 1989), 234.
5 Quoted in Seymour M. Hersh, *The Price of Power: Kissinger in the Nixon White House* (New York, 1983), 103.
6 William Shawcross, *Sideshow: Kissinger, Nixon and the Destruction of Cambodia* (New York, 1979), 80–1.

militarily," the men in uniform reported. Moreover, the North Vietnamese were on the run. In 1967, having fought an unsuccessful guerrilla war, the communists decided to change tactics. The result had been Tet, a disaster for the VC. This had been followed by NVA offensives in May and August 1968. Both had been turned back, and in the process, B-52s had pulverized enemy troop concentrations. The North Vietnamese had withdrawn forty thousand troops from the South and were in Paris because they had reached a dead end militarily.[7] If Goodpaster and the JCS were correct, the war was virtually won on the battlefield. America could afford to be tough and drive a hard bargain at the negotiating table.

Kissinger was much less sanguine about the military and particularly the political situation in Vietnam. The president was going to move toward a negotiated settlement and withdrawal, he told Averell Harriman nine days after the inauguration. Goodpaster was pushing Nixon to win the war in the next few months, but the president, he was sure, would act realistically.[8] As events would demonstrate, Kissinger was overestimating either Nixon's realism or his own influence with the new president.

There was no more willing congressional bride in the Nixon administration's honeymoon than J. William Fulbright. Calls for an immediate withdrawal of troops were premature, he told reporters: "I think we ought to give the people in Paris an opportunity to negotiate without making a serious change in the status quo," he informed *U.S. News and World Report*.[9] Indeed, later that month Fulbright got up at 5:00 a.m. to go to the airport to see Nixon off on his first overseas trip as president. At the same time, he let it be known that his tacit support stemmed from his belief that Nixon and Kissinger were committed to ending the war.

Some three weeks later, the chairman drove to the opposite end of Pennsylvania Avenue for a meeting with the president, Rogers, and Kissinger. In an effort to calm Fulbright and forestall a congressional uprising over Vietnam, Nixon had asked the chairman to come by and state his views. As usual, Fulbright was brutally frank. If the president did not liquidate the war by the midpoint of his first term, he warned, the administration "will be on an irreversible path toward repudiation."[10] Above all, he pleaded, do not

7 Notes of Presidential Meeting with President-elect Nixon, Nov. 11, 1968, Tom Johnson Meeting Notes, Box 3, Johnson Papers.
8 Memorandum of conversation with Henry Kissinger, Jan. 29, 1969, Box 481, Harriman Papers, LC. See also Haldeman Notes, Box 40, Papers of H. R. Haldeman, WHSpF, Richard M. Nixon Presidential Papers Project, National Archives, Arlington, Va. [hereinafter referred to as Nixon Project.]
9 "What U.S. Should Do about Vietnam: Survey of Key Senators," *U.S. News and World Report*, Feb. 10, 1969, 29–32.
10 Marcy to JWF, Mar. 20, 1969, Box 8, Jan.–Mar., Marcy Papers.

escalate the conflict in Vietnam. There was no need to take any military action beyond that necessary to defend American troops already in the country.[11] The president received Fulbright cordially, and Kissinger poured on the charm. For an hour and a half the two assured their guest that they would move quickly to end the war and would not repeat Lyndon Johnson's mistakes. "Just give us a year," Fulbright remembered them saying. He wished them well, the chairman said, but he reminded Nixon that public confidence in the presidency, in the military, and in the complex of rationales for Vietnam was rapidly disintegrating.[12]

After Fulbright returned to his office, Lee Williams came in with a message from Dan Blackburn of Metromedia. Instead of winding down the war, Blackburn confided, the Nixon administration had taken the offensive in Vietnam. Following his inauguration, the president had ordered General Abrams to intensify bombing activity above and below the seventeenth parallel and to apply full military pressure on the ground as well. In addition, Blackburn reported, rumor had it that the U.S. command in Saigon, in secret agreement with Prince Norodom Sihanouk, was planning to attack six North Vietnamese bases in Cambodia.[13] In fact, the bombing attacks on Cambodia had begun on March 18, 1969, three days before Fulbright's meeting in the Oval Office.

Nixon and Kissinger's strategy was to couple great-power diplomacy with force in an effort to win an "honorable" peace at the Paris negotiations. The president believed that military pressure had thus far failed because it had been applied in a limited and indecisive way. Encouraged by Goodpaster and the JCS, the president was prepared to threaten the very survival of North Vietnam in order to break the enemy's will. Analogizing between his situation and that faced by Eisenhower in Korea in 1953, Nixon believed that the threat of annihilation could be used just as effectively against Hanoi as it had against Pyongyang. His image as a hard-line anticommunist would make his warnings credible. "They'll believe any threat of force Nixon makes because it's Nixon," he told White House Chief of Staff H. R. Haldeman. "We'll just slip the word to them that, 'for God's sake, you know Nixon's obsessed about Communism . . . and he has his hand on the nuclear button.' "[14]

In March the president sent a personal message to Ho Chi Minh expressing his firm desire for peace and proposing as a first step the mutual withdrawal of American and North Vietnamese troops from South Vietnam and the restoration of the demilitarized zone as a temporary political boundary. He did not even wait for an answer. For years the JCS had urged Johnson to bomb

---

11 William C. Berman, *William Fulbright and the Vietnam War: The Dissent of a Political Realist* (Kent, Ohio, 1988), 108.
12 Interview with J. William Fulbright, Oct. 11–18, 1988, Washington, D.C.; and Berman, *Fulbright and the Vietnam War,* 107.
13 Lee Williams to JWF, Mar. 21, 1969, Series 48:17, Box 46:1, SPF.
14 Quoted in George C. Herring, *America's Longest War: The United States and Vietnam, 1950–1975,* 2d ed. (New York, 1986), 225.

communist supply routes and staging areas in Cambodia, but to no avail. Nixon gave the go-ahead but insisted that the bombing be kept secret from everyone. Under operation MENU, 3,360 B-52 raids were flown over Cambodia, dropping more than a hundred thousand tons of bombs. The stated military objective of the aerial assault was to limit North Vietnam's capacity to launch an offensive against the South, but Nixon's primary motive was to indicate that he was prepared to take measures that Johnson had avoided, thus frightening Hanoi into negotiating on his terms. The raids killed an untold number of civilians and accelerated the tragic destabilization of Cambodia. The North Vietnamese simply moved deeper into the Cambodian jungles.[15]

At a symposium on the military budget and national priorities held on Capitol Hill the morning after his meeting with the president, Fulbright appeared depressed. He was pessimistic about the war, he remarked to several of those present. Because the administration was bent on achieving an "honorable" peace, the present lull in Vietnam was probably "the calm before the storm."[16] He said nothing about the impending assault on Cambodia of which Dan Blackburn had warned. He knew that the administration was full of unscrupulous demagogues who would not hesitate to charge him with treason for discussing military operations then underway. Moreover, he had no hard evidence to prove that the bombing had taken place – and would not until the famous Moose–Lowenstein mission to Phnom Penh.

Fulbright well understood that it would be difficult for Nixon and Kissinger to withdraw from Southeast Asia – more difficult, perhaps, than it would have been for Lyndon Johnson. It was true that the long, protracted struggle and the antiwar movement had eroded support for the war even among hawks, but there were powerful forces at work with a vested interest in continuing the conflict indefinitely. The military–industrial complex of which Dwight Eisenhower had warned was larger and more formidable than ever. Indeed, in the chairman's view, Robert McNamara had created an $80-billion-a-year monster that would be difficult for Nixon and Kissinger to control even if they were so inclined. Finally, of course, there were the increasingly frustrated and alienated blue-collar workers to whom George Wallace appealed and for whom Nixon had to compete. It was on militarism, however, and specifically the military's growing influence on diplomacy, that Fulbright chose to focus.

The Arkansan's perception of the American officer corps was of an undereducated, isolated, overly professionalized body of men dedicated to creating a mission for themselves. Regular military officers "are a strong

15 Shawcross, *Sideshow,* 25–36, 90–3.
16 Quoted in Berman, *Fulbright and the Vietnam War,* 108.

breed," his longtime friend John Bell, then chief political officer at McDill Air Force Base, advised him. They divided civilians into two groups: those " 'for us' " and those " 'against us.' " They were generally ignorant of foreign cultures and, for that matter, of American society. The country and the world consisted not of cities but of bases and PXs that the officers and their families rarely left. The key word to the modern military was "require-ment": Once a requirement was established, it was seldom if ever reviewed; the test then became whether there was a "shortfall" in meeting the requirement. The concept included everything from chapels to wars.[17]

In February 1969 Fulbright learned that members of the officer corps were once again taking part in "national security seminars" conducted under the auspices of the Industrial College of the Armed Forces, an interservice in-stitution responsible directly to the JCS. The 1969 edition of the seminars emphasized not the threat of communist infiltration of American institutions but the need for the United States to continue to police the international community. "We must take over the guard all around the world, in order to fill the power vacuum left by the withdrawal of the British and other Western powers who no longer have the capacity," declared one beribboned confer-ence leader. "Our policy . . . is to contain Chinese imperialism – or com-munism – or whatever," proclaimed another. "To do this, we have to stay put as long as necessary to provide a balance of power in Asia."[18]

Predictably, Fulbright mounted the stump to warn his fellow Americans of the menace posed by the new militarism. Violence had become the coun-try's leading industry, he declared repeatedly during the spring of 1969. "We are now spending about $80 billion a year on the military, which is more than the profits of all American business,"[19] he told an audience at Denison University. Militarism permeated every aspect of the national life:

> Millions of Americans have acquired a vested interest in the expensive weapons systems, which provide their livelihood and indirectly, therefore, a foreign policy that has plunged the United States into a spiraling arms race with the Soviet Union, made us the world's major salesman of armaments, and committed us to the defense of freedom – very loosely defined – in almost 50 countries.[20]

But more than rhetoric was necessary. If the public were not educated and the Pentagon cut down to size, the chairman had become convinced, America would be plunged into one Vietnam after another and be bankrupted in the process.

On February 3 Fulbright announced that the SFRC was creating an Ad

17 Memorandum for the File, Military and Foreign Policy, Jan. 9, 1969, Box 8, Jan.–Mar., Marcy Papers.
18 "Fulbright Chokes on the Military's Rhetoric," *Baltimore Sun,* Feb. 22, 1969.
19 "Fulbright: Top Industry Is 'Violence,' " *Arkansas Gazette,* Apr. 20, 1969, 4001.
20 Ibid.

Hoc Subcommittee on United States Security Agreements and Commitments Abroad. Stuart Symington would chair the panel, which would include Fulbright, Sparkman, Aiken, Cooper, Mansfield, and Jacob Javits. Fulbright noted that under existing treaties the United States could possibly be committed to using its armed forces in forty-two countries. The United States provided military aid to forty-eight countries, and thirty-two percent of all Americans under arms were stationed outside the continental United States, most of them in an elaborate network of overseas bases. The tendency of the military to fill a void and create a mission for itself coupled with congressional delegation of authority to the executive had created a system in which the United States was pledged to defend other nations without the public's knowledge or permission. Following lengthy and thorough investigations, Fulbright told reporters, the Symington subcommittee would identify these commitments. The unspoken goal of the panel was to get the military out of the foreign-policymaking business and to compel the executive to once again seek congressional approval for the diplomatic commitments that it made. Because it raised a number of "complicated and unique questions," Vietnam would be excluded from subcommittee scrutiny, Fulbright declared.[21]

Symington's appointment was a stroke of genius. A former secretary of the air force, he had been one of the Senate's leading hawks on Vietnam until Fulbright had turned him. As a member of both the Armed Services and CIA oversight committees, the Missourian retained close ties with Senate conservatives and the Pentagon. No soft-headed peacenik, Symington could investigate the military with some credibility.

The day following the creation of the Symington subcommittee, Fulbright reintroduced the national commitments resolution. Promising his colleagues that the congressional statement of purpose that he proposed would not affect current military involvement in Vietnam, the chairman insisted that the resolution would redress a constitutional imbalance that was the product more of natural forces than of a conspiracy by would-be dictators. Napoleon long ago observed that "the tools belong to the man that can use them," he told the Senate. No executive could be expected to limit its freedom of action voluntarily. Congress would have to assert itself.[22]

The formation of the Symington subcommittee and the reintroduction of the national commitments resolution frightened and angered Richard Nixon. He, Haldeman, John Ehrlichman, Patrick Buchanan, and the other ad-agency types and ultraconservatives that made up the bulk of the White House staff detested Fulbright. Despite his segregationist record and conservative stance on many socioeconomic issues, they regarded him as a would-be intellectual and a tool of the "eastern establishment press." His relentless advocacy of

21 Fulbright press release, Feb. 3, 1969, Series 48:3, Box 17:1, SPF.
22 *Congressional Record,* Senate, Feb. 4, 1969, 4001.

the United Nations, his opposition to the war in Vietnam, and his sharp criticism of aspects of American culture marked him out in their minds as a "liberal." Nixon recalled the chairman of the SFRC's opposition to McCarthyism and his partisan attacks on the missile gap in 1959 and 1960. Philosophically and politically he qualified for a top spot on the president's "enemies list." Typically, Nixon saw the effort to rein in the military and limit the executive's ability to commit the United States to support other countries as a personal attack on him. Kissinger, who was infuriated at any effort to interfere with his freedom of action, raged against the Symington subcommittee and the national commitments resolution.[23] He was barely willing to brook opposition from the president of the United States, much less a committee of Congress and its Arkansas chairman. Remembering that Fulbright had led the fight against the Bricker amendment, Nixon put out the word to his underlings to label the national commitments resolution as nothing more or less than a reincarnation of that anachronistic and isolationist document.[24]

With the globalization of the Truman and Eisenhower doctrines, the Pentagon had in fact blanketed the world with a maze of bases and promises. In the feverish days of the early cold war, the air force had scrambled to acquire facilities for the medium-range B-47 bomber, which did not have range enough to reach potential targets in the Soviet Union from airfields on American territory. As Fulbright rightly suspected, however, over time the 429 bases that had been built overseas existed as much to ensure political stability in the host country as to deter the Soviet Union.[25] Fulbright and the staff of the SFRC were vaguely aware of the presence of American troops in Laos, Thailand, and perhaps Cambodia in connection with the Vietnam War. They also knew that the military had signed hundreds of agreements with governments in Latin America, Europe, Asia, and the Near East to cooperate in resisting communism; but the exact number and scope of those agreements were carefully guarded state secrets.

The task of the Symington subcommittee was to pull away that shroud of secrecy and define precisely the extent of existing commitments, whereas the goal of the national commitments resolution was to ensure that in the future Congress and the American people would be "in on the takeoff," to use Arthur Vandenberg's phrase, as well as the landing. Given Nixon and Kissinger's determination to control policy and the ongoing hysteria generated by the Vietnam War, Fulbright and Symington had set a formidable task for themselves.

---

23 Interviews with James Lowenstein, Oct. 3, 1991, and Richard Moose, June 29, 1989, Washington, D.C.

24 Nixon notation, Apr. 1969, WHSpF, President's Office File, Pres. Handwriting, Box 1, Nixon Project.

25 "Rival to the State Department?" *Chicago Daily News,* May 9, 1969.

In late February, Marcy named Walter Pincus and Roland Paul to be the chief investigators for the Symington subcommittee. Pincus was a tough-minded investigative reporter, and Paul was a Washington lawyer with a reputation for thoroughness and combativeness. It was obvious that two men could not cover the waterfront; as a result, Fulbright, Symington, and Marcy decided that the investigators would concentrate on Europe and Asia, exclusive of Vietnam, and look for "targets of opportunity."[26] The first target that presented itself was Spain – and it was a juicy one.

Shortly after Pincus and Paul joined the SFRC, stories began to appear in the national press that the Pentagon was about to conclude a multi-million-dollar bases deal with the government of aged dictator General Francisco Franco. The SFRC staff had learned not only that the administration was keeping the bases agreement secret from Congress but also that the Pentagon, specifically, JCS chief General Earle Wheeler and two-star general David A. Burchinal, deputy to the Supreme Commander of NATO – rather than the State Department – was negotiating terms. Fulbright called the Capitol Hill press corps together and told them he had serious questions as to whether or not the bases were strategically necessary and, if they were, why the United States should have to pay for the privilege of building and operating them.[27] What he suspected, but did not say, was that in "cooperating" with the Franco government the American military had made a de facto commitment to defend that autocratic regime against enemies both external and internal.

The decision to send Pincus and Paul abroad by themselves was a break with precedent. With one minor exception, SFRC staffers had never before ventured overseas without a member during Fulbright's tenure as chair. Freelancing by the staff offended prima donnas on the committee, and both Marcy and Fulbright knew that such forays would revive memories of the notorious Cohn–Schine trips of intimidation during the McCarthy period. Nevertheless, a majority of the SFRC was convinced that if Congress and the public were not to be involved in an endless series of Vietnams by the national security state, it would have to initiate its own intelligence-gathering effort.

In spite of the concerted efforts of U.S. military authorities in Spain to mislead them, the two congressional investigators learned first that the mission of the huge American military base at Torrejon outside Madrid was to provide forward support for a fighter-bomber squadron stationed in Turkey. That force, in turn, existed to rain atomic missiles on Georgia and the Ukraine

---

26 Background and Suggestions for Organization of Ad Hoc Subcommittee on U.S. Security Agreements and Commitments Abroad, Feb. 24, 1969, Box 8, Jan.–Mar., Marcy Papers.
27 "Rival to the State Department?"; and "Fulbright Panel Opens Probe on Spanish Bases," *Arkansas Gazette,* Apr. 3, 1969.

in case of war with the Soviet Union. Pincus and Paul also learned from sources at Torrejon that there were nuclear weapons stored in Spain.

After they had finished with Torrejon, the SFRC investigators visited Meron, a limited-manned base outside Seville. Meron was run by a skeleton crew and, as Pincus soon discovered, was used primarily for joint Spanish–American military exercises once a year. He also learned that the scenario for these exercises was a domestic insurrection in which the American military intervened to save the Spanish government. This was the same regime that was headed by Francisco Franco, one-time intimate of Adolf Hitler, brutal autocrat, cofounder of the fascist and anti-Semitic Falangist Party! It was the Spanish Civil War with the United States intervening on the side of the fascists, and Washington was willing to pay $175 million for the privilege.[28]

In early April, Symington and his colleagues issued their report, citing the Spanish bases arrangement as a classic example of executive usurpation of congressional authority in foreign affairs. During the current negotiations, Symington told the press while handing out copies of the report, JCS Chief Wheeler had assured the Spanish in writing that the presence of American armed forces in Spain "constitutes a more significant security guarantee to Spain" than would a written agreement.[29]

Nixon, Kissinger, the Pentagon, and the Spanish were infuriated. The Spanish ambassador, the Marquis de Merry bel Val, flatly denied that his government would ever ask American troops to fight against Spaniards and demanded that the chairman apologize.[30] In late April, Fulbright officially asked the administration to suspend negotiations on the Spanish bases agreement unless and until Congress was fully consulted.[31] Although neither Nixon, Rogers, nor Laird even bothered to reply, the Symington subcommittee had made an impact.

In June, Washington and Madrid announced that an agreement had been signed. The United States agreed to pay Spain $50 million in military assistance, with another $35 million in Export–Import Bank credits to follow. Instead of a ten-year renewal, however, the pact was limited to fifteen months. Both governments, their representatives told the press, had "serious reservations about any long-range extension."[32]

28 Interview with Walter Pincus, Mar. 11, 1990, Washington, D.C.
29 The 1953 executive agreement, kept secret until this time, and under which the 1969 pact had been negotiated, provided that an attack on joint Spanish–American facilities would be viewed as a matter of "common concern" and that the Spanish had the right to use the American-built bases with or without Washington's permission. See "Rival to the State Department?"
30 "Fulbright Assures Spain on Row," *Baltimore Sun,* Apr. 12, 1969.
31 JWF to Rogers, Apr. 22, 1969, Box 8, Apr.–June, Marcy Papers.
32 "U.S.–Spain Renew Military Agreement," *Iowa Daily Tribune,* June 21, 1969.

Fulbright did not need Lee Williams, Scotty Reston, or Walter Lippmann to tell him that a sure-fire way to discredit oneself with the American people, especially during wartime, was to appear to be antimilitary. Consequently, he scheduled a major address at the National War College, not, as one pundit put it, "to go into the lion's den to beard the lion" but to try and convince the nation's officer corps and the nation that he was opposed to militarism and not the military.

The atmosphere was electric as the nation's leading dove strode onto the stage of the huge auditorium at the National War College. His audience, composed of several hundred men who were committed to learning the art of war and sacrificing their lives for their country, greeted him with polite applause. Fulbright was a man of considerable personal courage; his voice did not quaver. "In the old Western movies," he began, "there was a standard climax in which the villain emerged from his hideout shielded behind the captive heroine and snarling:'Shoot me and the girl dies!' " It reminded him, he said, of those officials responsible for the war in Vietnam. Every time they were criticized, they wrapped themselves in the flag, hid behind the military, and declared, "Criticize me and the soldier dies."

The problem with contemporary American life was not the military but militarism, Fulbright declared. Every nation, he told the assembled officers, has a double identity; "it is both a power engaged in foreign relations and a society serving the interests of its citizens." In its role as arbiter of international affairs, the nation drew upon but did not replenish the people's economic, political, and moral resources. For three decades the United States had been preoccupied with its role as the world's greatest power "to the neglect of its societal responsibilities, and at incalculable cost to our national security." The 10-to-1 imbalance in military versus nonmilitary expenditures had undermined the nation's systems of education, welfare, health, and housing. The emergence of the national security state and the placing of the nation on what amounted to a permanent war footing had tipped the balance within the federal government dangerously in favor of the executive. The moral cost was reflected in the angry alienation of the nation's youth. "The 'dog of war,' which Jefferson thought had been tightly leashed to the legislature, has now passed under the virtually exclusive control of the executive," he warned.

When it came to the role that the military had played in this mounting tragedy, Fulbright did not mince words:

> Bringing to bear a degree of discipline, unanimity and strength of conviction seldom found among civilian officials, the able and energetic men who fill the top ranks of the armed services have acquired an influence disproportionate to their numbers on the nation's security policy. The Department of Defense itself has become a vigorous partisan in our

politics, exerting great influence on the President, on the military committees of Congress, on the "think tanks" and universities to which it
parcels out lucrative research contracts, and on public opinion.[33]

But there was a historic mistrust of power among the American people, and
"like a human body reacting against a transplanted organ, our body politic
is reacting against the alien values which, in the name of security, have been
grafted upon it."[34]

Perhaps stunned by Fulbright's audacity, the student body of the National
War College responded with the same polite applause with which they had
greeted him. Others were not so civil. His face working with emotion, Howard K. Smith, coanchor with Frank Reynolds on the *ABC Evening News,* accused Fulbright of inexcusable inconsistency. He had first promoted, then
denounced the Gulf of Tonkin Resolution. Having rejected his own offspring, the Arkansan then proved incapable of summoning up the courage to
work for its repeal. This southern conservative who had repeatedly voted
against raises in the minimum wage dared fault the executive for neglecting
social welfare programs. How could he talk about the well-being of underdeveloped peoples when he had consistently fought civil rights legislation?
Most viewers were not surprised at the hawkishness of Smith's editorial,
only its bitterness. Few knew that his son had been grievously maimed in
Vietnam.[35]

Generally, however, Fulbright's attack on the military-industrial complex
struck a responsive chord in academia and the national media. Richard Har-
wood and Laurence Stern devoted two pages in the *Washington Post* to a
description and analysis of the Pentagon and the defense industries that were
dependent on it. Former members of the Kennedy administration Richard
Goodwin and John Kenneth Galbraith stepped forward to accuse Robert Mc-
Namara of having created a military–industrial complex that was threatening
the nation's economic health, subverting its political institutions, and per-
verting its values.[36]

The first week in June, Nixon delivered a hard-hitting speech defending
the military in all its various roles and blasting Fulbright and his supporters
as neo-isolationists. Speaking at the Air Force Academy, he declared that the
current debate, centering as it did on America's proper place in the world,
was of immense importance. One school of thought favored "a downgrading
of our alliances and what amounts to a unilateral reduction of our arms."
According to Nixon, this "isolationist" worldview was based on the absurd
belief that "the United States is as much responsible for the tensions as the
adversaries we face." He would, he said, no more sanction a global American

33 *Congressional Record,* Senate, May 20, 1969, 13056.
34 Ibid.
35 Reuben Thomas, "Howard K. Smith on Fulbright," *Arkansas Gazette,* May 28, 1969.
36 Tom Huston, "The McNamara Legacy," June 16, 1969, WHSpF, Box 2, Nixon Project.

retreat than he would countenance a recommendation for "unilateral disarmament."[37]

The Nixon speech hit a Fulbright nerve. The president was, the Arkansan declared, engaging in "a form of demagoguery that was very fashionable in the time of his old colleague, Joe McCarthy."[38] He saw in the smoke of the president's fusillade the apparition of the old "America right-or-wrong attitude" that had been used to justify a generation of overinvolvement and to discredit those who dared criticize Pax Americana. It was the term "neo-isolationist" that rankled Fulbright, Marcy, Seth Tillman, and Lee Williams; but despite their denials and the fact that Nixon's motives were less than pure, by mid-1969, in many respects, the label was apropos.

At times Fulbright's critique of American foreign policy seemed to parallel that of the New Left, but there were many more differences than similarities. Although radical historians like Gabriel Kolko and Eugene Genovese as well as I. F. Stone and other left-wing columnists admired the Arkansan's stand on the war and frequently quoted him, they never considered him one of their own. Given his segregationist voting record, his republicanism and elitism, and personal revulsion at the burgeoning counterculture, how could they? He was a southerner, a conservative, and a champion of the Senate's undemocratic seniority system. Stone, who frequently hailed Fulbright in his weekly *Newsletter*, had no illusions. "He is not a liberal at all," he once remarked. "This is the landed civilized gentleman type . . . foreign to the American egalitarian tradition."[39] Yet, at the same time, they regarded Fulbright as perhaps the most important critic of the system they were themselves indicting.

Echoing anti-imperialists from George Washington to Abraham Lincoln to Charles Beard, Fulbright called on America to retreat within itself and work to perfect its own institutions and social system, and thus to become a beacon to the rest of the world. In early June 1969, in the midst of his indictment of the military–industrial complex, Fulbright exhorted the foreign policy establishment to abandon its effort to create a "Pax Americana – the imposition of peace by a force of arms paid for by the American taxpayer" – and instead make the United States a "humanistic example" to the rest of the world.[40]

Fulbright was uncomfortable with the notion that the war was immoral, although he did not hesitate to so label it, and instead periodically concentrated on the notion that Vietnam and American foreign policy in general were the products of flaws in the human psyche, flaws that were subject to being identified and controlled by modern social science. In mid-March Ful-

37 Quoted in Berman, *Fulbright and the Vietnam War*, 111.
38 William F. Buckley, "On Tormenting Senator Fulbright," *Pine Bluff Commercial*, June 10, 1969.
39 I. F. Stone, "An American Anthony Eden," *New York Review*, Dec. 29, 1966.
40 "Fulbright: Halt 'Absurd' Arms Race," *Chicago Daily News*, June 4, 1969.

bright convened a group of sociologists, anthropologists, and psychiatrists in the SFRC conference room. He listened to Lionel Tiger of Rutgers declare that war was not a human problem but a male problem: Unable to bond, modern males turned to more adolescent pursuits, of which war was one. He and Edward O. Wilson, a Harvard zoologist, described fantasies of aggression that people develop when their leaders insist they should adhere to policies over which they had no control.[41] Then, in June, the chairman had the renowned psychiatrist Karl Menninger testify before the SFRC in open session. Vietnam was, he proclaimed, "a destructive, futile, pointless military bonfire which has created haunting anxiety and depression that is near to despair."[42] "I think a psychological interpretation of many of our historical experiences . . . can be more persuasive with my colleagues in the Congress and the people than a poorly informed politician," he wrote Louis Halle, who had warned him that social scientists and academics possessed no magic formula to avoid war.[43]

41 "Fulbright and the Scholars," *Washington Evening Star,* May 16, 1969.
42 Ed Johnson, "Fulbright Panel 'Psychoanalyzes' Foreign Policy," *Arkansas Gazette,* June 20, 1969.
43 JWF to Louis J. Halle, July 22, 1969, Series 48:18, Box 56:6, SPF.

14

Of Arms and Men

Nixon and Kissinger's new world order called for a stable relationship with the Soviet Union. The two were committed to containment but were not adverse to the idea of dialogue, a position that had in part been responsible for the honeymoon with Fulbright. The national security adviser, however, believed that America's strategic position vis-à-vis the Soviet Union had steadily deteriorated under Jack Kennedy and Lyndon Johnson.[1] Implicit in Kissinger's version of détente was "linkage," an updated version of the old balance of power approach to international affairs. Instead of negotiating military, economic, and political issues piecemeal with the Soviets, Nixon and Kissinger would demand general settlements, linking problems such as Vietnam and the Middle East with concessions on trade and disarmament. In the area of arms control Kissinger and his boss saw negotiations with the Soviets as a means to extract concessions across a broad range of issues, including Vietnam. As far as the "balance of terror" was concerned, Kissinger, Nixon, and Secretary of Defense Melvin Laird were committed to establishing American supremacy, which, of course, they saw as the key to maintaining international stability.[2]

In 1966 U.S. intelligence discovered that the Soviet Union was in the research and development stage of a rudimentary antiballistic missile (ABM) system. The ultimate goal of that program was to ring Moscow and other cities with missiles that could destroy incoming enemy missiles and bombers in case of a nuclear attack. Possession of such a system by one of the superpowers and not the other would open up the possibility of a first strike (the possessor being invulnerable to retaliation) and thus upset the nuclear balance of power. But an ABM race would constitute a dangerous escalation of the arms race, one that could very possibly bankrupt the participants. Several times Johnson and Soviet Premier Aleksei Kosygin discussed conducting negotiations on limiting both offensive and defensive weapons, but

---

1 Kissinger to Nixon, Oct. 13, 1969, WHSpF, Box 3, Nixon Project.
2 See Seymour M. Hersh, *The Price of Power: Kissinger in the Nixon White House* (New York, 1983), 147–9.

nothing had ever come of their conversations. Consequently, in 1968 the president persuaded a reluctant Congress to pass legislation appropriating $1.195 billion for the construction of an American ABM system. When the Nixon administration took over the project, renamed it Safeguard, and announced that it was going to approach Congress for several billion more dollars, Fulbright and his colleagues decided that the time was propitious to make a stand against this particular weapons system and the military–industrial complex in general.[3]

As the battle lines formed, the national press predicted a major political confrontation, a "dramatic struggle" between "those who support the military budget and those who want to redirect resources toward solving hard social problems."[4] Cost estimates for the completed ABM system ran as high as $40 billion.[5] From the outset the opposition to Nixon's ABM system was deep and wide. Leading the revolt were Democrats Fulbright, McGovern, Symington, and Mansfield and Republicans Cooper, Javits, and Pearson. Even Everett Dirksen, responding to the cries of Chicagoans outraged at the scheduled construction of an ABM facility only thirty miles away, expressed reservations. However, the insurgents, as Laurence Stern pointed out, would be fighting an uphill battle. "The Defense Department has the biggest larder of benefits – money, real estate and plants – with which to foster friendliness and fealty. It maintains a congressional liaison establishment on Capitol Hill that is courteous, ever-willing and second to none among the executive agencies."[6] Taking point for the Pentagon were such proven cold war warriors as John Stennis, John Tower, Robert Dole (R–Kansas), Robert Byrd, and Strom Thurmond; but the heart and soul of the ABM team was Senator Henry M. "Scoop" Jackson, who, although a liberal Democrat on most domestic matters, was a tiger on defense issues. Jackson was a committed cold warrior both philosophically and politically. Without the aerospace industry, he believed, Washington's economy would collapse. The debate over ABM constituted the second chapter in the developing feud between Jackson and Fulbright.

Throughout March, Fulbright and the staff of the SFRC received a flood of information that the ABM system was technically deficient; that as soon as the installations were complete, they would be obsolete; and that the administration and defense contractors who would benefit from ABM were turning a deaf ear to criticism both from within the Pentagon and the scientific community at large. On March 27 Secretary of Defense David Packard ap-

3 Laurence Stern, "Political Winds Stir Change in Military, Defense Climate," *Washington Post,* Feb. 5, 1969.
4 National Committee for an Effective Congress, Mar. 10, 1969, Series 48:6, Box 24:3, SPF.
5 Tom Wicker, "The Overwhelming Case against ABM System," *Arkansas Gazette,* Mar. 13, 1969.
6 Stern, "Political Winds."

peared before the Disarmament Subcommittee. The Public Broadcast System was carrying the proceedings over the radio. Packard was reciting the usual litany when Fulbright interrupted him:

FULBRIGHT: Have you consulted outside experts on this system?

PACKARD: Yes, yes. Of course.

FULBRIGHT: Yeah, but who?

PACKARD: All the authorities.

FULBRIGHT: Yeah, but who?

PACKARD: I'm not sure I remember.

FULBRIGHT: Now, Mr. Secretary, you've consulted all these experts. Surely you can remember just one name.

PACKARD: [*After a long, pregnant pause*] I'll give one name. Dr. Wolfgang Panofsky at the Stanford Linear Accelerator.

Fulbright thanked him and the questioning continued.

A half hour later, the phone rang in the back of the hearing room. Jim Lowenstein answered. "This is Wolfgang Panofsky," the voice said. "He's not telling the truth. He ran into me in the airport and said, 'What do you think of the ABM system?' I said, 'I think it's for the birds. It won't work.' "[7]

The next day Fulbright called a press conference. The Nixon administration, he charged, had made "no serious scientific review" of the ABM program. The whole thing was a "political gimmick." "The Defense Department doesn't take this committee of the Congress seriously. . . . They think they can pull the wool over our eyes." He then told the Panofsky story.[8] In late April a group of anti-ABM physicists picketed the White House, carrying signs reading "Caution. The military–industrial complex is armed and dangerous" and "ABM is an Edsel."[9]

Nixon had staked his fragile ego on the ABM issue, and egged on by his top aides, he was determined to win. "A victory on this controversial issue is more than important; it is absolutely essential," Alexander Butterfield told him.[10] At Nixon's direction White House assistant Tom Huston lashed the troops to greater effort. "The attack on ABM and on defense spending has centered on the President because DOD, Congressional and Party officials are not doing their appropriate thing – sticking their necks out," he berated the cabinet and bureaucracy.[11] When National Educational Television ran a

7 Interview with James Lowenstein, Oct. 3, 1991, Washington, D.C.

8 "Fulbright Charges No Serious Review Made of Safeguard," *Arkansas Gazette,* Mar. 29, 1969.

9 *Congressional Record,* Senate, Aug. 12, 1969, 23469.

10 Butterfield to Nixon, June 11, 1969, WHSpF, Box 2, Nixon Project.

11 Tom Huston, "The McNamara Legacy," June 16, 1969, WHSpF, Box 2, Nixon Project.

series critical of the ABM specifically and military spending in general, Nixon exploded. "I want to use every possible discreet means to see that public funds for this left wing outfit are dried up," he ordered Herb Klein.[12] The White House persuaded Wall Street lawyer and well-known superhawk William Casey to establish the "Citizens Committee for Peace with Security" to lobby for passage of ABM. Amply funded by the major defense contractors who would profit from the Safeguard system, the Casey committee was tremendously effective in controlling the airways and pressuring key legislators.[13]

While Nixon and his aides mounted their television and print campaign in behalf of ABM, Fulbright and the opposition pursued two stratagems. They focused first on Laird's claim that the Soviets were mounting a first-strike capability and that, once achieved, the Kremlin intended to annihilate the West at the first opportunity. They then labored to bring to the public eye the fact that there were deep divisions within the administration over whether or not to go ahead with the system. Fulbright, Philip Hart (D–Michigan), and several other members of the opposition convened a scientific briefing at which anti-ABM scientists (which included virtually everyone except Edward Teller) briefed nineteen senators on the actual status of the Soviet arsenal.

The climactic debate over ABM began the first week in July. Leading the way for the defense establishment was Henry Jackson, the personification of liberal internationalism. The real issue, he told the Senate, was the nature of the threat facing the United States. Make no mistake about it, the Washingtonian proclaimed, "we face a very rough adversary, a very dangerous adversary, and an unpredictable one." That was not the issue at all, Fulbright responded. The issue was whether or not the Senate would be able "to reassert some control over the military department." If it did not, the United States would indeed become a national security state in which democracy, individual liberty, economic viability, everything, would be subsumed to the well-being of the military–industrial complex.[14]

After four weeks of debate, polls showed the Senate evenly divided with only Clinton P. Anderson (D–New Mexico) and John J. Williams (R–Delaware) uncommitted. The first and key vote would be on an insurgent amendment to continue research and development but to postpone actual construction of the first two Safeguard sites for a year. It was defeated on August 6 by a vote of 51 to 49.[15] The closeness of the vote was a triumph, Charles Percy (R–Illinois) told Fulbright in an effort to cheer him up. "In

---

12 Klein to Butterfield, July 10, 1969, WHSpF, Box 2, Nixon Project. In November, White House staffer Peter Flanigan offered the Corporation for Public Broadcasting a $5 million increase to enable it to supplant NET. Flanigan to Nixon, Nov. 4, 1969, WHSpF, Box 3, Nixon Project.

13 Peter Flanigan to John Ehrlichman, June 25, 1969, WHSpF, Box 42, Nixon Project.

14 *Congressional Record,* Senate, July 9, 1969, 18914.

15 David R. Boldt, "ABM Wins Crucial Senate Test," *Washington Post,* Aug. 7, 1969.

winning the support of half of all Senators, we established the principle that the Senate is no longer willing to accept without question the judgment of the military that a particular weapons system is vital to national survival."[16]

While Fulbright was publicly inveighing against the threat posed by the military–industrial complex, the investigative team of Pincus and Paul had shifted their attention from Spain to Laos. In 1967 and 1968, as the fighting in Vietnam escalated, so too did the level of violence in Laos. While American personnel, including Ambassador William Sullivan, insisted that the United States was respecting Laotian neutrality as provided for under the 1962 Geneva Accords, hundreds of military advisers, CIA operatives, and Air America personnel flooded into that unfortunate country and directed the Royal Laotian armed forces in operations against NVA enclaves and parts of the Ho Chi Minh Trail. By 1968 American fighter-bombers stationed in Thailand were pounding the Plain of Jars, a fertile region in northeastern Laos that had been under Pathet Lao control since 1964.[17]

With Nixon's election, Sullivan became deputy assistant secretary of state. Replacing him as ambassador in Vientiane was George McMurtrie Godley, whose experience in the Congo in 1964–5 had given him a taste for action. Washington ordered all restrictions on bombing, including the use of B-52s, removed. Godley, who personally directed air operations from a command post in the U.S. embassy, quickly acquired the nickname "air marshall." In the summer of 1969 Pincus and Paul arrived in the middle of this secret war. To their delight, it proved to be a simple task to uncover the Pentagon's covert operation.

The American embassy seemed not to have gotten the word that Nixon and Kissinger wanted the secret war in Laos kept secret, especially from Congress. Godley, whom Pincus referred to as the American "proconsul" in Laos, thoroughly enjoyed his responsibilities and could not stop talking about them. The SFRC investigator was delighted:

> We proved that we had to go in and support one of the two groups in Laos in order to get them to allow us to go into Laos to support the war. It meant that the commitment was to perpetuate a group in Laos in order to help the war. What we were doing was we were showing that we were creating commitments way beyond what people knew.[18]

Throughout the summer of 1969 the Symington subcommittee deliberately maintained a low profile[19]; then on September 30, the long-awaited public

16 Percy to JWF, Aug. 12, 1969, Series 48:6, Box 24:5, SPF.
17 Marilyn B. Young, *The Vietnam Wars, 1945–1990* (New York, 1991), 235.
18 Interview with Walter Pincus, Mar. 11, 1990, Washington, D.C.
19 Marcy to Lindsay Rogers, July 18, 1969, Box 8, Folder July–Sept., Marcy Papers.

hearings on unauthorized national commitments began. As the magnitude of the work done by Pincus and Paul became apparent, the White House momentarily panicked. "Symington Committee staffers have obtained from DOD, State and field missions a vast amount of highly sensitive information," Kissinger wrote Nixon. "Much of this is the type that has never been given to the Legislative Branch in previous administrations. Their information includes such things as type and locations of nuclear weapons and data on covert operations in Laos."[20] After meeting with Symington and futilely attempting to persuade him to desist, Nixon ordered all executive branch personnel to stonewall on the location of nuclear weapons and on all military "contingency" plans. It was a proverbial barn-door order.

The last week in October the Symington subcommittee turned its attention to Laos and Cambodia. "It's time people knew the facts," Fulbright told the Capitol Hill press corps. With copies of the Pincus–Paul report in their hands, Fulbright, Symington, and Mansfield grilled CIA Director Richard Helms, Secretary of Defense Laird, and military personnel brought back from Laos and Thailand specifically at the subcommittee's request. To the administration's enragement, Fulbright would regale reporters with tidbits of information gleaned by committee investigators after the closed-door hearings had ended. After Helms testified on October 29, Fulbright emerged from the committee room and announced to a phalanx of reporters that the United States had been fighting a secret war in Laos in direct violation of the 1962 Geneva Accords, which prohibited the introduction of foreign troops into that country. The CIA was illegally arming and training a clandestine Laotian army, he insisted, and the United States Air Force was operating inside Laos.[21]

The chairman and his supporters intended the hearings to be a prelude to concrete congressional action to prohibit U.S. involvement in overseas conflicts made under secret agreements. The White House knew what the anti-imperialists had in mind, but they did not know when or how they would act. On December 15 Fulbright and his cohorts struck. During a debate on the military appropriations bill, the chairman asked the measure's floor manager why it included $90 million for U.S. military assistance to neutral Laos. Before he could respond, Frank Church rose to propose that the Senate amend the Pentagon budget bill to bar the use of new defense funds "to finance the introduction of American ground combat troops in Laos and Thailand." In a massive show of force, hawks and doves banded together to approve the Church amendment by a vote of 73 to 17. When the dust had settled, Congress had slashed $5.3 billion from the administration's military spending bill.[22]

20 Kissinger to Nixon, Oct. 1, 1969, WHCF, Box 20, Nixon Project.
21 "U.S. Waging War in Laos on the Sly, Fulbright Asserts," *Arkansas Gazette,* Oct. 29, 1969.
22 Warren Unna and Richard Homan, "Hill Acts to Curb Asia Role," *Washington Post,* Dec. 16, 1969.

Fulbright recognized an essential truth about the nature of North Vietnamese resistance that seemed to escape Nixon, Goodpaster, and the JCS. Ho Chi Minh and the soldier-citizens around him were willing to sacrifice everything to reunify the country under their leadership. They were not subject to threats. There was no significant evidence of a division within Ho's ranks. The United States had moved more tonnage of equipment and weaponry into Vietnam than it had into the European Theater of Operations during World War II. American body count put enemy deaths as of 1969 at 520,219. Nevertheless, the communists persisted. "There are some kinds of wars that can't be won by force, and some kinds of people that will die before they will surrender," Fulbright wrote Mrs. Albert Gore. The nature and origin of their motivation were irrelevant. Even if the NVA and VC soldiers were hopeless automatons, turned into suicide machines by a totalitarian government (which he did not believe), "the United States has taken on a hopeless task."[23]

Despite congressional and public impatience with the Nixon administration's policies in Vietnam, the president was no more willing to make the hard choices than Kennedy or Johnson had been. He was aware at the intellectual level of how strategically and politically counterproductive the war was; but he was convinced that an immediate, unnegotiated withdrawal would be interpreted by the Russians as a sign of weakness and lack of control. In addition, there continued to be powerful psychological forces at work that kept the president from withdrawing. Once Nixon became president and inherited responsibility for the war, he acquired ownership in it. He was enthralled with the notion of being commander in chief and terrified of being viewed by the military as weak. Like Johnson, he came to believe that those who criticized the conflict were criticizing him. Indeed, the war and the debate over it activated Nixon's near-obsessive fear of defeat and humiliation. Those who opposed what he wanted to do in Southeast Asia, whatever that happened to be at the time, became in his mind "doctrinaire leftists."[24] What differentiated Nixon from his predecessors and made possible the prolongation of the war was that he was more successful in convincing both hawks and doves that he was heeding their advice and in diverting popular impatience to his critics.

On May 14, 1969, the president had addressed a national television audience on Vietnam. "I know that some believe I should have ended the war immediately after my inauguration by simply withdrawing our forces from Vietnam," he said. "That would have been the easy thing to do and it might have been a popular move." But he could not do it, the president declared somberly. To simply withdraw would have been to have "betrayed my solemn responsibility as President." He intended to end the war permanently,

23 JWF to Mrs. Albert Gore, July 22, 1969, Box 8, July–Sept., Marcy Papers.
24 News Summary, May 20, 1969, WHSpF, Box 30, Nixon Project.

Nixon declared, ''so that the younger brothers of our soldiers in Vietnam will not have to fight in the future in another Vietnam some place in the world.'' The United States had given up on winning a purely military victory, Nixon told the American people, but neither would his government accept a settlement in Paris that amounted to a ''disguised defeat.'' The United States would agree to withdraw its troops from Vietnam according to a specified timetable if North Vietnam would agree to withdraw its forces from South Vietnam, Cambodia, and Laos according to a specified timetable.[25]

Shortly thereafter, William Rogers testified before the SFRC in executive session on his recent tour of Vietnam. As the secretary of state launched into his optimistic review, the chairman interrupted him:

> You sound exactly like Mr. McNamara and Mr. Taylor when they used to report to us year after year, and always the generals were always first-rate, the morale was fine, Bunker was fine, everything was just fine, which again leads me to believe that there is not the slightest idea of changing anything that the previous administration has been doing.[26]

Two weeks after Rogers's appearance Fulbright announced on ABC's *Issues and Answers* that the SFRC would hold a new series of hearings on Vietnam. The president's ''new isolationist'' speech at the Air Force Academy, he said, indicated that his policy was as bankrupt as Johnson's.[27] The first witness would be Clark Clifford, who had just recommended in *Foreign Affairs* that a hundred thousand troops be brought home by the end of 1969 and that all combat troops be removed by the end of 1970.[28]

Meanwhile, Nixon's secret diplomacy and implied military threats were having no impact on Hanoi. Ho Chi Minh agreed with Fulbright: There was no significant difference between Nixon's negotiating position and Johnson's. To have accepted the notion of mutual, calibrated withdrawal that left the Thieu government in place and the NLF outside the power structure would have been to have relinquished goals for which Ho and his colleagues had been fighting for a quarter century. The North Vietnamese delegation publicly dismissed the proposal made in Nixon's May television address. They would, if necessary, sit in Paris ''until the chairs rot,'' they said.[29] Certain that American public opinion would eventually force Nixon to withdraw from Vietnam,

25 Text of Televised Speech by the President on Vietnam, May 14, 1969, Series 1:1, Box 4:3, SPF.

26 Briefing on Secretary Rogers's Trip, June 6, 1969, Executive Sessions, SFRC, RG 46, NA.

27 Robert C. Jensen, ''Fulbright Will Reopen Probe of Vietnam Policy,'' *Washington Post*, June 23, 1969.

28 JWF to Clark Clifford, June 21, 1969, Series 48:3, Box 17:1, SPF.

29 Quoted in George C. Herring, *America's Longest War: The United States and Vietnam, 1950–1975*, 2d ed. (New York, 1986), 226.

the North Vietnamese were prepared to wait him out, no matter how many soldiers and civilians had to die and how long it took.

Fulbright's and the SFRC's mounting frustration with the Nixon administration was accompanied by a revival of the antiwar movement, disorganized, demoralized, and largely dormant since the disastrous Chicago convention. As the threat of ghetto uprisings subsided somewhat, a development having more to do with exhaustion than with satiation of demands, a wave of protest and demonstrations disturbed nearly four hundred of the nation's twenty-five hundred college campuses. The 1969 disorders were more confrontational and violent than previous eruptions. Nerves on both sides of the picket line were raw. Patience was at a premium. Occupation of administration buildings seemed almost always to end with beatings and arrests. Authorities hauled away over four thousand students on campuses from San Francisco State to Swarthmore, while seven percent of the country's schools reported violent protests involving property damage or personal injury.[30]

Despite this violence, or perhaps because of it, the main burden of regenerating the antiwar movement fell in 1969 upon its more conservative elements, primarily liberals who wanted to work within the system. The activities and makeup of the participants reflected this shift. The resurgence of springtime activism culminated in the organization of the moratorium and the New Mobilization, which, according to Charles DeBenedetti and Charles Chatfield, "combined . . . to rally the most potent and widespread antiwar protests ever mounted in a western democracy." On June 30, the Vietnam Moratorium Committee issued its call for a nationwide work stoppage to demonstrate opposition to the war in Southeast Asia. The New Mobilization Committee to End the War in Vietnam was determined to organize the broadest possible spectrum of antiwar citizens in "a legal and traditional protest action";[31] in pursuance of that goal, it called for a national demonstration in Washington to begin on November 13. Participants would demand America's immediate withdrawal from Vietnam.

30 Charles DeBenedetti with Charles Chatfield, *An American Ordeal: The Antiwar Movement of the Vietnam Era* (Syracuse, 1990), 242–3.
31 Ibid., 248; quote on 250.

15

Sparta or Athens?

The first week in October 1969 J. William Fulbright observed to the Senate of the United States that President Nixon had been in office nine months, "the normal period of gestation for humans." During the fall campaign the president had told the American people that he had a "secret plan" to end the war. What had happened to that alluring scheme? Noting that nearly ten thousand American soldiers had died in Vietnam since the new administration had come to power, he proclaimed that it was time for the United States to leave Vietnam; it was time for the Vietnamese to fight their own war. Fulbright also announced his support for the national moratorium scheduled for October 15, declaring it to be "in the best American tradition of peaceful protest for the redress of grievances."[1]

As the antiwar movement veered sharply toward the political and cultural center in 1969, Fulbright became more closely identified with it and important to it. Partial proof of that was the fact that he became anathema to the movement's more radical elements.

No less than Richard Nixon or Lyndon Johnson, the Arkansan perceived that the battle on the home front was a struggle for the political center. It was to patriotic, law-abiding, churchgoing, property-owning Americans to which the movement would have to appeal. To this end, Fulbright repeatedly and publicly repudiated the tactic of draft resistance. Throughout 1967, 1968, and 1969, young men planning to burn their draft cards or flee to Canada wrote the chairman of the SFRC, asking for his advice. His response was always the same: Your decision "is a profoundly personal one," he would write, and consequently, his advice had "no more than limited relevance." Although the war in Vietnam was unjustified, "I believe that if I were drafted I would serve," he wrote. "I would do so because I believe that our country, despite grave defects and mistakes, is basically a decent society and one, therefore, whose laws and requirements I would wish to comply with." The individual citizen could do more to correct the nation's

1 *Congressional Record*, Senate, Oct. 1, 1969, 2781–3.

"transgressions" by "staying within the system and laws than by going outside them."[2]

On October 15 the first phase of the Vietnam Moratorium Committee's operation began. The day started with a memorial service for American war dead held on Massachusetts's sea coast, and it spread westward as the day unfolded, attaining, in the words of DeBenedetti and Chatfield, "a diversity, pervasiveness and dignity unprecedented in the history of popular protest."[3] Moratorium activities ranged from lonely picketing to mass rallies, from public demonstrations to private conversations. Managers of businesses such as the Itek Corporation and Midas Muffler encouraged workers to take time off to support the moratorium. In New Haven, no less an establishment figure than Malcolm Baldrige, 1968 Connecticut Chairman for Citizens for Nixon–Agnew, denounced the war to a group of Yale students.[4] Fulbright was delighted. "They seemed to me to be extremely well-behaved and a very serious demonstration of disapproval of the tragic mistake . . . in Vietnam," he wrote a disgruntled constituent.[5]

His advisers might have been split over the sincerity and integrity of the antiwar movement, but Richard Nixon remained convinced that it continued to be led and organized by the Students for a Democratic Society, which he perceived to be a collection of Marxists, radicals, and anarchists, and that the goal of the student movement was destruction of the established political order.[6] Indeed, the president's true feelings were articulated by Spiro Agnew, who addressed a Republican gathering a few days after the October demonstrations. The Vietnam Moratorium Day activities were wrongheaded and dangerous demonstrations "encouraged by an effete corps of impudent snobs who characterize themselves as intellectuals," he proclaimed.[7] Most important, the president refused to believe that the antiwar movement included significant portions of the American center. The law-abiding, property-owning, churchgoing public would not tolerate defeat in Vietnam.

Nixon had justified the fall draft cancellations as part of his "new" policy of Vietnamization. Actually, it was an approach he had inherited from Lyndon Johnson. This approach, Melvin Laird explained, involved reliance "on indigenous manpower organized into properly equipped and well-trained armed forces with the help of materiel, training, technology and specialized

2 JWF to Richard H. Cook, Nov. 29, 1967, Series 48:18, Box 50:3, SPF.
3 Charles DeBenedetti with Charles Chatfield, *An American Ordeal: The Antiwar Movement of the Vietnam Era* (Syracuse, 1990), 255.
4 Butterfield to Haldeman, Oct. 21, 1969, Box 138, WHSpF, Nixon Project.
5 Quoted in William C. Berman, *William Fulbright and the Vietnam War: The Dissent of a Political Realist* (Kent, Ohio, 1988), 116.
6 Arthur Burns to Nixon, May 26, 1969, Box 2, WHSpF, Nixon Project.
7 "Agnew Says 'Effete Snobs' Incited War Moratorium," *New York Times,* Oct. 19, 1969.

military skills furnished by the United States."[8] Vietnamization seemed to Nixon to offer the alluring prospect of reducing U.S. casualties and of terminating American involvement in an honorable fashion regardless of what North Vietnam did.

In a major television address on November 3 the president spelled out his Vietnamization policy in some detail. He also announced a schedule for further troop withdrawals. Having apparently placated critics of the war, Nixon then went out of his way to antagonize them. He dismissed the protesters as an irrational and irresponsible rabble and accused them of sabotaging his diplomacy. He openly appealed for the support of those he labeled the "great silent majority," and he finished his speech with a dramatic flourish: "North Vietnam cannot humiliate the United States. Only Americans can do that."[9]

In fact, Vietnamization was designed to appeal not to doves but to hawks and former supporters of the war who had become alienated. In the spring of 1969 Pat Buchanan and his conservative coworkers had identified the core of Nixon's political support and advised him on how best to enlarge it. Aside from the well-to-do industrialists, financiers, and professional people who traditionally voted Republican, Nixon's broadest potential appeal was to the lower middle class who, ironically, had been converted into haves from havenots by the New Deal. Above all, they were preoccupied with preserving their newly won wealth (modest though it was) and social status.

Tactically, the "silent majority" speech was a brilliant stroke. As the Democratic National Committee put it, "[T]he national mood on Viet Nam is at the same time glum and tired, but unwilling to accept outright defeat."[10] Having announced a plan for ending the war, Nixon denounced those who had been demanding its end. In so doing he made it possible for the Americans who had at one time or another supported the war in Vietnam, but who had turned against it, to support a scheme for American withdrawal without seeming to oppose the war. A Gallup poll indicated that seventy-seven percent of Americans backed the president's plan, with only six percent in opposition, and that by a 6-to-1 margin people agreed with him that antiwar protests actually harmed the prospects for peace.[11] Nixon was so thrilled with these opinion surveys that he twice called newspeople and camera crews into the Oval Office to see them;[12] and he had Bryce Harlow send Fulbright "personal" copies of the Gallup poll "in the event you had not noted it in the papers."[13]

8 Quoted in Marilyn B. Young, *The Vietnam Wars, 1945–1990* (New York, 1991), 240.
9 Quoted in George C. Herring, *America's Longest War: The United States and Vietnam, 1950–1975,* 2d ed. (New York, 1986), 229.
10 "Richard Nixon – One Year Later," Democratic National Committee, Dec. 19, 1969, Series 1:1, Box 4:4, SPF.
11 DeBenedetti and Chatfield, *American Ordeal,* 259.
12 "Nixon Thinks He Has Won a Referendum on the War," *Baltimore Sun,* Nov. 5, 1969.
13 Harlow to JWF, Nov. 5, 1969, Series 1:1, Box 4:4, SPF.

Not surprisingly, the "silent majority" speech angered and depressed Fulbright. It was all he could do to contain himself when Bob Hope wrote proposing that the Arkansan join him in cochairing a "week of national unity."[14] President Nixon, Fulbright told reporters, "now has fully and truthfully taken on himself the Johnson war, and I think it is a fundamental error."[15]

A major assumption of the political strategy espoused by Buchanan, Kevin Phillips, and other conservative intellectuals, and embraced by Nixon, was that their opponents were totally out of touch with the forgotten American. In the case of the chairman of the SFRC, they were quite right. No public figure was more remote from, or less simpatico with, the silent majority than the junior senator from Arkansas. The chairman of the SFRC lived in a world that took no notice of pickup trucks, country music, celebrity sports, or religious fundamentalism. His and Betty's only concession to popular culture were addictions to *Bonanza* and the soap operas. Socially secure himself, Fulbright did not understand the fears and anxieties of those who were not. He had never experienced personal debt; he once expressed amazement that his secretary and her husband had assumed a mortgage to pay for their house. Fulbright did not worry about blacks moving into his neighborhood; blacks already lived there – Ghanaian, Zambian, and Moroccan diplomats. His opposition to forced integration stemmed from his constitutional views and his old-fashioned progressive conviction that the government owed to the people equality of opportunity and not equality of condition. For the forgotten American the war in Vietnam was a test the nation could not afford to fail, a contest it dare not lose. Defeat meant loss of face, personal as well as national humiliation. Because Fulbright related primarily to the "international community," which was in fact a fairly close-knit network of well-educated political and cultural elites, rather than to the parochial, sports-minded, undereducated Americans who constituted the silent majority, it was the war itself that threatened the nation with humiliation: The worst thing that could have happened in Vietnam was for America to have won a military victory.

In mid-November Joseph Starobin, former editor of the *Communist Daily Worker*, then laboring in self-imposed exile as an assistant professor at York University, contacted Fulbright and told him that he had twice acted as a go-between for Henry Kissinger and North Vietnamese delegate Xuan Thuy in Paris. Charges made by Nixon in the silent majority speech that North Vietnam had rejected all overtures for a peace settlement, public and private, were untrue. Prior to the speech, the DRV had made several attempts to break the diplomatic logjam but had been rebuffed. Although Starobin had been

14 Bob Hope to JWF, Nov. 6, 1969, Series 48:1, Box 9:4, SPF.
15 "Fulbright Critical of Nixon's Address," *Fort Smith Southwest Times Record,* Nov. 4, 1969.

for much of his adult life a communist, and there were questions concerning his reliability, Fulbright decided to break the story. He suspected, correctly, that Nixon had chosen to substitute ''Vietnamization'' for negotiation. In fact, on November 21 two top members of the U.S. delegation in Paris, Henry Cabot Lodge and Lawrence Walsh, resigned in apparent disgust at the administration's intransigence; but the Starobin revelation was a public relations bust. Agnew and company simply cited the incident as further proof that the Arkansan was a willing or unwilling dupe of the communists.[16]

Late in 1969 Fulbright initiated a Senate debate on Laos. Six weeks earlier, in late October, with Roland Paul at their side, Fulbright and Symington had questioned former ambassador William Sullivan and CIA Chief Richard Helms on America's secret war in that unfortunate land. Under tough cross-examination, they admitted that during the period from 1964 to 1969 B-52s operating out of Korat air base in Thailand had flown from seven hundred to fifteen hundred sorties against the Ho Chi Minh Trail and Pathet Lao positions in the Plain of Jars. There were 125 U.S. Air Force (USAF) officers assigned to the Air Attaché's Office in Vientiane. In addition, they conceded that the U.S. ambassador had complete authority to ''validate'' targets in Laos.[17]

When subsequently Fulbright began to describe American activities to the Senate, members of the Armed Services Committee jumped to their feet. The senator from Arkansas was leaking classified information of military use to the enemy, they charged. The executive branch had involved the United States in an undeclared war in Laos without the knowledge or consent of Congress or the American people, Fulbright replied. He was going to say what he was going to say. Mansfield quickly seized the floor and guided the Senate into executive session. As the chairman detailed American secret activities in Laos, his colleagues became visibly outraged. Some like Mansfield insisted that air strikes in Laos were necessary to the prosecution of the war in Vietnam, but all agreed that Congress had a right to know. Several days after the executive session, the House and Senate passed an amendment to a military appropriations bill sponsored by John Sherman Cooper and Frank Church forbidding the use of American ground troops in Laos without Congress's approval.[18]

16 ''Fulbright Quotes Intermediary,'' *Pine Bluff Commercial,* Nov. 12, 1969; Marcy, memo of conversation, Nov. 20, 1969, Box 8, Folder Oct.–Dec., Marcy Papers; and ''Nixon Seen as Downgrading Talks, Stressing Vietnamization,'' *Arkansas Democrat,* Nov. 21, 1969.
17 Hearings on Laos, Executive Sessions, SFRC, RG 46, NA.
18 Berman, *Fulbright and the Vietnam War,* 119.

To say that J. William Fulbright welcomed the Nixon administration with high hopes when it assumed office in January 1969 would be an overstatement. He harbored no illusions concerning Richard Nixon's altruism; but he believed that the president's political opportunism boded well for the future. The election, Fulbright was convinced, had been a repudiation of Lyndon Johnson and his policies in Southeast Asia. During his conversations with the president and Henry Kissinger in the spring, both had assured him that they realized that their political future as well as the interests of the nation would be served by the earliest possible exit from Vietnam. Instead of scaling down the war and making meaningful concessions in negotiations with the North Vietnamese, however, Nixon had actually escalated the level of violence, continued a clandestine war in Laos, and engaged in the secret bombing of Cambodia.

By the summer of 1969 Fulbright had decided that, like Lyndon Johnson, Richard Nixon had become a prisoner of forces – the radical right, the military–industrial complex, his own psyche – of which he was only dimly aware and which he could not control even if he had so desired. The country was frightened and exhausted, afraid to lose in Vietnam, but increasingly convinced that it could not win. The junior senator from Arkansas was not optimistic about his or the Senate's ability to lead the country out of the wilderness – he did not think in such terms anyway – but someone had to sound the tocsin, and Congress was the only power center available around which to build support for an end to the war and a new foreign policy based on reason and restraint.

"The true patriot," J. William Fulbright told the Senate in 1971, "is one who gives his highest loyalty not to his country as it is, but to his own best conception of what it can and ought to be." Those among his colleagues with an eye to history recalled William Lloyd Garrison and his invocation of a higher law. That speech, delivered during the height of the slavery controversy, had presaged a denunciation of the Constitution and the Fugitive Slave Act, and an appeal by Garrison to his abolitionist followers to ignore the law when it violated their moral scruples. But Fulbright's invocation of a higher loyalty foreshadowed instead a campaign to restore constitutional democracy to America. It was a call to arms to combat what he referred to as an "elective dictatorship" – what Arthur Schlesinger would subsequently dub "the imperial presidency."

As Congress began its deliberations in early 1971, Fulbright delivered an updated version of "The Legislator," the speech he had given at the University of Chicago some twenty-seven years earlier. From time immemorial, presidents, prime ministers, premiers, generalissimos, and tribal chieftains, elected or otherwise, had grasped for greater power; it was their nature. It was the duty of legislatures to remain forever vigilant against this threat; but

America's had failed. "Out of a well-intentioned but misconceived notion of what patriotism and responsibility require in a time of world crisis, Congress has permitted the President to take over the two vital foreign policy powers which the Constitution vested in Congress," Fulbright proclaimed: the power to declare war and the power to approve foreign commitments.[19] Theoretically, Congress had the authority to end the war in Vietnam; whether or not it had the will was the issue. One did not have to be a student of Plato, Thucydides, or Montesquieu to understand that the Vietnam War was not only polarizing the country but eroding the political liberties of its citizens. In the heat of war and frustrated by the nation's inability to win a clear-cut victory, Congress and the American people during the Johnson years had deferred to an avaricious executive in thrall to a burgeoning military–industrial complex whose existence was justified on the grounds that it was bringing social justice, a higher standard of living, and at least the possibility of democracy to those peoples of the world threatened by international communism. Although that crusade had proved to be an illusion, private interests and ideological fanatics had joined hands to perpetuate it. If Congress did not act, the nation would be dragged into one foreign adventure after another until, morally and financially bankrupt, it disappeared from the face of the earth like other empires before it.[20]

Not only had the trend toward executive domination of American foreign policy accelerated dramatically under Richard Nixon and Henry Kissinger, but there was no idealism in their notion of American exceptionalism. As a nationalist and card-carrying superpatriot, Richard Nixon continually paid lip service to the notion of American cultural superiority; but as an outsider and an episodic paranoid, he attached himself to those aspects of American culture that he felt would make him popular – sports, for example. He had no genuine passions or even hobbies beyond politics, much less a utopian vision or even a commitment to a moral code. Indeed, like the public relations men with whom he surrounded himself, Nixon was completely amoral, a humorless man seeking in the exercise of power the comfort and security that he was unable to find elsewhere.[21] Repeatedly referring to himself in the third person as "RN" in memos to his aides, Nixon hammered away at the person he wanted them to create in the public mind: "strong convictions came up through adversity . . . cool . . . unflappable . . . a man . . . who is steely but who is subtle and appears almost gentle."[22]

19 *Congressional Record,* Senate, Feb. 5, 1971, 1867–8.
20 Ibid.
21 Late in 1970 the president directed H. R. Haldeman to assign a designated "anecdotalist" to any public meeting or interview involving the president. That person was to be sure that out of every such encounter the press received a "warm human interest story" that portrayed Nixon as a sensitive, caring human being. Haldeman to Chapin, Dec. 9, 1970, WHSpF, Box 70, Nixon Project.
22 Nixon to Kissinger, July 19, 1971, WHSpF, Box 151, Nixon Project.

The Nixon regime, because it was less idealistic than the Johnson administration, was both more and less formidable an adversary for Fulbright and those who wanted to end the war in Vietnam, reduce American commitments abroad, and restrict the power of the executive. Unlike Johnson, Nixon had no agenda for uplifting the downtrodden at home or abroad. He tried the new Republicanism in the form of the Family Assistance Plan but abandoned it. Indeed, Richard Nixon cared nothing for domestic reform because he could not win with it. "International affairs is *our* issue," he told White House staffers John Haldeman and John Ehrlichmann, and the Democrats must not be allowed to usurp it. Leave domestic affairs to them "because Libs can *always* promise more."[23] However, he thought of international relations in terms of power and control, not understanding and interdependence. His approach to the Fulbright exchange program was to view its participants as agents of cultural imperialism. He repeatedly told Kissinger that the United States should send more of its students abroad and accept less from foreign countries. Indeed, at times he blamed campus unrest on "radical" exchange students from other parts of the world.[24]

No one ever accused Henry Kissinger of being a bleeding heart, either. The notion of replicating America around the globe seemed absurd to him, both because he had contempt for so much of what was American and because he recognized the pitfalls of "welfare imperialism," to use Fulbright's phrase. Like Nixon, Kissinger was interested in power for power's sake. As numerous historians have noted, the national security adviser aspired to be nothing less than arbiter of the international political system. For Kissinger as well as for Nixon to satisfy their needs, America had to be respected, and respect, they were convinced, was built primarily on fear. The vision of America as a moral exemplar and benefactor to the rest of the world – champion of human rights, elevator of living standards – held no attraction for them. Bases, bombs, missiles, and ships gave the United States credibility. In *A World Restored,* Kissinger acknowledged that diplomacy was "the art of restraining power," but he also observed that "in any negotiation it is understood that force is the ultimate recourse."[25] Those assumptions and goals placed the administration on a collision course with J. William Fulbright and the growing anti-imperialist clique within the United States Congress.

Throughout 1970 and 1971 Fulbright, together with George McGovern, John Sherman Cooper, and Mark Hatfield (R–Oregon), hammered away at the system of bases and overseas commitments and at the military–industrial complex that underlay them. Using the issue of executive usurpation of congressional prerogatives to attract conservatives and capitalizing at every op-

23 Notes on News Summary, Nov. 13, 1971, WHSpF, Box 35, Nixon Project.
24 News Summaries, Jan. 3, 1971, WHSpF, Box 32, Nixon Project.
25 Chalmers Roberts, "Kissinger vs. Fulbright," *Washington Post,* Apr. 26, 1970.

portunity on the widespread discontent created by American involvement in Cambodia, Laos, and Vietnam, they sought to persuade the nation to redefine its foreign policy objectives in a rational, restrained way, one that would take into account cultural diversity and match America's ends to its diminishing means.

In 1969 Carl Marcy persuaded Richard Moose to join the staff of the SFRC. Moose, an Arkansan and career foreign service officer, had worked first for Walt Rostow on the staff of the NSC and subsequently for Henry Kissinger in the same capacity. He left the White House for a variety of reasons: he was tired of looking out his office window and watching his wife marching to protest the very war that he was planning; He was increasingly influenced by his radical friend I. F. Stone; and it soon became clear that ''Henry'' had his knife sharpened for him. A bright, personable man with a fine sense of irony, Moose found a kindred spirit in Jim Lowenstein.

Both Moose and Lowenstein had had a conversion experience over Vietnam, and they attacked American involvement there with all the ferocity guilty consciences could muster. In the fall of 1969 the pair approached Carl Marcy and asked him about the feasibility of a fact-finding mission to Southeast Asia. Led by Spiro Agnew, supporters of the war were insisting almost daily that Fulbright himself go to Vietnam and find out the truth, a suggestion that the chairman had steadfastly resisted on a number of grounds. An SFRC staff mission, argued the two, would hopefully spike the vice-president's guns. Moreover, Vietnamization had temporarily mesmerized the country and many members of Congress. With George Aiken and John Sherman Cooper openly supporting the policy, all momentum toward withdrawal had been lost.[26] Moose and Lowenstein suspected that the military/political situation was not as promising as the administration portrayed it and that the GVN and ARVN were no more prepared to assume responsibility for the future of their country than they had been during the Johnson era.

Marcy hesitated. He had had a hard time selling committee members on the Pincus–Paul expedition, and there had been no partisan split on the committee as there was in 1970. After consulting Fulbright, however, he gave the go-ahead. The chairman was convinced that Vietnamization was a sham, and he decided that the Lowenstein–Moose mission was necessary to prove it.

As soon as the two SFRC investigators arrived in Saigon on December 4, the two broke away from their uneasy hosts and struck out for the delta. Traveling at times by bicycle and at times by rickety automobile, they were passed from source to source, interviewing peasants, village chiefs, and field-grade American officers. In the company of a journalist friend of Lowen-

26 Interview with James Lowenstein, Oct. 3, 1991, Washington, D.C.

stein's the two spent the night in a supposedly secure hamlet, only to wake up the next morning to find that the headman's throat had been cut. In Saigon, Moose and Lowenstein were met with hostile contempt by Ellsworth Bunker and the military command, but the two SFRC staffers quickly learned that the upper echelon's control did not reach very far down into the ranks. Lowenstein recalled:

> The situation in the military was very bad by then. A lot of officers would talk to us about it ... a lot of junior officers – lieutenants, captains majors – who were very well educated. Out of the military academies. They were very upset. All the lies that went into the business about body counts were so flagrant and so obvious.[27]

The Moose–Lowenstein team returned to Washington just before Christmas to deliver its report. After describing the situation as they had found it – a much less optimistic image than that being projected by the administration – the SFRC investigators argued that Vietnamization would work only if there emerged a broad-based government capable of commanding the allegiance of all major groups, if ARVN became a highly motivated, efficient fighting machine, and if Hanoi continued its low level of military activity in the South. "Dilemmas thus seem to lie ahead in Vietnam, as they have throughout our involvement in this war that appears to be not only far from won but far from over," they concluded.[28]

No sooner had the two investigators filed their analysis with the SFRC than Carl Marcy leaked it to the press. Lowenstein recalled that the result was astonishing. All the major dailies carried front-page excerpts, and the nightly news anchors read portions of the text on the air.[29] At once the sense of tranquillity over Vietnam that Nixon and his minions had labored so hard to establish was shattered. All the old anxieties came flooding back. Nixon was furious. "This shows there *is* an establishment for peace at any price," he wrote Kissinger. "Have your letters team give them hell – we must keep our silent majority group involved."[30]

Throughout February and March 1970 Fulbright and the SFRC staff received word from various sources that the secret war in Laos was escalating. Those rumors turned out to be true. Nixon had come under intense pressure from the air force to resume bombing North Vietnam. Kissinger pleaded with him not to take that dangerous step, a step that was sure to derail his private negotiations with Le Duc Tho and to breathe new life into the antiwar move-

27 Ibid.
28 Quoted in Berman, *Fulbright and the Vietnam War,* 120.
29 See John W. Finney, "War-Policy Basis Is Called Dubious," *New York Times,* Feb. 2, 1970.
30 Notes on News Summary, Feb. 2, 1970, WHSpF, Box 31, Nixon Project.

ment. Nixon compromised by authorizing massive new bombing of North Vietnamese positions in Laos and the portions of the Ho Chi Minh Trail that ran through that country.[31] From the secret hearings that the Symington subcommittee had held in October 1969, Fulbright and the other members knew that there were hundreds of American military advisers in Laos and that American planes based in Thailand were flying numerous missions each week in support of the Royal Laotian Army's effort to clear the Pathet Lao out of the Plain of Jars. They had also learned that the U.S. military and the CIA had for years supplied and trained a secret army under Major General Van Pao. Van Pao's force, composed of Laotians but separate from the Royal Laotian Army, felt free to cross into Vietnam and Cambodia in pursuit of the communists.[32]

Despite the fact that Fulbright had detailed some of this activity to his Senate colleagues in executive session, the Nixon administration continued to argue privately that its operations in Laos were classified and to deny publicly that they existed at all. Indeed, so determined was Washington to hide its involvement, particularly on the ground, that CIA operatives killed in northeast Laos were routinely maimed by their fellows to prevent identification. "The Americans have orders they must not be captured," a Laotian official working with the CIA confided to a foreign correspondent. "If they are killed, other members of their patrol put a grenade on their face or shoot them up with their machine guns till they can't be recognized."[33]

Although he would not release verbatim portions of the transcript or cite precise numbers of advisers and sorties, Fulbright began giving Kissinger-style "backgrounders" to the press. The conflict in Laos had already turned into a Vietnam, he told an Arkansas reporter. The only difference was that because there were only three million Laotians, the number killed could never equal the number of Vietnamese killed.[34] The first week in March Fulbright backed a move by George McGovern to have the Senate once again go into executive session to consider the Laotion situation.[35] Still the Nixon administration refused to allow the SFRC to release its information.

Then on March 9, in an effort to head off the gathering storm, Nixon went on a national television hookup to inform the nation that there were four hundred American advisers in Laos and that American warplanes were bombing the trail and flying support missions for Prince Souvanna Phouma's Royal Laotian Army. But he stated that no Americans had died in combat in Laos; he would, moreover, abide by the 1969 congressional directive not to intro-

31 Ibid., Feb. 9 and Mar. 13, 1970.
32 "Rogers Explains His Stand on Laos," *New York Times,* Mar. 18, 1970.
33 "CIA Reportedly Maims Its Dead on Lao Patrols," *Washington Evening Star,* June 10, 1970.
34 "Concern Grows Over Laos," *Fort Smith Southwest Times Record,* Feb. 22, 1970.
35 George C. Wilson, "Secret Session on Laos Sought by McGovern," *Washington Post,* Mar. 4, 1970.

duce American ground troops into that country. Three days later newspapers across the nation reported that Captain Joseph K. Bush, Jr., had been cut down by North Vietnamese machine-gun fire in northeastern Laos. Assistant Press Secretary Gerald Warren admitted to reporters at Key Biscayne that Bush was the twenty-seventh American combat death in Laos but that the president had been unaware of the statistic when he had delivered his speech.[36] Fulbright suspected that Warren was lying, and he was not satisfied with the president's pledge. Three days after the White House statement, he introduced a resolution prohibiting the use of U.S. forces "in combat in or over Laos" without prior congressional approval. "If the Senate is to remain silent while the President uses air forces in an Asian country without authority from Congress," he declared, "we should remain silent about his use of ground combat forces."[37]

The first week in April 1970, Fulbright delivered a speech entitled "New Myths and Old Realities," an ironic play on the title of his famous 1964 address. He called for nothing less than American acquiescence in the communization of Vietnam:

> The master myth of Vietnam . . . is the greatly inflated importance which has been attached to it. From the standpoint of American security and interests, the central fact about Indochina, including Vietnam, is that it does not matter very much who rules in those small and backward lands. At the risk of being accused of every sin from racism to communism, I stress the irrelevance of ideology to poor and backward populations.[38]

The notion of a monolithic communist threat bent on conquering the world was an illusion. The Soviet Union was a "traditional, cautious, and rather unimaginative great power" incapable of co-opting nationalism in Southeast Asia. If the United States had not interfered in Vietnam, "we might now be dealing with a stable, independent, unified Communist country – no more hostile to the United States than Yugoslavia itself is today." North Vietnam was the paramount power in Indochina, and the sooner the United States recognized that fact, the better. "We are fighting a double shadow in Indochina," he proclaimed: "the shadow of the international Communist conspiracy and the shadow of the old, obsolete, mindless game of power politics."[39]

Although Nixon and Kissinger would never have admitted it, there was much in "New Myths and Old Realities" with which they agreed. "What

36 UPI 6, Mar. 9, 1970.
37 "Use of Planes for Laos War Called Illegal," *Arkansas Gazette,* Mar. 12, 1970.
38 *Congressional Record,* Senate, Apr. 2, 1970, 10150–6.
39 Ibid., 10150–6.

happens in those [developing] parts of the world is not, in the final analysis, going to have any significant effect on the success of our foreign policy in the foreseeable future," Nixon wrote Kissinger in March.[40] They did not, however, regard power politics as old, obsolete, or mindless. Nor did they perceive the Soviet Union and especially Communist China to be satiated, unimaginative powers; rather, these countries would seize markets, bases, and political influence wherever and whenever they could, and it was up to the United States to contain and even dominate its adversaries. Nixon and Kissinger wanted to extricate the United States from Vietnam because the war weakened the nation's ability to combat Moscow and Peking and to influence events in other, more important regions of the globe. But America could not simply pull out. To do so would lessen its credibility with friend and foe alike and cause division at home that would impair the administration's ability to arbitrate abroad in those areas that were of vital interest.

"New Myths and Old Realities" was accorded a very different reception than the earlier speech to which it alluded. In 1964 Fulbright had conjured up visions of a better world based on peaceful coexistence. In 1970 he urged Americans to recognize that they had for the past seven years been involved in a long, bloody, and pointless failure in Vietnam. In the end, he said, it did not matter whether communism prevailed in Southeast Asia, and it had never mattered. The United States should negotiate the best deal it could and get out. "This is strong stuff," editorialized the *Washington Post*[41] – indeed, still too strong for most Americans. "Fulbright Would Surrender" proclaimed the *Richmond Times-Dispatch*.[42]

---

40 Nixon to Haldeman, Ehrlichman, and Kissinger, Mar. 2, 1970, WHSpF, Box 138, Nixon Project.
41 Benjamin C. Bradlee, ed., "Vietnam: The Missing Ingredient," *Washington Post,* Apr. 5, 1970.
42 "Fulbright Would Surrender," *Richmond Times-Dispatch,* Apr. 5, 1970.

16

Cambodia

In April 1970 Fulbright became the longest-reigning chairman of the SFRC in American history. One after another, the members of the club rose on the floor of the Senate to pay tribute. John Sparkman, Gale McGee, and Russell Long, with all of whom he had differed sharply over Vietnam, praised him as a conscientious, independent, thoughtful statesman. Jacob Javits, whose unflinching support of Israel had repeatedly pitted him against the Arkansan, lauded him as "a man of very deep insight . . . a fine intellect." And virtually every member of the SFRC, Republican as well as Democrat, paid him homage.[1]

By the spring of 1970 the flaws in Nixon's policy of Vietnamization were becoming apparent. In an effort to build on the tranquillity that followed in the wake of the silent majority speech, the president announced in March 1970 the withdrawal of one hudred and fifty thousand additional troops during the next year. No matter how useful Vietnamization was in terms of quelling domestic dissent in the United States, however, it was counterproductive to the goal of forcing North Vietnam to negotiate a settlement that would leave the Thieu government intact. The logic of the situation was that Hanoi had only to wait and refuse to make concessions; eventually the Americans would be gone, and the pitifully weak Thieu regime could be summarily dispatched. Indeed, Creighton Abrams had bitterly protested the new troop withdrawals, warning that they would leave South Vietnam dangerously vulnerable to enemy military pressure. Increasingly impatient with the stalemate in Southeast Asia, Nixon began once again looking around for an opportunity to demonstrate to the North Vietnamese that "we were still serious about our commitment in Vietnam."[2] One was not long in coming.

Throughout the Vietnam War, Prince Norodom Sihanouk had worked des-

---

1 "Fulbright Praised by Fellow Senators," *Arkansas Gazette,* Apr. 24, 1970.
2 Quoted in George C. Herring, *America's Longest War: The United States and Vietnam, 1950–1975,* 2d ed. (New York, 1986), 234.

perately to insulate Cambodia from the fighting. As part of an early understanding with Hanoi, Sihanouk agreed to ignore sanctuaries established by the Vietcong on the Vietnamese–Cambodian border. In exchange, Hanoi promised not to aid the small Cambodian communist movement, the Khmer Rouge. The decision by the Nixon administration in 1969 to embark on its top secret bombing campaign inside Cambodia helped upset the delicate balance Sihanouk had established. In March 1970, while he was in Europe, the prince was overthrown by Prime Minister Lon Nol, who had the support of Cambodia's intensely anticommunist military commanders. Although the United States had played no direct role in the coup, according to George Herring and William Shawcross,[3] Lon Nol was well aware of Washington's disapproval of Sihanouk's neutralism and therefore believed that the United States would not only tolerate but reward a pro-Western coup. Following Sihanouk's overthrow, the United States quickly recognized the new government and began providing it with covert military aid.

For years the American military had wanted to do more than just bomb North Vietnamese and Vietcong sanctuaries in Cambodia. The JCS longed to invade and destroy the communist enclaves on the ground. With a friendly government now in power they could act. Henry Kissinger, Melvin Laird, and William Rogers were all opposed to an incursion, but Nixon was determined to strike. Attacks on the sanctuaries could now be justified in terms of sustaining a friendly Cambodian government as well as easing the military threat to South Vietnam. The president knew the move would touch off a firestorm of controversy at home, but he was in one of his black moods. Angry with the Senate for having rejected two of his nominees to the Supreme Court and for criticizing his handling of the war, he was determined to "show them who's tough." Nixon perceived himself as an individual who thrived on crises, even if he had to manufacture one. "When you bite the bullet, bite it hard – go for the big play," he subsequently told Nelson Rockefeller in describing his decision to invade Cambodia.[4] The mixed Western/football metaphor was vintage Nixon.

On April 29 South Vietnamese units with American air support attacked an enemy sanctuary on the Parrot's Beak, a strip of Cambodian territory thirty-three miles from Saigon. On the thirtieth, American forces assaulted Fishhook, a North Vietnamese base area fifty-five miles northwest of Saigon. That night Nixon went on national television and justified the invasion as a response to North Vietnamese "aggression." The real target of the operation, he explained, was the Central Office for South Vietnam (COSVN), the "nerve center" of North Vietnamese operations, although the DOD had made clear to him that it was uncertain as to where COSVN was located or whether

---

3 Ibid., 234; William Shawcross, *Sideshow: Kissinger, Nixon and the Destruction of Cambodia* (New York, 1979), 122.
4 Quoted in Marilyn B. Young, *The Vietnam Wars, 1945–1990* (New York, 1991), 247.

it even existed.[5] At a subsequent press conference on May 8, Nixon promised that all American units would be out of Cambodia by the second week of June and that all Americans, including advisers, would be out by the end of the month.

Although the administration had worked assiduously during the weeks preceding the invasion to conceal its plans from Fulbright and the SFRC, they had almost been able to anticipate the incursion. By late April, Washington was full of rumors that the Nixon administration was secretly funneling unauthorized military aid to the Lon Nol government. Dick Moose and Jim Lowenstein were certain something more was afoot, and they subsequently convinced Marcy and Fulbright to send them out to investigate. "Maybe by going out there . . . if you can send us some information . . . maybe this won't happen," Moose remembered Fulbright as saying. The two investigators did not arrive in time. "We were in Hong Kong when the invasion of Cambodia occurred and we landed in Saigon the first day after it had happened," Moose recalled. "We were too late but we were able to dig right in to the rationale of the administration for doing what they had done."[6]

After taking in the standard round of briefings in Saigon, Moose and Lowenstein drove directly to Fishhook and the Parrot's Beak. They were shown mounds of captured equipment and heard how COSVN had been surrounded. "We've got them in the bottle; all we've got to do is put the stopper in," the U.S. commander told them. "It was all pure bullshit," Moose recalled. "If Lowenstein and I knew the attack was coming, you can be goddamn sure the NVA knew they were coming."[7]

Nixon's Cambodian incursion had in fact produced only limited tactical results. According to the U.S. command, American troops killed some two thousand enemy troops, cleared over sixteen hundred acres of jungle, destroyed eight hundred bunkers, and captured large stocks of weapons. The invasion no doubt helped relieve pressure on ARVN and the Thieu government, thereby buying some time for Vietnamization; but COSVN turned out to be little more than a handful of thatched huts sitting atop a network of tunnels, and the NVA moved back into the area as soon as the Americans and South Vietnamese left.[8] Coming as it did in the wake of Sihanouk's overthrow, the invasion shattered Cambodian neutrality. "I think the effect is going to be – and already is – a terrible destruction to a rather fine little country that was not bothering anybody," Fulbright remarked prophetically to a group of reporters.[9]

---

5 Herring, *America's Longest War,* 236.
6 Interview with Richard Moose, June 29, 1989, Washington, D.C.
7 Ibid.
8 Herring, *America's Longest War,* 236.
9 Mike Trimble, "Allied Troops' Invasion to Destroy Cambodia, Fulbright Forecasts," *Arkansas Gazette,* June 17, 1970.

Immediately Fulbright and other senators questioned the legal and constitutional power of the president, even as commander in chief, to send troops into a neutral nation. In a bitter Senate speech Mike Mansfield, a longtime friend of Sihanouk's, condemned the invasion and criticized Nixon personally. The time had come, he said, for the nation's leaders to show "a fitting sense of humility."[10] Senator Stephen Young (R–Ohio), attacking the "hallucination of victory in Vietnam," introduced a resolution to censure the president. In behalf of the SFRC, Fulbright requested a face to face meeting with Nixon, the first such conference since Woodrow Wilson had met with Henry Cabot Lodge's committee in 1919.[11]

Within minutes of the president's televised address, antiwar activists took to the streets in New York and Philadelphia, and in the days that followed, protests erupted across the country. In Cambridge, Massachusetts, students occupied Harvard buildings to protest the university's refusal to take a stand against the Vietnam War or to withdraw its investments in racist South Africa. At Berkeley, Governor Ronald Reagan mobilized a battalion of police to confront more than five thousand students and community residents who had seized a vacant lot and turned it into a "people's park." Armed helicopters sprayed tear gas on the demonstrators from above, while police shotgun fire blinded one student and killed another. The first week in May, Kent State students protested the Cambodian invasion by rioting downtown and firebombing the ROTC building. Upon hearing the news, Nixon called the student demonstrators a bunch of "bums" at an informal briefing session at the Pentagon. Meanwhile, Ohio Governor James Rhodes called out the National Guard and declared martial law. When he ordered guardsmen onto the campus of Kent State, students held a peaceful demonstration to protest. Suddenly the troops turned and opened fire. Their fusillade left four students dead and eleven wounded. Two of the young women killed were simply walking to class. Within days, a million and a half students were participating in a boycott of classes, shutting down about a fifth of the nation's campuses for periods ranging from one day to the rest of the school year. Even the University of Arkansas, attended for the most part by conservative southern students, held a memorial service, and students and faculty circulated petitions calling for Nixon's impeachment.[12] Aroused by both the invasion and the Kent State shootings, more than a hundred thousand people gathered in Washington to show their disapproval.

In the summer of 1970, in the wake of the Cambodian demonstrations, an embittered president declared virtual warfare on those he considered his en-

10 "Fulbright Panel Wants Session on Troop Move," *Washington Evening Star,* May 1, 1970.
11 "Lawmakers Demand President Explain Cambodia Decision," *Arkansas Gazette,* May 2, 1970.
12 Brenda Blagg, "Mullins Declines Class Dismissal, Backs Memorial," *Arkansas Gazette,* May 7, 1970.

emies: the "madmen" on the Hill, the "liberal" press, those who marched in protest. "Within the iron gates of the White House," Charles Colson later wrote, "a siege mentality was setting in. It was 'us' against 'them.' Gradually, as we drew the circle closer around us, the ranks of 'them' began to swell."[13] The day following the massive demonstration in Washington, Spiro Agnew, with a hundred National Guardsmen on duty for his protection, defended U.S. entry into Cambodia and accused J. William Fulbright of trying to "rekindle the debilitating fires of riot and unrest." In his address to a Republican campaign dinner at Boise, he classified Fulbright as one of America's Jeremiahs – "a gloomy coalition of choleric young intellectuals and tired, embittered elders."[14]

The Nixon administration's panicked reaction to criticism following Cambodia and Kent State sowed the seeds of its downfall. Shortly before the invasion of Cambodia, the Weathermen faction of the SDS had bombed the New York headquarters of three major U.S. corporations, including the Bank of America. Tom Huston subsequently told H. R. Haldeman that not only was the SDS determined to overthrow the government by force but it was fully capable of doing so.[15] In response to his aide's hysteria, the president authorized Huston to assemble a team of "countersubversives" who would ferret out and neutralize enemies of the Republic (and of Nixon – to him the two were interchangeable). In addition under the Huston plan, intelligence agencies were directed to install wiretaps, open mail, and even break and enter to gather information that could be used to thwart opponents of the administration.

The May demonstrations in Washington heartened Fulbright because he saw in them the beginnings of a return by American liberals to the values of the 1930s and 1940s. The students who had come to the nation's capital, he noted in the *Progressive*, "seem to be in the process of becoming lobbyists for peace, making their views known, in a concerted, persistent, but peaceful and orderly way, to the elected representatives." They were following the path trod by American farmers, businesspeople, and labor unionists over the decades and, in the process, were reaffirming democracy. Although he was only dimly aware of the gathering storm of paranoia in the White House, Fulbright could not have disagreed more with Huston, Buchanan, and Nixon's views on the sources of instability in American society. Fulbright insisted that

> [i]f there is any bias in our history, . . . it is not toward the Left but toward the Right. The "Red scares" of our past, from Sacco–Vanzetti to Alger Hiss to the "effete snobs" . . . of more recent vintage, have never amounted to much as far as threatening our society is concerned,

13 Quoted in Herring, *America's Longest War,* 239.
14 "Spiro Defends U.S., Blasts Fulbright," *Paragould Daily Press,* May 9, 1970.
15 Huston to Haldeman, Mar. 12, 1970, WHSpF, Box 152, Nixon Project.

but the anti-Red reactions have amounted to a great deal. [It is] the right wing bias of our past, the intense, obsessive fear of Communism, the disruption wrought by thirty years of chronic war, the power of the military–industrial–labor–academic complex which war has spawned [that threatens America].[16]

Fulbright continued to believe that with liberal internationalism discredited the best bet for checking the right-wing radicalism spawned by the cold war was traditional conservatism. He remained convinced that the principal rallying point in his campaign to end the war and contain the burgeoning American empire was the Constitution. Only that hallowed document would offer sufficient political protection for those who would be accused of endangering America's national security. In addition, while Fulbright was convinced that the war in Vietnam was immoral, he had come to the conclusion that it was unwise, perhaps impossible, to build a politically effective anti-imperialist campaign on abstract notions of right and wrong.[17]

Carefully, meticulously, Fulbright and Marcy had been building support for the notion that the administration – first Johnson's and now Nixon's – was making international commitments and involving the country in future wars without its permission or even its knowledge and, in so doing, was violating the basic law of the land. Not coincidentally, in the summer of 1970 the antiwar movement began to focus for the first time on the constitutional issue, both because its new leaders saw its potential for ending the war and because the new, more conventional majority tended to think in traditional political and legal terms. After the Cambodian invasion, Congress was inundated with the heaviest volume of mail on record. Fulbright alone received a hundred thousand telegrams and letters the first week. By mid-July the count was three hundred and fifty thousand. Clara Buchanan and the rest of the secretarial staff found their desks surrounded by mountains of mailbags each day. The chairman's letters and telegrams ran 60 to 1 against the decision to invade.[18]

Five days after Nixon announced the incursion, members of the SFRC accused him of usurping the legislature's warmaking power and denounced the "constitutionally unauthorized, Presidential war in Indochina."[19] The charge quickly became a rallying cry inside and outside of Congress.

On April 10, 1970, the SFRC voted unanimously to repeal the Gulf of Tonkin Resolution and at the same time approved the Cooper–Church amendment to the 1971 military sales bill. Authored by John Sherman

16 J. W. Fulbright, "What Students Can Do for Peace," *Progressive* (June 1970).
17 Ibid.
18 The count was much closer, 3 to 2, among the three thousand letters from Arkansas. JWF to David C. Rains, July 10, 1970, Series 48:18, Box 61:3, SPF.
19 Quoted in Charles DeBenedetti and Charles Chatfield, *An American Ordeal: The Antiwar Movement of the Vietnam Era* (Syracuse, 1990), 284.

Cooper and Frank Church, the amendment would cut off funds for U.S. military operations in Cambodia after June 30, 1970, the date Nixon had set for withdrawal in the midst of the postinvasion brouhaha. Fulbright was wildly enthusiastic about the latter proposal. The president ought to be completely supportive of Cooper–Church, he told the Senate. Had he not promised to pull all American troops out anyway? Congress was just helping him keep his word. The administration did intend to keep its word, did it not? he asked.[20]

The Nixon White House, being a collection of public relations experts, was uniquely equipped to deal with the daunting public relations problems posed by Cambodia and Kent State. Typically, Nixon and his men decided to take the offensive. "As in all battles the tide in this one ebbs and flows," H. R. Haldeman observed. "At this particular point the opposition has shot their wad. . . . We now have a chance to frighten off the enemy [antiwar critics] but we've got to do it in a strong, positive fashion and without any delay – without any letup."[21] Indeed, Pat Buchanan saw an opportunity in the situation. The administration should take the offensive and make Congress the whipping boy. "We are the beneficiaries of the visceral patriotism of the lower middle class," he told his boss, and now was the time to call on it. Haldeman and the president were enthusiastic. "Run a roll of shame," Haldeman suggested; administration spokespeople should imply that supporters of Cooper–Church were nothing less than traitors, willing to deny ammunition to American GIs and to see them die as a result. That was the ticket, Buchanan declared, but the president should appear to remain above it all: "[F]or the President . . . no epithets . . . for the Vice President, let's cut loose and see how much blood we can spill."[22]

What followed in the spring and summer was a campaign of calculated divisiveness waged by the administration. Nixon and his henchmen attempted to make Vietnam a symbol of the integrity of the presidency and of the nation's core values. Administration figures brandished the symbols of American nationalism at every opportunity. The White House sponsored a lavish "Honor America Day" in the capital on the Fourth of July. The president and his supporters began wearing flag jewelry. Throughout the summer, the American Legion, the John Birch Society, the Christian Crusade, and other right-wing organizations charged that the peace symbol was a Marxist emblem, an anti-Christian insignia, or a sorcerer's signature.[23]

20 JWF to Lewis W. Douglas, May 12, 1970, Box 9, Apr.–June, Marcy Papers; and *Congressional Record,* Senate, May 15, 1970, 15726.
21 Talking Papers, May 20, 1970, Haldeman Papers, WHSpF, Box 152, Nixon Project.
22 Buchanan to Nixon, June 17, 1970, WHSpF, Box 139, Nixon Papers.
23 DeBenedetti and Chatfield, *American Ordeal,* 288–9.

Fulbright was one of the first to feel the lash. In mid-May, White House loyalist Hugh Scott escorted the national commanders of the American Legion and the Veterans of Foreign Wars to the Senate Press Gallery for a press conference. Denouncing Fulbright and other doves by name, the two declared that the Cooper–Church amendment amounted "to a declaration of surrender to Communist forces and constitutes a stab in the back for our boys in combat."[24] Fulbright's hate mail became frighteningly explicit. "Inevitably you will be caught off guard, sometime, somewhere, somehow, and then bingo! a bullet right between the eyes," warned Edward Pretarski of Santa Ana, California. "Yes, Billy boy, the Vigilantes are coming."[25]

Despite the activities of the revived antiwar movement, public opinion polls taken in early June were still showing majority support for the incursion into Cambodia. Moreover, the politics of polarization began to take its toll on the tenuous anti-imperialist coalition as Robert Dole (R–Kansas), Hugh Scott (R–Pennsylvania), and other administration supporters prolonged the congressional debate over Cooper–Church and pointed out the political consequences for those who voted to cut off funds for troops in the field.

As a result, the White House decided it was time for a test of strength. Nixon and Laird persuaded the flamboyant, conservative Robert Byrd of West Virginia, a man not known for political courage in the mildest of circumstances, to propose an amendment to Cooper–Church. It would authorize the president to send U.S. troops back into Cambodia after July 1 if he thought redeployment was necessary to protect American forces in South Vietnam. Predictably, Fulbright, Javits, and McGovern denounced the Byrd proposal as nothing less than a scheme to "gut" Cooper–Church.[26]

In a major miscalculation, the Nixon administration forced a vote on the Byrd amendment on June 12. In what the *Washington Post* termed a "key rebuff" and "one of the most important foreign policy votes in years," the Senate rejected the Byrd amendment by a vote of 52 to 47. The coalition of thirty-nine Democrats and thirteen liberal Republicans had held firm.[27] Acting on orders from the White House, Scott, Dole, and company hurriedly put together a filibuster to prevent a vote on Cooper–Church itself.

No sooner had the clamor over the Byrd amendment died than Dole, a gravel-voiced veteran who had been maimed during World War II, interrupted the proceedings to propose repeal of the Gulf of Tonkin Resolution. Administration supporters, he explained, were tired of being called warmongers. Fulbright leapt to his feet to object. A repealer had already been ap-

24 "Scott Apologizes for Attack on Stand of 4 Colleagues," *Arkansas Gazette,* May 17, 1970.
25 Petrarski to JWF, June 7, 1970, Series 52, Box 310, SPF.
26 *Congressional Record,* Senate, June 10, 1970, 19181.
27 Spencer Rich, "52–47 Vote Deals Nixon Key Rebuff," *Washington Post,* June 12, 1970.

proved by the SFRC and had been placed on the calendar for debate after the Senate finished with Cooper–Church. He accused the Kansan of departing from established Senate procedure, which called for all measures to go through committee before being voted on by the Senate as a whole. Hugh Scott interrupted. The senator from Arkansas had often spoken of the need to repeal the resolution he had once so ardently supported. Now he had the chance. What was the problem? he asked mischievously.

Fulbright was trapped. If the Senate went ahead and passed the Cooper–Church amendment as altered by Robert Byrd and then repealed the Gulf of Tonkin Resolution, the net effect would be "to give the president a clear legislative history that Tonkin meant nothing when it was passed and means nothing by its repeal – thus confirming the president's claim to the power to do what he pleases as Commander in Chief."[28]

Confused, exhausted, angry, the U.S. Senate on June 24, 1970, voted to repeal the Gulf of Tonkin Resolution by a vote of 81 to 10. On the surface, it appeared to be a groundbreaking victory for opponents of the war and the imperial presidency. Fulbright, who voted no, knew better and said so. "We are in the process of making legislative history of the kind which, I predict, we will regret as much as many of us have regretted our precipitant approval of the Tonkin resolution in 1964," he declared bitterly.[29]

Two days after his ironic vote on the Tonkin repealer, Fulbright rose on the floor of the Senate to vent his usually well-controlled spleen. The *Washington Post*, which had recently compared Vice-President Agnew to Joe McCarthy, had it wrong, he declared. Agnew was reminiscent of Joseph Goebbels, chief propagandist and hatemonger of Hitlerian Germany. Goebbels and Agnew spoke with the power of the state behind them, whereas McCarthy had not.[30]

During his long career in the Senate, J. William Fulbright had been alternately frustrated and gratified that the Congress of the United States was a deliberative body in the most complex, slow-moving, and inefficient sense of the word. At no time was he more grateful for that ponderousness than in the summer of 1970. With Dole and the White House in apparent command of the constitutional and political field, the doves regrouped and counterattacked. Three days before the scheduled showdown vote on Cooper–Church, the Senate by a vote of 73 to 0 approved a proposal by Jacob Javits that stated: "Nothing contained in this section shall be deemed to impugn the congressional powers of the Congress including the power to declare war and

28 *Congressional Record,* Senate, June 23, 1970, 20988.
29 Philip D. Carter, "Senate Voids Resolution on Tonkin, 81–10," *Washington Post,* June 25, 1970.
30 William C. Berman, *William Fulbright and the Vietnam War. The Dissent of a Political Realist* (Kent, Ohio, 1988), 131.

to make rules for the government and regulation of the armed forces of the United States."[31] The Javits proviso seemingly canceled out the Byrd amendment. Or put another way, the Senate had reasserted the respective powers of the executive and legislative branches in the area of foreign affairs. What was left was a warning that all funds for U.S. military action in Cambodia would be cut off in three days.

The last week in June, after six weeks of tumultuous debate, the U.S. Senate approved the Cooper–Church amendment to the military sales bill by a vote of 58 to 37. It was a momentous occasion, the first time the upper house had passed a clear-cut anti–Vietnam War resolution. Fulbright, McGovern, Church, Javits, and Marcy sensed the possibility of victory in their grueling struggle to end the war in Indochina, place restraints on the burgeoning American empire, and reassert congressional prerogatives in the area of foreign policy.

On the eleventh Fulbright in behalf of the SFRC introduced the original repealer of the Gulf of Tonkin Resolution. Dole's bill had been an amendment to another, broader piece of legislation and, as such, subject to presidential veto. The Fulbright repealer was in the form of a concurrent resolution and consequently was not vulnerable to a veto. Fulbright alerted his colleagues to the difference:

> The two forms of repeal of the Tonkin resolution . . . , though nominally leading to the same result, in fact have radically different connotations. The one, coupled as it is with a legislative enactment which can be read as acquiescence in the Executive's claim to plenary war powers, represents an act of resignation, an attempt by Congress to give away its own constitutional war powers. The other, favored by the committee, would eliminate an illegitimate authorization and, in so doing, reassert the constitutional authority of Congress to "declare war," "raise and support armies," and "make rules for the Government and regulation of the land and naval forces."[32]

Even if Nixon did not veto the repealer, the Dole resolution would enhance the power of the executive by making it possible for him to do so. The SFRC resolution passed by a vote of 57 to 5.

Shortly before enactment of the second Tonkin repealer, the House, still much more conservative and hawkish than the Senate, rejected Cooper–Church by almost 2 to 1. Mike Mansfield warned that unless the House reconsidered, the Senate would simply refuse to pass the huge arms sales bill to which the Cambodian amendment was attached;[33] but Thomas E. ("Doc")

31 "Senate Approves Javits Plan Citing War Policy Roles," *Washington Evening Star,* June 27, 1970.
32 *Congressional Record,* Senate, July 10, 1970, 23711.
33 Philip D. Carter, "Senate Again Votes to Repeal Tonkin," *Washington Post,* July 11, 1970.

Morgan, just as much a champion of the war and of executive prerogatives under Richard Nixon as he had been under Lyndon Johnson, refused to be intimidated. The measure remained locked up in conference committee for the next six months.

Cooper–Church was really a flank attack on the war in Southeast Asia. Emboldened by their success in the Senate, the doves decided to stage a frontal assault. George McGovern and Senator Mark Hatfield proposed attaching an amendment to a pending arm sales bill cutting off funds for all U.S. military operations in Southeast Asia after December 31, 1970. It was the ultimate end-the-war measure.

To McGovern's surprise and dismay, Fulbright and Marcy were initially opposed to the proposal. Indeed, Fulbright went to McGovern and urged him to support a different, weaker resolution, one that stated that Congress would not fund a troop level beyond two hundred and eighty thousand after April 1, 1971. Nixon had already announced that he would pull one hundred and fifty thousand soldiers out of Vietnam by that date, leaving two hundrd and eighty thousand. As had been the case with Cooper–Church, the Senate could argue that it was merely helping the president keep his word.[34]

Apparently Fulbright's sudden reticence about an end-the-war resolution was the product of Henry Kissinger's influence. In spite of the bitterness of the fight over Cooper–Church and the chairman's anger over Cambodia, the two men had managed to maintain a working relationship. They continued to see each other at Washington social functions, and during crucial periods, Kissinger would come to Fulbright's house on Belmont Road. In their talks, Kissinger continually emphasized his long-range goals: détente with the Soviet Union and China and a new pragmatic foreign policy free of the hysterical anticommunism and missionary zeal that had been responsible for missteps like Vietnam. "It was deeply satisfying to Fulbright to sit and exchange ideas [with Kissinger]," recalled Richard Moose, who had worked for them both. "He was aware that Kissinger was a remarkable man. To be able to sit and talk about a great purpose in which they were both opposed by people who didn't understand" was heady stuff.[35]

Shortly after McGovern–Hatfield was conceived, Kissinger once again pleaded with Fulbright not to do things that would anger Nixon, that would tempt him to lash out at his domestic critics and the North Vietnamese. Fulbright was sympathetic. McGovern later recalled that the Arkansan told him that he did not want to coerce Nixon; there must be a more "civilized" way. McGovern refused to go along with the chairman's troop-level com-

---

34 Draft Amendment to the Military Procurement Bill, Aug. 21, 1970, Box 9, July–Sept., Marcy Papers.

35 Moose interview.

promise, and Fulbright's name was not among the twenty-three cosponsors of the McGovern–Hatfield amendment.[36]

Fulbright had reservations about McGovern–Hatfield that had nothing to do with his relationship with Kissinger. The chairman's experience with the Gulf of Tonkin Resolution and the legalistic maneuverings of Nicholas Katzenbach had made him very wary of inadvertent actions by the Senate that could be used by the executive to further usurp Congress's prerogatives. Repeal of the Gulf of Tonkin Resolution had had the support of strict constructionists who believed President Johnson had exceeded his authority, as well as of blind supporters of executive power who were convinced, like Katzenbach, that "the President has full authority to make war under his powers as Commander in Chief, with or without Congressional approval." McGovern–Hatfield imposed restrictions on the use of the armed forces. Given the fact that Congress had not in the first place authorized the use of such forces, the resolution could be interpreted to mean that in the absence of restrictions "the President can do whatever he pleases – anything goes, that is, unless it is explicitly prohibited."[37]

By the summer of 1970 Richard Nixon was locked in a fierce struggle with congressional doves for control of the political middle ground on Vietnam. J. William Fulbright's dream was at long last coming true. No longer was the antiwar movement a protest of the liberal left. A majority of Democrats and a sizable minority of Republicans were now actively opposed. Not for a hundred years had Congress mounted such a challenge to a commander in chief with troops fighting in the field as that mounted against Richard Nixon. In fact, by late June, polls showed that nearly half of all Americans advocated getting out of Vietnam immediately and only fifteen percent favored staying in.[38]

36 Berman, *Fulbright and the Vietnam War,* 133.
37 *Congressional Record,* Senate, Feb. 5, 1971, 1868–9.
38 DeBenedetti and Chatfield, *American Ordeal,* 290.

17

A Foreign Affairs Alternative

One of the few things that J. William Fulbright and Richard Nixon had in common was a belief that American Zionists exerted too much influence on U.S. foreign policy.[1] Although Nixon's national security adviser was himself a Jew, he too favored a "balanced" approach toward the Middle East. During their musings on a new world order, Kissinger and Fulbright did not fail to outline a lasting settlement of the Arab–Israeli conflict, one that included an Israeli willingness to trade peace for land and an Arab willingness to recognize the legitimacy of the Jewish state and to sign peace treaties with it. Indeed, in 1970 Fulbright decided to jeopardize his carefully constructed anti-Vietnam coalition and to propose an extension, rather than reduction, of American commitment overseas as part of an effort to bring a lasting peace to the Middle East.[2]

Most of the Arab world had severed formal ties with the United States in the aftermath of the Six-Day War in 1967 in which the Israelis, utilizing American arms and supplies, had crushed the Soviet-supplied Egyptian and Syrian forces. During the fighting, the Israelis seized and occupied vast portions of Egypt, Syria, and Jordan. As of 1969 Israel controlled all of the Sinai Desert up to the western bank of the Suez Canal; the Gaza Strip, a narrow coastal area jutting toward Tel Aviv from the Sinai; the Golan Heights, a strategic hill area from which, before the war, Syrian and Palestinian gunners had lobbed artillery shells into Jewish settlements; and East Jerusalem and the West Bank, both of which had been seized from Jordan. The West Bank and Gaza Strip teemed with Palestinian refugees, whereas the Palestine Liberation Organization mounted frequent guerrilla raids into Israel from bases in the Sinai and southern Lebanon. Meanwhile, the Soviet Union increased its military and economic aid to Syria, Egypt, and Iraq, and to the alarm of

---

1 Nixon, note to Haldeman, News Summaries, Feb. 1970, WHSpF, Box 31, Nixon Project.
2 Complicating Fulbright's efforts to assemble and maintain an antiwar consensus in the Senate was the fact that a number of prominent doves – Javits, Goodell, and McGovern, for example – were ardent advocates of aid to Israel. See Goodell to JWF, Mar. 23, 1970, Box 3, JWF Papers, SFRC, RG 46, NA.

Western diplomats, the Soviet Mediterranean fleet began calling frequently at Arab ports.

The dilemma facing the Nixon administration in 1969 was stark. The Arabs insisted that Israel give up its conquered lands before serious negotiations leading to normalization of relations could start, whereas the Israelis demanded recognition of Israel's right to exist as a state as the price for talks on disengagement. Yasir Arafat, head of the PLO, insisted that much of Israel belonged to his people by right of two thousand years of continued occupancy. The goal of the radical fedayeen movement that he led was the creation of a "democratic secular state" in which Jews, Arabs, and Christians would live together with equal rights."[3]

As 1970 came to a close the level of conflict between the Palestinians and Egypt, on the one hand, and Israel, on the other, increased to the point where the Nixon administration decided it would have to take a gamble in an effort to break the diplomatic impasse and avert a general war. During an address to an audience of foreign service officers, Secretary of State Rogers suggested that Israel withdraw to its pre-1967 boundaries in return for recognition from Egypt. He also called for a broadly based settlement in the Middle East, involving negotiations between Israel and Jordan over the West Bank, the future of United Jerusalem, and the Palestinian refugee problem.[4] Israel and American Zionists immediately denounced the Rogers plan, as it was called, as a sellout of Israeli interests.

Fulbright was not unmindful of the historical burden borne by world Jewry; he understood the fears created in Jewish minds by the Holocaust. "As survivors of genocide, they [Jews] can hardly be expected to distinguish with perfect clarity between Nazi crimes and Arab rhetoric," he once remarked.[5] He understood that Jerusalem with its Wall of the Temple was sacred to the Jews. Fulbright never questioned the legitimacy of a Jewish state in the Middle East, and he recognized the precarious strategic situation faced by a tiny nation of three million surrounded by millions of hostile Arabs.

However, the Arab–Israeli conflict was not, Fulbright insisted, a case of right against wrong, good versus evil. It was, as I. F. Stone, another Jewish intellectual, put it, a classic tragedy, a case of "right against right," in which good men do evil to each other.[6] More than a million Palestinians had been dispossessed by the 1948 war, and their demand for a return to their lands was legitimate, Fulbright believed. The areas taken in the 1967 conflict were conquered territories; Egypt, Syria, and Jordan would never let Israel live in peace until their return. Israel would have to trade land for peace unless it

3 Quoted in Seymour M. Hersh, *The Price of Power: Kissinger in the Nixon White House* (New York, 1983), 215.
4 Ibid., 217, 219–20.
5 *Congressional Record,* Senate, Aug. 24, 1970, 29804.
6 Ibid., 29796.

was willing to conquer and hold the entire Arab world – a clear impossibility, a proposition, Fulbright was convinced, even more absurd than an American effort to conquer and hold Vietnam. Given unconditional American backing of Israel and the general sympathy in the West for the Jewish state, it was natural for the Arabs to view Zionism as another form of Western imperialism. The tighter the Israeli–American embrace, the more intense became Arab nationalism.

The Arab–Israeli conflict was to Fulbright's mind no less an indigenous phenomenon than the civil war in Vietnam; but the cold war had come to the Middle East just as it had to Southeast Asia, infusing into a regional struggle the potential for a worldwide nuclear war. For this reason, if for no other, he was convinced, the Middle East crisis had to be settled. As it was, every fedayeen raid, every Israeli retaliation, brought the Soviet Union and the United States to the brink of war.

The last week in August 1970 Fulbright rose from his seat in the Senate to make a startling proposal. As part of an effort to establish a lasting peace in the Middle East, the United States should enter into a formal ''treaty of guarantee'' with Israel under which the United States would, through use of armed force if necessary, promise to protect ''the territory and independence of Israel within the borders of 1967.'' The treaty would also obligate Israel itself never to violate those borders. Under Fulbright's plan the American commitment would become effective only after the Security Council itself guaranteed such a settlement. In that way the Great Powers, including the Soviet Union, would be committed to recognize the pre-1967 boundaries of Israel. According to Fulbright's scheme, as Israeli troops withdrew from the Golan Heights, the Gaza Strip, and the West Bank, they would be replaced by UN peacekeeping troops. Israel would agree to accept a certain number of Palestinians as Israeli citizens and help resettle the rest in a Palestinian state outside Israel. Fulbright made it clear that U.S. military action to defend Israel, once the guarantee went into effect, would not depend on prior Security Council action and that the Israelis would be free to defend themselves against fedayeen attacks.[7]

The Fulbright peace plan created an instant international furor. ''Fulbright Urges US–Israel Treaty'' ran the front-page headline of the London *Sunday Times*.[8] American observers of foreign affairs were enthusiastic. There was no hobgoblin in this Arkansan's large mind, declared Joseph Kraft. No matter that Fulbright had been straining every nerve and sinew since 1967 to reduce American commitments abroad. Never mind that he had been warning since 1960 of the insidious machinations of the American Zionist lobby to make America an Israeli cat's-paw in the Middle East. ''A deep inner logic'' governed Fulbright's ideas, Kraft declared. ''He is one of the few actors on the

7 Ibid., 29796–809.
8 ''Fulbright Urges US–Israel Treaty,'' *Sunday Times* (London), Aug. 23, 1970.

world stage who knows how to take the cue of history.'''[9] James Reston, writing in the *New York Times,* agreed and predicted that Fulbright's proposal would carry great weight because of his reputation as an opponent of foreign entanglements and as a friend of the Arabs. Fulbright's "switch," Reston declared, was not unlike that made by another chairman of the SFRC. In January 1945, Arthur Vandenberg, a senator famed for his staunch isolationism, had shocked the Senate and the nation by calling for a system of treaties with other democracies to defend Western Europe against the scourge of communism. That speech had transformed American policy in the postwar world. Hopefully, Fulbright's would do the same for the nation's contemporary Middle Eastern policy.[10] No doubt the Arkansan shuddered at the comparison. Somewhat surprisingly, so did the Israeli government.

In 1970 Israel was still clearly in control of its own destiny, and the government of Golda Meir was not about to give up the territories won in the 1967 war. Fulbright's proposal came in the midst of a ninety-day cease-fire with Egypt and UN-sponsored peace talks in New York. Israeli militants in the Knesset were furious with the Nixon administration for blocking the sale of 125 jet fighters to their government and angry with Washington for agreeing to a cease-fire. On August 25 Foreign Minister Abba Eban, speaking to the Israeli legislature, flatly rejected the Fulbright peace plan. A UN or U.S. guarantee, he said, was no substitute for an iron-clad treaty signed by all the Arab states recognizing Israel, including the territories taken in the 1967 war.[11]

With Tel Aviv up in arms, and Henry Jackson and American Zionists on the warpath, the administration immediately distanced itself from the Fulbright proposal. Most people applauded Nixon's efforts to arrange a cease-fire, but opinion polls showed that forty-six percent of the public sympathized with Israel, whereas only six percent supported the Arabs. The country was evenly divided over whether or not U.S. troops should intervene, even if Israel was about to be overrun by Soviet-backed Arab armies.[12]

The whole affair disgusted Fulbright. The Israelis were not even willing to act in their own self-interest, he lamented. At one point he suggested that the United Nations, backed by the force of a unilateral American guarantee, impose a peace on the Middle East. There was little chance of that, however, he admitted to a California supporter. The United States was in thrall to the Zionist maximalists, who were in turn "extremely powerful . . . especially in the field of communications. The most prestigious newspapers in this country

---

9 Joseph Kraft, "Fulbright Cuts Through the Middle East Miasma," *Arkansas Gazette,* Aug. 25, 1970.

10 James Reston, "Washington: Fulbright's Startling Proposal," *New York Times,* Aug. 23, 1970.

11 "Israel Rejects Fulbright Plan," *Baltimore Sun,* Aug. 26, 1970.

12 News Summaries, Sept. 14, 1970, WHSpF, Box 32, Nixon Project.

are devoted to this cause, and most of the TV networks are owned by people sympathetic to the same cause.''[13]

One of the primary reasons the vast majority of Americans supported Israel was its demonstrated ability to fight its own battles – unlike the people of Southeast Asia. The Cambodian incursion may have bought some time for Vietnamization, but it also imposed clear-cut, if implicit, limits on the future use of American combat forces, and it increased pressure on the Nixon administration to speed up the pace of withdrawal. Nixon's efforts to intimidate his enemies at home and abroad produced just the opposite effect. Domestic divisiveness increased dramatically in the summer and fall of 1970. North Vietnamese and Vietcong delegates boycotted the formal Paris talks and promised they would not return until American troops had been withdrawn from Cambodia. The secret talks lapsed as well. Hanoi was content to bide its time, secure in the belief that the antiwar movement, with Fulbright among the vanguard, would destroy America's will to fight.

In an effort to keep Hanoi and the antiwar movement off balance, Nixon in October 1970 launched what he described as a ''major new peace initiative.''[14] On a nationally televised broadcast, he proposed a cease-fire in Indochina, the immediate release of all prisoners of war (POWs), the convening of a Great-Power conference on Southeast Asia, and the creation of a political process that would express the will of the people of South Vietnam. ''I thought the President's speech represented a considerable improvement . . . in tone,'' Fulbright wrote David Bruce, the new American negotiator in Paris, ''but I regret to say that I do not think that it is an offer the other side will accept.''[15] He was right. Hanoi promptly rejected the president's suggestion for a cease-fire in place, which, it perceived, would restrict the Vietcong to areas they then controlled without assuring them of any role in a political settlement.

In fact, the October speech was intended primarily for domestic consumption. The midterm congressional elections were coming up, and the White House dreamed of a Republican landslide. Nixon followed up his address by touring ten states, angrily denouncing the antiwar protesters and urging the voters to elect men who would ''stand with the President.''[16] The White House hoped for a majority in the Senate because it would mean, among other things, the end of J. William Fulbright's tenure as chairman of the

13 JWF to Ronald Harris, Sept. 24, 1970, Series 48:15, Box 40:3, SPF.
14 Quoted in George C. Herring, *America's Longest War: The United States and Vietnam, 1950–1975,* 2d ed. (New York, 1986), 239.
15 Quoted in William C. Berman, *William Fulbright and the Vietnam War: The Dissent of a Political Realist* (Kent, Ohio, 1988), 134.
16 Quoted in Herring, *America's Longest War,* 240.

SFRC.[17] Agnew conducted his own tour in behalf of Republican candidates. He was particularly obnoxious, even for Agnew, and frequently singled out Fulbright for abuse. The GOP managed to defeat three leading Senate doves – Albert Gore (D–Tennessee), Charles Goodell (R–New York), and Joseph Tydings (D–Maryland) – but about that number of hawks were also defeated. The bellicose Thomas Dodd lost in the Democratic primary in Connecticut. The Republicans gained only two seats in the Senate and lost nine in the House. The 1970 midterm elections were hardly the conservative, forgotten-American landslide that Nixon's political advisers had predicted.

By 1970 the number of American POWs held by the communists or listed as missing in Southeast Asia ran into the thousands, and the issue of their treatment and return had become one of the most sensitive of the war.[18] Both hawks and doves labored to take maximum propaganda advantage of the situation. To Fulbright's enragement, the administration arranged through House Speaker John McCormack to allow Texas billionaire H. Ross Perot to hang a life-sized "tiger cage" in the rotunda of the Capitol. The bamboo cages, suspended several feet off the ground and exposed to the elements, were allegedly used by the North Vietnamese to house American POWs.[19] The rotunda display, the chairman of the SFRC asserted, was a public relations stunt that would only further inflame public opinion and prolong the war. In 1969 Fulbright had appealed directly to Ho Chi Minh – and after his death in September, to Pham Van Dong, who succeeded Ho as premier – to publish an official list of those held and to repatriate the sick and wounded. The North Vietnamese, who had succeeded in coercing some of their American prisoners to tape "confessions" and appeals for peace, refused and used the occasion to tell POW families that their loved ones would return to them if only President Nixon would halt his war of aggression.[20]

Throughout the fall of 1970 Fulbright met repeatedly with the wives of POWs and servicemen missing in action (MIAs), most of whom were then pressing for a quick end to the war as a means for getting their husbands home. It was significant that the innately hawkish families of missing and imprisoned servicemen were by the close of Nixon's second year in office willing to turn for help to a man they had once reviled as "Hanoi's little helper." During October, the national networks ran footage of POW–MIA wives going into and out of Fulbright's office.[21] The Arkansan assured the

---

17 News Summaries, Oct. 13, 1970, WHSpF, Box 32, Nixon Project.
18 Neil Sheehan, "U.S. Information on P.O.W.'s Appears Limited," *New York Times,* Nov. 24, 1970.
19 "Fulbright on the Prowl," *Washington Post,* Aug. 6, 1970.
20 JWF to Pham Van Dong, June 24, 1970, and Ho Chi Minh to JWF, July 25, 1969, Series 48:6, Box 27:6, SPF.
21 News Summaries, Oct. 6, 1970, Box 32, WHSpF, Nixon Project.

families that he was continuing to work to persuade the North Vietnamese to treat the POWs as a humanitarian issue unconnected to military and political considerations.[22]

Two weeks after the midterm elections in November, Nixon made a bold move to take the POW issue away from Fulbright and the doves. Early one Saturday, 250 American fighter-bombers struck targets across the DMZ and within the Hanoi–Haiphong "doughnut," the first resumption of bombing since the Johnson-initiated pause in the fall of 1968. The attacks were, however, a diversionary tactic to cover a daring raid by U.S. Air Force and Army Special Forces units on the Son Tay prison camp twenty-three miles west of Hanoi. American fighters swooped in and blasted guard towers and concertina-wire fences; but when the U.S. helicopters nestled in and disgorged their commandos, there was no sign of life. The communists had cleared out days before and taken their prisoners with them.[23]

Fulbright suspected from the first that the Son Tay prison raid was a public relations ploy. Indeed, when a somber but self-satisfied Melvin Laird – with Colonel Arthur Simonds, who had led the Son Tay raid, in tow – told newspeople that the "daring mission" highlighted the administration's "dedication" to the POWs and its determination to "do everything that we can in our power to accomplish their early release," Fulbright was sure of it.[24] The Arkansan dared not voice his suspicions without clear cut proof, however, and he had none. Moreover, such raids were for the most part popular with the public, providing a temporary respite from the ever-present feeling of powerlessness that had set in in the wake of the Tet offensive. In fact, so positive was public comment that Laird called Fulbright and volunteered to testify on Son Tay before the SFRC.[25] Fulbright could not deny the request, and the DOD took full advantage of the opportunity. Laird acknowledged that operations like Son Tay were risky, but with a view to defusing criticism from the POW–MIA families, he refused to rule out future raids. "If this country is willing to abandon its military men to death and captivity, we will have truly lost our national morality and our humanity," he declared sanctimoniously.[26]

Within days of Laird's appearance before the SFRC, however, the administration's story had begun to unravel. Laird claimed during his testimony that he and the president had authorized the raid upon hearing that several American POWs had died at Son Tay; but the two Americans from whom the administration claimed to have gotten that information – private citizens

22 See JWF to Olaf Palme, July 11, 1970, Series 48:3, Box 17:4, SPF.
23 William Beecher, "U.S. Rescue Force Landed Within 23 Miles of Hanoi, But It Found P.O.W.'s Gone," *New York Times*, Nov. 24, 1970.
24 JWF to Harry Ashmore, Dec. 3, 1970, Series 48:18, Box 59:1, SPF.
25 "Critics Symied as Laird Invokes Honor, Morality," *Washington Post*, Nov. 25, 1970.
26 "1st Foray Justified, Hill Told," *Washington Post*, Nov. 25, 1970.

who had traveled to Hanoi and had brought back the names of seventeen Americans killed over North Vietnam – denied that any of those had died at Son Tay or any other prison camp. "It [the list] could mean they were dead on hitting the ground, or found dead after wandering around in the mountains for weeks after they crashed, or died from wounds suffered while they were being shot down," Peter Weiss, a lawyer representing the POW families, told reporters.[27] Writing in the *Washington Star*, Clayton Fritchey observed that even if the Son Tay raid had been successful, it would have subjected other Americans in captivity to torture and death. "There is a smell of desperation about this adventure," he mused. "It is not the considered action of a great power."[28]

On Sunday, November 9, Fulbright appeared on *Face the Nation* opposite Vice-Premier Nguyen Cao Ky, who was a guest on NBC's *Meet the Press*. Fulbright astounded Marvin Kalb and his other questioners by accusing Laird of "misrepresenting the facts" about the Son Tay raid and the bombing of North Vietnam. "Now I wouldn't ever call anybody a liar in public except by inadvertence," he declared, but he made it clear that that was what he was doing. He then launched into an unprecedented indictment of the DOD and its representatives in Congress. Son Tay and the resumed bombing of the North were just symptoms of a general malady, the chairman of the SFRC declared. The Defense Department had completely eclipsed State and was not only making American foreign policy but, with $80 billion a year to spend, selling and implementing that policy. "This is muscle, this is influence, this is power," the chairman observed. "It [the Pentagon] controls and influences everything that goes on in our government." Representing the interests of the military establishment in the Senate, he told Kalb and the others, were Richard Russell, John Stennis, Henry Jackson, and other members whose home states brimmed with defense plants. These men were the real power in the Senate. Compared with them, his position as chairman of the SFRC was "very secondary," comparable, he said, to the subsidiary position State was then occupying in relation to Defense. His journalist-hosts should not have been surprised. The Arkansan's new book, *The Pentagon Propaganda Machine*, had been published earlier in the month; it was a devastating attack on the military–industrial complex.[29]

As Congress prepared to reconvene in January 1971 Carl Marcy, as was his wont, surveyed the events of the previous year. He did not like what he saw.

---

27 "Laird Accused of Distorting POW Deaths," *Arkansas Gazette,* Nov. 26, 1970.
28 Clayton Fritchey, "That Dubious Raid to Free the Hanoi Prisoners," *Washington Star,* Nov. 30, 1970.
29 "Bombing Facts Misstated, Fulbright Says," Los Angeles Times, Nov. 30, 1970; and "Fulbright Says U.S. Action in Vietnam Has Intensified," *Baltimore Sun,* Nov. 30, 1970.

The administration had systematically continued the erosion of congressional prerogatives in the areas of warmaking and treaty ratification, he concluded. As the Cambodian invasion, the clandestine war in Laos, and the secret commitments to Thailand, Spain, and other countries indicated, the Nixon administration not only was proceeding unilaterally but was deceiving Congress and the American people. In addition, Nixon and Kissinger were manipulating the bureaucracy in ways that allowed them to conceal their intentions and actions from the SFRC.[30]

Marcy's analysis also noted that the executive had systematically withheld vital information from the committee – the Thai contingency plan, the Tonkin Gulf command-and-control study, and the Spanish bases agreement. Diplomatic correspondents, foreign diplomats, and selected members of certain pro-administration committees had greater access to foreign policy information than had the SFRC.[31] While Rogers, Kissinger, and Laird gave frequent "backgrounders" to friendly congresspeople and members of the press corps, they had been unavailable for testimony in public session. When they or other executive branch officers did agree to appear, State Department officials would come to the Hill and brief individual SFRC members so that they would not show up for the scheduled meeting, thus embarrassing Fulbright and preventing a confrontation en masse.[32] "The Committee has had more significant meetings this year with Abba Eban, Willy Brandt, Suharto, and others than it has had with high level officers of the U.S. Government," Marcy lamented to Fulbright.[33] When executive branch officers did testify with any candor, the administration declared their remarks classified, thus preventing their release to the public.

On the positive side, the committee would remain Democratic and under the chairmanship of J. William Fulbright until at least 1974. Gore was gone, but there was still a "Fulbright majority" on the committee, to use Richard Moose's term. Stuart Symington and his subcommittee would continue to uncover clandestine commitments. The relentlessly dovish George McGovern would be back. In response to the bombing and invasion of Cambodia, Mike Mansfield had abandoned his long-held view that the Senate majority leader should be the handmaiden of the president no matter what his party, and he was apparently prepared to work openly for the defeat of administration measures. Although Fulbright did not completely trust him, Frank Church, the boy orator from Idaho with the slicked-back hair and burning ambition, still perceived opposition to the war as good politics. The gaggle of Republican liberals – the chain-smoking and inarticulate John Sherman Cooper, the brilliant Jacob Javits, and the morally driven Clifford Case – could also return to strengthen

30 Marcy to JWF, Jan. 22, 1971, Box 10, Folder Jan.–Mar., Marcy Papers.
31 Marcy to JWF, Sept. 30, 1970, Box 9, Folder July–Sept., Marcy Papers.
32 Marcy to JWF, Jan. 22, 1971, Box 10, Folder Jan.–Mar., Marcy Papers.
33 Marcy, memorandum, Nov. 5, 1970, Box 9, Folder Oct.–Dec., Marcy Papers.

the anti-imperialist coalition. "Between the conservatives of 15 years ago and the liberal internationalists of today," one journalist noted after surveying the new Congress, "there is a common concern over the president's ability to enter into foreign agreements without the consent or knowledge of Congress."[34]

On February 1, 1971, the *New York Times* reported that B-52s were bombing enemy supply bases in southern Laos around the clock. Rumor had it that a massive South Vietnamese invasion, backed by American aircraft, was afoot. Because the MACV in Saigon had clamped an embargo on news coming out of both Laos and South Vietnam, stories about a possible incursion could not be confirmed immediately.[35] An alarmed Fulbright, believing that the administration had decided to cast caution to the wind and go for broke, summoned the Capitol Hill press corps. If the raids in Laos failed to hamper the enemy, he told them, "it would be logical to go on further north" and overrun North Vietnam itself. He pointed out that there was no congressional restriction on the use of American troops for an invasion of North Vietnam; indeed, the Cooper–Church amendment was being interpreted as authorization for all actions not specifically forbidden.[36]

The Laotian incursion fueled the movement in the Senate to impose both specific and general limitations on the president's warmaking powers. Hatfield and McGovern asked Fulbright to join them in cosponsoring a reworked version of their 1970 Ammendment to"End the War." It would "propose" that the president set a timetable for the withdrawal of all American armed forces from Vietnam by December 31, 1971. After that date, funds would remain available only for release of prisoners of war, protection of South Vietnamese "who might be endangered," and continued assistance to the government of South Vietnam.[37] Fulbright refused, primarily because the new Hatfield–McGovern amendment included continued aid for the Thieu regime. "Even our concept of 'peace' has been drastically modified," he told an assemblage of students and teachers at Florida State. "Where once it referred to a condition in which nobody is killing anybody, it now refers to a future state of affairs in which Asians will be killing Asians with American guns, bombs and air support." Quoting another critic of the war, he declared that "American policy in Indochina was being shaped 'as though America had no concern for the sanctity of human life, as such – as though, somehow, Americans cared only about American lives.' "[38]

34 "Case Offers Bill to Disclose Pacts," *New York Times,* Dec. 3, 1970.
35 Terence Smith, "U.S. B-52's Strike Foe's Laos Bases Around the Clock," *New York Times,* Feb. 1, 1971; and Marcy to JWF and Williams, Feb. 1, 1971, Box 10, Jan.–Mar., Marcy Papers.
36 UPI 27, Feb. 8, 1971, Series 48:3, Box 18:1, SPF.
37 Hatfield to JWF, Jan. 21, 1971, Series 48:17, Box 46:2, SPF.
38 *Congressional Record,* Senate, Mar. 12, 1971, 6395.

Nor did Fulbright join other legislative efforts designed to limit the war-making powers of the president. In mid-February Javits introduced the measure that would eventually become the War Powers Act. It required the president to end any future military action overseas after thirty days unless it was authorized by Congress. Javits's bill compelled the commander in chief to "report fully and promptly" to Congress, explaining the reason and authority for military actions taken in the absence of a declaration of war. Unless authorizing legislation was forthcoming, the chief executive would have to terminate the action.[39]

Fulbright's apparent apathy puzzled the press. the *New York Times* reported that the Arkansan was "in a mood of despairing resignation, bored with criticizing the Administration and uninterested in pushing legislation." Fulbright admitted to being frustrated and pessimistic, but his intermittent despondency stemmed not from his belief that Congress would never pass an end-the-war resolution but from his suspicion that such specific prohibitions were too little, too late.[40] That he was willing to let others take the lead on various end-the-war measures was merely indicative of the fact that he had decided to challenge the imperial presidency on other fronts.

39 "Javits Offers War Curb Bill," *Washington Evening Star,* Feb. 10, 1971.
40 JWF to Mrs. William Maloney, Mar. 2, 1971, Series 48:18, Box 63:1, 3PF.

18

Privileges and Immunities

Since 1967 J. William Fulbright had decried and described the corrosive effect the war was having on both Vietnamese and American society. By 1971 his focus was almost entirely on the havoc being wrought on the U.S. economy, its Constitution, and its common ideals. "When a war is of long duration, when its objectives are unascertainable, when the people are bitterly divided and their leaders lacking in both vision and candor, then the process of democratic erosion is greatly accelerated," he declared in his Florida State speech. "Beset by criticism and doubt, the nation's leaders resort increasingly to secrecy and deception." That was what was happening in America in 1971, and as a result, the very institutional foundations of the Republic were at risk. "When truth becomes the first casualty," he warned the Senate, quoting a familiar aphorism, "belief in truth, and in the very possibility of honest dealings, cannot fail to become the second."[1]

In mid-March Fulbright decided to attack the whole concept of executive privilege. It lay, he was convinced, at the very heart of the imperial presidency, and it was being used to conceal American involvement in Southeast Asia and other real and imagined trouble spots around the world. By 1971 Nixon and Kissinger had succeeded in shifting most diplomatic policy and decision making from the cabinet departments to the NSC, which was part of the office of the president and as such exempt from congressional accountability. Unwilling to see anything slip through the veil of secrecy, however, the president extended executive privilege beyond the confines of the White House to cover even communications between regular cabinet officers and the president. Perhaps most important, the Nixon administration refused not only to provide information but even to debate the rationale for the war or to discuss its plan for ending it. During an SFRC hearing earlier in the year, a high-ranking administration official had been asked if the government intended to withdraw from Southeast Asia unconditionally or whether it was determined to leave only after it had firmly established anticommunist gov-

---

1 *Congressional Record,* Senate, Mar. 12, 1971, 6395.

ernments. The official had declined to answer on the grounds that such information would aid the enemy.[2]

The Nixon administration based its virtually unlimited interpretation of executive privilege on a 1958 Justice Department memo: "Congress cannot, under the Constitution, compel heads of departments by law to give up papers and information; regardless of the public interest involved," it read; and anyway, "the President is the judge of that interest." That definition had had the same effect on the legislative and executive branches as a severance of relations would have on two sovereign nations, Fulbright declared. The notion that the president, and the president alone, was the sole judge of the public interest was absurd, a mortal threat to the system of checks and balances. "As James Madison said in *The Federalist*," Fulbright argued to the Senate, "neither the executive nor the legislature can pretend to an exclusive or superior right of setting the boundaries between their respective powers."[3]

In an effort to create momentum in behalf of a congressional show of force against executive privilege, Fulbright submitted a bill requiring employees of the executive branch to appear in person before Congress or the appropriate committee when duly summoned. The chairman reasoned that even if, upon their arrival, the president's men did nothing more than invoke executive privilege, they would have put Congress and the public on notice that the administration was operating in secret.[4] He hoped the claim would have the same damning effect that witnesses' invocation of the Fifth Amendment had had during the McCarthy, McClellan, and Kefauver committee hearings. At the same time, he put Marcy to work on a draft amendment to the Constitution providing for censure or removal of a president without subjecting the country to the trauma of impeachment. Among those actions warranting censure or removal under the Fulbright–Marcy plan were "ignoring provisions of law such as the Cooper–Church amendment" and "the refusal of lawful requests for information."[5]

Amid Fulbright's ruminations on executive privilege and impeachment, one of the decisive events of the entire Vietnam era transpired. Following five months of testimony and investigation, a military court at Fort Benning, Georgia, convicted Lieutenant William Calley of murdering twenty-two in-

---

2 Ibid., Mar. 5, 1971, 5232.
3 Ibid.
4 Ibid., Mar. 12, 1971, 6396.
5 Referring to the 1867 impeachment trial of Andrew Johnson, Marcy observed that Congress and the courts had traditionally held that impeachment ought to be for "treason, bribery, and other high crimes and misdemeanors," and that referred only to criminal acts, not resistance to the will of one or both of the other branches of the federal government. Marcy to JWF, Apr. 27, 1971, Box 10, Apr.–June, Marcy Papers.

nocent men, women, and children in the village of My Lai and sentenced him to twenty years in prison. The trial was conducted with scrupulous regard for the rights of the defendant. The six judges were all combat veterans, and five had served in Vietnam. After the evidence was presented, there was no doubt in their minds or in the minds of the vast majority of professional soldiers everywhere that Calley was guilty and that his conduct was inexcusable. "This is the guy," William Greider reminded his readers in the *Washington Post*, "who picked up a baby, threw him into a ditch and shot him. He is the soldier who butt-stroked an old man in the face, then shot him at point-blank range and blew away the side of his head."[6] As Aubrey Daniels, the Army's chief trial counsel, put it, "[I]t is unlawful for an American soldier to summarily execute unarmed and unresisting men, women, children, and babies."[7]

Nonetheless, Calley's conviction seemed to outrage Americans as had no other incident in the war. The White House and various congressional offices were deluged with tens of thousands of letters of protest from both hawks and doves. Hawks felt the trial, not to mention the sentence, was grossly unfair and final proof that the nation did not have the will to win. War was a collective decision to murder, they pointed out; once that line was crossed, conventional moral standards went out the window. Everyone knew that it was impossible to distinguish friend from enemy in Vietnam. "The most innocent looking child or old person can kill a person with a gun or grenade," a Little Rock woman declared. "Men are trained in the Army to kill the enemy and this is what happened at My Lai."[8]

Those who had served in Vietnam, who had lost relatives in the war, or who had relatives serving in Southeast Asia felt betrayed. "We have never been in sympathy with the Vietnam War, but our son went when his draft call came," Mrs. Ralph Barnett wrote Fulbright. "Our boys should not be tried and sentenced for killing the enemy when they are sent over to do just that." Mrs. Barnett's son had been killed in action three months earlier.[9]

Opponents of the war did not deny that Calley was guilty. Indeed, since 1969 they had been insisting that My Lai was a disgraceful emblem of American imperialism and the ultimate example of the brutality of the war in Vietnam. But in the wake of Calley's conviction, doves insisted that the commander of Charlie Company had been made a scapegoat and called for an immediate end to the war, followed by Nuremberg-type war crime trials for those officials who had originally been responsible for committing Amer-

6 William Greider, "Calley's Trial: The Moral Question and Battlefield Laws," *Washington Post,* Apr. 5, 1971.
7 Daniels to Nixon, Apr. 3, 1971, WHSpF, Box 16, Nixon Project.
8 Debbie Tyler to JWF, Apr. 1, 1971, Series 4:10, Box 18:3, SPF.
9 Barnett to JWF, Mar. 30, 1971, Series 4:10, Box 18:3, SPF.

ica to war.[10] Fulbright's views on the trial were typical. It was "a rather questionable principle" to single out Calley for prosecution, he told reporters. He had been "put in a situation created by policy supported by the principal political authorities in this country." It was Johnson, Westmoreland, and Abrams who should be held accountable, he said. "The principle that we applied to Yamashita [Japanese General Tomoyuki, commander of Japanese forces in Southeast Asia, executed as a war criminal in 1946] should be applied here."[11]

"Tide of Public Opinion Turns Decisively Against the War" ran the headline of a Louis Harris poll taken in the wake of the Calley trial. By 60 to 26 percent, Americans indicated they would favor continued withdrawal of U.S. troops from Vietnam, "even if the government of South Vietnam collapses." For the first time, by 58 to 29 percent, a majority of the public agreed that it was "morally wrong" for the United States to be fighting in Vietnam.[12]

Buoyed by signs of pervasive disillusionment with the war, Fulbright and the SFRC, the last week in April, opened hearings on the various end-the-war resolutions pending before Congress. Among the witnesses were former Johnson administration officials McGeorge Bundy, Arthur Goldberg, and George Reedy, all of whom endorsed the notion of setting a deadline and enacting legislation placing limits on the executive's ability to wage war.[13] One of the star witnesses at the 1971 hearings was John Kerry, a leading light in the newly formed Vietnam Veterans against the War (VVAW). Kerry and his compatriots, clothed symbolically in faded fatigues adorned with battle ribbons and peace symbols, had come to Washington from Detroit, where in a Howard Johnson's motel room they had conducted their "Winter Soldiers" investigation of U.S. war crimes in Indochina. Kerry's band gathered on the Capitol steps, bore witness to their own misdeeds in Vietnam, and ceremoniously tossed away their medals. Several days later, Fulbright met Kerry at a Georgetown party and invited him to appear before the SFRC.[14]

As the hearings opened, the committee room was filled with Vietnam veterans. Kerry, thrice wounded as a riverboat commander, was eloquent in his appeal for an immediate end to the war. "How do you ask a man to be the last to die in Vietnam?" he asked the senators. "How do you ask a

10 See Jack Baker to JWF, Mar. 31, 1971, Series 4:10, Box 18:5, SPF.
11 "Nixon Orders Calley Freed from Stockade," *Arkansas Gazette,* Apr. 2, 1971.
12 Louis Harris, "Tide of Public Opinion Turns Decisively Against the War," *Washington Post,* May 3, 1971.
13 Marcy to JWF, May 6, 1971, Series 48:3, Box 18:1, SPF; and "Harriman Assails Thieu on '68 Talks," *Washington Evening Star,* May 25, 1971.
14 Interview with Carl Marcy, Oct. 10, 1988, Washington, D.C.

man to be the last to die for a mistake?''[15] Newspaper reporters and television commentators declared Kerry's testimony to be among the most dramatic of the war, and everyone complimented the veterans on their comportment.[16]

Later, however, as Fulbright and the SFRC were listening to various establishment figures testify on the need to get out of Vietnam as soon as possible, the committee room was invaded by members of the Mayday Tribe, a new counterculture, antiwar organization that had come to Washington with the stated intention of ''shutting the government down.'' While their comrades were outside conducting ''lie-ins'' on bridges and major thoroughfares and at the entrances of government buildings, three ''tribesmen'' interrupted Fulbright to accuse him and everyone involved in the proceedings of being imperialists and war criminals. The committee was ''doing the dirty work of the administration'' by acting as a safety valve and diverting the attention of the antiwar movement. Both Aiken and Fulbright lost their tempers.

''Why the hell do you stay here if other countries are so much better?'' the white-haired Republican asked. ''If you were in an authoritarian country,'' Fulbright told the demonstrators, ''you'd all be in jail.''[17]

Positive public and press response to the end-the-war hearings seemed to stiffen the Senate's resolve. In mid-May the upper house began debate on the new Hatfield–McGovern amendment, which proposed to cut off funds for further military operations by the end of the year. Mike Mansfield revived his bill calling for a fifty percent reduction of American troops in Europe.[18] Stuart Symington asked for and got a secret session of the Senate during which he briefed his colleagues on the extent of American bombing in Laos. He flatly accused the Nixon administration of deceiving Congress and the American people and of violating the law.[19]

When the debate had ended, the doves seemed to have little to show for their efforts, however. The second Hatfield–McGovern amendment was defeated by a vote of 55 to 39 on June 16.[20] Shortly before, supporters of the

15 Herbert Rainwater to JWF, June 3, 1971, Series 48:18, Box 63:3, SPF.
16 Actually Kerry was something of an establishment figure. While in Washington he stayed in the Georgetown townhouse of a friend of the Kennedy family's. Adam Yarmolinsky, a former Kennedy administration official, had helped script his SFRC testimony. In early June the VVAW leadership denounced him for using their organization to further a prospective political career.
17 UPI 28, Apr. 28, 1971.
18 *Congressional Record,* Senate, May 18, 1971, 15550–1.
19 Spencer Rich, ''Senate Told Nixon Aid to Laos Illegal,'' *Washington Post,* June 8, 1971.
20 William C. Berman, *William Fulbright and the Vietnam War: The Dissent of a Political Realist* (Kent, Ohio, 1988), 145.

administration had managed to down the Mansfield proposal to cut U.S. troops in Europe by a 63 to 36 tally.[21] These seemingly hawkish votes were somewhat deceiving, however. The Nixon administration was then justifying its opposition to end-the-war resolutions almost solely on the grounds that it needed maximum leeway to protect American troops as they withdrew from Vietnam. The decisive defeat of the Mansfield bill stemmed from the fact that in May Soviet leader Leonid Brezhnev had called for a mutual reduction of forces in Europe, and the administration had begged the Congress not to give away a bargaining chip in advance.[22] Moreover, while the House simultaneously voted down its own end-the-war resolution, the antiwar tally of 158 was the largest in the history of the Vietnam conflict.[23] Perhaps most important, the Senate's most effective and consistent hawk, John Stennis, announced to his startled colleagues that he was introducing his own legislation to curb the power of presidents to commit the nation to war without the consent of Congress. Fulbright, Symington, and McGovern joined with Sam Ervin, John Sparkman, and the *New York Times* to hail Stennis's speech as a potential turning point in contemporary American history, a key action that could lead to the redressing of the balance of power between Congress and the executive.[24]

Fulbright had not been on hand for the second vote on Hatfield–McGovern. Cambridge University had invited him to address its commencement exercises, and because he was able to arrange a pair (i.e., aggree not to vote) with an opponent of the end-the-war proposal, he went. Fulbright's speech, delivered amid the medieval towers and rolling meadows of one of the world's most picturesque and prestigious universities, the site of his lacrosse triumph when he was at Oxford, was a study in irony. Twenty-five years earlier he had created an academic exchange program that had as one of its primary objectives the training of the best and the brightest for government service; but the ensuing participation by intellectuals in government, he told the graduates, had been a mixed blessing, to say the least:

> I very much doubt that America's brilliant strategy in Vietnam could have been shaped without the scholarship and erudition of two Rhodes scholars and one former Harvard dean. More recently, we have been served at the highest policy level by an illustrious historian and strategic thinker whose special gift is an ability to shape American strategy in

21 Spencer Rich, "Senate Defeats Compromises on NATO Cutback," *Washington Post,* May 20, 1971.

22 Ibid.

23 "Senate End-the-War Faction Is Close to Majority, But . . . ," *Washington Evening Star,* June 20, 1971.

24 John W. Finney, "Stennis Seeks War Curb on President," *New York Times,* May 12, 1971.

Southeast Asia in the light of the experience of Weimar Germany and Metternich's stewardship of the Hapsburg empire. . . . Eschewing false modesty, I am bound to confess that my country has solved the problem of drawing intellectuals into government. The problem is . . . how do we get them out?[25]

While he was in London, the *New York Times* began publishing the first portions of the *Pentagon Papers*, the top secret Defense Department study of the war commissioned by Robert McNamara in 1967. The person who had furnished them to the *Times* was Daniel Ellsberg, a former DOD and Rand Corporation employee, an intellectual who had become intensely disillusioned with the war, and a newly converted activist who wanted to spread that disillusionment as widely as possible.[26] As a DOD employee with a top secret clearance, he was granted access to the forty-seven-volume, seven-thousand-page study commissioned by McNamara. That compilation, he concluded, was a record of deceit and misjudgment without parallel in American diplomatic history. Its publication would be the final blow that would collapse the Vietnam consensus. In the late spring of 1970 Ellsberg summoned an old friend of his named Neil Sheehan to Massachusetts Institute of Technology (MIT), where Ellsberg was then working as a research fellow. Sheehan received the papers and subsequently succeeded in persuading his employer, *Times* publisher Arthur Sulzberger, to print them.[27]

From London, where, having received his honorary degree from Cambridge, he was attending the British–American Parliamentary Conference, Fulbright hailed the decision to publish the *Pentagon Papers.* "I think it's very healthy for a democratic country like America to know the facts surrounding their involvement in such a great tragedy as the war in Vietnam," he told reporters. The chairman revealed for the first time that he and the SFRC had known of the study's existence and had unsuccessfully attempted to secure a copy from the administration. He himself had never seen the Pentagon documents, Fulbright insisted.[28]

Upon his return the chairman of the SFRC asked the *Times* to turn over its copy of the *Pentagon Papers* to Congress so that the study could be published in its entirety. When Sulzberger refused, Fulbright officially requested a copy from Melvin Laird.[29] As he had in the past, Laird, after consulting with Nixon, said no. The study was a "compilation of raw materials to be used at some unspecified, but distant, future date." Giving the

25 Quoted in Berman, *Fulbright and the Vietnam War,* 144.
26 Stanley Karnow, *Vietnam: A History* (New York, 1984), 633.
27 Sanford J. Ungar, "Daniel Ellsberg: The Difficulties of Disclosure," *Washington Post,* Apr. 30, 1972.
28 UPI 22, June 7, 1971.
29 JWF to Sulzberger, *New York Times,* June 16, 1971; and Sulzberger to JWF, June 19, 1971, Box 10, Apr.–June, Marcy Papers.

history to the SFRC ''would clearly be contrary to the national interest,'' Laird concluded.[30] Meanwhile, the *Times* continued to run choice excerpts on its front page.

Publication of the *Pentagon Papers* shocked and angered both Nixon and Kissinger. At Nixon's direction the Justice Department filed suit to block further publication. Both men were worried that this ''hemorrhage of state secrets,'' as Kissinger described the release, would undermine American credibility abroad and affect negotiations with both North Vietnam and China that were then under way.

Nixon was also angry that such a monumental leak had taken place during his watch. Shortly after the Supreme Court turned down his request to block further publication by the *Times*, he threw a tantrum: ''I want to know who is behind this and I want the most complete investigation that can be conducted. . . . I don't want excuses. I want results. I want it done, whatever the costs.''[31] In early July the White House formed a secret internal police unit and began domestic operations aimed at destroying the credibility of Ellsberg and others in the antiwar movement.

On June 22 Fulbright announced that the SFRC would soon launch a full-scale investigation into the history of U.S. involvement in Vietnam, and he once again asked the administration to furnish the Senate with a complete copy of the *Pentagon Papers*. The following day Nixon agreed, although he told reporters that the report was still classified and it would be available only for senators to see and take notes. The papers would be guarded, and they would not be made public.[32] What persuaded the president to make this ''concession'' was the knowledge that Fulbright and the SFRC staff had had a copy of the *Pentagon Papers* in their possession for almost two years.

The first week in November 1969, Ellsberg, convinced that the Nixon administration was deliberately escalating the war in Vietnam in hopes of winning a military victory while deceiving Congress and the American people as to its true intentions, had gone to Washington and called on Jim Lowenstein. He and Lowenstein had first met during the latter's trip to Vietnam with Philip Hart. Ellsberg had also met Dick Moose while Moose was working for Henry Kissinger. Ellsberg told Lowenstein that he had in his posses-

---

30 James M. Naughton, ''Laird Refused '69 Fulbright Request for the Pentagon Study on Vietnam,'' *New York Times*, June 17, 1971.

31 Quoted in Karnow, *Vietnam: A History*, 633.

32 John Herbers, ''Nixon Will Give Secret Study to Congress,'' *New York Times*, June 24, 1971; and Elsie Carper, ''Part of Study in Hand, Fulbright Seeks Rest,'' *Washington Post*, June 23, 1971.

sion "a classified Executive Branch document regarding Vietnam" that would be useful to the committee.[33] After talking to Carl Marcy, Lowenstein set up a meeting that afternoon between Fulbright and Ellsberg.

Ellsberg was very familiar with Fulbright's views on the war and particularly with his belief that Lyndon Johnson and Robert McNamara had lied to him and the Senate during the Gulf of Tonkin incident. The Arkansan, Ellsberg believed, was the perfect person to receive and publish the papers. As a leader of the antiwar movement, Fulbright would draw attention to the secret history and maximize its impact on Congress and the public. His imprimatur would, moreover, help legitimize what some would characterize as an act of espionage. Most important, perhaps, Ellsberg realized that if the *Pentagon Papers* were published under the auspices of Fulbright and the SFRC, he could avoid prosecution. Senators acting as senators were immune to prosecutorial action by the courts and Justice Department. Logic seemed to dictate that that protection would extend to their sources.[34]

During the forty-five-minute meeting, Ellsberg briefly described what he had in his possession. To whet Fulbright and Marcy's appetite, he had given them a copy of the Gulf of Tonkin command and control study prepared by the DOD's Institute of Defense Analysis. The secret history of the war McNamara had ordered was a sordid tale of deception and ineptitude whose publication was sure to accelerate disillusionment with the war, he insisted. Fulbright expressed interest and suggested that the best approach might be to have Ellsberg testify before an executive session of the SFRC. He instructed Lowenstein and Jones to follow up. The next day Ellsberg brought a single-volume summary of the *Pentagon Papers* to Jones. The two agreed to lock the summary in the committee safe.[35]

The next day Fulbright huddled with his staff to decide how to proceed. Marcy and Jones urged the chairman to use caution. Ellsberg was a volatile personality, and he had obviously broken the law. "If the Committee had decided to hold hearings on the papers," Jones later observed, "the focus would have been on how the Committee came into possession of the documents and not their contents. It would have side-tracked the Committee's efforts to mobilize opinion against the war, thus playing into the Administration's hands." In addition, the climate in Congress was "already bitter," Fulbright's aides told him, and release of the purloined documents would impair his efforts to weld hawks and doves into an anti-imperial coalition. Finally, there was little in the excerpts that Ellsberg had given them that they

33 Lowenstein to Jones, Mar. 23, 1973, Ellsberg File, Papers of Norvill Jones (in his possession)[hereinafter referred to as Jones Papers].

34 See Donald A. Ritchie, interviewer, *Carl A. Marcy: Oral History Interviews* (Senate Historical Office: Washington, D.C., 1983) and Ungar, "Daniel Ellsberg."

35 "Ellsberg Matter," undated, Ellsberg File, Jones Papers; and Ungar, "Daniel Ellsberg."

did not already know, namely, that the Johnson administration had engaged in deception "which amounted to fraud."[36]

Fulbright, Marcy, and Jones perceived, correctly, that Ellsberg being who he was, the *Pentagon Papers* would find their way into the public domain through another sphere. Why not use the situation to embarrass the administration and discredit the use of "executive privilege"?[37] If the SFRC could get Laird to deny Congress access to the papers, citing executive privilege, and then the documents became public, it would be clear for all to see that the Nixon administration was abusing the classification power and the claim of executive privilege merely to cover up a trail of executive branch misdeeds.

In late February, Norvill Jones began receiving in the mail copies of twenty-five of the forty-seven volumes of the secret study. Some of them Ellsberg simply mailed at the post office in the Brentwood section of Los Angeles. After looking them over, Jones and Marcy conferred with Fulbright. The purloined volumes were subsequently locked away in the safe in the committee's offices on the fourth floor of the New Senate Office Building.

Ellsberg's two children from his first marriage had helped photocopy the documents, and they had kept their mother apprised of what was transpiring, including their father's decision to mail copies of certain volumes to Fulbright. Shortly thereafter, FBI agents, casting their net widely for incriminating information on former administration officials who had turned against the war, interviewed the first Mrs. Ellsberg. She told all, including her ex-husband's liaison with the chairman of the SFRC. When Ellsberg learned that Hoover's men were on his trail, he resigned from Rand and took the position with MIT. Meanwhile, FBI agents made inquiries at Rand and were told that the documents in Ellsberg and Fulbright's possession did not involve national security. Despite its doubts, the bureau immediately dropped its investigation. They did so primarily out of fear of the link to Fulbright. The chairman was too powerful; officials decided that further inquiry could "embarrass the bureau."[38]

In the weeks that followed, Ellsberg pressed Fulbright to hold hearings for the specific purpose of revealing the contents of the *Pentagon Papers*. The chairman refused. Norvill Jones told Fulbright:

> I am very leery about Dan Ellsberg and believe that we should keep him at arm's length. I have repeatedly warned him about not getting the Committee's name involved in any way in his efforts to do something

---

36 "Why the Committee Did Not Act on the Pentagon History of the War," undated, Ellsberg File, Jones Papers.

37 Ibid.

38 Seymour M. Hersh, *The Price of Power: Kissinger in the Nixon White House* (New York, 1983), 327. See also SAC, Los Angeles to Director, July 7, 1970, 62–71126, FBI Files.

with the material he wants to get out, but I fear that for his own purposes sometime he may let it be known that he has supplied the Committee with a copy.[39]

Indeed, during his various contacts with Ellsberg in the spring of 1970, he found the former DOD official increasingly frantic. He knew that the FBI was tailing him, Ellsberg told Jones, and he was certain that he was going to jail. Ellsberg was a loose canon, Jones told Marcy, and it would be best to keep Fulbright and the SFRC out of his way.[40]

On July 10, 1970, Fulbright had written Secretary of Defense Laird again asking that the papers be made available to the committee. Three days later Laird had written back to say no. Fulbright had then denounced the decision on the floor of the Senate. "Nothing is secret for long in Washington," he had noted. "I hope that the first enterprising reporter who obtains a copy of this history will share it with the committee."[41]

Ellsberg had seen Fulbright one final time before publication in June. On March 31, after his meeting with the Sheehans, he had met with the chairman in Washington. Ellsberg had stressed that he was ready to go to jail if necessary to help bring the war to a close. At the same time, he had pleaded with Fulbright to read a portion of the papers into the *Record* or to help him find a senator or congressperson who would. Fulbright had told him that in his opinion publication of the papers would have minimal impact on the course of the war and would do little to help the various end-the-war resolutions. Ellsberg had called several times after that, but upon the advice of his staff, the chairman had not responded.[42]

Ellsberg did manage to secure congressional protection, but only after the *Times* had begun publication. Two days after the initial installment appeared, Senator Mike Gravel (R–Alaska) convened a meeting of his Buildings and Grounds Subcommittee and began reading portions of the *Pentagon Papers*. After bursting into tears several times, Gravel finally stopped at 1:12 a.m.[43]

The revelation that Fulbright and the staff of the SFRC had had a copy of the *Pentagon Papers* for months before their publication in the *Times* caused little outcry among either hawks or doves. Fulbright and the committee were far too valuable to the antiwar movement to have jeopardized their credibility by releasing the documents, opponents of the war concluded. Administration supporters muttered that the chairman of the SFRC should have turned Ellsberg over to the proper authorities, but by being circumspect Fulbright and company had avoided giving their enemies any real opening.

39 Jones to JWF, Apr. 1, 1971, Ellsberg File, SPF.
40 Interview with Norvill Jones, June 29, 1989, Washington, D.C.
41 Ungar, "Daniel Ellsberg."
42 "Background of Contacts with Daniel Ellsberg," undated, Ellsberg File, Jones Papers.
43 Spencer Rich, "Gravel Appears Unlikely to Be Disciplined by Senate," *Washington Post,* July 1, 1971.

Although Fulbright never succeeded in forcing the Nixon administration to invoke executive privilege over the *Pentagon Papers*, the president's efforts to have the Supreme Court block publication had the effect of casting him in the role of an enemy of the First Amendment and as a tacit partner of Lyndon Johnson in an ongoing conspiracy to deceive the public. The whole affair, as Fulbright had hoped, further aroused strict constructionists, mostly southern conservatives, in Congress. For months Fulbright had been wooing the epitome of that breed, Senator Sam Ervin (D–North Carolina). During 1970 and 1971 he wrote Ervin several times arguing that whatever he thought of the war in Vietnam, he must admit that it was extraconstitutional. Its continuation and expansion without congressional approval or input were destroying the system of checks and balances.[44] Fulbright ostentatiously supported Ervin's fight to eliminate the "no-knock" provisions from John Mitchell's notorious Omnibus Crime Bill. Although Ervin was grateful, he resisted suggestions that he extend his fight against the imperial presidency into the field of foreign affairs.

Fulbright's persistence, however, coupled with the brouhaha over the *Pentagon Papers* and John Stennis's declared intention to seek a congressional limit on the warmaking powers of the president, finally turned Ervin. In August the self-styled "country lawyer," his jowls shimmying and eyes flashing, opened hearings before his Judiciary Subcommittee on various pending measures designed to keep the executive branch from withholding information from Congress. The first item on the agenda was the Fulbright bill, and it was clear from the beginning that the measure had the North Carolinian's full support.[45]

Despite his defiant posture, Richard Nixon could feel the foundations of the Republic shaking beneath his feet during the summer and fall of 1971; or, more important from his perspective, he could see his prospects for reelection in 1972 diminishing by the day. The *Chicago Sun-Times* warned the president that it was "3rd and 20" for him on the war.[46] A team of Library of Congress researchers declared the Vietnam conflict to be "the second most expensive war in American history," and the once-proud American military team in Vietnam continued to disintegrate slowly on the nightly news before the eyes of an anguished public.[47] As the purpose of the war became increasingly obscure to American GIs, occurrences of individual and mass disobedience

44 JWF to John Stennis, July 7, 1971, Series 48:1, Box 10:2, SPF.
45 "Senate G.O.P. Chief Backs Restrictions on President's Warmaking Powers," *New York Times,* July 27, 1971.
46 News Summaries, June 7, 1971, WHSpF, Box 33, Nixon Project.
47 "Impact of War Totaled," *Arkansas Democrat,* July 11, 1971.

mounted. More than two thousand incidents of "fragging" – attempted murder of officers, often by grenade – were reported in 1970. The U.S. command estimated that as of that year as many as sixty-five thousand American servicemen were using drugs. At the same time, racial tensions were becoming palpable; in some encampments, black and white soldiers segregated themselves. "A sense of uselessness and lack of accomplishment dwells within our ranks," SP5 Donald Young wrote Fulbright from his fire base camp. "We do not believe our President when he says it must take time to bring our men home. Why does it take one day to become involved in a situation, but eleven years to admit our possible wrong and then gradually withdraw?"[48]

Although determined not to be stampeded, Nixon and Kissinger were sufficiently concerned about the course of the war and the state of the home front to try once again to break the stalemate in Paris. Kissinger repeatedly expressed fear that the administration might be hamstrung at any moment by Congress "giving the farm away."[49] Most important, Nixon suspected that he would need a peace settlement in order to win reelection. As a result, in May, Kissinger secretly presented to the North Vietnamese the most comprehensive peace offer yet advanced by the United States. In exchange for release of the American prisoners of war, Washington would withdraw all troops within seven months after an agreement had been signed. The United States also abandoned the concept of mutual withdrawal, insisting only that North Vietnam stop further infiltration in return for the removal of American forces.

In the midst of his Paris shuttle, the NSC adviser made a trip to Pakistan, ostensibly to consult American officials there. His agenda included a secret detour to China to make last-minute arrangements for an official visit by Nixon in 1972. Mao proved receptive, and on the evening of July 15, Nixon told a national television audience that he was going to Beijing to negotiate a normalization of relations with Communist China.[50]

Nixon's announcement stunned the nation and the world. No hatred was more sacred to anticommunists than that they harbored toward Mao's China. No bilateral relationship was more shrouded in mythology. Republicans had been pummeling the Democratic Party for the "loss" of China with great profit for a generation. During the early years of that drama, its star had been

48 Young to JWF, Aug. 30, 1971, Series 48:19, Box 53:4, SPF.
49 Quoted in George C. Herring, *America's Longest War: The United States and Vietnam, 1950–1975,* 2d ed. (New York, 1986), 244.
50 Stephen E. Ambrose, *Nixon,* vol. II, *The Triumph of a Politician, 1962–1972* (New York, 1989), 450–3.

Richard Nixon. Jiang Jie-shi's government was appalled at Nixon's opening to mainland China, but outside of radical right circles, the forthcoming trip was hailed as a coup by foreign policy observers and politicians at home and abroad.[51]

Long before Nixon or Kissinger sought to open the door to China, Fulbright had advocated a fresh approach to Mao's regime. His China hearings in 1966 had gone far to demythologize the entire subject. Ironically, as Kissinger shuttled back and forth between Beijing, Paris, and Washington, Fulbright's committee was holding new hearings on China, this time focusing on the issues of representation in the United Nations and the status of the Formosa Resolution of 1955, which authorized the president to use force to defend the Nationalist government.

Fulbright was generally positive about Nixon and Kissinger's gambit. "I would like to go to Peking. . . . I used to play Ping-Pong twenty years ago," he joked with reporters.[52] Indeed, he had been urging such openings to the communist world ever since Nikita Khrushchev had made his impassioned appeal for peaceful coexistence before the SFRC in 1959. At the same time, Fulbright used the 1971 hearings to launch a major attack on the policy of containment and to make sure that the right would not force the administration to retreat. To the enragement of Dean Acheson and other architects of the cold war, Fulbright's new China hearings depicted a Truman administration that had deliberately misled Congress and the American people as to the threat posed to their interests by Communist China and as to the true nature of Jiang Jie-shi's corrupt, repressive regime. John Stewart Service and John Paton Davies, the two foreign service officers savaged by Joe McCarthy twenty-five years earlier for allegedly betraying China to the communists, came out of seclusion to reveal that their reports criticizing Jiang had been suppressed.[53] "We've been deceived for a long time," Fulbright told the Capitol Hill press corps, "much longer than we thought and much more profoundly."[54] Over the objections of the State Department, which declared that such action would "send the wrong signal" prior to Nixon's forthcoming visit to China, the SFRC voted to repeal the 1955 Formosa Resolution.[55]

As in the past, the whipping boy for senators frustrated by their exclusion from the foreign policy process was foreign aid. That was so not only because it was one of the few areas in which the executive was vulnerable to legis-

51 Weekend News Review, July 19, 1971, WHSpF, Box 33, Nixon Project.
52 "Fulbright Begins to Like Ping-Pong," *Washington Post,* Apr. 15, 1971.
53 UPI 11, July 21, 1971.
54 "Fulbright Panel Told Data on China Was [*sic*] Suppressed," *Baltimore Sun,* June 29, 1971.
55 Marcy to JWF, July 21, 1971, Box 10, July–Sept., Marcy Papers; and Henry Tanner, "Senate Unit Acts to Repeal Taiwan Defense Measure," *New York Times,* July 22, 1971.

lative pressure but also because it was an expression of the liberal internationalism that Fulbright, Mansfield, and Symington were convinced had been
responsible for American overcommitments around the world, including Vietnam. Throughout late 1970 and early 1971 a coalition consisting of traditional
conservative opponents of foreign aid and antiwar activists waged a guerrilla
war against various foreign aid "supplementals" for Cambodia and Laos.[56]
As the date for the final vote on the administration's 1972 request approached, the White House applied maximum pressure. Dozens of lobbyists
from the White House, State Department, Defense, and AID swarmed
through Senate corridors and twisted arms in the off-floor office of Vice-
President Spiro Agnew.[57]

No foreign aid bill had ever gone down to defeat in the history of the
program; both the White House and the Republican leadership were confident
– too confident. As the vote proceeded, however, the gallery began to buzz.
One by one, former supporters of the program answered no: Bayh, Cranston,
Magnuson, Saxbe, Smith, Spong. Defeat of a major bill on the floor of either
house was very rare; usually the dirty work was done in committee.[58] When
the final ballot was cast, the U.S. Senate had voted 41 to 27 on October 29,
1971 to kill the entire foreign aid program.

The Sunday after his victory Fulbright appeared on *Face the Nation*. He
praised the Senate for defeating the foreign aid bill, which he denounced as
a mechanism to ensure continued U.S. dominance over small nations. The
way was now open to write a new bill emphasizing nonmilitary aid funneled
through multilateral channels and featuring a multiyear authorization. At the
same time, Senate Minority Leader Hugh Scott, white-faced with anger, appeared on *Meet the Press*. He charged "left wing Senators" with leading the
bill to "slaughter." These people, he declared, were guiding the nation down
the dangerous path of neo-isolationism.[59] Nixon's reaction was reflected in a
bitter commentary by his friend Joe Alsop: "The proof is now clear," he
wrote the day following the vote, "that Senate majority leader Mike Mansfield and the chairman of the Foreign Relations Committee, Sen. J. William
Fulbright, are actively, unashamedly eager to see the United States defeated
in war."[60] In the end, the Senate voted to approve $1.14 billion for economic
and humanitarian aid and $1.5 billion for foreign military support. The total
was nearly a billion dollars less than the amount the administration had originally requested.[61]

---

56 *Congressional Record,* Senate, Feb. 18, 1971, 3009–11.
57 Marcy, memorandum, Nov. 12, 1971, Box 10, Oct.–Dec., Marcy Papers.
58 Neil MacNeil, "Foreign Aid: Scrambling to the Rescue; How the Senate Foreign Aid Bill
    Died," *Time,* Nov. 15, 1971, 13–15.
59 News Summaries, Nov. 1, 1971, WHSpF, Box 35, Nixon Project.
60 Joseph Alsop, "Undercutting the War," *Washington Post,* Nov. 5, 1971.
61 Spencer Rich, "Military Aid Voted in Senate; $1.5 Billion Provided for Revived Bill,"
    Washington Post, Nov. 12, 1971.

In the spring of 1972 the SFRC, using the *Pentagon Papers* as a basis, held a series of hearings on the origins of American involvement in Southeast Asia. Among those testifying were Noam Chomsky and Arthur Schlesinger, Jr., two academics whose views on the Vietnam War reflected two principal strains in revisionist historiography. In his testimony, Schlesinger attributed the disaster to policies made out of "ignorance, improvisation and mindlessness."[62] He stressed the importance of the ideology of anticommunism, a belief system that equated capitalism with freedom and democracy, and state socialism with oppression and totalitarianism. Chomsky presented the structuralist or classic New Left interpretation. He contended that the war was an outgrowth of American opposition to a peasant-based revolutionary movement and as such was the product of "rational imperialism" rather than blind anticommunism. The overriding objective of American foreign policy and the raison d'être for the war in Vietnam, he said, was to prevent "any nibbling away at areas that provide Western industrial powers with free access to markets, raw materials, a cheap labor force and the possibilities for the export of pollution and opportunities for investment."[63]

Fulbright believed that both interpretations were equally credible. He had always fancied himself a pragmatist in both thought and action. Taken to task by a constituent for reversing himself on the issue of presidential power over foreign policy formulation, he replied:

> As a political officeholder, I do not make speeches designed to formulate abstract principles for all time, but I respond to the circumstances as I see them . . . for the purpose of trying to direct the policies of the country in a useful and orderly direction, preserving, if possible, our security and our prosperity.[64]

As a pragmatist he could accept both Chomsky's and Schlesinger's interpretation of the origins of the war in Vietnam. In analyzing any diplomatic problem, Fulbright believed, an informed person had to take into consideration such historical constants as ideology, economics, geopolitics, domestic politics, and after 1945, bureaucratic momentum; but each episode and movement was unique and had to be evaluated as such.

In January Fulbright and Tillman had published in the *New Yorker* a scathing indictment of the containment policy. "The anticommunism of the Truman Doctrine has been the guiding spirit of American foreign policy since the Second World War," they wrote. "Stalin and Mao Tse-tung and even

62 Berman, *Fulbright and the Vietnam War,* 155. On the whole, Chomsky's views tended to be more extreme and conspiratorial than other New Leftists, particularly historians such as William Appleman Williams, Lloyd Gardner, Barton Bernstein, Thomas Paterson, and Walter LeFeber.

63 Quoted in ibid.

64 JWF to Kenneth Jones, Apr. 3, 1973, Series 48:18, Box 65:3, SPF.

Ho Chi Minh replaced Hitler in our minds as the sources of all evil in the world. We came to see the hand of 'Moscow communism' in every disruption that occurred anywhere.'' In this piece, entitled "In Thrall to Fear," and in subsequent articles and speeches, the Arkansan explained that in an effort to sell Congress and the American people on a massive foreign aid program and military buildup to combat a threat that they believed to be authentic, Harry Truman and his cohorts oversold the evil of communism and the danger posed by Soviet imperialism. "The Truman Doctrine, which made limited sense for a limited time in a particular place, has led us in its universalized form to disaster in Southeast Asia and demoralization at home," he wrote. As 1972 opened, the Arkansan called upon America "to return to the practical idealism of the United Nations Charter," which he conceived to be peaceful coexistence and tolerance for cultural diversity;[65] but Vietnam, the ultimate manifestation of America's cold war paranoia and its counterrevolutionary policies, would not go away.

In mid-February Richard Nixon paused in his ongoing battle with Hanoi and American doves to embark on the greatest adventure of his presidency – the much-anticipated journey to mainland China. The trip was more of a public relations triumph than the buildup, if that was possible. The American people watched in disbelief as the man who had based his early career on professional anticommunism, who had for two decades derided the Democrats for "selling out" China to the communists, was escorted around the Forbidden City and shown the Great Wall by his Red Chinese hosts. He and Mao traded smiles and toasts, and much of the world hailed him and his German-accented adviser as pragmatic geniuses.

Richard Nixon and Mao Zedong discussed Southeast Asia during their summit, and the Chinese leader promised to help bring the war to an end. Whether or not he was sincere is unclear. What is certain is that he was unsuccessful. In March 1972, a hundred and twenty thousand North Vietnamese troops, led by phalanxes of Soviet tanks, smashed their way across the DMZ and drove into northern South Vietnam. At that point, there were only six thousand American combat troops, out of a total of ninety-five thousand personnel, in Vietnam. Hanoi reasoned that with a presidential election imminent Nixon would not dare reverse the course of Vietnamization and put additional troops in Vietnam. It was also logical to assume that a major escalation in the fighting during an election year would generate irresistible pressure for peace in the United States.

Initially, the NVA offensive was an unqualified success. Communist troops advanced across the DMZ, in the Central Highlands, and across the Cam-

---

65 "Fulbright Traces Foreign Failures to Truman Policy," *Arkansas Gazette,* Jan. 5, 1972.

bodian border northwest of Saigon. Thieu dispatched thousands of troops to defend the besieged towns of Quang Tri in the north, Kontum in the highlands, and An Loc just sixty miles north of Saigon. In the process, he opened the door for increased Vietcong activity in the Mekong Delta and the heavily populated areas around Saigon.

Richard Nixon would not be reconciled to the fall of South Vietnam. Typically, he convinced himself that the offensive was a tactic designed to force him out of the 1972 election, as Lyndon Johnson had been driven from the field in 1968.[66] The president quickly approved B-52 strikes across the demilitarized zone and followed up with massive air attacks on fuel depots in the Hanoi–Haiphong area.

Sensing trouble ahead, Kissinger arranged to meet with Fulbright for two hours at Taylor House on Lafayette Square one evening during the last week in March.[67] The administration had had to react to the North Vietnamese offensive, he explained. The only way the United States could withdraw from Vietnam was with the Thieu government intact and the military situation stabilized. Fulbright said that he understood but that he had to react as well. There were still plenty of hawks in the administration who believed that a military victory was possible, and plenty of doves who would be less understanding of Kissinger's position than he was.

The resumed bombing of the North on a massive scale maddened Fulbright because he feared that it portended a return to the strategy of "military victory" in Vietnam and, more important, that it would destroy détente with the Soviet Union. Following months of tedious negotiations, Kissinger had arranged for Nixon to go to Moscow and meet with Soviet Premier Leonid Brezhnev in late May. The Kremlin denounced U.S. bombing in the harshest terms, and after four Soviet transports were damaged in Haiphong harbor in mid-April, it warned of "possible dangerous consequences."[68] For Fulbright this new outbreak of violence at a time when the superpowers seemed to stand on the brink of an era of peace and reconciliation was heartbreaking.

"Reports from Vietnam are getting worse," Carl Marcy confided to Fulbright on May 2. "The President is going to find himself in a box – he must threaten to escalate the bombing (and do so if Hanoi doesn't come to an agreement) or, in the alternative, reach an agreement which may humiliate him."[69] De-

66 News Summaries, Feb. 7, 1972, WHSpF, Box 38, Nixon Project.
67 Ibid., Mar. 28, 1972, Williams Papers.
68 "Nixon Halts Bombing of Haiphong, Hanoi; Waits for Response," *Arkansas Gazette,* Apr. 18, 1972.
69 Marcy to JWF, May 2, 1972, Box 11, Apr.–June, Marcy Papers.

spite his several encounters with humiliation, Nixon had not accommodated himself to it. On May 8 the president decided to respond to General Abrams's warning that Hué and Kontum might soon fall unless Washington authorized decisive action. Ignoring Rogers and Laird's admonition that drastic measures could possibly push Congress over the edge and precipitate an end-the-war resolution with teeth in it, Nixon intensified the war against North Vietnam. "The bastards have never been bombed like they're going to be bombed this time," he told a staff member.[70] On May 8 Nixon announced to a startled nation the sharpest escalation of the war since 1968. The navy had been instructed to mine Haiphong harbor and impose a blockade on all of North Vietnam, he told the American people. Meanwhile, air force and navy planes would bomb the enemy forces until they ceased their aggression.

The following day Fulbright met with members of the Democratic caucus, who passed by a vote of 29 to 14 his resolution "disapproving the escalation of the war in Vietnam." That was not enough, the Arkansan declared. Nixon had violated his pledge, given to him personally in the spring of 1969, to end the war by negotiation and not to continue his predecessor's suicidal policies. If the Democratic majority had no confidence in the president, it must demonstrate the courage of its convictions. By a 2-to-1 margin, the caucus approved the most recent end-the-war measure, an amendment sponsored by Clifford Case and Frank Church that would cut off funds for American troops in Vietnam after December 31, 1972.[71]

The mining of Haiphong harbor and the bombing escalation did not produce the public outcry that Rogers and Laird had feared. The American public had always considered bombing a more acceptable alternative than the use of ground forces, and many Americans felt that the North Vietnamese invasion justified Nixon's response. Moreover, the blows that Nixon rained down on the North seemed to have averted defeat in South Vietnam. The conventional military tactics employed by the North Vietnamese in the summer of 1972 depended heavily on vast quantities of fuel and ammunition, and the intensive bombing attacks, along with the blockade, made resupply extremely difficult. In South Vietnam itself, U.S. bombers flew round-the-clock missions, pummeling North Vietnamese supply lines and encampments. With the assistance of American airpower, the ARVN managed to stabilize the lines in front of Saigon and Hué, and it even mounted a small counteroffensive. Meanwhile, the build-down of American forces in Vietnam continued. "In 1965," explained an antiwar leader, "the American people knew there was a war, and we had to convince people it was wrong. In 1972,

70 Quoted in Herring, *America's Longest War,* 247.
71 Marcy to JWF, May 9, 1972, Box 11, Apr.–June, Marcy Papers; and John W. Finney, "Democratic Caucus in the Senate Condemns the 'Escalation' in Vietnam by 29 to 14," *New York Times,* May 10, 1972.

people know the war is wrong, but we have to convince them that there is a war."[72]

Seymour Hersh has noted that in 1972 Henry Kissinger began "to travel his own path inside the White House." The national security adviser desperately wanted the Moscow summit to occur as scheduled. As he flew back and forth from Paris to Moscow during the spring of 1972, he labored to convince the Kremlin that Richard Nixon really did favor a policy of détente and Richard Nixon that détente was in his political interest.[73] In his frequent talks with Dobrynin and other Soviet officials and journalists, Fulbright proved to be an invaluable ally in that effort.

The last week in May, Nixon and Kissinger journeyed to Moscow, where they met face-to-face six times with the leaders of the Soviet Union during five days of intense negotiations. The event dominated American newspapers and television, leaving little room for the Democrats and their election-year attacks on the administration. No less than five major bilateral agreements dealing with issues of trade and scientific cooperation were signed during the second, third, and fourth nights of the summit. The conclave culminated with the inking of the Strategic Arms Limitation Treaty (SALT). SALT I included two basic agreements. The first, in the form of an official treaty requiring a two-thirds vote of the Senate, would limit each side to two hundred anti-ballistic missiles for defense to be divided equally at two sites, one in the capital and the other at an offensive missile site at least eight hundred miles away. The theory underlying the ABM pact was that with such severe restrictions on its defense each country would be deterred from launching a missile attack against the other, lest its own population be wiped out. The second was a five-year executive agreement that put limits on land-based and submarine-launched missiles.[74]

Nixon and Kissinger favored SALT I for a variety of reasons. First, it would enable the president to run in 1972 as the peace candidate. Second, the administration had not budgeted for increased missile production for the five-year life of the Interim Agreement anyway. Kissinger saw SALT as a major step toward his new world order. For their part, the Soviets were interested in reducing defense expenditures and in gaining access to the U.S. grain market.[75]

As soon as the official party returned to Washington, Nixon submitted both the SALT treaty and the Interim Agreement to Congress for its consideration.

72 Quoted in Charles DeBenedetti with Charles Chatfield, *An American Ordeal: The Antiwar Movement of the Vietnam Era* (Syracuse, 1990), 323.
73 Hersh, *Price of Power*, 508, 509, 523.
74 "Nixon Makes Plea for Arms Accord," *New York Times*, June 16, 1972.
75 Hersh, *Price of Power*, 529, 531.

Following a meeting with the president at the White House,[76] Fulbright enthusiastically agreed to floor-manage the pacts. He wrote Tris Coffin:

> I think the agreements on missiles are most significant, as I believe they indicate a changed attitude on the part of the Russians, and, hopefully, the Americans. I personally think the Russians are fed up with spending so much money on useless arms and will be inclined to do what they can to implement the agreements. If the President means what he says . . . there could be quite a change in our approach.[77]

As had happened so often in the past, however, Fulbright's hopes would be crushed under the massive political weight of the military–industrial complex.

Indeed, Secretary of Defense Melvin Laird and the JCS had agreed to go along with SALT only in return for White House approval for the new Trident submarine system and a sixteen percent overall increase in the defense budget. In mid-June the Pentagon submitted an appropriation request bloated with funds for the immediate construction of not only the Trident but the B-1 bomber as well. If Congress should refuse to fund these systems, Laird announced, he would recommend to the president that he not sign the SALT agreements even if Congress should approve them.[78]

Fulbright was first incredulous, then furious. When Laird and JCS chairman Admiral Thomas Moorer dutifully trooped up to the Hill to testify on SALT, Fulbright blistered them. The Pentagon was doing nothing less than blackmailing Congress, he charged. Are you trying to "sabotage the whole spirit" of SALT? Most certainly not, Laird replied. The new weapons systems would simply permit the United States to negotiate future accords from a position of strength.[79]

On August 4, 1972, the Senate approved the ABM portion of SALT by a vote of 88 to 2.[80] When Congress then turned its attention to the five-year interim pact, the military–industrial complex's personal representative to the Senate, Henry Jackson, dropped a bombshell. The second portion of SALT had imposed a five-year freeze on ICBMs (intercontinental ballistic missiles) and SLBMs (submarine-launched ballistic missiles). At that time the United States had an estimated 1,054 land-based missiles plus another 656 deployed aboard the Polaris submarine fleet. The Soviets possessed 1,607 land-based missile launchers and 740 SLBMs. Soviet superiority in number of missiles was offset by the United States' 3-to-2 advantage in MIRV (multiple independent targeted reentry vehicle) warheads.[81] Nonetheless, Jackson added an

---

76 Appointments calendar, June 2, 1972, Williams Papers.
77 JWF to Tris Coffin, June 7, 1972, Series 48:16, Box 42:3, SPF.
78 "Treaty without New Arms Unacceptable, Laird Says," *Washington Evening Star,* June 20, 1972.
79 "Fulbright Says Laird Jeopardizing Accord," *Arkansas Gazette,* June 22, 1972.
80 "Senate Backs Defensive Half of Missile Pact," *Baltimore Sun,* Aug. 4, 1972.
81 Hersh, *Price of Power,* 529.

amendment to the Interim Agreement stipulating that in any future negotiations the president only sign agreements that provided equality in number of missiles. The first week in August, the White House announced that the Jackson amendment was "consistent" with administration policy.[82]

Led by Fulbright, the SFRC voted 11 to 0 to reject the Jackson amendment. "This [the Jackson amendment] means the President made a bum agreement," he told reporters. "How the President could agree to it is beyond my comprehension." It appeared that the junior senator from Washington was determined, he said, to perpetuate the arms race.[83] Huddling with Mansfield and the rest of the Senate leadership, the Arkansan announced that he would vote against the Interim Agreement if the Jackson amendment was part of it;[84] but in the end, he could not bring himself to do so. In mid-September the Senate approved the Jackson amendment 56 to 35 and then endorsed the Interim Agreement by 88 to 2. Fulbright voted against the amendment but for the agreement.[85] In a fit of pique, Fulbright attempted to block funding for a $11.5 million federal pavilion at Spokane's Expo '74. "The only reason you guys support this bill," he told members of the SFRC, "is because it is sponsored by two powerful senators [Jackson and Magnuson] and they have gotten more than their share."[86]

In reality, the seemingly inconsistent stance taken by the Nixon administration over arms control in 1972 was carefully orchestrated by Nixon to obtain maximum political advantage. Indeed, it paralleled his policy of stepped-up bombing coupled with troop withdrawals in Vietnam. "We must stay right on the tightrope," he told Alexander Haig, Kissinger's assistant. "Hold the hawks by continuing adequate defense – Hold the doves by pointing out that without SALT the arms budget would be much larger."[87]

The specter of the administration simultaneously negotiating an arms control agreement and coupling it with a demand for two major new arms systems once again deflated and disillusioned Fulbright, but he refused to blame the national security adviser. He and Kissinger had tried, Fulbright wrote a constituent, but the Pentagon's and Nixon's ingrained Russophobia was too strong. Kissinger was sincere and no doubt influential with the president, he observed, but "the President's own experiences, especially his early ones in running against Jerry Voorhis and Helen Gahagan Douglas . . . created an

82 The White House had not been enthusiastic about the Jackson amendment, but it had agreed reluctantly to endorse it in return for the Washingtonian's much-needed vote on the Trident sub, a project for which he had little enthusiasm. Rowland Evans and Robert Novak, "The Politics of Defense," *Washington Post,* Aug. 10, 1972.
83 "Jackson Arms Act Stand Rebuffed by Fulbright Panel," *Washington Evening Star,* Aug. 11, 1972.
84 Marcy to JWF, Sept. 6, 1972, Box 11, July–Sept., Marcy Papers.
85 "Senate Approves Pact with Soviet on Strategic Arms," *New York Times,* Sept. 18, 1972.
86 "Fulbright Trying to Block Expo 74 Fund," *Seattle Times,* Oct. 4, 1972.
87 Kissinger to Haig, minute, News Summaries, June 20, 1972, WHSpF, Box 40, Nixon Project.

attitude which I do not think Henry Kissinger . . . can change. In short, I believe the President is incapable of bringing himself to compromise with any communist regime."[88] With the Pentagon deluging the country with propaganda on the need to build the Trident and B-1, and American bombing of North Vietnam intensifying daily, Fulbright took a sudden and intense interest in the election of 1972.

88 JWF to Reuben Thomas, Dec. 30, 1972, Series 48:18, Box 64:7, SPF.

19

The Invisible Wars

For J. William Fulbright and Richard Nixon, Vietnam and the 1972 presidential election were inextricably intertwined. The president's diplomacy and policies toward Southeast Asia in the summer and fall of 1972 were keyed almost exclusively to securing victory over George McGovern and the Democrats. Fulbright, for his part, saw the election and McGovern's candidacy as a means to hasten the end of the war in Vietnam. Privately he was quite candid about the South Dakotan's chances for winning, but he believed that the nomination of a peace candidate would push Nixon toward an early and decisive end to the war.[1]

Ironically, given his conservatism and his aversion to radical politics, it was Fulbright more than any other figure who molded and articulated the foreign policy program of the new Democratic Party. In the late summer of 1972 Random House published *The Crippled Giant*. Convinced that there was an extensive market for a sequel to *The Arrogance of Power*, the huge publishing house had approached Fulbright in 1971. After some deliberation, the chairman agreed to pen another critique of American foreign policy and society, and over the next year, Seth Tillman put together a manuscript based on material he had prepared for Fulbright going back to 1967. Included in the synthesis were the *New Yorker* and *Progressive* articles, speeches at Yale and Dennison universities, and various statements Fulbright had made on the floor of the Senate.

Although the book was not a commercial success, it was widely read by the new leadership in the Democratic Party and did much to define their views on foreign policy. Indeed, Carl Marcy took great pains to see that McGovern and his advisers were supplied with galleys during the crucial weeks of July and August when the campaign was writing its position papers.[2] *The Crippled Giant* was a thoroughgoing, systematic rejection of the

---

1 "Bumpers, Fulbright Back Vietnam Plank; End of War Seen," *Arkansas Gazette,* July 12, 1972.
2 Marcy to Purvis, June 8 and Aug. 7, 1972, Box 11, Folders Apr.–June and July–Sept., Marcy Papers.

cold warriorism of Democratic traditionalists like George Meany and Henry Jackson and of the liberal activism of moderates such as Arthur Schlesinger. At the heart of Fulbright's critique was the argument that the United States had been using its vast power recklessly and irresponsibly – thus "fostering a world environment which is, to put it mildly, uncongenial to our society." This pattern of behavior, Fulbright believed, resulted from the Truman administration's oversell of the communist menace, the inability of American policy assumptions to change with the changing international situation, the development of a military–industrial complex with a vested interest in the continuation of the cold war, and the misdirected altruism of Americans committed to the notion that they had a mission to reshape the world in their own image. The result had been the globalization of U.S. commitments with a concomitant weakening of America's position abroad and a "material and spiritual drain" at home.[3] In a sense, Vietnam was the end product of these combined forces and the chief contributor to the nation's deteriorating position. By being more "selective" in its commitments and by disavowing ideological crusades, the United States could avoid future disasters like Vietnam. Increasingly, *The Crippled Giant* advised, the nation should emphasize its domestic priorities. "I am dubious about the proposition that we have a certain obligation as the richest nation in the world to help underdeveloped countries," he wrote Robert McCord, a columnist with the *Gazette*. "I believe the primary duty of this country at present is to get its economic house in order, and to set an example for other nations of prudent and wise government."[4]

From a historiographical perspective, Fulbright's interpretation was soft revisionism. He abjured the economic and systemic determinism of the New Left, instead viewing Russophobia and missionary globalism as aberrations that could be corrected. It should always be remembered that his perspective was that of a Fulbrighter abroad. He wanted to fashion a foreign policy that students and academics could be proud of when they were interacting with their enlightened counterparts in Europe, Asia, Africa, and Latin America. From a political perspective, *The Crippled Giant* articulated the foreign policy views of the McGovernite wing of the Democratic Party. But it was all for naught.

Disillusioned with the past and anesthetized by the present, the American people returned Richard Nixon to office by a record margin in November. Having identified himself as a forthright champion not only of minorities and the antiwar movement but of the effort within the party to wrest control from the traditionalists and moderates, McGovern found it difficult to capture the vitally important center. Many longtime party stal-

3 Quoted in William C. Berman, *William Fulbright and the Vietnam War: The Dissent of a Political Realist* (Kent, Ohio, 1988), 162.
4 JWF to McCord, Mar. 14, 1973, Series 78:3, Box 26:5, SPF.

warts had been offended by the new Democratic rules, which they associated with McGovernism. In addition, on October 10 he had called for an American withdrawal from Vietnam in ninety days and the termination of all military aid to the Thieu regime, a proposal about which even Fulbright had expressed reservations.[5]

As Americans were preparing to celebrate Hanukkah, the birth of Christ, and the advent of 1973, the president once more ordered air force and navy planes into the skies over North Vietnam. Nixon was interested in more than a token show of force against the enemy. "I don't want any more of this crap about the fact that we couldn't hit this target or that one," he stormed at Admiral Thomas Moorer, chairman of the JCS. "This is your chance to use military power to win this war and if you don't I'll consider you responsible."[6] Over the next twelve days, the United States launched the most devastating attacks of the war, dropping more than thirty-six thousand tons of bombs, an amount exceeding the total for the entire period from 1969 through 1971.

The prevalent reaction to the Christmas bombing in the United States was outrage. Critics denounced Nixon as a "madman" and accused him of waging "war by tantrum." Nixon's popular approval rating dropped overnight to thirty nine percent. On January 4, Senate Democrats met in caucus and passed a resolution calling for an immediate cutoff of funds for the war in Indochina, "subject only to the release of U.S. prisoners and the accounting of those missing in action."[7]

Following a New Year's vacation in San Juan and St. Martin, Fulbright returned to Washington determined to force both Rogers and Kissinger to explain to the SFRC why the bombing had been resumed.[8] Before they could appear, Nixon suspended the bombing of the North and induced Hanoi to return to the negotiating table. Fulbright and, to an extent, Marcy were very nervous. If the committee began work on a fund cutoff bill, and Kissinger suddenly engineered a peace accord, the SFRC would be left with mud on its face. Nonetheless, the chairman and his chief of staff decided to press ahead; Nixon and Kissinger could use antiwar sentiment in Congress as a bargaining chip in their negotiations with Thieu. On January 2 the committee

---

5 The chairman did not want to do anything to tie Kissinger's hands: The national security adviser, as Fulbright knew, was then negotiating furiously in Paris to secure a peace agreement prior to the election. "Fulbright Backs Peace Proposal of McGovern," *Arkansas Gazette,* Oct. 12, 1972.

6 Quoted in George C. Herring, *America's Longest War: The United States and Vietnam, 1950–1975,* 2d ed. (New York, 1986), 253–4.

7 Quoted in Berman, *Fulbright and the Vietnam War,* 166.

8 Marcy to JWF, Dec. 27, 1972, Box 11, Folder Sept.–Dec., Marcy Papers.

voted to start work on legislation to cut off funds for the war if Nixon had not negotiated peace by Inauguration Day. "The consensus of everyone present was that we did not wish to do anything to prejudice the negotiations starting next Monday," Fulbright told the press. "But if some settlement is not reached by the 20th, then it is our intention to employ legislative power to bring the war to a close."[9]

The negotiations resumed in Paris on January 8. By January 20 Kissinger and Le Duc Tho had hammered out an agreement that was acceptable to both sides. "Peace with honor" permitted American extrication from the war and secured the return of the POWs while leaving the Thieu government intact. At the same time, North Vietnamese troops remained in the South and the People's Revolutionary Government (PRG) gained recognition as a legitimate political force. The major question over which the war had been fought – the political future of South Vietnam – was left to be resolved at a later date. The diplomats insisted that the future would be defined through the political process, but realists, including Saigon and Hanoi, recognized that the fate of their country would be decided by force.

As part of an effort to persuade Thieu to accept what he had henceforth steadfastly rejected, Nixon secretly promised that if South Vietnam would go along with the accord, the United States would continue massive military aid and would "respond with full force" if North Vietnam violated the agreement, that is, if it attempted a military conquest of the South. At the same time, he made it clear that if Thieu did not acquiesce, Congress not only would cut off funds for continued American activity in Southeast Asia but would veto further aid, military and nonmilitary, to his government. Thieu stalled for a few days and then gave in. "I have done all that I can for my country," he resignedly told reporters.[10]

When Nixon announced the cease-fire agreement on the twenty-third, Fulbright at once called to congratulate him on his achievement. "It's later than I hoped, but it's good," he subsequently told reporters. When Nixon summoned twenty-five congressional leaders to the White House to brief them on the accords, the mood was one of relief and even euphoria. Nixon's announcement that he would not submit the agreement to the Senate for its advice and consent seemed to have no effect on most of those assembled. "I'm so relieved, I don't care what the agreement is called," Mike Mansfield told the press.[11] Fulbright was a bit more sanguine, remarking after the meeting that "it is inevitable that many difficulties will arise out of the liquidation of this long and costly and bitter struggle."[12]

Although he did not share the euphoria of many of his colleagues, Ful-

9 Richard Lyons, "Senate Unit Set to Act on Jan. 20," *Washington Post,* Jan. 3, 1973.
10 Quoted in Herring, *America's Longest War,* 255.
11 UPI 892, Jan. 24, 1973.
12 Quoted in Berman, *Fulbright and the Vietnam War,* 167.

bright was in the mood for reconciliation. Tragically, Lyndon Johnson had died the day before Nixon announced the Vietnam cease-fire.

In mid-February, Fulbright extended an olive branch to the Nixon administration as well. The end of the war, he told Secretary of State Rogers, should pave the way for a new era of cooperation between the SFRC and the executive branch.[13] The affable Republican was willing enough to participate in such a rapprochement, but his chief was not. It quickly became apparent that although he had won a landslide victory in the fall and that he was well on his way to extricating America from its ten-year ordeal in Southeast Asia, Richard Nixon, egged on by members of the White House staff, was in a bitter and vindictive mood. "When you go to the Capitol you must at all costs give no quarter whatever to the doves," Haldeman instructed Kissinger at Nixon's request. "You should flatly indicate . . . that the resolutions passed by the House and Senate caucuses . . . prolonged the war."[14] On February 1, White House counselor Charles Colson told television interviewer Elizabeth Drew that "a sellout brigade" which included Clark Clifford, William Fulbright, George McGovern, Frank Church, and Edward Kennedy, had kept the president from ending the war much earlier.[15] Throughout February, Nixon and his spokespeople emphasized again and again that they had not simply abandoned an ally, as the doves had demanded, but had hammered out a peace accord that left in place a strong, independent Vietnam.

Fulbright may have wanted a rapprochement with the Nixon White House, but it was to be on his own terms. Now that the war was due to end, he decided, the administration had less reason than ever to upset the balance of power within the federal government, overcommit the United States overseas, and act in unconstitutional ways. Revelations relating to the break-in at the headquarters of the Democratic National Committee in the Watergate complex and the subsequent cover-up concerned the Arkansan, but not nearly as much as did Nixon's policy priorities and his arrogance toward Congress. The second Tuesday in February he and Walter Lippmann spent two hours together over drinks.[16] Both agreed that the SFRC should play a role in implementing a lasting peace whether the administration wanted it to or not. The only lever available, as usual, was congressional control of the purse strings.

Meanwhile, Moose and Lowenstein were winging their way to Phnom Penh again to investigate rumors of continued American military activity in Cambodia. The two were well known to, and thoroughly disliked by, American

---

13 Rogers to JWF, Feb. 16, 1973, Series 48:3, Box 18:3, SPF.
14 Haldeman to Kissinger, Jan. 25, 1973, WHSpF, Box 178, Nixon Project.
15 Quoted in Berman, *Fulbright and the Vietnam War,* 168.
16 Appointments calendar, Feb. 13, 1973, Williams Papers.

diplomatic and military personnel in the Cambodian capital. When the SFRC investigators arrived the first week in April, their journalist friends told them that they suspected that American spotter planes were flying out of Phnom Penh airport, locating Khmer Rouge targets for U.S. fighter-bombers and B-52s. "Lowenstein and I would go out at odd moments and try to get into the far end of the airport and poke around," Moose remembered. "We could never quite do it."[17]

The second Sunday morning they were there, the two investigators wandered over to the small office shared by the local *Washington Post* stringer and the United Press International (UPI) correspondent to check on the baseball scores. When they arrived one of the correspondents was standing, listening intently to a small transistor radio.

"Dick, listen to this," she said.

"I heard unmistakably a flight of American air force planes identifying themselves: 'Blue Six, this is Fox Four, what is your location?' and so on. Finally one of them addressed the Embassy," Moose recalled. "Let's get over there while the planes are still in the air," Moose urged his partner.

As Moose and Lowenstein parked the car beside the embassy, who should emerge but the air attaché. They had previously interviewed the man, and he had flatly denied that he or his staff were spotting for the air force. Moose confronted him: "I believe that you are controlling air strikes from within the embassy and that you're putting forward spotter planes out of the airport here. I have just heard the ground-to-air and air-to-air communications." The officer paled, hesitated, and then declared, "I'm not going to answer any more questions."

Lowenstein and Moose were not able to prepare a report for release until April 27, but even before he received confirmation that Ambassador Thomas Enders and his staff were violating the specific congressional ban on the use of combat troops in Cambodia, Fulbright had decided to make an issue of the post–cease-fire air offensive in that benighted country. The war in Vietnam might be over for all intents and purposes, and Henry Kissinger might be poised to establish a new world order based on détente, but, as Cambodia revealed, there was nothing to prevent Nixon or a future president from plunging the United States into another undeclared war such as Vietnam. Indeed, although the substance of American foreign policy seemed to be improving, the great issue of restoring a balance between Congress and the executive remained to be dealt with. Testifying on Capitol Hill on March 28, Assistant Secretary of State William Sullivan had been asked about Nixon's authority to bomb Cambodia. He had replied that two State Department lawyers were currently working on the problem, then added that, "[F]or now, I'd say the justification is the reelection of President Nixon."[18]

17 Interview with Richard Moose, June 29, 1989, Washington, D.C.
18 Quoted in Berman, *Fulbright and the Vietnam War,* 171.

In early 1973 most observers predicted that Congress would never be able to stand up to the imperial presidency. Hamstrung by massive inefficiency and by rules that ensured delays, boredom, and interruption of business, run by crotchety and sometimes senile men sheltered by the seniority system and insensitive to the public will, so the argument ran, Congress could not hope to compete with the modern executive, especially in the person of Richard Nixon. That argument, however, did not take into account the burgeoning Watergate scandal.

By April 15, the political climate in Washington was beginning to change dramatically. Watergate was mushrooming into a major political and legal problem for the administration and a personal nightmare for Nixon. While Kissinger urged him to expand the bombing from Cambodia into North Vietnam to punish it for its alleged persistent violations of the Paris agreements, Nixon refused to act. To those who saw him, he seemed shell-shocked, and he spent endless hours with Haldeman, Ehrlichman, and White House counsel John Dean searching for some way to contain the crisis.

Fulbright sensed that Watergate was a window of opportunity. Appearing on *Face the Nation* on April 15, the chairman noted that break-in by Committee to Reelect the President (CREEP) operatives had made it possible for Congress not only to discuss but to act against executive encroachments on its powers. The presidency and the president were no longer sacrosanct, able to operate above the law.[19]

On April 11 the SFRC opened hearings on Jacob Javits's war powers bill. The immediate backdrop for the debate that ensued was the continuing bombing campaign in Cambodia. On March 27 Fulbright had risen in the Senate to address his colleagues. "I noted on the back page of the press . . . a statement that United States Air Force planes had just completed the 19th consecutive daily B-52 bombing attack in Cambodia," he declared. Why and under what authority were these raids being conducted? There were no more Americans (the sixty-day withdrawal period provided for in the Paris accords had lapsed) in Vietnam to protect. Was there some secret commitment to Lon Nol? "Does the President assert – as the Kings of old – that as Commander in Chief he can order American forces anywhere for any purpose that suits him?"[20]

On April 29 Stuart Symington released the Lowenstein–Moose report on Cambodia. There was yet another secret, unauthorized war raging in Southeast Asia in which the United States was participating, they declared. The struggle in Cambodia did not involve Cambodians fighting North Vietnamese but rather Cambodians fighting Cambodians. It was a civil war, pure and simple. They went on to point out that until he and his comrades overthrew

19 Ibid., 172.
20 Statement by J. W. Fulbright, Mar. 27, 1973, Box 11 , Folder Jan.–Mar., Marcy Papers.

Prince Sihanouk in 1970, Lon Nol and his generals had actively supported the NVA and VC. Declared Stuart Symington:

> At this late date in this long war in Indochina, it is indeed tragic to witness the beginning of another wasteful and immoral episode, one which had nothing to do with the security of the United States, one which finds us dropping bags of rice to some Cambodians and five hundred pound bombs on others.[21]

Throughout April and May, Fulbright was deluged with anguished letters from American servicemen flying missions over Cambodia – the so-called B-52 Letters. "It is hard to impart to you sir, the frustration of being on continuous temporary duty with no end in sight," wrote one B-52 gunner who was in his thirteenth month of combat missions against Cambodia and Laos. "I for one, sir, do not wish to die as a mercenary for a foreign dictator!" He commended Fulbright for his efforts "to have a legal end to this war declared."[22]

An airman from Blytheville, Arkansas, provided an exact chronology of the post-Paris bombing of Cambodia:

> On approximately the 15th of February, we ceased all bombing operations in all parts of Southeast Asia. We were told at that time that as soon as the North Vietnamese and Viet-Cong started a timely release of the P.O.W.'s our B-52's and personnel would begin to return to our home bases. On approximately the 17th of February we started bombing operations against the Republic of Laos. We were again told that as soon as a cease fire was accomplished in Laos, we would cease operations on Guam [home base for B-52s flying missions over Southeast Asia]. . . . In the latter part of February a cease fire was signed in Laos. We stopped bombing on the day the cease fire was signed in Laos for approximately 12 hours and then we started bombing in Cambodia. When we made inquiries as to the reason why . . . no one seemed to be able to give us a reason. We have been bombing for approximately 41 days now.[23]

And yet, faced with irrefutable proof that Nixon had ordered the illegal and unconstitutional bombing of Cambodia, the Senate still hesitated. Neither house of Congress had yet voted an absolute fund cutoff for military action in the field, and that reluctance remained. John Finney noted in the *New York Times* that Congress did not want to be accused of "losing" Cambodia. Reports, even from impartial sources, indicated that without daily American bombing and strafing Lon Nol's army would collapse, and Cambodia would fall to the Khmer Rouge – the same Khmer Rouge that would slaughter 1.2

---

21 "Report on Air War in Cambodia," Apr. 29, 1973, Series 28:7, Box 27:1, SPF.
22 SSgt. Charles E. Shinn to JWF, Apr. 17, 1973, Series 48:18, Box 65:5, SPF.
23 SSgt. Robert E. Walker to JWF, Apr. 24, 1973, Series 48:17, Box 46:4, SPF.

million people, the same Khmer Rouge rendered infamous by the Academy Award–winning *Killing Fields.*[24] Indeed, in 1971 following one of their trips to Cambodia Moose and Lowenstein had reported that "there is considerable support for the government of Gen. Lon Nol" and that many Cambodians favored American air strikes to contain the NVA and control the Khmer Rouge.[25]

Far more important in restraining Congress than fear of contributing to the rise of the Khmer Rouge – most Americans were ignorant of the dynamics and goals of that organization in 1973 – was apprehension over Richard Nixon's political clout. Senators and representatives could not forget the unprecedented landslide the president had fashioned. Haldeman, Colson, and John Mitchell's mean-spirited declarations convinced many that a political purge was in the offing; but just as it seemed Congress would get cold feet again, Watergate heated up to warm them. As evidence mounted that the White House had been deeply involved in the "plumbers'" operation and that there was a conspiracy to cover up the Watergate break-in, Nixon went on television on April 30 to announce the resignation of H. R. Haldeman and John Ehrlichman and the firing of John Dean. Suddenly the president seemed imminently vulnerable. Doves and hawks alike began circling for the kill.

The first week in May the SFRC voted 13 to 3 to recommend a cutoff of funds for continued U.S. bombing raids in Cambodia.[26] Five days later the House passed a supplemental appropriations bill for the DOD that would deny money for continued operations in Cambodia.[27]

Sensing that at last the time was ripe, Frank Church informed the Senate on May 14 that he and Clifford Case had obtained thirty-eight cosponsors for their proposal to cut off funding for all American military forces involved "in hostilities in or over from off the shores of North Vietnam, South Vietnam, Laos, or Cambodia." Fulbright was not among the sponsors. The bill reached the floor of the Senate on June 14 – just as Henry Kissinger was concluding a follow-up round of talks on the peace agreement in Paris and just before Leonid Brezhnev flew into Washington for a summit with Richard Nixon. The resolution, attached to a State Department authorization measure, passed the Senate by a wide margin.

Frank Church later remarked that he would have welcomed Fulbright's cosponsorship, and he expressed the view that the Arkansan had held back

24 "U.S. Will Continue Raids in Cambodia," *New York Times,* Mar. 28, 1973.
25 According to Moose, Fulbright was furious at the content of their report, especially after he told the chairman that it was based in part on interviews with twenty former Fulbrighters. The chairman at first attempted to bury the report but then eventually released it; Moose interview; and "Fulbright Panel Aides Support Cambodia Help," *Washington Evening Star,* Feb. 2, 1971.
26 "2 Senate Panels Vote to Cut Off Bombing Funds," *Arkansas Gazette,* May 5, 1973.
27 *Congressional Record,* House, May 10, 1973, H509.

in order not "to trouble" Henry Kissinger.[28] There was some truth to Church's observation. Kissinger was engaged in intensive discussions with Le Duc Tho throughout the spring of 1972 on postwar aid, Cambodia, Laos, and the post–cease-fire political and military situation in South Vietnam. He continued to call Fulbright on a regular basis, reporting to him and asking for his cooperation. They lunched several times at the Metropolitan Club.[29] The reasons for Fulbright's failure to cosponsor and vote for Church–Case were multiple, however.

At times during the spring of 1973, J. William Fulbright suffered from bouts of intense cynicism about, and disillusionnment with, public life. Watergate and the bombing of Cambodia and Laos coming in the wake of Richard Nixon's landslide victory were profoundly discouraging. Perhaps, he mused in the quiet of his office or on his screened-in porch overlooking Rock Creek Park, the Republic really had been perverted. Several times during the hearings on the Cambodian bombing, he remarked that it did not matter what law Congress passed: Nixon and his henchmen would find "some specious legal justification for doing exactly what it wishes to do."[30] On *Face the Nation* he declared that if Nixon "decided to bomb Burma tomorrow, I don't know how we could stop him from it."[31]

By the first week in June the noose was beginning to close on the Nixon administration over Cambodia. White House aide William Timmons reported to the president that there were pending in Congress no fewer than five cutoff amendments, several of them attached to bills that would be very difficult to veto.[32]

In the midst of the brouhaha over Cambodia, Leonid Brezhnev arrived in Washington for his summit with the beleaguered president. Fulbright was delighted – with Kissinger and the Russians, if not the rest of the Nixon administration. Indeed, by 1973 the Arkansan's Russophilia had become part of his public persona. On the eve of the summit, he assembled the White House press corps and called for a thorough reappraisal of the military budget, arguing that by all accounts the Soviets were cutting back on their defense expenditures. Fulbright also arranged for a luncheon at Blair House for Brezhnev so that the Soviet leader could meet with twenty influential senators, including most members of the SFRC. During the course of their three-and-a-half-hour session, Brezhnev declared "the cold war was, as far as we are concerned, over."[33]

On June 21 Kissinger, freshly arrived from Paris, met secretly with the

28 Quoted in Berman, *Fulbright and the Vietnam War,* 174–5.
29 Appointments calendar, Mar. 9, 1973, Williams Papers.
30 Quoted in Berman, *Fulbright and the Vietnam War,* 172.
31 Ibid.
32 William Timmons to Nixon, June 15, 1973, WHSpF, Box 42, Nixon Project.
33 "Brezhnev Urges Senators to Help Work for Peace," *Arkansas Gazette,* June 20,1973.

SFRC. Fulbright had arranged the conference following several private conversations with the NSC adviser. Kissinger told the senators that there was about a 50–50 chance for a comprehensive settlement of all outstanding issues relating to Indochina by early September, and he pled with them not to vote for an immediate fund cutoff.[34]

Nixon had hoped that the Brezhnev visit would divert public attention from the harrowing ordeal of Watergate and strengthen his hand in his confrontation with Congress over Cambodia. It did neither. On June 25 – the day Brezhnev left for Moscow – Sam Ervin resumed his Watergate hearings, which he had postponed for a week at the president's request. John Dean, Nixon's former counsel, took the stand and mesmerized the nation with his tale of intrigue, cover-up, and "blind ambition."

While Dean spilled his guts, to use a Nixonian phrase, and the SFRC considered Henry Kissinger's request, both houses passed a continuing resolution with an immediate fund cutoff attached. Nixon at once vetoed it, and an override measure failed in the House. At that point Fulbright stepped in and led the fight for a compromise on Cambodia, but the price he extracted from the administration was high.

On June 29 Fulbright rose on the floor of the Senate to inform his colleagues that the SFRC by a vote of 15 to 2 had approved an amendment to the general appropriations bill, then stalled in Congress, prohibiting the continuation of hostilities by U.S. forces anywhere in Indochina after August 15, 1973. The acceptance of the August 15 date "in no way" constituted recognition of the president's authority to be there in the first place, he declared. In return for this six-week extension, the administration had agreed not to resume hostilities after that date without the express approval of both houses of Congress. Was that not correct? he asked Hugh Scott, Senate minority leader. That was correct, Scott reluctantly declared.[35] Mike Mansfield, increasingly cut out of the decision-making process by the Kissinger–Fulbright relationship, led the fight against Fulbright's proposal. He denounced the compromise as a "capitulation and abdication of the Constitutional powers of the Senate."[36] His opposition was not enough. A reluctant and divided Senate voted 63 to 26 for the Fulbright compromise, and the House followed suit 236 to 169.[37] In effect the chairman had traded six more weeks of bombing in Cambodia for an explicit promise by the administration not to initiate further hostilities without congressional consent. Never during the history of the war in Indochina had any president conceded Congress the right to veto military action.

34 "Adm. Trying to Find Right Neg. in Cambodia," *Washington Post,* June 30, 1973.
35 *Congressional Record,* Senate, June 29, 1973, 12560.
36 "Nixon Accepts a Cut-off," *New York Times,* July 1, 1973.
37 "Bombing to End by Aug. 15," *Washington Evening Star,* June 30, 1973.

Despite everything that the Americans could throw at them, the Khmer Rouge made steady progress during the next month and a half, chewing up Lon Nol's army at a rate of twelve hundred casualties a month. By the first week in August, Phnom Penh was a city under siege. Every day American jets could be seen wheeling in the sky over the beleaguered city. Black clouds of smoke rose on the outskirts of town, and at night the undersides of the monsoon clouds glowed pink in the false dawn of exploding bombs. Nixon appealed to Congress to repudiate the Fulbright compromise, and he warned that the fall of Cambodia to the Khmer Rouge would be its responsibility; but Congress would not relent. As Lon Nol's army went down the drain, hearings before the Armed Services Committee brought to light for the first time that the bombing of Cambodia had continued unabated past the 1970 invasion in direct contravention of Congress's expressed will. The military, moreover, had lied to cover up.[38] The Cambodian government collapsed in the spring of 1974, and the Khmer Rouge assumed control of Phnom Penh on April 17.

Kissinger later argued that the congressionally mandated bombing halt denied him the leverage necessary to force Hanoi, and through it the Khmer Rouge, into accepting a cease-fire in Cambodia. Up to August 15, Communist China had proven willing to help engineer a halt to the fighting and had indicated a willingness to support a coalition government under Prince Sihanouk; but, according to Kissinger, Beijing seemed to lose interest after the August 15 cease-fire went into effect. The NSC adviser blamed Watergate for robbing Nixon of the will to resist Congress, and Congress for interfering in the diplomatic process and making possible the rise of Pol Pot and his gang of murderers.

The Nixon administration, however, had had the opportunity to facilitate the installation of a coalition government in Cambodia under Sihanouk much earlier and had chosen not to do so. The United States, seeing Cambodia as merely a pawn in the Vietnam War, encouraged the coup that overthrew Sihanouk and then supported Lon Nol, all as part of the Vietnamization strategy which called for destruction of North Vietnamese sanctuaries in Cambodia. Although the Nixon administration was not responsible for the rise of the Khmer Rouge, its growth paralleled the policy of Vietnamization. Perhaps Congress did misunderstand the situation in Cambodia in the summer of 1973, but, as William Berman has argued, Nixon and Kissinger, along with Hanoi, bear the responsibility for destabilizing Cambodia. In the process, they chose to ignore the recommendation of seventy-five senators who, by

---

38 H. D. S. Greenway, "Cambodia: 'It Is Never Quiet Here,' " *Washington Post,* Aug. 4, 1973; John W. Finney, "Nixon Sees Peril in Bombing Halt; Warns Congress," *New York Times,* Aug. 4, 1973; and Seymour M. Hersh, "Senators Are Told U.S. Bombed Cambodia Secretly after Invasion in 1970," *New York Times,* Aug. 8, 1973.

voting for the Cooper–Church amendment on June 30, 1970, had urged that the United States stay out of that unfortunate country.[39]

The movement to undermine the imperial presidency's warmaking powers culminated with congressional passage of the War Powers Act in the fall of 1973. Ironically, J. William Fulbright was less than enthusiastic about the measure, which required the president to inform Congress within forty-eight hours of the deployment of American military forces abroad and obligated him to withdraw them in sixty days in the absence of explicit congressional endorsement. In Fulbright's opinion, Jacob Javits's bill gave the president far too much latitude to involve the United States in foreign conflicts. America had learned once again during the long, painful Vietnam experience how difficult it was politically to compel the withdrawal of troops in the field once they were committed. In Fulbright's opinion the Constitution bound the president to ask for and secure a declaration of war – or at the very least congressional approval as provided in the National Commitments Resolution – before committing troops abroad.

Despite the sixty-day window, Nixon informed Minority Leader Gerald Ford (R–Michigan) that if the Javits bill reached him in any form, he would veto it. Meanwhile, each new day brought fresh revelations concerning Watergate, revelations that further undermined Richard Nixon's power. A thrill of excitement and anticipation shot through Congress and the nation when Alexander Butterfield informed the Ervin committee on July 16 that the president had employed a taping system inside the Oval Office and that the hundreds of hours Nixon, Haldeman, Ehrlichman, and Dean had discussed Watergate (and its cover-up) were recorded and available if the committee subpoenaed them.

When the war powers bill reached the floor of the Senate in mid-July, Fulbright offered several amendments designed to tighten it. The most important simply conformed to the Constitution, reiterating that the president had authority to commit troops to combat only when the nation was being threatened with invasion or its security directly imperiled. All of his amendments were overwhelmingly defeated, as was that of Thomas Eagleton (D–Missouri), which would have included CIA covert activities in the bill's coverage, a step Fulbright strongly favored. On July 20 the Senate approved the war powers legislation by a wide margin and sent it to the House, which had already passed a similar measure. Fulbright not only voted for the Senate measure but headed the Senate conferees who subsequently worked out a compromise with Representative Clement Zablocki (D–Pennsylvania) and his delegation. As he had promised, Richard Nixon vetoed the War Powers Act, but Watergate had so weakened him that he could only protest when on November 6, 1973, Congress voted to override. The following week the House and Senate endorsed an amendment to the Military Procurement Au-

39 Berman, *Fulbright and the Vietnam War*, 179.

thorization Act banning the funding of any U.S. military action in any part of Indochina, and American involvement in the Second Indochina War effectively came to a halt.[40]

The end of American participation in the Vietnam War and the circumscription of presidential powers in the area of foreign policymaking brought little joy to J. William Fulbright. His long struggle had been, to his mind, to right a wrong, to correct an endless series of mistakes, to bring a halt to years of brutality and suffering. The country was exhausted, its confidence shaken, and Fulbright to an extent shared that malaise. There was little consolation in the thought that thousands more might have died and that democracy might have been seriously compromised in the United States, had it not been for his efforts. America's great crusade in Southeast Asia had contained the seeds of its own destruction. The fact that he had perceived that fact early on and sounded the clarion call was of no comfort. Fulbright could not get the Gulf of Tonkin Resolution out of his mind; he could not forget that he had once embraced and been chief purveyor of the liberal activism that had been responsible for the horror that was Vietnam. Moreover, he realized that it was not just the ancient Greeks who killed messengers bearing bad tidings.

40 Marily B. Young, *The Vietnam Wars, 1945-1990* (New York, 1991), 285; "War Measure Approved," *Arkansas Democrat,* July 21, 1973; and Richard L. Madden, "Congress Leaders Confident on Bill to Curb President," *New York Times,* Oct. 5, 1973.

20

Conclusion

In 1974 Fulbright encountered political opposition in Arkansas from an un-expected source – its progressive and immensely popular governor, Dale Leon Bumpers. Bumpers viewed the governor's office as a political graveyard and very much wanted to go to Washington. Fulbright had failed to make his preemptive tour of the state in early 1973, and Bumpers and his advisers sensed, correctly, a weakening of political will. They were not alone. Indeed, preliminary polls indicated that any one of a number of people, including Orval Faubus, could beat the incumbent junior senator in 1974. To save Arkansas and the national Democratic Party from the humiliation of Faubus in the Senate, and to realize his own ambition, Bumpers decided to challenge Fulbright.

The incumbent was never in the race. Arkansans were angry with Fulbright for his stands on Vietnam, the Middle East, and Watergate and for his per-ceived neglect of the state. The junior senator was ill at ease with the cam-paign techniques necessary to win in the new media age, whereas the challenger was perfectly at home with them. Bumpers was conservative enough to satisfy those on the political right and liberal enough to please those on the left. As a result, on election day he outpolled the state's most famous citizen by 320,798 to 174,734.[1]

Fulbright's defeat was mourned and cheered around the nation and the world. Scoop Jackson's staff broke out a case of whiskey in celebration. As news of Fulbright's resounding defeat came across the wire services in Phnom Penh, members of the American embassy staff stood in their chairs and cheered wildly.[2] Vice-President Gerald Ford, only recently appointed to replace the disgraced Spiro Agnew, walked off the eighteenth hole of the Kemper Open and observed to reporters that after thirty years Fulbright had simply lost touch with his constituents. Tass, the Soviet news agency, de-

---

1 "Fulbright Beaten in Arkansas," *Arkansas Gazette,* May 28, 1974; and Ernest Dumas, "Bumpers Shatters Fulbright; Pryor takes Narrow Victory," *Arkansas Gazette,* May 29, 1974.
2 Interview with Hoyt Purvis, Jan. 19, 1990, Fayetteville, Ark. and interview with Richard Moose, June 29, 1989, Washington, D.C.

scribed the election as a victory for "American reaction, the military–industrial complex, and influential Zionist elements."[3]

James Reston, Tom Wicker, and Tom Braden wrote bittersweet eulogies. "The lesson to be learned is not that Fulbright should be younger, more handsome, better on TV," Braden wrote in the *Washington Post*. "The lesson is that we need to find a way to avoid the waste of our best-educated talent."[4] An editorial in the *Toronto Globe* lamented, "The voice of William Fulbright has been a courageous, and often lonely, countervailing force when the need has been greatest. . . . The choice may, in one sense, be a vindication of the lonely stands Mr. Fulbright has taken in the past."[5]

After 1975 most Americans wanted to forget J. William Fulbright. He was a man shunned, a living, breathing reminder of the humiliation of Vietnam. It took years after the final marine helicopter lifted off the roof of the U.S. embassy in Saigon before the nation was ready to come to grips with the war, to heal the wounds it had inflicted. Fulbright was not destined to be part of that process. Americans were angry with themselves, angry with the political system, angry with the world, and angry particularly with Fulbright. For hawks he remained a symbol of betrayal, a reminder of the nation's lack of resolve, a key factor in America's decision not to make an all-out effort in Southeast Asia. For doves Fulbright continued to be a hero of a sort, but they still viewed him as a fixture of the system that had been discredited by Vietnam, and they could not forget that he had voted against every civil rights measure proposed in Congress between 1945 and 1970. At a huge commemorative anti–Vietnam War conference held in Toledo, Ohio, in 1990, Fulbright was barely mentioned. For those in the middle, Fulbright was an I-told-you-so emblem of their monumental error. The 1974 election had indeed cast the junior senator into the wilderness.

For the next quarter century Fulbright was feted overseas and ignored at home. He and Betty chose to remain in Washington, and from his law offices in Hogan and Hartson, the former chairman of the SFRC followed foreign affairs with his always critical eye. He despaired of Jimmy Carter's human rights campaign, seeing it as a throwback to Wilsonian interventionism and a threat to détente. Fulbright deplored Ronald Reagan's simple-mindedness and anticommunist fixation. As always, however, Fulbright had his gaze fixed on improved Soviet–American relations, and when the cold war began grinding to a halt during the latter stages of the Reagan and early months of the Bush administration, he was more than willing to give the Republicans credit.

3 Quoted in "Lost Touch with Voters," *Arkansas Democrat,* May 30, 1974.
4 Tom Braden, "A Place for the Fulbrights," *Washington Post,* June 8, 1974.
5 "A Canadian Viewpoint,"*Northwest Arkansas Times,* June 18, 1974.

For Fulbright, however, the hero of détente was Mikhail Gorbachev. In the spring of 1989 Fulbright and Seth Tillman published *The Price of Empire*, an update of the world according to Fulbright. It was a paean to Gorbachev, who, by introducing elements of democracy and capitalism in the Soviet Union, had allegedly undercut ideologues and the military–industrial complex in both his country and the United States. The United States must refrain from gloating, the two longtime collaborators wrote, and concentrate on perfecting American democracy. Only after the United States had eliminated the last vestiges of racism, sexism, and poverty from its own society could it declare victory in the cold war. Above all, the United States must initiate a massive military build-down in order to protect both Gorbachev's and Bush's right flanks.[6] What Fulbright and Tillman did not recognize was that Gorbachev had set in motion events that he could not control – that the Soviet people, at least in the short run, would settle for nothing less than the breakup of the empire that Lenin and Stalin had so carefully and brutally crafted and the sweeping away of the old communist order within the Soviet Union. Nor did they anticipate the difficulty that future American leaders would have in building consensus for any foreign policy initiative given the absence of an overarching enemy.

In 1992 former mailroom boy and Fulbright protégé William Jefferson Clinton was elected president. Fulbright was absolutely delighted. Actually, he had been quite pleased with George Bush, declaring him to be one of the most knowledgeable men ever to be in charge of American foreign policy; but Clinton was an Arkansan, a Rhodes scholar, an educated, pragmatic, interested man who had opposed the war in Vietnam. The election of his protégé seemed a redemption to Fulbright, a repudiation of the true believers, a fitting response to those who had heaped aspersions on Arkansas through the years, a last laugh on Lyndon Johnson. Although rumors concerning Fulbright's intervention in his behalf to keep him out of the draft had caused Clinton difficulty during the presidential campaign, the president took pains to acknowledge his debt to Fulbright and to embrace him publicly. In May 1993, at a gala ceremony in Washington, Clinton presented an overwhelmed Fulbright with the Medal of Freedom.[7] That summer Fulbright's amazing body finally failed him. The splendid physical and mental athlete suffered a massive stroke that left him wheelchair bound and both his speech and memory severely impaired. He died in his sleep at one o'clock in the morning on February 9, 1995. President Clinton delivered the eulogy at a moving ceremony in Washington National Cathedral. That the service ended with Aaron Copland's ''Fanfare for the Common Man'' was both fitting and ironic.

6 ''Our New Opportunity to Beat Swords into Plowshares,'' *Chicago Tribune,* Apr. 19, 1989.
7 Phil McCombs, ''An 88-Candle Salute to Senator Fulbright,'' *Washington Post,* May 6, 1993.

At the close of World War II and the dawn of the cold war, Fulbright perceived the central problem of U.S. foreign policy to be how to preserve Anglo–American civilization from destruction. Appalled by the bombing of Hiroshima and Nagasaki, he decided that the world was far too dangerous a place for the members of the Atlantic community simply to go their own way. As part of a universal effort to control the forces of nationalism and fascism, the Western democracies would have to surrender a portion of their national sovereignty within the context of an international collective security organization. Only in this way could aggression be nipped in the bud and eventually the socioeconomic roots of war be eliminated. Subsequently confronted with the reality that neither his country nor its wartime allies were willing to relinquish their freedom of action in a regional association of nations, much less an international one, Fulbright resigned himself to working toward the rehabilitation of Western Europe and the containment of Soviet and Chinese communism. Thus did he support not only the Marshall Plan – which, according to John Gaddis, represented the most perfect conflation of American ideals and self-interest in the postwar era – but military aid to Greece and Turkey, foreign aid in general, and limited intervention into foreign societies threatened by communism. He did not, however, buy into the globalist assumptions inherent in the Truman Doctrine, agreeing with George Kennan that America's response ought to be commensurate with the actual threat to its interests.

During the Eisenhower years, Fulbright sensed a rigidity and moral absolutism in American policy that hindered America's drive for competitive coexistence with the Soviet Union; yet it was not so much rigid anticommunism for which the Arkansan attacked Dulles and Eisenhower but their unimaginative and inflexible approach to combating America's enemies. Their emphasis on military aid and alliances, he charged, allowed the Soviet Union under Khrushchev to identify itself with anticolonialism and, through pragmatic aid programs and support of indigenous nationalist movements, to win the battle for the developing world.

Frightened by the resurgence of the radical right that began with the establishment of the John Birch Society in 1959, and mightily impressed by Nikita Khrushchev's conciliatory visit to the United States that same year, Fulbright moved beyond competitive coexistence and embraced the concept of détente. He was well pleased with the Kennedy administration's flexible response to the communist threat and, following the Berlin and Cuban missile crises, with its willingness to make a fresh start with the Soviet Union. Indeed, he greeted the signing of the nuclear test ban treaty as nothing less than the dawning of a new age. Although he continued to be troubled by the structure of foreign aid and the vast sums spent on the military–industrial complex by Robert McNamara, the new chairman of the SFRC had every reason to believe that Kennedy's flexibility and the search for détente would continue under Lyndon Johnson. The "old myths and new realities" speech was designed to point the nation and the administration further down that road.

With the burgeoning of the military–industrial complex, the penetration of the military by the radical right, far-reaching covert operations by the CIA, and the onset of the Vietnam War, however, Fulbright decided that the United States was acting in ways that were counterproductive to its strategic and economic interests. The factors that underlay Fulbright's opposition to the war were indeed multiple. Some have argued that the Arkansan acted out of personal pique, miffed at President Johnson's decision not to make him secretary of state; but there was more to the Arkansan's dissent than resentment over thwarted ambition. At various times he blamed the war on the radical right and its hysterical fear of communism, on the increasingly powerful military–industrial complex, and on Lyndon Johnson's Texas heritage and Alamo mentality. In the end, however, Fulbright came to believe that the very liberal internationalist philosophy that he had espoused from 1944 through 1964 was equally culpable. In his view, the union of New Deal liberalism with militant anticommunism had spawned a foreign policy that was at the same time both altruistic and imperialist. Like Chester Bowles, Arthur Schlesinger, Jr., and John Kenneth Galbraith, Fulbright had accepted the need after World War II to embrace anticommunism and link it with a higher ideal. That heritage made his critique of contemporary American foreign policy all the more devastating. He was among the first cold war activists to see that in harnessing their obsession with social justice to anticommunism, liberals had turned the cold war into a missionary crusade that blinded the nation to the political and cultural realities of Southeast Asia. It also made possible an unholy alliance between realpolitikers preoccupied with markets and bases, and emotionally committed to the domino theory, and idealists who wanted to spread the blessings of freedom, democracy, and a mixed economy to the less fortunate of the world.

By the summer of 1969 Fulbright had concluded that, like Lyndon Johnson, Richard Nixon had become a prisoner of the radical right, the military–industrial complex, his own psyche, and other forces of which he was only dimly aware and which he could not control even if he had wanted to. The country was frightened and exhausted, afraid to lose in Vietnam but increasingly convinced that it could not win. The liberal internationalism of the Kennedy–Johnson years was dead, thoroughly discredited by events in Southeast Asia. The void in American foreign policy was being filled by the true believers, vested interests, and political opportunists who had a stake in the continuation of the war in Vietnam, the perpetuation of the cold war, and the maintenance and expansion of the network of bases and commitments that it had spawned. If Congress did not act, the nation would be dragged into one foreign adventure after another until, morally and financially bankrupt, it disappeared from the face of the earth like other empires before it.

With the activism of the Kennedy–Johnson years in disrepute, Fulbright reasoned, the best bet for checking the right-wing radicalism spawned by the cold war and extricating America from Vietnam was traditional conservatism. From the summer of 1969 until the Arkansan's departure from the Senate in 1975, the Constitution served as the principal rallying point in his campaign to end the war and contain the burgeoning American empire. Only that hallowed document, he perceived, offered sufficient political protection for those who were sure to be accused of endangering America's national security. Carefully, meticulously, Fulbright and his chief of staff, Carl Marcy, built support for the notion that first the Johnson and then the Nixon administrations were making international commitments and involving the country in future wars without its permission or even its knowledge and, in so doing, were violating the basic law of the land. The movement that began with passage in 1969 of Fulbright's national commitments resolution was transformed into a relentless juggernaut by Cambodia, Kent State, and Watergate.

Fulbright's participation in the crusade against civil rights during the postwar period enabled him to communicate with disgruntled hawks when other members of the antiwar movement could not. And, in fact, the White House was not entirely wrong in believing that Fulbright's critique of liberal internationalism stemmed from his conservative, southern roots. As a southerner and a segregationist, not to mention the founder of the international exchange program that bore his name, Fulbright was especially jealous of the sanctity of indigenous cultures. Like so many other leaders of the New South, he never forgot that Arkansas and the entire region were onetime economic colonies of the North. Both his views on the South as an economic appendage of the North and his resentment at what he believed to be that region's efforts to impose its racial views on Dixie instilled in him an intense commitment to the principle of cultural and political self-determination. As an individual with a strong sense of class, kinship, and place, he believed it no less abhorrent that the United States should force its culture, political institutions, and economic theories on Vietnam than that the North should impose its mores on the South. In the end Fulbright's insights into the causes of the war as well as his effectiveness as an opponent of the war stemmed in no small part from his experiences as a crusader in behalf of two apparently contradictory causes: internationalism and segregation.

It is difficult to categorize and label the Arkansan's foreign affairs philosophy. Fulbright, Seth Tillman, and Carl Marcy vehemently rejected the term "neo-isolationist," a label that the Nixon administration sought to apply to them. They pointed out that the chairman of the SFRC remained a strong supporter of the United Nations, multilateral aid, and a multinational peace corps. He was not against international cooperation but American unilateralism, they insisted. Fulbright readily admitted that he had repudiated liberal internationalism and the globalist foreign policy to which it had led, but like Gerald P. Nye, the famous isolationist of the Roosevelt era with whom he struck up a brief correspondence in 1969, he preferred the term "noninterventionist."

Above all, Fulbright considered himself a realist, and he perceived that the great goal of his labors was to restore American foreign policy to a rational basis. A self-proclaimed disciple of University of Chicago political scientist Hans Morgenthau, Fulbright in *The Price of Empire* and *The Arrogance of Power* advocated an Asian policy that resembled that espoused by Herbert Hoover in 1950 or even Alfred Thayer Mahan in 1895. The executive, he wrote, should abandon its efforts to "extend unilaterally its power in such a way as to promote its conception of 'world peace' generally, or the defense of 'free people' and seek to maintain such base facilities there as will protect the sea and air routes of the area from domination by hostile forces."[8] Morgenthau and other realists thought him dangerously naive concerning the threat posed by the Soviet Union and Communist China. Fulbright was convinced that the cold war was responsible for sustaining absolutism and paranoia in the Soviet Union rather than, as Henry Jackson and other cold warriors believed, that Russian imperialism was an inevitable by-product of communist totalitarianism.

Fulbright's stature as a prophet is debatable. From the very beginning of the cold war, J. William Fulbright saw no reason why the Western democracies and the Soviet Union could not peacefully coexist. Like Mikhail Gorbachev, Fulbright never believed that communism and the Soviet empire would die a sudden death; rather, he surmised that the Soviet Union would evolve economically and then perhaps politically. A new generation of leaders, untrammeled by history and ideology and anxious for popular support, would introduce a mixed economy, shift resources from military to nonmilitary production, and demythologize international relations. Perhaps the USSR and its satellites would never become multiparty democracies, but given the deep-seated nationalism, xenophobia, and political fragmentation of Eastern Europe, that might very well be for the best. He warned John F. Kennedy of the perils involved in the Bay of Pig operations but subsequently recommended a course during the missile crisis that might have provoked nuclear war. On Vietnam, his opposition was largely an articulation of the views of disaffected scholars and diplomats. His contribution lay in his personal courage, his stature as a conservative, and his tactical skill. He made the Constitution and the issue of executive usurpation an umbrella under which hawks and doves, liberals and conservatives, idealists and cynics could gather.

There is no doubt that Fulbright transcended Arkansas and the U.S. Senate. In America, Western Europe, and Japan he came to epitomize the struggle of reason and restraint against excess. He was – as Cipriana Scelba, longtime

8 Summary Proposal for Disengagement in Vietnam, May 18, 1967, Box 7, Folder Apr.–June, Marcy Papers.

head of the Italian Fulbright program, put it – what non-Americans wanted America to be. To their minds, his sophistication, cosmopolitanism, and cultural humility stood in sharp contrast to the traits they associated with the bulk of Americans: parochialism, xenophobia, materialism, and cultural aggression. Most mistakenly wrote off his civil rights record to political expediency and focused instead on his foreign policy views. In the 1940s he endeared himself to Europeans by participating in the crusade to save them from Stalinism, in the 1950s by laboring to prevent a nuclear Armageddon, and in the 1960s and 1970s by working to save the world from America and America from itself. His attacks on colonialism, advocacy of nonviolent change, and paeans to neutrality won him plaudits in the developing world. All the while, the Fulbright program was endearing him to intelligentsia and cultural elite the world over.

Indeed, Fulbright was better known and respected abroad than in the United States. Part of the reason is that this man – a man who had so much to do with articulating the liberal–New Left critique of American foreign policy, who was as early as 1958 calling on his countrymen and -women to recognize the difference between Sino–Soviet imperialism and Marxism–Leninism as a socioeconomic principle– was a southerner, a segregationist, and an elitist. For a generation American academics, independent intellectuals, and social activists, the "New Class" of neo-conservative nightmares, have viewed the anti–Vietnam War movement as exclusively their own. The anti-imperial onslaught against the military–industrial complex was to their minds their creation, an extension of the liberal tradition. Despite *The Arrogance of Power*, *The Price of Empire*, and *The Crippled Giant*, the nation's intelligentsia found it very difficult to give this quintessential conservative his due.

Whatever his errors and misperceptions, America was well served by J. William Fulbright, this rational man combating an irrational and immoral world. He was a voice, sometimes a lone voice, calling the nation to move ahead, to abandon old myths for new realities. His emotional and intellectual journey from cold war activism to anti-imperialism comprised not so much a reflection as a counterpoint to some of the dominant trends in American foreign policy. When the isolationism of Taft and Hoover threatened America's efforts to save the world from the scourge of Stalinism, Fulbright denounced it. When in the name of anticommunism Lyndon Johnson and Richard Nixon intervened in Latin America and attempted to impose a Pax Americana on Asia, he invoked the neo-isolationist theories he had once attacked. When Congress seemed to be dominated by nationalism and parochialism, he called for an activist presidency, one with maximum freedom to act in the international sphere. When he perceived the executive to have been taken over by militarists and imperialists, he campaigned for a restoration of congressional prerogatives. He insisted throughout his career that governmental agencies and departments not allow themselves to be used by vested interests, ideologues, and unscrupulous politicians to deceive and propagandize the American people. If Fulbright was not always right, he was generally healthy, a foreign affairs gyroscope dedicated to keeping the ship of state in trim.

Index